Steve
Buttery

Tony & Von
Mij & Ronni ... ret. 15/

new voices 3

in Literature, Language, and Composition

Jay Cline

Dan Donlan

James Flood

Coleen Goodwin

Russell Hill

Robert Probst

Ken Williams

Harry L. Walen,
Consultant in Career Education

Consultants
Margaret Adelman
Marion Heather

Ginn and Company

C19915
ISBN: 0-7702-0801-0

BCDEFGHIJK 08543

PRINTED IN CANADA

contents

3

A degree sign (°) following a word or phrase in the text indicates that that word or phrase is explained in the Dictionary.

1

Night Drive

forestudy

Foreshadowing

Suppose that a story begins like this:

"Jim tucked the stone into his baseball glove and looked at it skeptically. It really wasn't quite round enough, but it was the right size. He decided that his father probably wouldn't notice. He could stroll casually into the house, holding the mitt tightly closed, and walk directly to his room, where he could deposit glove and stone in a dark corner of his closet. It was too bad, he thought, that he had been too lazy to walk the extra kilometre to the empty field—away from all those houses."

What do you think has happened? What do you think is going to happen? Though you don't know directly what the story is all about, the writer *has* given you some clues and perhaps has caused you to wonder about just what's going on. What's more, if the writer is skilful enough, you will be wondering about exactly what he/she *wants* you to wonder about.

What questions *do* come to mind as you read that opening paragraph? Here, at least, are a few:

1. Why is Jim concerned that the stone looks like a baseball?
2. Why is he concerned about the best way to enter his house?
3. Why is he concerned about his father?
4. Why does he regret not having gone to the empty field?

You can no doubt make some pretty good guesses about possible answers to those questions—and to others that you might have asked. Of course, you can't be absolutely sure that your guesses are correct, but you can be fairly sure that you're on the right track and asking the right questions.

And then there's this to consider: You won't be surprised if, later on in the story, the stone and the missing baseball take on considerable importance. Nor will you be surprised if some kind of conflict develops between Jim and his father. The writer, you see, has supplied clues to crucial events to come by causing you to raise questions about details that seem to have some importance. In other words, the writer has FORESHADOWED future events. For example, Jim's desire to hide the stone from his father FORESHADOWS a conflict between Jim and his father.

In FORESHADOWING events, the writer must be skilful enough to emphasize the right details—details that will prompt you to raise the "right" questions. You'd feel cheated, for instance, if you read through the entire story, wondering about that missing baseball, about the stone, about a conflict between Jim and his father, only to discover that none of those concerns mattered at all. And you'd be justified in condemning the story as not worth the paper it's written on.

A writer who knows what he/she is doing will take care to lead you, the reader, in the right direction; he/she will see to it that you raise relevant questions. In short, a good writer will emphasize only those details/circumstances that FORESHADOW the outcome of the story.

In "Night Drive" the author has used FORESHADOWING to good effect. When you have read the story, you may want to go back and identify some of the clues that foreshadowed the outcome of events.

Night Drive

Will F. Jenkins

Madge was all ready and in the act of turning out the livingroom lights when the telephone rang. She picked it up, and Mr. Tabor identified himself. He sounded as if he had a bad cold. Madge barely knew him, but in a small town people don't stand on ceremony. He said apologetically° that his niece Eunice had stopped in town to see him this afternoon, and he'd heard that Madge—he called her Mrs. Haley, of course—was driving over to Colchester tonight. It was an imposition° for him to ask, but it would be a great favor if she'd let his niece ride with her.

Madge felt uncomfortable—for Mr. Tabor to mention the Colchester road would make anybody uncomfortable—but she said cordially that she'd be glad to give his niece a lift.

"I was just about to leave, though," she said. "I hope she can be ready fairly soon."

"She's ready now, Mrs. Haley," said Mr. Tabor's muffled voice over the phone. "She'll be waiting for you on the porch. I have to leave, so I'll thank you now, on her behalf."

He hung up, and Madge felt that twinge of uneasiness which comes of being reminded of something one would rather not remember. She turned off the light and went out to the car, feeling queasy. No woman liked to think about Mrs. Tabor before driving a car at night, alone. There was the other girl, too, but it wasn't quite the same thing. Nobody knew who the other girl was or how it had happened. But Madge had known Mrs. Tabor.

The car started briskly and she went two blocks underneath the trees, and one to the right, and there was a lonely looking figure sitting on the steps of Mr. Tabor's already dark house. As Madge pulled in to the curb, the figure picked up a small suitcase and came forward. Madge opened the right-hand door.

"You're Eunice?" she asked cheerfully. "I'm Mrs. Haley."

"It's very good of you," the girl said in a flat voice. "I thought it was a lot for my uncle to ask."

"Nonsense!" said Madge. "I'm glad to have company! Put your bag in the back seat and climb up here with me."

The girl obeyed silently. She was a little angular° and a little clumsy. Her hat was severely plain. She wore spectacles that

11

seemed to be tinted, even at night. She sat primly, her hands folded in her lap, as Madge turned and headed out of town.

It was really a beautiful night, with all the nice summery smells that make one glad to be alive and glad that it's cool and dark. Presently the houses drew back from the road, and street lights ended, and there were fields on either side of the road with dark masses that were woodland beyond them. Madge settled down for the 60 km run to Colchester. She touched the headlight switch and had bright lights for a long way ahead. The road flowed smoothly toward them. But still she thought about Mr. Tabor—Mrs. Tabor, really. She hadn't known them well, but in a small town everybody knows everybody else to speak to, at least, so Mrs. Tabor's death had been especially horrible because she was a bride and Mr. Tabor had been so happy and so proud of her.

"It's nice having someone with me,"

said Madge. "I really don't like driving at night. But Sam—my husband, you know—gets into Colchester at ten-ten tonight; and if he waited for a bus, he wouldn't get home until after three in the morning. We have terrible bus service!"

The girl was silent for a second, and then said, "Yes." Her voice was flat and low-pitched. Then she seemed to realize that she sounded curt.° She added, "It isn't bad in the daytime."

"No," agreed Madge. She was silent for a while, and said, "How did Mr. Tabor know I was driving over?"

The girl seemed to consider. Then she said, "I guess somebody mentioned it."

"They'd hardly—" Then Madge stopped. She would never speak of the Colchester road to Mr. Tabor, but some people might. "Oh . . . I got the gas and oil and tires checked today. I mentioned to Bob—the filling-station attendant—why I was being so finicky. I guess that's the answer."

12

The girl said, "Probably," and sat quiet, her hands in her lap. The dotted center line of the highway became a solid streak, and the road made a wide curve. Woodland bracketed it—the air was almost chilly among the trees—and abruptly it was clear again. They were maybe six kilometres on their way.

"Mrs. Haley," said the girl's flat voice, "do you carry a pistol, driving at night?"

Madge jumped a little. Then she laughed, not quite at ease.

"Good Heavens, no! Why—" Then she said, "I see. Your uncle thinks women should."

She felt queer. She was going to drive over the highway on which Mrs. Tabor had been killed a year before. There had never been any clue to the killer. It was just assumed that somehow Mrs. Tabor— on her way to meet her husband, too— had been persuaded to stop her car and pick someone up. The car was found, ultimately. It had been sprinkled with gasoline and set on fire, and any clues it might have yielded were destroyed. Mrs. Tabor, herself, had been bludgeoned to death. There were other details, but that was the way the local paper phrased it. And Madge couldn't understand how her husband kept on living in the same town and in the very house to which he'd brought Mrs. Tabor as a bride.

She heard herself saying with morbid° interest, "He and Mrs. Tabor hadn't been married long, had they?"

"About three months," said the girl tonelessly. She added in the same expressionless manner, "We're near the turn-off, aren't we?"

"Why, yes," said Madge. She grew confused. One doesn't expect a newcomer to know such things. She didn't remem-

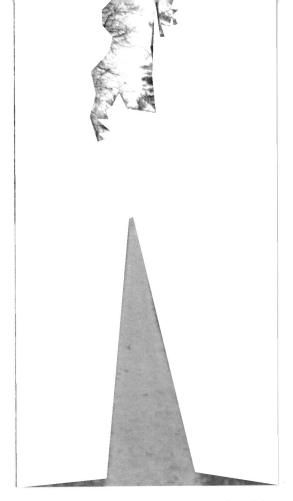

ber Mr. Tabor's niece ever visiting him before, and she'd more or less assumed that she was a complete stranger. As far as that went, Mr. Tabor wasn't a long-time resident himself. He'd come to town a little more than a year ago to accept a rather good position. Three months later he married and brought his bride to a bungalow he'd bought.

Only three months later still, Mrs. Tabor drove on her way to Colchester one night but never reached her destination. Madge shivered at the thought of what she'd heard about that killing. Her most vivid single memory of Mr. Tabor was of the first time she'd seen him after the murder. He was a small man, and **13** he'd looked shrunken and mummylike. But he didn't leave town. He stayed on, living in the house he'd spent his honeymoon in. Madge couldn't understand his doing that.

The car came to the turn-off. There was nothing conspicuous about it. It was just a secondary road—well-paved enough—that branched off the main highway and wound across-country to Colchester. In 50 km there was one crossroads store and maybe four or five farmhouses which could be seen from the highway. Most of the road's length ran through woodland.

Madge turned into it. Within a kilometre tall and columnar tree trunks engulfed the road. The air was fragrant with the aromatic° smell of dropped pine tags and cones. It was cooler, too. But one no longer had the feeling of being in empty open space. Above and ahead there was a narrow ribbon of sky in which stars shone brightly. The headlights stabbed on before and showed the pavement, and pine tree trunks alongside, and more pine tree trunks. There was a bare screen of underbrush at the road's edge.

The angular figure beside Madge said, "Lonely out here, isn't it?"

Madge pressed harder on the accelerator. The car picked up speed.

"One thing's certain," she said, trying to smile; "nobody could make me stop to pick them up on this road!"

"Mrs. Tabor—Aunt Clara, I suppose I should say," said Eunice without emotion, "didn't pick people up. But that night she did."

Madge set her lips and drove. Presently she said awkwardly, "I wouldn't ask ordinarily, Eunice, but has Mr. Tabor ever gotten any idea of who—er—killed Mrs. Tabor?"

"There's always the chance that the man who did it will be caught." There was a slight pause. "Another girl was killed six months later, you remember," the flat voice said impassively.°

Madge suddenly regretted deeply that she had not made some excuse to avoid having Mr. Tabor's niece ride with her. It was bad to be reminded of Mrs. Tabor. But to be reminded—and at the same time—of that other battered, half-burnt body of an unknown girl made it worse. The girl had surely been murdered somewhere, but nobody knew where, or by whom, or even when. Hunters had found the remains of a huge bonfire deep in the woods. There was a young girl's body in the ashes. The police were never able to find out even so much as her name. All that was known was that she had been dead six weeks or so when her body was found.

"Your uncle," said Madge distastefully, because of the memory, "is staying in town, then, in hope of catching his wife's murderer?"

Eunice's voice said monotonously, "The same man killed that other girl. There was a scorched automobile road map under her body, as if she'd been driving, too. Only the killer got rid of her car. It hasn't ever been found. But it was the same man."

Madge said, shocked, "But that means—"

"The killer is still around," said the flat voice. It hadn't any human quality to it at all. "He was even mentioned to the police, by name. But they didn't believe it for an instant. He's too well thought of."

"You—you talk as if you know who the killer is!" protested Madge.

"Of course," the flat voice said almost scornfully.

The car swept past a small clearing, filled now with shoulder-high weeds. The road dived into woods again. Just before the trees re-enveloped the car, there was a sudden sweetness in the air. Honeysuckle. Then the damp, aromatic smell of pine woods once more. Madge was sensitive to scents. Consciously or otherwise, she associated some scent with everyone she knew. All her friends, certainly. Now she suddenly realized one thing that made this girl Eunice seem strange. She did not use scent. Not even a scented soap. But she was hardly a really feminine type, anyhow.

Madge's forehead began to knit into a faint frown, and her heart began to pound oddly as if in anticipation of something that would occur to her presently. She was uneasy.

"If Mrs. Tabor's murderer were caught, I can see that it might be hard to convict him now. My husband's a lawyer, and he says the evidence in such cases has to be airtight because the crime's so horrible."

The detached voice beside her said, "There's no motive for the man to kill that particular woman rather than another. A jury wants to see a motive for a crime. Naturally. Preferably a motive they could feel themselves. Naturally!"

Madge admitted uncomfortably, "My husband said something like that . . . ."

She fumbled in the handbag beside her.

"You drive," said the flat voice. "I'll light your cigarette."

Madge felt unreasonably shaky, but she was driving fast. She couldn't take her eyes off the road. She felt one of her own cigarettes touched to her lips. She accepted. Eunice snapped a lighter. Its tiny flame rose up before Madge's lips. She glanced down. The car wavered. Then the wheel resisted. It was held. Madge felt sheer paralysis° numb every muscle in her body.

"I've got the wheel," came tonelessly from beside her.

Madge remembered to puff. The cigarette was lit. The lighter was withdrawn and went off. The wheel was released.

Everything was as before. The car went swiftly between crowded tall tree trunks that rose to where their branches joined to form a roof over all the forest. The sound of the motor echoed back from the wood with a singing note added to it. There was the same clean damp smell of wood mould and pine tags. Everything was exactly as before.

But everything was different. Madge's legs were stiff and icy. Her whole body was cold. Every muscle was tense. Her heart was hammering with an hysterical tempo: beat—beat—beat—beatbeat beat-beat . . . .

Because in that one glance down at the flame as it was held to her cigarette, she had seen Eunice's hand closely and clearly lit. The fingernails were innocent of nail polish. Their ends were not rounded, but square like a man's. The knuckles were like a man's. There were short, black hairs on the back of the hand. Like a man's.

Eunice was a man.

A yammering voice inside Madge's brain chattered hysterically.° *"You didn't*

who sat beside her in the appearance of a woman, with tinted spectacles and an unbecoming hat and a flat and toneless voice.

But it was too late now . . . .Before she fully realized her lost opportunity, it was gone forever. She went driving on through the night with the muscles of her throat constricted° and an icy horror filling all her veins. It was a beautiful night. It was a warm and an odorous and a softly romantic night. The car sped through the darkness, its headlights flaring before it, and now and again a moth fluttered helplessly in their rays; and once there was something feral glittering by the roadside, and as the car sped past it could be seen to be a cat—kilometres from any house—crouching in the grass at the gravel's edge. It had stared at the approaching car, and its eyes had reflected the headlights.

"Women really ought to carry pistols when they drive at night," said the passionless voice beside her. "But maybe they wouldn't have the nerve to use them."

Madge made an inarticulate° sound. Then a desperate cunning came to her. If she could keep him in talk. . . .

"I doubt that I could shoot anyone," she said. Listening to her own voice, she was astounded. It sounded quite human. It was almost convincing. "I couldn't imagine harming a human being."

The uninflected° voice said meditatively, "I don't know that the man who killed Mrs. Tabor and that girl would be called human. Possibly he couldn't help it. But—there used to be stories about werewolves."

Madge said quickly, while her tongue tried to cleave to the roof of her mouth,

know it was Mr. Tabor on the phone. He talked like he had a cold! It could have been anybody! It wasn't Mr. Tabor at all! It was somebody who wanted to ride with you! He called you and sat on Mr. Tabor's front steps and waited for you! It's the way Mrs. Tabor was killed! It's the way Mrs. Tabor was killed. . . . "

There was a light by the side of the road ahead. Numbed as she was, Madge drove on blindly. She saw other lights, which were windows, and dumbly knew that it was the single store between the cut-off and Colchester. But she was half a kilometre beyond it when she realized that she could have stopped there. She could have swerved the car and crashed it against something, and people would have run out and she would have been safe. Injured, perhaps, or even killed, but at any rate safe from the man

"Oh, but that's nonsense! People can't turn into wolves!"

"Some people turn into something," said the figure beside her. It spoke without heat. "They aren't insane. I think they're cursed. Once in a year, or once in six months, they feel something stirring inside them. Their eyes change. They glow—bright and restless and terribly intent. The accursed ones feel a horrible, unbearable tension inside. They're obsessed. And they have to kill."

Madge expected to hear herself scream. But her voice said brightly while she felt horror unspeakable, "Then the psychiatrists ought to watch out for bright-eyed people, don't you think?"

"Ah, but they're cunning!" said the figure softly. "They don't let anybody notice their eyes!" The head with its unbecoming woman's hat turned, in the dim light from the instrument-board. The tinted spectacles, which were like sunglasses—worn at night!—regarded Madge with a monstrous unhumanness. She could not see the eyes behind them. There was the plain, angular outline of a face, and merely the seeming of two holes for eyes. "You see," said the voice confidentially, "I've studied them. I wanted to understand. And it seems that there have always been such people. In olden days they killed like wolves, and wolves were blamed, but no wolves were ever as clever as they were! So the story of the werewolf began—of a person who got into a house in human form and then turned into a wild beast to kill and rend and tear his victim. It was wonderfully clever of the people who killed, to start that story!"

The figure in the seat beside Madge seemed mirthlessly° amused. "They start-

ed, too, the tradition that werewolves couldn't face garlic, and that they could only be killed by silver bullets. Those legends were very useful to the accursed people. . . . Now they help spread the story that such killers only need to be treated by psychiatrists to be cured, and that they're really to be pitied . . . . That's useful to them, too.

"I—but I can't believe—" then Madge's throat clicked and she could not speak at all.

The person beside her sat quite still. The hands were folded primly. Somehow it was more horrible that the figure sat quiescent,° awaiting its own time, than any snarled menaces would have been. Madge's hands and arms were stiff. They did not tremble, because they were paralyzed. But the wheel did not waver. Automatically, her body moved to keep the car in the road.

"I suppose they're frightened after they have killed," said the figure reflectively. "They would be. But they learn cunning. They never live in one place very long. They kill once or twice, or maybe three times, and then they move away. But they're very nice people, and their friends are sorry to see them go. They go to church, and they act like everybody else. But they never dare get too prosperous. When you're prosperous you can't move on easily. It would be a temptation to stay on and kill—maybe a fourth or fifth time. That wouldn't be wise! Oh, they're cunning! They have to be. Because they're cursed."

The wood broke away from one side of the road. Far, far away, a single unwinking dot of light told of an isolated farmhouse, far from any neighbors. Then the trees closed in once more, and Madge knew that from here to the very outskirts of Colchester there would be no other light. She heard her voice say brightly, "Oh, but let's talk of something else! Why choose such a gruesome subject, Eunice?"

"Mrs. Tabor was killed somewhere along here," said the voice, softly.

Then Madge's hands began to shake. It was not a mere trembling, but an uncontrollable shake. The road was very straight, here, and a long way ahead there was a light. A tiny red light. She did not speak. She could not. She pressed on the accelerator and found herself offering an agonized prayer that the man beside her in a woman's dress wouldn't notice until she had caught up with it. And then she would scream and swerve in front of it and brake . . . .

But the toneless voice said, "You had your car checked today, Mrs. Haley. You mentioned at the filling station that it was because you would be driving to meet your husband on the ten-ten train in Colchester. That wasn't discreet. People still talk about Mrs. Tabor's murder. The filling station boy mentioned that you'd be driving the same way tonight—the same way she did. If the killer heard about it. . . . "

Madge tried hysterically to keep him talking until she caught up with whatever was ahead . . . .

"Oh, but I'm sure no one would think—"

"Someone would," murmured the figure with the tinted spectacles that hid its eyes to make it unrecognizable. "Somebody who was obsessed, who was accursed, who felt a horrible unbearable tension inside. Someone who knew the time had come when he had to kill."

"Why—" said Madge brightly, and gasped for breath between every word, "why—you speak—as if someone—planned to kill me!"

"I wouldn't be surprised. I wouldn't be surprised at all," the figure beside her said softly. Then the voice changed. "There's something on the road ahead."

Madge made a sound which by no possibility could be considered a word. It was merely a noise formed by her throat and lips.

"It looks like an accident," said the figure beside her, tensely. "If someone's hurt—"

The light was not moving. She overhauled it swiftly. She knew she was ashen white now and that her throat was dry, but if she could only get to where someone else was, no matter who . . . . Then she knew not only what was in the road ahead, but who. It was the red motorcycle on which the young man, Bob, at the filling station dashed madly about the countryside during his time off. It lay on the road, its lights still shining brightly slanting across the road. There was Bob, limping out into the bright glare and spreading out his arms in a plea for the car to stop. There was an improvised bandage on one leg.

"I've—got to stop," Madge said, choking. "I know him! It's Bob at the filling station. He checked my car today."

The figure beside her seemed to relax. A crazy, frantic hope came to Madge. The masquerading man must be armed. But he would hesitate to try to kill two people—a man and a woman together—where a woman alone would be a certain victim. Maybe—maybe if she could get Bob into the car, the figure that pretended to be Eunice might sit quietly, and get out of the car in Colchester, and nothing would happen at all . . . .

The brakes squealed shrilly. The car stopped. There was some spilled gasoline on the road. There was Bob, limping—almost hopping—in the headlight rays. He came to the window beside Madge.

"Mrs. Haley!" he said, relieved. "I was hoping you'd be coming long behind me, instead of having gone on ahead. I hit something in the road and skidded, and my leg's all messed up—"

He stopped. He'd seen that Madge was not alone. She said unsteadily, "Bob, this is—Eunice. She's Mr. Tabor's niece. She's riding to Colchester with me."

"Oh," said Bob.

"Get in the back seat," said Madge feverishly. "You'll want a doctor. I'll rush you over to Colchester."

Bob hesitated. Then he said, "I don't know. . . . I hate to leave my motorcycle. There's nothing really the matter with it. All I need is somebody to help me stand it up. With one bum leg I can't do it, but I don't need much help. It's not too heavy—"

The soft, emotionless voice beside Madge said, "I'll help. I've got a pair of work gloves in my suitcase. I'll get them out and help, if you'll pull up a little so you won't block the road, Mrs. Haley."

Madge was wrenched by agonizing hope. She pulled ahead and over to the side of the road.

The figure in the car said softly, "A little farther. . . . Don't stop the motor, Mrs. Haley. . . . "

Then the right-hand door was open. The angular figure was getting out. It opened the back door and pulled out the small suitcase. Bob went hopping back to his motorcycle to wait.

And then the figure of Eunice—which was not Eunice—said with an extraordinary hushed passion, "Mrs. Haley. . . . I'm not a woman. I'm John Tabor. My wife was killed near here by someone she knew. She'd had her car checked that day at the filling station, being worried about driving alone at night."

Madge gasped, and tried to speak, and could not.

"I watched everybody's eyes," said the figure very, very softly. "I picked him out because I saw his eyes glowing six months ago. But nothing happened. But—then they found that other girl's body. Then I knew I was right. He's very happy now. He knew you were coming. He said so. And you'd have stopped for him. My wife did."

Madge's throat made a bubbling sound.

"Oh, but he's happy!" said the small figure softly. "He thinks I'm a girl. I'll start back. Then he'll call to you to stop your motor and help. He's quite sure he'll have both victims tonight."

The person who was not Eunice turned away.

"But—what shall I do?" Madge gasped.

"Just drive on," said John Tabor in a gentle voice. "That's all. Just drive on. He killed my wife. He's going to try to kill me—thinking I'm a woman. I think he's going to be surprised."

The small, angular figure went back through the night, along the highway's edge. The car idled softly. Katydids shrilled stridently in the dark. There were faint rustling sounds which were tree branches moving in the night wind.

Everything was utterly peaceful. But Madge cringed in her seat at the wheel of the idling car. Little choked sounds came from her throat with every breath. John Tabor went back—clicking absurd high heels on the roadway—to kill Bob, of the filling station. Or perhaps Bob waited to kill him, waited with glowing, feral° eyes to commit the unspeakable. If she—Madge did not scream to warn Bob, there would be murder done. But if she did scream there would be John Tabor killed instead, and Bob could overtake the car on his motorcycle and he could force her off the road and—

There was no light except the narrow straight ribbon of stars overhead and the slanting skewed patch of road and tree trunks which was lighted by the motorcycle's headlight. Bob wasn't in that beam. But he was silhouetted against the lighted space. He watched the small, skirted figure as it approached him. And as Madge looked, whimpering senselessly, Bob seemed to change.

He was a black shape against a lighted background. And the shape changed—very gradually and very terribly—from that of a tall and well-made young man favoring an injured leg, to a crouched horror which was wholly animal and an embodiment° of blood-lust. The outlines of humanity remained, but one of the arms moved slowly, and it came back into silhouette holding something drawn from a hiding place. It was a bludgeon, a club, a thing with which to batter in lustful frenzy at a body helpless to resist any longer. The hand held it, swayed it gently back and forth, making ready . . . .

Then a voice came. But the voice was wholly human, and humorously appealing, and productive of stark hysteria because it told of cunning past all madness.

"Mrs. Haley," called the voice cheerfully, "if you'll turn off your motor and come help too, it won't be any job at all to get the bike up and going!"

Madge's heart stopped beating. The crouched figure moved toward the blob

20

of light print dress which was Eunice—but which was not Eunice. The crouched figure moved with a swift, rolling, ape-like gait toward the angular small figure that Bob from the filling station thought was a girl. And it did not limp; the injured leg was a trick, too!

Then there was a sound in the darkness.

Madge let in the clutch. It was her body that did it, taking charge while her mind screamed soundlessly. It was her body which drove with an insane skill and speed away from that place. She never remembered driving the seven kilometres to Colchester. Her mind was gibbering° that this was the way Mrs. Tabor had been killed. She'd stopped at the filling station—as Madge had done—to check her car for the night drive. She chatted with Bob—as Madge had done—and told him why. And Bob had been respectful and friendly—as with Madge—and did not let her see his eyes. The unknown girl too had been driving through. She'd stopped for gasoline, no doubt. Maybe she'd asked about the roads. And Bob had been respectful and friendly and helpful—keeping his eyes averted. . . .

And ever since then Mr. Tabor had been watching the eyes of all the people in the town, and he'd seen that horrible glitter only once, but Bob had been too cunning for him, and he wasn't sure he was right until the body of the unknown girl was found, weeks later. And then there was nothing for the police to go on. Mr. Tabor's talk of glittering eyes wasn't enough even to justify an investigation. It wasn't anything at all . . . . So Mr. Tabor could only wait patiently for that glitter to come into Bob's eyes again, and then find out what woman would be driving alone, and drive with her. He even had to pretend to be a girl, or Bob would have been too cunning to attempt any crime. . . .

Madge drove like a madwoman until the lights of Colchester showed through the trees. Then her body slowed the car, and took it sedately into Colchester, and even stopped at the town's one red traffic light, and parked it with trembling precision by the railroad station where her husband would presently descend. Then she sat still, shaking. She couldn't speak. She couldn't tell anyone . . . .

But she clung hysterically to her husband when he arrived. He drove back home the long way—she wouldn't go through the cut-off—concerned over the terror she couldn't attempt to explain. She wasn't able to tell him until the next day. Then she wept horribly.

He went out. An hour later he came back, very white.

"Bob isn't back at the filling station," he

said sternly. "He told his boss last night he was leaving. Mr. Tabor is at his desk in the mill. Nothing's happened. Nothing! Understand?"

And that was one time that Madge obeyed her husband. She stayed indoors for days, shivering. The first time she went out, she saw Mr. Tabor on the street. He lifted his hat politely. She nodded distantly and hurried on.

He moved to another town shortly after that.

follow-up

Discussing "Night Drive"

1. Do you think it was right for Mr. Tabor to disguise his voice when he talked to Madge on the telephone? Why? Why not?
2. Why, do you think, didn't Mr. Tabor tell Madge what he was up to so that both of them could work together in exposing the murderer?
3. In your opinion, was Mr. Tabor justified in seeking on his own to trap Bob? Why didn't he call upon the police to help?
4. What right has anyone to terrify another person? Even if causing terror has a beneficial outcome, is it still justified?
5. Identify at least three clues that FORESHADOWED the outcome of the story.

Writing Dramatic Dialogue

Suspense stories like "Night Drive" are often adapted into dramatic form—scripts—for the stage, for the movies, for radio plays, or for television plays. Because drama is meant to be seen and heard by an audience, the words to be spoken by the actors are written in a special form of dialogue called DRAMATIC DIALOGUE. Not only does the dramatic dialogue form indicate what the actors are to say, but that form also gives easy-to-follow directions that tell the actors what they are to do on stage or on camera. The following examples from "Night Drive" illustrate the essential differences between narrative (story) dialogue and dramatic dialogue.

Narrative (story) dialogue

"The angular figure beside Madge said, "Lonely out here, isn't it?" Madge pressed harder on the accelerator. The car picked up speed. "One thing's certain," she said, trying to smile, "nobody could make me stop to pick them up on this road!

"Mrs. Tabor—Aunt Clara, I suppose I should say," said Eunice without emotion, "didn't pick people up. But that night she did."

Madge set her lips and drove. Presently she said awkwardly, "I wouldn't ask ordinarily, Eunice, but has Mr. Tabor ever gotten any idea of who—er—killed Mrs. Tabor?"

"There's always the chance that the man who did it will be caught." There was a slight pause. "Another girl was killed six months later, you remember," the flat voice said impassively.

Dramatic dialogue

EUNICE: Lonely out here, isn't it?

(MADGE *presses harder on the accelerator. The car picks up speed.*)

MADGE (*trying to smile*): One thing's certain; nobody could make me stop to pick them up on this road!

EUNICE (*without emotion*): Mrs. Tabor—Aunt Clara, I suppose I should say, didn't pick people up. But that night she did.

(MADGE *sets her lips and continues driving.*)

MADGE (*after a long pause, she speaks awkwardly*): I wouldn't ask ordinarily, Eunice, but has Mr. Tabor ever gotten any idea of who—er—killed Mrs. Tabor?

EUNICE: There's always the chance that the man who did it will be caught. (*A slight pause, then the flat voice continues impassively.*) Another girl was killed six months later, you remember.

Practice 1. Discussion

1. What specific differences, if any, do you find between the two forms of dialogue? (Hints: Consider word arrangement, punctuation, verb tense.)

2. From what you know of the various forms of drama, in which form do you think the scene above would be most effective—as a television play, as a radio play, or as a stage play? Why?

Practice 2. Writing

Using the dramatic dialogue above as a model, choose another short scene from "Night Drive," and rewrite it as a dramatic dialogue.

Practice 3. Oral reading and performance

When you think your dramatic dialogue is ready for presentation, follow this procedure:

Have the *narrative dialogue* from the story read aloud. (That is, have the scene from the story read aloud just as the author of "Night Drive" wrote it. You yourself might do the reading, or you might ask a classmate to do so.)

With one or two classmates (depending on the number of speakers/characters involved), perform your dramatic dialogue for the class. (You yourself will no doubt be one of the performers. Use whatever props—equipment— you think necessary.)

At the conclusion of your performance, invite your audience to comment about the effectiveness of your dramatic dialogue.

Bookshelf

The Little Girl Who Lives down the Lane, by Laird Koenig. Coward, 1974. A story about the sweet young murderess who lives next door.

Murder on Board, by Agatha Christie. Dodd, 1974. A collection of several of Miss Christie's shorter murder mysteries.

Tales of Terror and Suspense, ed. by Stewart H. Benedict. Dell, 1963. Benedict has collected some of the best stories of the greatest writers of horror and mystery.

Three Plays about Crime and Criminals, ed. by George Freedley. Washington Square Press, 1962. Three mystery plays, suitable for reading on rainy nights or for performing in class.

2

The In-Group

forestudy

Drama and Human Nature

Plays are written to be performed—on a stage before a live audience or before motion picture or television cameras (for later viewing by large audiences). Plays are written because playwrights have something they want to say to you about people and their behavior, about the predicaments that individuals get themselves into—and sometimes out of—about this world in which we find ourselves through no choice of our own.

Some plays, including movies and television plays, are memorable because of what happens. "Sorry, Wrong Number" is a good example. Other examples include "Trifles," "The Pharmacist's Mate," "The Clod," and such movies/TV shows as *The Man in the Iron Mask* and *The French Connection*.

On the other hand, some plays—including TV plays—are memorable because of the characters in them. *Romeo and Juliet* is a good example. Other examples include "Visit to a Small Planet," in which Kreton is the memorable character; "All in the Family," in which Archie Bunker figures prominently; *To Kill a Mockingbird*, (the movie, as well as the novel), in which Scout Finch was the principal character.

Of course, no play focuses exclusively on character or on plot/situation or on idea/theme. It's simply that one of those elements usually receives greater emphasis than another.

When a playwright stresses idea/theme in a play, the plot/situation may strike you as unreal—even nonsensical. The reason might well be that the playwright presents what he/she sees as a general condition of life rather than a specific situation affecting specific individuals. What's more, the characters

25

in such a play may or may not seem like real people. In fact, they may not even have names! Again, one important reason is that the playwright's interest is not centered on one person and his/her problems. Instead, the playwright wants you to see how people in general behave under certain kinds of circumstances.

In short, when a play focuses on idea/theme, the playwright wants to show you something about human nature and how various *kinds* of people behave in typical human situations.

It's very nice being the only member of the group, or is it?

The In-Group

Paul T. Nolan

Characters

ONE	
TWO	*dressed in white*
THREE	
FOUR	
FIVE	*dressed in blue*
SIX	
SEVEN	
EIGHT	*dressed in white and black*
NINE	
TEN	
ELEVEN	*dressed in green*
TWELVE	

Reprinted by permission from *Drama Workshop Plays for Young People*, by Paul T. Nolan. Plays, Inc., Publishers. Copyright © 1968 by Plays, Inc. This play is for reading purposes only. For permission to produce this play, write to Plays, Inc., 8 Arlington St., Boston, MA 02116.

Setting

An elevated platform, on which are three kitchen stools, is at centre, slightly upstage. Several mats and pillows are downstage from the platform. Five chairs and an easel are down left, and down right are five more chairs and a typewriter on a table.

AT RISE: ONE, TWO, *and* THREE *are sitting on the stools.* FOUR, FIVE, *and* SIX *are sitting on the mats.* SEVEN *and* EIGHT *are sitting in chairs left, reading, and* NINE *stands in front of the easel, painting.* TEN *and* ELEVEN *are sitting in chairs right, and* TWELVE *sits at typewriter, ready to type.* (NOTE: *The action of the actors in the areas around the platform is done in exaggerated pantomime,° as quietly as possible.*)

ONE: I don't think anyone could honestly say we are snobbish.

TWO: But let's face it, One. We are the in-group.

THREE: It may not be fair, but . . .

ONE: We are better than other people.

TWO: We are all dressed in white.

THREE: And sit on fine stools.

ONE: On a fine platform.

TWO: Which naturally makes us better than other people.

ONE: I am very grateful.

TWO: I am, too.

ONE: *That* proves we're not snobbish.

TWO: Snobs *think* they are better than other people.

ONE: But we really are.

TWO: Everyone would like to be in our group.

ONE: Naturally, Two.

THREE: But we have no room for anyone else.

ONE: We have only three stools, and there are three of us.

THREE: Of course, we could make some more stools.

ONE: Then we would be crowded, Three.

TWO: Besides, there are plenty of seats for everyone—over there. (*Points to area left*)

THREE: And over there. (*Points to area right*)

ONE   (*snickering*): And down there. (*Points to area down centre*)

TWO: But up here, there are just enough stools for the members of the in-group.

ONE: That's the way it should be, because we were born to sit on stools and look down on the out-groups around us.

TWO: I am very grateful that I am a member of the in-group.

THREE: I am, too.

ONE: Everyone would like to change places with us and sit on a fine stool on this fine platform and have such a fine view of the world below.

TWO: They certainly would.

THREE: But . . .

ONE: But what?

TWO (*to* ONE; *indicating* THREE):   Are you sure Three belongs to our group? He sounds like a dangerous radical.°

ONE: Or a reactionary,° which is just as bad.

TWO: Or a conservative.

ONE: Or a liberal.

TWO: Or a moderate.

ONE: Or even a middle-of-the-roader.

TWO: Whatever that is.

THREE: I just said *but*.

ONE: I wish we had soap. I'd wash his mouth out.

TWO: I've always been suspicious of him.

ONE: Now he'll be accusing us of exploiting° the lower classes.

TWO: Or revolting against the upper classes.

ONE: Or selling out to the middle classes.

TWO: Or of advocating a classless society.

ONE: Or of joining . . . of joining . . .

TWO: We've run out of classes.

ONE: It's Three's fault. He's the one who brought up this whole class business.

TWO: I agree. I think there's entirely too much talk about class. (*Pointing to other groups*) They talk about class, but *we* don't.

THREE: I didn't say anything about class.

ONE: You did, you did. (*to* TWO) Didn't he, Two?

TWO: I don't think so. He said *but*.

ONE: That's the same thing.

THREE: I wasn't even thinking of class. I was just thinking.

(NINE, *the painter, throws his hands in the air in glee, steps back and looks at easel. All, except those on the platform, rush over and look at the picture. They clap* NINE *on the back, shake his hand, admire picture.* ONE, TWO, *and* THREE *walk to edge of platform nearest easel and look.*)

ONE: What are they doing now?

TWO: They are looking at a picture he painted.

THREE: Is it any good?

ONE: I don't know whether it's any good or not. I can't even see it.

TWO: I can see it.

THREE: Is it any good?

TWO: I don't know anything about art. I know what I like, but that's as far as I go.

THREE: Do you like it?

TWO: I'd rather not say. I might be wrong. (ONE, TWO, *and* THREE *return to stools. Others return to original positions.* ONE *and* TWO *sit, but* THREE *remains standing.*)

ONE (*to* THREE):   Well.

THREE: Well, what?

ONE: Sit down.

THREE: I don't want to sit down.

ONE: You don't want to sit down?

TWO: On a stool?

THREE: No.

ONE: You just want to stand there?

TWO: Forever?

THREE: I want to sit down. There! (*Points to left area*)

ONE: Traitor!

TWO: Quisling![1]

ONE: Benedict Arnold!

TWO: George Washington!

ONE (*turning to* TWO, *somewhat aghast*): George Washington? What does George Washington have to do with this? He was no traitor.

TWO: I was thinking of the matter from the British point of view.

ONE: You *do* have a point, but I wish you hadn't made it. (*to* THREE) I suppose you feel sorry for them.

THREE: Why should I feel sorry for them? They look happy.

TWO: Don't listen to him, One. It's just that business with the painting. He thinks they have a group.

THREE: I do not. My back is tired, and I want to sit down. That's all.

ONE: Are you saying that their chairs are more comfortable than our stools?

THREE: Yes, I am.

TWO: That's a crime. Every day in every way we are better than anyone else. Even if we are too polite to say so.

ONE: Look, Three, I've always liked you. Perhaps those chairs do *look* more comfortable than our stools.

TWO: The grass always looks greener in the other fellow's pasture.

ONE: *Perhaps*—and mind you, I say *perhaps*—their chairs might be a little more comfortable. Are you going to sacrifice your position in our group for that?

THREE: What's so great about our group?

TWO: Oh, I do wish we had soap to wash out his mouth.

ONE: Patience, Two, patience. After all, he is a member of our group.

TWO: I know. And that means he is worth saving. At least in theory.

ONE: At least, he deserves a chance.

1. *quisling:* see Follow-Up, page 38.

(*to* THREE) What was that question again?

THREE: What's so great about our group?

ONE: What's so great about our group?

THREE: There must be an echo in here. That's exactly what I asked.

ONE: Don't be fresh.

TWO: Or insolent.°

ONE: Or outlandish.

TWO: Or freakish.

ONE: I'll tell you what's so great about our group. We're the in-group.

THREE: So's the group at the State Penitentiary.

ONE: But they don't dress in white.

TWO: Or sit on fine stools.

ONE: And they weren't born into their group.

THREE: I wish I hadn't been.

ONE: You may leave, you know.

THREE: May I really?

TWO: Right now, if you wish. (THREE *walks to edge of platform and puts one foot over edge as though testing the water. He wiggles his foot.*)

THREE: It seems pleasant enough out here.

ONE: Of course, once you leave, you can't come back.

TWO: Never.

ONE: That's a rule.

TWO: Of long standing.

THREE: I wonder if they'll have me.

ONE: Of course.

TWO: Why not?

ONE: There's always room at the bottom.

TWO: So stop being silly. Come back and sit down.

THREE: No, I'm going to do it. (*Starts to step forward*)

ONE: Well, go ahead.

TWO: But you'll be sorry.

ONE: Forever.

THREE (*stepping back*): I suppose I will. (TWELVE *gets up from typewriter, waves sheet of paper in air. All except* ONE, TWO, *and* THREE *rush around him. He pantomimes reading from paper. Others take out large handkerchiefs and pantomime crying.*) What are they doing now?

ONE: Twelve has written a poem.

THREE: Twelve?

ONE: That's his name. People out there have very funny names. Like Four, Five, Six, Seven, Eight, Nine, Ten, Eleven, Twelve.

TWO: Some you can't even pronounce.

ONE: If they belonged to the in-group, they would have nice names.

TWO: Like Two.

ONE: And One.

THREE: And Three?

ONE: I suppose.

THREE (*looking at them carefully*):   Why are they crying?

ONE: The poem.

TWO: It's very sad.

ONE: They cry a great deal in the out-group.

TWO: They are sad.

ONE: It's their own fault. If they want to listen to poetry, they must expect to be sad. (*Others pantomime laughter, clap* TWELVE *on back, and shake his hand.*)

THREE: Now they're happy.

ONE: Of course. They are not very dependable.

THREE: I think I'll join them.

TWO: You'll be sorry.

THREE: I *am* going to join them. (*He steps off platform carefully, looks about, smiles, flexes his muscles, runs over to a chair in left group, and sits.*)

TWO (*staring after* THREE):   He did it.

ONE: He did what?

TWO: He left us. He deserted our group. (*Gets up*)

ONE: Who deserted our group?

TWO: Three did. See him sitting there? (*Others return to their original positions.* EIGHT *gives* THREE *a book, and* THREE *starts to read.*) See, he's reading.

30   ONE: Who's reading?

TWO: Three is.

ONE: I never heard of him.

TWO: Oh. Oh, of course not. (*Still staring at* THREE) But he does look like someone I used to know.

ONE: Stop that, Two. Come back and sit down. (TWO *returns, but can't decide which of the two empty stools to take.*)

TWO: Where shall I sit?

ONE: On the stool, of course.

TWO: But there are two stools.

ONE (*looking at* TWO, *puzzled*):   Is there only one of you?

TWO: Why, yes, I think so.

ONE: Are you sure?

TWO (*pointing to himself*):   One. (*Seems about to point to a second*) Yes, I'm sure. There is only one of me.

ONE (*rising and looking concerned*):   This does present a problem.

TWO: Maybe I could sit on two stools.

ONE: Not if there's only one of you.

TWO: Maybe we could just leave one stool empty.

ONE: That would utterly ruin property values.

TWO: What are we going to do?

ONE: It's all your fault. You drove what's-his-name off.

TWO: I did not. He left of his own free will.

ONE: I don't like that expression—*free will*. It sounds . . . well . . . unruly.

TWO: Unruly?

ONE: Yes, undisciplined. If people just go around doing things from free will, what happens to law and order?

TWO: And what happens to the extra stool?

ONE: Exactly. (SEVEN *walks up to platform.*)

SEVEN: Psst!

ONE: Two, did you hear something?

TWO: No.

ONE: I didn't either.

SEVEN: Psst. Hey, I mean you.

TWO: Are you sure you didn't hear anything, One?

ONE: Not unless you did.

TWO: I heard . . . well—(*points at* SEVEN)

ONE: Do you want to speak to him?

TWO: Do you?

ONE: Not unless you do.

TWO: You speak first. You're One.

ONE: All right. (*Goes over near* SEVEN *and bends over as though speaking down from a great distance*.) Did you call us?

SEVEN: I sure did. Is that stool empty?

ONE: Why do you want to know?

SEVEN: I'd like to sit on it.

TWO: It's not as easy as that. These stools are for members of the in-group only.

SEVEN: I know; I want to join your in-group.

ONE: You can't just *join* our group. You have to be born into it.

SEVEN: I know. I want to be born into it.

ONE: Oh. (*Turning to* TWO) What do you think?

TWO: What do *you* think?

ONE: Do you want me to speak for the group?

TWO: Yes, of course.

ONE: Will you give me authority to speak with one voice for the whole group?

TWO: Yes, of course.

ONE: And you won't complain later?

TWO: I probably will.

ONE: If that's understood, I'll speak to him. (*Returns to* SEVEN) In our group, we all sit on stools.

SEVEN: I like stools.

ONE: We all wear white.

SEVEN: I am wearing black and white.

(ONE *reaches out, takes* SEVEN's *hand, and helps him onto platform.*)

ONE: Welcome aboard, then.

SEVEN: Shouldn't we all sit down?

ONE: Of course. (*Goes to stool and sits*)

TWO: To be sure. (*Sits on stool*)

SEVEN: It's perfectly natural. (*Sits on stool*)

ONE: Everyone would like to be in our group.

TWO: Naturally.

SEVEN: But we have no room for anyone else.

ONE: We have only three stools, and there are three of us.

TWO: Of course, we could make some more stools.

SEVEN: But then we would be crowded. Besides, there are plenty of seats for everyone.

ONE (*pointing left*): Over there.

TWO (*pointing right*): And over there.

SEVEN (*snickering*): And down there. (*Points to area down centre*) But up here, there are just enough stools for the members of the in-group.

ONE: And that's the way it should be.

SEVEN: Because we were born to sit on stools and look down on the out-groups around us.

ONE: I'm grateful.

TWO: Me, too.

SEVEN: Everyone would like to change places with us and sit on a fine stool on this fine platform and have such a fine view of the world below.

ONE: I guess they would.

TWO: But . . .

SEVEN (*rising and pointing at* TWO): He said *but*. Two said *but*. Did you hear him, One?

ONE: I heard him.

SEVEN: Are you sure he belongs to our

group? He sounds like a dangerous non-conformist.° (ONE *shrugs.*) A radical. A conservative. A liberal. A moderate. A middle-of-the-roader.

ONE: Whatever that is.

TWO: I did say *but*, and that's what I meant.

SEVEN: I wish I had soap. I'd wash out his mouth.

TWO (*standing and walking to edge of platform right*): I'm going to write a poem, too.

SEVEN: You'll never do it. It's easy enough to talk. But you'll never leave. You'll never do it. You know which side your bread's buttered on. You'll never go. (TWO *steps off platform and goes to typewriter. He taps* TWELVE *on shoulder.* TWELVE *looks around, sees* TWO, *gets up, and goes to another chair.* TWO *sits down at typewriter.*) He did it.

ONE: I hope he writes a short poem. I hate long poems.

SEVEN: It's all your fault. You've become soft in your position, One. You've been up on top too long.

ONE (*getting off stool and rubbing his hip*): I think I have been.

SEVEN: I think there should be an election for a new leader.

ONE: All right.

SEVEN: Isn't it the tradition of our in-group that people don't vote for themselves?

ONE: Of course. We are ladies and gentlemen. We serve only when we are forced to do so.

SEVEN: All right then, how many votes for One? (*Looks about to count*) No votes. Now then, how many votes for Seven? (*Looks at* ONE) Aren't you going to vote for me?

ONE: I don't think so.

SEVEN: Why not?

ONE: I don't like you. You're too traditional.

SEVEN: Oh. (*Raises hand*) And how many votes for Seven? (*Looks up at own hand*) One. Gentlemen, I accept this high office that has been forced upon me. Although I would prefer to lead a private life, tending my sheep, collecting stamps, whistling Brahms,[2] I know my duty. Since you, my fellow citizens, have insisted that I take the helm of state, I can do no less than accept. (*Bows*)

ONE: You broke the tradition of our in-group when you voted for yourself.

SEVEN: I have just started a new tradition.

ONE: Very well. I submit.

SEVEN: Well, then, let's all sit down. (*Sits on stool*)

ONE: Which stool shall I sit on?

SEVEN: Is that my job to decide?

ONE: Of course, you're the leader.

SEVEN: It's not easy to lead, is it?

ONE: I wouldn't know.

SEVEN: True. Only we who have accepted the burden of command know its weight.

ONE: What stool shall I sit on?

SEVEN (*pointing to one stool*): How about that one?

ONE (*pointing to other*): That one will be empty then.

SEVEN: Then why not sit on that one?

ONE: Then that one (*points to other stool*) will be empty.

SEVEN: There does seem to be a problem. Why can't one stool be empty?

ONE: Ruins property values.

SEVEN: Couldn't you sit on both stools?

ONE: That would be pushy.

2. *Brahms*: Johannes, a famous German composer (1833–1897)

32   ONE: I don't think so.

SEVEN: Couldn't we burn the stool?

ONE: That would be wasteful.

SEVEN: Oh, the burden of command. (NINE *moves away from easel, stretches, and walks up to platform.* SEVEN *looks down at* NINE.) Hello there, Nine.

NINE: Hi, Seven, what's new?

ONE: You are not supposed to speak to those out there.

SEVEN: I used to know him.

ONE: We never used to know anyone out there.

SEVEN: I didn't know him very well.

ONE: You're not supposed to know him at all.

NINE: Hey, Seven, is it all right if I take that stool up there?

SEVEN (*to* ONE): Is it?

ONE: It's up to you.

SEVEN: It would solve our problem.

ONE: Of course, he'd have to be a member.

SEVEN: Nine, do you want to be a member of the in-group?

NINE: Will I be able to sit on the stool if I do?

SEVEN: Of course.

NINE: And look down on the rest of the world?

SEVEN: Of course.

NINE: All right, I'll join.

SEVEN (*giving him a hand to help him onto the platform*): You're very lucky, you know. Everyone wants to be a member of our group.

NINE: I know.

SEVEN: Let's all sit down. Everything is solved now. (NINE *and* SEVEN *sit on stools.* FOUR *rises from his mat and stands on his head. Others rush over and applaud. After he rights himself, they shake his hand and clap him on the back. Then they return to their original positions.*)

33

ONE: I could do that, too.

SEVEN: Do what?

ONE: Do what Four down there just did. Stand on my head.

NINE: That's an odd ambition. In all my years as a member of the in-group, I never heard any of our members express a desire to stand on his head.

SEVEN: One hasn't been feeling well, I'm afraid.

NINE: Are you sure he's a member of our group?

ONE: It shouldn't be too hard. (*Yells down to group down centre*) Hey, Four, I can do that. Did you hear me?

NINE: Of course, he didn't hear you.

SEVEN: We have no communication with them, and they have no communication with us.

NINE: We don't speak the same language.

SEVEN: Or use the same accent.

NINE: I am grateful that I am a member of the in-group.

SEVEN: Everyone would like to change places with us and sit on a fine stool on this fine platform and have such a fine view of the world below.

ONE (*yelling again*): Hey, Four. I can stand on my head, too.

SEVEN (*to* NINE; *indicating* ONE): Are you sure he belongs to our group

NINE: He sounds like an outsider. Or an inside-outer. Or an upside-downer.

ONE (*yelling again*): Hey, Four, I can do that.

SEVEN: You're just wasting your time, One. There is a wall between our world and theirs.

NINE: They can't hear us, and we can't hear them.

ONE: But I hear them.

SEVEN: Oh.

NINE: Well.

SEVEN: We hear them, but we can't understand them. Not really.

NINE: They are just different.

ONE: I understand them. I understand them all. (*Points to right area.*) They are writers and orators, and they like to write poetry and cry and laugh. (*Points to left area*) And they are painters and builders and plumbers and artists like that. They like to paint things and build things and plumb things. (*Points to downstage area*) And they are athletes, and they like to do things. They are just like us.

SEVEN: They are not like me.

NINE: I don't like to do anything.

ONE: Some of them don't like to do things, either.

NINE: Those are just the bums.

ONE: You talk in circles.

SEVEN: Talking in circles is the proper way to talk.

NINE: If you really and truly belong to the in-group.

SEVEN: So stop that nonsense of trying to talk to the people out there and sit down. (FOUR *stands on his head again.*)

ONE: There, he did it again.

SEVEN: Really, One, you are being quite tiresome.

ONE (*shouting to* FOUR): Hey, Four, I can do that.

NINE: He can't hear you.

ONE: How do you know he can't?

NINE: I shouldn't tell you, but I will. People out there—doing things, crying, laughing, and standing on their heads—they don't know what it is like just to *be* something. They are always proving things, doing things.

SEVEN: Helping people and hurting people and things like that.

NINE: Every day they want to do something new.

SEVEN: It's always just a lot of fuss and bother.

NINE: And they forget all about what group they are in.

SEVEN: And even how much more important the group is than anything else.

NINE: They write poems.

SEVEN: Poems that aren't even about their group.

NINE: They wander from group to group, just as if there were no walls separating people from each other.

SEVEN: I could forgive them if they would stay the same, even if they were always doing things.

NINE: But they don't. Look. (FOUR *goes over to* TWO *at typewriter, taps him on the shoulder,* TWO *gets up, and* FOUR *sits down.* TWO *goes to center and stands on his head.*)

SEVEN: You see. Everybody does everything out there.

ONE: Hey, Two, I can do that.

NINE: He can't hear you.

ONE: That's Two. I used to know him. He was a member of our in-group.

SEVEN: It doesn't make any difference. They can't hear us out there unless they come to us.

ONE: I'm going out there, too.

SEVEN: You won't like it.

NINE: You'll try to stand on your head and fall.

SEVEN: Then where will you be?

NINE: Do you want to be a failure?

ONE: I might not fail.

SEVEN: Stay here, One, and you know you can't fail.

ONE: I might succeed.

NINE: Stay here, One, and you know you can't succeed. We are safe here. We don't fail. We don't succeed. We just are.

ONE: We never laugh here.

SEVEN: We sneer a lot.

ONE: That's not the same. We don't laugh.

NINE: But we don't cry, either.

ONE: It doesn't matter if you don't cry as long as you don't laugh.

SEVEN: You may cry a lot out there.

ONE: It's better to cry than to do nothing. I'm going to go.

NINE: You'll be back.

SEVEN: We've been there. We know.

ONE: I *am* afraid to go. Hey, Two, help me to join you.

SEVEN: He won't help you.

ONE: You said that people out there help each other.

NINE: You're not out there.

SEVEN: They don't even know you exist.

ONE: I'm going out there.

SEVEN: You're afraid.

ONE: I know it. But I'm going to go anyway.

NINE: Suit yourself.

ONE: Goodbye, Nine. Think about me when I'm gone.

NINE: We never think about anyone here.

SEVEN: If we tried, it would ruin our in-group.

ONE: I'll think about you.

NINE: You won't have time.

SEVEN: Out there, you just do things. You'll forget all about us.

ONE (*stepping off platform*): Goodbye. (*Looks about, then goes to* TWO) I can stand on my head, too.

TWO: That's nice. To whom were you speaking?

ONE: When?

TWO: Just then.

ONE (*looking around without seeing* SEVEN *and* NINE):   I must have been speaking to myself. There's no one else around.

TWO: I used to live over there. (*Points to typewriter*) I was a poet when I was young.

ONE: I am going to be a poet someday.

TWO: Next year, I am going to be a painter.

ONE: Say, that would be fun. I might try that, too. But now, I am going to stand on my head. I've always wanted to. (ONE *tries to stand on his head, falls, laughs, and*

TWO *watches, smiling.* ONE *tries again and succeeds.* SEVEN *and* NINE *get up.*)

SEVEN: He has forgotten us.

NINE: You said he would.

SEVEN: We don't need him.

NINE: Or any of them.

SEVEN: We are the in-group.

NINE: We are better than other people.

SEVEN: We are all dressed in black and white.

NINE: And sit on fine stools.

SEVEN: On a fine platform.

NINE: While out there, they are alive.

SEVEN: And that means being unhappy and trying and failing.

NINE: And crying and writing poetry and fixing the plumbing.

SEVEN: Come on, Nine, let's sit down.

NINE: Where shall we sit? There are three stools, and there are only two of us.

SEVEN: Just sit on any one. Someone else will be along soon.

(SEVEN *sits on a stool and looks glumly out.*)

NINE (*hesitating a moment, then selecting a stool*):   I am very grateful that I am a member of the in-group.

SEVEN: I am, too.

NINE (*sighing*):   Everyone would like to be in our group.

SEVEN (*sadly*):   Everyone envies us.

NINE: But we need a new member. Isn't someone somewhere tired of being alive? (SEVEN *and* NINE *sit, looking out, chins on hands.*)

ONE: Do you know what we ought to do? We ought to have a party.

TWO: And invite everyone?

ONE: Everyone who wants to come.

THREE (*coming to centre*): I want to come. (*Others join group at centre.*)

FOUR: I'll bake a cake.

FIVE: I don't have a thing to wear, but I'll come anyway.

SIX: I'll have a friend I want to bring. I'm going out and make a friend right now. (*Runs off stage*)

EIGHT: I used to have some friends just like me. I wish they were here.

SEVEN: Eight is talking about us, Nine.

NINE: It will probably be a wonderful party.

SEVEN: I don't want to go, do you?

NINE: Not if everyone is invited.

SEVEN: Let's have a party of our own.

NINE: It wouldn't be the same.

SEVEN: Why not?

NINE: We don't have anyone to invite.

SEVEN: Then I'm going to One's party. Hey, wait for me. (SEVEN *leaps off platform and joins others, who form a line.*)

ALL (*chanting*): We're having a party. (*They march off right, chanting.*)

NINE (*sadly*): It's very nice being the only member of the in-group. That means I'm really exclusive. But it does get lonely. (*Pretending to phone*) Hello, Operator? Do you have a phone number for the Lonely Hearts Club? . . . But that's my number. . . . No, thank you. Don't bother to ring. There will be no one there. Goodbye, Operator. (*Hangs up*) Hey, wait for me. I'm coming, too. (*Leaps off platform*) Wait for me. (*Runs off right, chanting*) I'm going to a party. I'm going to a party. (*Curtain*)

---

follow-up

Discussing "The In-Group"

1. What do you understand the "in-group" to be? Why do people want to be in it?
2. What do you understand the "out-group" to be? Why do people want to be in the "out-group"? Why might they want to be out of the "out-group"?
3. How do you see yourself? Do you tend to be like those who joined—or wanted to join—the "in-group" or like those who joined—or wanted to join—the "out-group"?
4. How do you see your friends? Are they "in-group" joiners or "out-group" joiners?

Our Changing Language

Our English language is like people. It grows and changes just as people do. Not only do words come into the language, **37** but their meanings can and do change. Some words last longer than others. Some words die out altogether.

Take the word *quisling* (p. 28) for instance. That word came into our English language in 1945, and so it's just a youngster when compared to English words that have been around since about 1350. *Quisling*, incidentally, came from the name of a Norwegian politician—Vidkung Quisling—who collaborated with the Nazi invaders of Norway in 1945. His name has become synonymous with the word *traitor*. Other relatively new words that have come into the language within the last 50 years are *middle-of-the-roader* (p. 27) and *pushy* (p. 32).

New words come into the language from a number of sources. As people move from one place to another, they have new experiences. They find that the old words aren't really adequate under new conditions, and so they coin new words. *Bucket seat*, for example, is a fairly new term, as also are *jive*, *mooch*, *cloning*, *recap*, *supermarket*, and *Laundromat*.

New words also come into the language as a result of scientific research. *Television, antibiotics, radar, sonar, jeep, transistor, moonwalk, microwave*—these are among the many words—like *quisling*—that have come into our English language within the last 60 years.

Not only does the English language acquire *new* words. Many words that have been around a long time have come to mean something different today than they did originally. Take *stink* for instance. Originally, the word meant "any odor" and was a perfectly respectable word to use. Shakespeare, for instance, spoke of the "stink of roses." Today, however, the meaning has changed. If something stinks, you can bet it doesn't smell like roses!

Meat is still another word whose meaning has changed. Originally, *meat* meant "food in general." Maybe you've seen or heard the expression "meat and drink." It means "food and drink." Today, however, *meat* refers primarily to "the flesh of animals used for food."

Finally, some words die out altogether. Take *yclept*, for example. It's an old, old English word that meant "named" or "called." It was used in this way: The maiden *yclept* Dawn has captured his heart. Another outdated word is *wellaway*, which meant "alas." And consider every word in this sentence, except *not*: *Dost thou* not *ken, varlet, thy liege*? Except for *not* and for *thou* and *thy* (which we hear today only in connection with religious matters), not one of those words is used anymore. (Incidentally, what that question asks is this: Don't you know, you scoundrel, who your superior, or boss, is?)

New words, words whose meanings have changed, and outdated—archaic—words all give lasting proof that English is a dynamic, living language.

Practice 1. Writing

The following words are relative newcomers to our language. In your own words, write a brief definition of each one. Then select any five of them, and use each in an original sentence. You may want to consult a recently published dictionary—one that was published within the last ten years.

1. allergy	4. emcee	7. jitney	10. smog
2. astronaut	5. fallout	8. microfilm	
3. brainwash	6. jinx	9. motel	

Be prepared to read your definition of at least one of the words aloud. Then read the sentence in which you've used the word. Do your classmates agree that your definition and your use of the word are accurate? clear?

Practice 2. Writing

Each of the words in Column A below means something different today from what it meant originally. In Column B, you'll find the original meaning of each word. *Column C: Today's Meaning* is for you to complete. On your paper, copy the items in Column A and in Column B as they appear here. Then, in Column C, write *today's* meaning of each word. Be brief; use your own words.

	Column A Word	Column B Original Meaning	Column C Today's Meaning
Example 0:	meat	any food	animal flesh used for food
1.	cheap	inexpensive	
2.	fame	rumor	
3.	homely	homelike; kind	
4.	insane	not healthy	
5.	nice	fastidious; finicky	
6.	pretty	cunning; crafty	
7.	steeped	stupefied; stunned	
8.	villain	a country person	

Be prepared to read your definition of at least one word aloud. Compare your definition with those your classmates have written.

Practice 3. Writing

The italicized word in each of the following sentences is one that we don't use anymore. After you consult a dictionary to find out what the italicized word meant, rewrite the sentence, expressing the idea in words we use today.

1. The king dreamed of seven fat *kine* and seven lean *kine*.
2. *Fain* would I go with you.
3. I *wist* not where the ship was headed.
4. *Meseems* the speaker was wrong.
5. *Forsooth*, sir, I mean you no harm.

Be prepared to read one of your rewritten sentences aloud. First tell what the outdated italicized word meant; then express the idea in today's words. Do your classmates agree that your sentence conveys the correct meaning?

Bookshelf

Bitter Is the Hawk's Path, by Jean McCord. Atheneum, 1971. A group of stories about people who gradually come to understand and accept their uniqueness, their differences from everyone around them.

A Girl Called Al, by Constance C. Green. Viking 1969. Two friends try hard to find themselves by refusing to conform to their group.

The Loners: Short Stories about the Young and Alienated, ed. by M. L. Schulman. Macmillan, 1970. A collection of stories about the pain of growing up and assuming adult responsibility.

Very Special People, by Frederick Drimmer. Bantam, 1976. A nonfiction account of the lives of people whose problems are complicated by severe physical deformities.

3

Youth and Age—Age and Youth

We tend to group people into age groups—childhood, adolescence, adulthood, old age. Each age has its satisfactions and pleasures, its pains and fears. In general, the young are free of major responsibility; yet they may have fears because of ignorance, because of the unknown. In general, adults have the satisfaction of achievement; yet they bear heavy responsibilities. In general, old people have the satisfaction and pleasure of wisdom; yet they may fear sickness and death.

The young are often not as practical, as hard-headed, as adults. And yet don't people lose a certain something by growing up? For instance, take the speakers in the next two poems.

The Centaur[1]

May Swenson

The summer that I was ten—
Can it be there was only one
summer that I was ten? It must

have been a long one then—
each day I'd go out to choose
a fresh horse from my stable

which was a willow grove
down by the old canal.
I'd go on my two bare feet.

1. *centaur:* in Greek legend, a creature that had the head, arms and chest of a human, and the body and legs of a horse

But when, with my brother's jack-knife,
I had cut me a long limber horse
with a good thick knob for a head,

and peeled him slick and clean
except a few leaves for a tail,
and cinched my brother's belt

around his head for a rein,
I'd straddle and canter him fast
up the grass bank to the path,

trot along in the lovely dust
that talcumed over his hoofs,
hiding my toes, and turning

his feet to swift half-moons.
The willow knob with the strap
jouncing between my thighs

was the pommel and yet the poll[2]
of my nickering pony's head.
My head and my neck were mine,

yet they were shaped like a horse.
My hair flopped to the side
like the mane of a horse in the wind.

My forelock swung in my eyes,
my neck arched and I snorted.
I shied and skittered and reared,

10

20

30

2. *poll:* the nape of a horse's neck

stepped and raised my knees,
pawed at the ground and quivered.
My teeth bared as we wheeled

and swished through the dust again.
I was the horse and the rider,
and the leather I slapped to his rump

spanked my own behind.   40
Doubled, my two hoofs beat
a gallop along the bank,

the wind twanged in my mane,
my mouth squared to the bit.
And yet I sat on my steed

quiet, negligent riding,
my toes standing the stirrups,
my thighs hugging his ribs.

At a walk we drew up to the porch.
I tethered him to a paling.   50
Dismounting, I smoothed my skirt

and entered the dusky hall.
My feet on the clean linoleum
left ghostly toes in the hall.

Where have you been? said my mother.
Been riding, I said from the sink,
and filled me a glass of water.

What's that in your pocket? she said.
Just my knife. It weighted my pocket
and stretched my dress awry.   60

Go tie back your hair, said my mother,
and Why is your mouth all green?
Rob Roy, he pulled some clover
as we crossed the field, I told her.

    A: That's pretty dumb. What a way for anyone to waste an
       afternoon!
    B: But didn't she have as much fun on her make-believe
       horse as she would have had on a real horse?
    A: You mean that imagining something can sometimes be
       as enjoyable as the real thing?

When I Was One-and-Twenty

A. E. Housman

When I was one-and-twenty
  I heard a wise man say,
'Give crowns and pounds and guineas[3]
  But not your heart away;
Give pearls away and rubies
  But keep your fancy free.'
But I was one-and-twenty,
  No use to talk to me.

When I was one-and-twenty
  I heard him say again,
'The heart out of the bosom
  Was never given in vain;
'Tis paid with sighs a plenty
  And sold for endless rue.'[4]
And I am two-and-twenty,
  And oh, tis true, tis true.

> A: There. You see? He was a childish dreamer, not
>   listening to the voice of wisdom. And now he regrets it.
> B: But wasn't there at least a chance for some happiness
>   in his falling in love? Don't you sometimes have to
>   take risks?
> A: Not me! I learn from *other* people's mistakes!

3. *guineas:* a former British gold coin worth one pound
and one shilling

4. *rue:* sorrow, regret

From "A Shropshire Lad"—Authorized Edition—from THE COL-
LECTED POEMS OF A.E. HOUSMAN, Copyright 1939, 1940,
© 1965 by Holt, Rinehart and Winston. Copyright © 1967, 1968
by Robert E. Symons. Reprinted by permission of Holt, Rinehart
and Winston, Publishers, and the Society of Authors as the literary representative of the Estate of A.E. Housman; and Jonathan
Cape Ltd., publishers of A.E. Housman's COLLECTED POEMS.

Learning from mistakes—other people's and our own, too—can do a lot to make life more livable. What's more, learning from successes—again, other people's, as well as our own—can certainly help us progress further than those who have come before us. It's much like the progress scientists make as they build upon the discoveries their predecessors have made.

But life's sort of strange, isn't it? Scientific information is passed along from one generation to another. (That's one reason why we today can all ride in automobiles rather than on horseback.) But we still haven't found the secret of passing along the knowledge that will insure all of us a full, happy life. In fact, on that score, we're not much better off than were the ancient Greeks and Romans. Yet there *are* times when a person from one generation does pass along some information that might help persons of a younger generation. Is that the case in this next poem?

Death of a Salesman

David Wevill

By the big Shell sign I turned left
Around the cloverleaf, and drove out north
Across the boundary river into Quebec.
Beside me a boy on a bicycle raced
Abreast of me, level with my door—
I could feel the beat of his heart against the wind
And whirl of his knees spinning against my
Engine, straining to lose
Not a foot, as I pushed the car faster.

But where the road forked
Right, into Hull, I lost him; looked back to see if he'd stopped
Fallen, or gone in another direction.
Nowhere in sight... I waited a moment,
Smoked, reflected: thinking I'd betrayed him,
Not given him a chance,
All that effort lost in the wind—
Game I used to play myself to win.

From A CHRIST OF THE ICE-FLOES by David Wevill. Reprinted by permission of Macmillan, London and Basingstoke.

But now on this road, not exulting, what had happened?
Between those tall dreaming elms at the intersection
He'd given it up, as he knew he must,
Though his heart thumped faster still, ahead of him,
    hot to outrace me.

In the mirror I see
Just the empty road behind me,
The vanished boy, and the wheels loitering back slowly...

And the whipped heart retreats to pride, my loss,
His victory will come when he owns a car.
His loss will follow when he wins this race.

    If the older generation could inform the younger generation
of wisdom gained by experience, could youth learn—what their
predecessors had been unable to learn from their youth? Are there
some lessons that can only be learned by living?
        X: What kind of jerk is that—racing his bike against a car?
        Y: For fun. He knows he can't win, but it's a gas...ha, ha...to try.
        Z: Not so much fun for the old guy in winning as for the kid
           in losing.
    It may be that adults don't learn from the young any more than
youth from age. Isn't that what the so-called generation gap is all
about—adults forgetting what they learned as children and so
unable to do anything but set false models for youth? They can only
be painfully reminded of kid stuff when exposed to it, rather than
really relate to it. And, of course, it's impossible to hand down to
younger folk something you've lost—except perhaps the realization
of loss.

A Dream of Mountaineering

Po Chü-i

(Written when he was over seventy)

At night, in my dream, I stoutly climbed a mountain,
Going out alone with my staff of holly-wood.
A thousand crags, a hundred hundred valleys—
In my dream-journey none were unexplored
And all the while my feet never grew tired
And my step was as strong as in my young days.
Can it be that when the mind travels backward
The body also returns to its old state?

And can it be, as between body and soul,
That the body may languish, while the soul is still strong?
Soul and body—both are vanities:
Dreaming and waking—both alike unreal.
In the day my feet are palsied and tottering;
In the night my steps go striding over the hills.
As day and night are divided in equal parts—
Between the two, I *get* as much as I *lose*.

—*translated by Arthur Waley*

> M: Is he saying that as the body ages and grows weaker,
>   the imagination grows stronger?
> N: Yes, something like that. What's more, he seems to be
>   content with that trade-off.
> M: Well, then, isn't he like the ten-year-old girl in "Cen-
>   taur"—the one who rode the imaginary horse?
> O: Do you suppose the poet is suggesting that when you
>   get old, you re-learn some of the things you knew and
>   enjoyed as a child?

And then, in the end, there is death. Or is there?

For My Grandmother

Countee Cullen

This lovely flower fell to seed;
  Work gently, sun and rain;
She held it as her dying creed
  That she would grow again.

> A: How could she be sure that she would grow again?
> B: I guess you can't be sure of anything beyond death. All
>   you can do is believe—or hope.
> A: Do you think that by "grow again" she meant that she
>   would live on in her children and her grandchildren
>   and her great-grandchildren and her——?

Discussion "Youth and Age—Age and Youth"

1. What can the old teach the young? What can the young teach the old? Can they learn from each other? How?
2. Maybe you can recall one year in your life that seems to you the happiest, the best. On the other hand, maybe you look forward to some future time that you think could be the happiest, the best. If you could spend your entire life at *one age*—12 or 16 or 21 or 55 or some other—which one would you choose? Why?

4

An Ounce of Cure

forestudy

Viewpoints

Much of what you say and much of what you do depends on your POINT OF VIEW. For instance, consider this poem about the bull calf.

The Bull Calf

Irving Layton

The thing could barely stand. Yet taken
from his mother and the barn smells
he still impressed with his pride,
with the promise of sovereignty in the way
his head moved to take us in.
The fierce sunlight tugging the maize[1] from the ground
licked at his shapely flanks.
He was too young for all that pride.
I thought of the deposed Richard II.[2]

'No money in bull calves,' Freeman had said.
The visiting clergyman rubbed the nostrils
now snuffing pathetically at the windless day.
'A pity,' he sighed.
My gaze slipped off his hat toward the empty sky
that circled over the black knot of men,
over us and the calf waiting for the first blow.

1. *maize:* corn
2. *Richard II:* a king of England in the fourteenth century who thought that he should have absolute power. He was defeated by noblemen and was forced to give up the throne

From COLLECTED POEMS by Irving Layton. Reprinted by permission of The Canadian Publishers, McClelland and Stewart Limited, Toronto.

Struck,
the bull calf drew in his thin forelegs
as if gathering strength for a mad rush...
tottered...raised his darkening eyes to us,
and I saw we were at the far end
of his frightened look, growing smaller and smaller
till we were only the ponderous mallet
that flicked his bleeding ear
and pushed him over on his side, stiffly,
like a block of wood.

Below the hill's crest
the river snuffled on the improvised beach.
We dug a deep pit and threw the dead calf into it.
It made a wet sound, a sepulchral gurgle,
as the warm sides bulged and flattened.
Settled, the bull calf lay as if asleep,
one foreleg over the other,
bereft of pride and so beautiful now,
without movement, perfectly still in the cool pit,
I turned away and wept.

    Point of view! Who is right—the farmer who has to make a living or the poet who feels for the helpless calf? Doesn't it depend on point of view?

    Your point of view depends on *what* you experience and *where* you are when you experience it. Your view of an experience also depends on how closely you are involved in it. A roller-coaster, for example, seems different to those riding in it than it does to the person who's selling tickets for the roller-coaster ride.

    Take another example. Two children start a neighborhood tale that an old dilapidated house is haunted and that the little old lady with a shawl, who is often seen in its gardens, is a witch. None of this is true, of course. The lady may be a respectable person who has inherited a house which is beyond her means to keep up. But the house looks to the children as if it should be haunted, and the lady, seen only from a distance, is changed by the children's imaginations.

    In summary, the way a person views an event or scene depends mainly on three conditions:

    (1) the kind of event or scene it is,
    (2) where the person is in relation to it, and
    (3) the meaning he/she reads into it at a given moment in his/her life.

Practice 1. Reading/Discussion

Read the following passage. Then with your classmates, discuss the questions following it.

> The traffic changed as my little sports convertible glided up the on-ramp and into the right lane of 99N. A big tractor-trailer roared from behind, its lights flooding the night. And when it passed, slapping a great wall of air against my car, I felt as if I had been stiff-armed by a huge mechanical fullback racing to make a touchdown. Then two white headlight lances loomed on the dull asphalt ribbon ahead, fused into a blinding flash, and hissed a sinister near miss while bolting past.

1. What details appeal to the eye? to the ear? to the sense of touch?
2. What seems to be the writer's mood? Which words reveal it?
3. Is the writer observing from a distance, or as a part of the scene itself?
4. How do you think the writer's mood and approach would have been different if he/she had observed the scene from a distance?

Practice 2. Reading/Discussion

Read the following passage and discuss the questions after it.

> We were flying at 300 m. I looked down from the plane's cabin window, through the dark, to the city lights, soft green and amber and yellow and rose. There seemed to be endless lines of autos crawling around city blocks and up and down the ribbon freeway, like countless illuminated ants.

1. What does the short first sentence do for you, the reader?
2. In the second sentence what is the general base statement? What detail-phrases help focus the viewpoint?
3. What is the base statement of the third sentence? What details in that sentence reinforce the viewpoint already expressed?
4. Which detail-phrase do you think adds most to the whole picture? Why? How does it depend on previous details?
5. In what way does the view from a distance seem to affect the writer's mood? How does that mood, in turn, affect the writing as compared with the passage in Practice I?

Practice 3. Writing

Choose either A or B below. Then write two or more sentences, with details, describing the two situations given.

A

How the fans of a winning championship basketball team feel
How the fans of a losing team feel

B

How you felt about a special gift as a child
How you felt about the same gift months or years later

Practice 4. Discussion

People often say things in the heat of emotion that they would not say later. "Count to ten," goes the saying. Similarly, if a person describes a tragic incident at the time it happens, with its shattering emotional impact, his/her style of expression will very likely differ from a later description of the same event. The reason: The person is looking *back* at the event from a *different* point of view.

Read passages A and B and then compare them in the questions that follow.

A

My head sank back; I closed my eyes. And at once opened them, opened them wide, threw myself out of the chair and down the hall and reached—thank God, thank God—the Berrymans' bathroom, where I was sick everywhere, everywhere, and dropped like a stone.

B

What was it that brought me back into the world again? It was the terrible and fascinating reality of my disaster; it was *the way things happened*.

1. What repetition does the speaker use that reinforces the desperation of her situation?
2. The second sentence of A is a long strung-out sentence with a spontaneous interjection in the middle of it. What does this suggest about the speaker's relation to this section of her story?
3. In B, the speaker has removed herself from the immediacy of the events. How does she show us that she is more detached and distanced in time from the agony of the events?

An Ounce of Cure

Alice Munro

My parents didn't drink. They weren't rabid[3] about it, and in fact I remember that when I signed the pledge in grade seven, with the rest of that superbly if impermanently indoctrinated[4] class, my mother said, "It's just nonsense and fanaticism°, children of that age." My father would drink a beer on a hot day, but my mother did not join him, and—whether accidentally or symbolically—this drink was always consumed *outside* the house. Most of the people we knew were the same way, in the small town where we lived. I ought not to say that it was this which got me into difficulties, because the difficulties I got into were a faithful expression of my own incommodious[5] nature—the same nature that caused my mother to look at me, on any occasion which traditionally calls for feelings of pride and maternal accomplishment (my departure for my first formal dance, I mean, or my hellbent preparations for a descent on college) with an expression of brooding and fascinated despair, as if she could not possibly expect, did not ask, that it should go with me as it did with other girls; the dreamed-of spoils of daughters—orchids, nice boys, diamond rings—would be borne home in due course by the daughters of her friends, but not by me; all she could do was hope for a lesser rather than a greater disaster—an elopement, say, with a boy who could never earn

3. *rabid:* unreasonably extreme
4. *indoctrinated:* taught a doctrine or belief
5. *incommodious:* not roomy enough

his living, rather than an abduction[6] into the White Slave[7] trade.

But ignorance, my mother said, ignorance, or innocence if you like, is not always such a fine thing as people think and I am not sure it may not be dangerous for a girl like you; then she emphasized her point, as she had a habit of doing, with some quotation which had an innocent pomposity[8] and odor of mothballs. I didn't even wince at it, knowing full well how it must have worked wonders with Mr. Berryman.

The evening I baby-sat for the Berrymans must have been in April. I had been in love all year, or at least since the first week in September, when a boy named Martin Collingwood had given me a surprised, appreciative, and rather ominously° complacent° smile in the school assembly. I never knew what surprised him; I was not looking like anybody but me; I had an old blouse on and my home-permanent had turned out badly. A few weeks after that he took me out for the first time, and kissed me on the dark side of the porch—also, I ought to say, on the mouth; I am sure it was the first time anybody had ever kissed me effectively, and I know that I did not wash my face that night or the next morning, in order to keep the imprint of those kisses intact. (I showed the most painful banality[9] in the conduct of this whole affair, as you will see.) Two months, and a few amatory° stages later, he dropped me. He had fallen for the girl who played opposite him in the Christmas production of *Pride and Prejudice*.

I said I was not going to have anything to do with that play, and I got another girl to work on Makeup in my place, but of course I went to it after all, and sat down in front

with my girl friend Joyce, who pressed my hand when I was overcome with pain and delight at the sight of Mr. Darcy[10] in the white breeches, silk waistcoat, and sideburns. It was surely seeing Martin as Darcy that did for me; every girl is in love with Darcy anyway, and the part gave Martin an arrogance and male splendor in my eyes which made it impossible to remember that he was simply a high-school senior, passably good-looking and of medium intelligence (and with a reputation slightly tainted°, at that, by such preferences as the Drama Club and the Cadet *Band*) who happened to be the first boy, the first really presentable boy, to take an interest in me. In the last act they gave him a chance to embrace Elizabeth (Mary Bishop, with a sallow complexion and no figure, but big vivacious eyes) and during this realistic encounter I dug my nails bitterly into Joyce's sympathetic palm.

That night was the beginning of months of real, if more or less self-inflicted, misery for me. Why is it a temptation to refer to this sort of thing lightly, with irony, with amazement even, at finding oneself involved with such preposterous emotions in the unaccountable past? That is what we are apt to do, speaking of love; with adolescent love, of course, it's practically obligatory; you would think we sat around, dull afternoons, amusing ourselves with these tidbit recollections of pain. But it really doesn't make me feel very gay—worse still, it doesn't really surprise me—to remember all the stupid, sad, half-ashamed things I did, that people in love always do. I hung around the places where he might be seen, and then pretended not to see him; I made absurdly roundabout approaches, in conversation, to the bitter pleasure of casually

6. *abduction:* carrying off (a person) unlawfully and by force

7. *White Slave:* woman or girl held unwillingly for purposes of commercial prostitution

8. *pomposity:* self-importance

9. *banality:* commonplaceness

10. *Mr. Darcy:* one of the characters in *Pride and Prejudice*

mentioning his name. I daydreamed endlessly; in fact if you want to put it mathematically, I spent perhaps ten times as many hours thinking about Martin Collingwood—yes, pining and weeping for him—as I ever spent with him; the idea of him dominated my mind relentlessly and, after a while, against my will. For if at first I had dramatized my feelings, the time came when I would have been glad to escape them; my well-worn daydreams had become depressing and not even temporarily consoling. As I worked my math problems I would torture myself, quite mechanically and helplessly, with an exact recollection of Martin kissing my throat. I had an exact recollection of *everything*. One night I had an impulse to swallow all the aspirins in the bathroom cabinet, but stopped after I had taken six.

My mother noticed that something was wrong and got me some iron pills. She said, "Are you sure everything is going all right at school?" *School!* When I told her that Martin and I had broken up all she said was "Well so much the better for that. I never saw a boy so stuck on himself." "Martin has enough conceit to sink a battleship," I said morosely and went upstairs and cried.

The night I went to the Berrymans was a Saturday night. I baby-sat for them quite often on Saturday nights because they liked to drive over to Baileyville, a much bigger, livelier town about 30 km away, and perhaps have supper and go to a show. They had been living in our town only two or three years—Mr. Berryman had been brought in as plant manager of the new door-factory—and they remained, I suppose by choice, on the fringes of its society; most of their friends were youngish couples like themselves, born in other places, who lived in new ranch-style houses on a hill outside town where we used to go tobogganing. This Saturday night they had two other couples in for drinks before they all drove over to Baileyville for the opening of a new supper-club; they were all rather festive. I sat in the kitchen and pretended to do Latin. Last night had been the Spring Dance at the High School. I had not gone, since the only boy who had asked me was Millerd Crompton, who asked so many girls that he was suspected of working his way through the whole class alphabetically. But the dance was held in the Armouries, which was only half a block away from our house; I had been able to see the boys in dark suits, the girls in long pale formals under their coats, passing gravely under the street-lights, stepping around the last patches of snow. I could even hear the music and I have not forgotten to this day that they played "Ballerina," and—oh, song of my aching heart—"Slow Boat to China." Joyce had phoned me up this morning and told me in her hushed way (we might have been discussing an incurable disease I had) that yes, M.C. *had* been there with M.B., and she had on a formal that must have been made out of somebody's old lace tablecloth, it just *hung*.

When the Berrymans and their friends had gone I went into the living room and read a magazine. I was mortally depressed. The big softly lit room, with its green and leaf-brown colors, made an uncluttered setting for the development of the emotions, such as you would get on a stage. At home the life of the emotions went on all right, but it always seemed to get buried under the piles of mending to be done, the ironing, the children's jigsaw puzzles and rock collections. It was the sort of house where people were always colliding with one another on the stairs and listening to hockey games and Superman on the radio.

55

I got up and found the Berrymans' "Danse Macabre" and put it on the record player and turned out the living-room lights. The curtains were only partly drawn. A street light shone obliquely[11] on the windowpane, making a rectangle of thin dusty gold, in which the shadows of bare branches moved, caught in the huge sweet winds of spring. It was a mild black night when the last snow was melting. A year ago all this—the music, the wind and darkness, the shadows of the branches— would have given me tremendous happiness; when they did not do so now, but only called up tediously familiar, somehow humiliatingly personal thoughts, I gave up my soul for dead and walked into the kitchen and decided to get drunk.

No, it was not like that. I walked into the kitchen to look for a coke or something in the refrigerator, and there on the front of the counter were three tall beautiful bottles, all about half full of gold. But even after I had looked at them and lifted them to feel their weight I had not decided to get drunk; I had decided to have a drink.

Now here is where my ignorance, my disastrous innocence, comes in. It is true that I had seen the Berrymans and their friends drinking their highballs as casually as I would drink a coke, but I did not apply this attitude to myself. No; I thought of hard liquor as something to be taken in extremities, and relied upon for extravagant results, one way or another. My approach could not have been less casual if I had been the Little Mermaid drinking the witch's crystal potion. Gravely, with a glance at my set face in the black window above the sink, I poured a little whisky from each of the bottles (I think now there were two brands of rye and an expensive

Scotch) until I had my glass full. For I had never in my life seen anyone pour a drink and I had no idea that people frequently diluted their liquor with water, soda, et cetera, and I had seen that the glasses the Berrymans' guests were holding when I came through the living room were nearly full.

I drank it off as quickly as possible. I set the glass down and stood looking at my face in the window, half expecting to see it altered. My throat was burning, but I felt nothing else. It was very disappointing, when I had worked myself up to it. But I was not going to let it go at that. I poured another full glass, then filled each of the bottles with water to approximately the level I had seen when I came in. I drank the second glass only a little more slowly than the first. I put the empty glass down on the counter with care, perhaps feeling in my head a rustle of things to come and went and sat down on a chair in the living room. I reached up and turned on a floor lamp beside the chair, and the room jumped on me.

When I say that I was expecting extravagant results I do not mean that I was expecting this. I had thought of some sweeping emotional change, an upsurge of gaiety and irresponsibility, a feeling of lawlessness and escape, accompanied by a little dizziness and perhaps a tendency to giggle out loud. I did not have in mind the ceiling spinning like a great plate somebody had thrown at me, nor the pale green blobs of the chairs swelling, converging, disintegrating, playing with me a game full of enormous senseless inanimate malice. My head sank back; I closed my eyes. And at once opened them, opened them wide, threw myself out of the chair and down the hall and reached—thank God,

11. *obliquely:* in a slanting way

57

thank God—the Berrymans' bathroom, where I was sick everywhere, everywhere, and dropped like a stone.

From this point on I have no continuous picture of what happened; my memories of the next hour or two are split into vivid and improbable segments, with nothing but murk and uncertainty between. I do remember lying on the bathroom floor looking sideways at the little six-sided white tiles, which lay together in such an admirable and logical pattern, seeing them with the brief broken gratitude and sanity of one who has just been torn to pieces with vomiting. Then I remember sitting on the stool in front of the hall phone, asking weakly for Joyce's number. Joyce was not home. I was told by her mother (a rather rattlebrained woman, who didn't seem to notice a thing the matter—for which I felt weakly, mechanically grateful) that she was at Kay Stringer's house. I didn't know Kay's number so I just asked the operator; I felt I couldn't risk looking down at the telephone book.

Kay Stringer was not a friend of mine but a new friend of Joyce's. She had a vague reputation for wildness and a long switch of hair, very oddly, though naturally, colored—from soap-yellow to caramel-brown. She knew a lot of boys more exciting than Martin Collingwood, boys who had quit school or been imported into town to play on the hockey team. She and Joyce rode around in these boys' cars, and sometimes went with them—having lied of course to their mothers—to the Gayla dance hall on the highway north of town.

I got Joyce on the phone. She was very keyed-up, as she always was with boys around, and she hardly seemed to hear what I was saying.

"Oh, I can't tonight," she said. "Some kids are here. We're going to play cards. You know Bill Kline? He's here. Ross Armour—"

"I'm *sick*," I said, trying to speak distinctly; it came out an inhuman croak. "I'm *drunk*, Joyce!" Then I fell off the stool and the receiver dropped out of my hand and banged for a while dismally against the wall.

I had not told Joyce where I was, so after thinking about it for a moment she phoned my mother, and using the elaborate and unnecessary subterfuge that young girls delight in, she found out. She and Kay and the boys—there were three of them—told some story about where they were going to Kay's mother, and got into the car and drove out. They found me still lying on the broadloom carpet in the hall; I had been sick again, and this time I had not made it to the bathroom.

It turned out that Kay Stringer, who arrived on this scene only by accident, was exactly the person I needed. She loved a crisis, particularly one like this, which had a shady and scandalous aspect and which must be kept secret from the adult world. She became excited, aggressive, efficient; that energy which was termed wildness was simply the overflow of a great female instinct to manage, comfort and control. I could hear her voice coming at me from all directions, telling me not to worry, telling Joyce to find the biggest coffeepot they had and make it full of coffee (*strong* coffee, she said), telling the boys to pick me up and carry me to the sofa. Later, in the fog beyond my reach, she was calling for a scrub-brush.

Then I was lying on the sofa, covered with some kind of crocheted throw they had found in the bedroom. I didn't want to lift my head. The house was full of the smell of coffee. Joyce came in, looking very pale; she said that the Berryman kids had wakened up but she had given them a cookie and told them to go back to bed, it was all right; she hadn't let them out of their room and she didn't believe they'd remember. She said that she and Kay had cleaned up the bathroom and the hall though she was afraid there was still a spot on the rug. The coffee was ready. I didn't understand anything very well. The boys had turned on the radio and were going through the Berrymans' record collection; they had it out on the floor. I felt there was something odd about this but I could not think what it was.

Kay brought me a huge breakfast mug full of coffee.

"I don't know if I can," I said. "Thanks."

"Sit up," she said briskly, as if dealing with drunks was an everyday business for her, I had no need to feel myself important. (I met, and recognized, that tone of voice years later, in the maternity ward.) "Now drink," she said. I drank, and at the same time realized that I was wearing only my slip. Joyce and Kay had taken off my blouse and skirt. They had brushed off the skirt and washed out the blouse, since it was nylon; it was hanging in the bathroom. I pulled the throw up under my arms and Kay laughed. She got everybody coffee. Joyce brought in the coffeepot and on Kay's instructions she kept filling my cup whenever I drank from it. Somebody said to me with interest. "You must have really wanted to tie one on."

"No," I said rather sulkily, obediently drinking my coffee. "I only had two drinks."

Kay laughed, "Well it certainly gets to you, I'll say that. What time do you expect

they'll be back?" she said.

"Late, after one I think."

"You should be all right by that time. Have some more coffee."

Kay and one of the boys began dancing to the radio. Kay danced very sexily, but her face had the gently superior and indulgent, rather cold look it had when she was lifting me up to drink the coffee. The boy was whispering to her and she was smiling, shaking her head. Joyce said she was hungry, and she went out to the kitchen to see what there was—potato chips or crackers, or something like that, that you could eat without making too noticeable a dint. Bill Kline came over and sat on the sofa beside me and patted my legs through the crocheted throw. He didn't say anything to me, just patted my legs and looked at me with what seemed to me a very stupid, half-sick, absurd and alarming expression. I felt very uncomfortable; I wondered how it had ever got around that Bill Kline was so good looking, with an expression like that. I moved my legs nervously and he gave me a look of contempt, not ceasing to pat me. Then I scrambled off the sofa, pulling the throw around me, with the idea of going to the bathroom to see if my blouse was dry. I lurched a little when I started to walk, and for some reason—probably to show Bill Kline that he had not panicked me—I immediately exaggerated this, and calling out, "Watch me walk a straight line!" I lurched and stumbled, to the accompaniment of everyone's laughter, towards the hall. I was standing in the archway between the hall and the living room when the knob of the front door turned with a small matter-of-fact click and everything became silent behind me except the radio of course and the crocheted throw inspired by some delicate malice of its own slithered down around my feet and there—oh, delicious moment in a well-organized farce—there stood the Berrymans, Mr. and Mrs., with expressions on their faces as appropriate to the occasion as any old-fashioned director of farces could wish. They must have been preparing those expressions of course; they could not have produced them in the first moment of shock; with the noise we were making, they had no doubt heard us as soon as they got out of the car; for the same reason, we had not heard them. I don't think I ever knew what brought them home so early—a headache, an argument—and I was not really in a position to ask.

Mr. Berryman drove me home. I don't remember how I got into that car, or how I found my clothes and put them on, or what kind of a goodnight, if any, I said to Mrs. Berryman. I don't remember what happened to my friends, though I imagine they gathered up their coats and fled, covering up the ignominy[12] of their departure with a mechanical roar of defiance. I remember Joyce with a box of crackers in her hand, saying that I had become terribly sick from eating—I think she said *sauerkraut*—for supper, and that I had called them for help. (When I asked her later what they made of this she said, "It wasn't any use. You *reeked*.") I remember also her saying, "Oh, no, Mr. Berryman I beg of you, my mother is a terribly nervous person I don't know what the shock might do to her. I will go down on my knees to you if you like but *you must not phone my mother*." I have no picture of her down on her knees—and she would have done it in a minute—so it seems this threat was not carried out.

Mr. Berryman said to me, "Well I guess you know your behaviour tonight is a pretty serious thing." He made it sound as if I might be charged with criminal negligence or something worse. "It would be very wrong of me to overlook it," he said. I suppose that besides being angry and disgusted with *me*, he was worried about taking me home in this condition to my strait-laced[13] parents, who could always say I got the liquor in his house. Plenty of Temperance people would think that enough to hold him responsible, and the town was full of Temperance people. Good relations with the town were very important to him from a business point of view.

"I have an idea it wasn't the first time," he said. "If it was the first time, would a girl be smart enough to fill three bottles up with water? No. Well in this case, she *was* smart enough, but not smart enough to know I could spot it. What do you say to that?" I opened my mouth to answer and although I was feeling quite sober the only sound that came out was a loud, desolate-sounding giggle. He stopped in front of our house. "Light's on," he said. "Now go in and tell your parents the straight truth. And if you don't, remember I will." He did not mention paying me for my baby-sitting services of the evening and the subject did not occur to me either.

I went into the house and tried to go straight upstairs but my mother called to me. She came into the front hall, where I had not turned on the light, and she must have smelled me at once for she ran forward with a cry of pure amazement, as if she had seen somebody falling, and caught me by the shoulders as I did indeed fall

12. *ignominy:* loss of one's good name   13. *strait-laced:* very strict in matters of conduct

61

down against the bannister, overwhelmed by my fantastic lucklessness, and I told her everything from the start, not omitting even the name of Martin Collingwood and my flirtation with the aspirin bottle, which was a mistake.

On Monday morning my mother took the bus over to Baileyville and found the liquor store and bought a bottle of Scotch whisky. Then she had to wait for a bus back, and she met some people she knew and she was not quite able to hide the bottle in her bag; she was furious with herself for not bringing a proper shopping-bag. As soon as she got back she walked out to the Berrymans'; she had not even had lunch. Mr. Berryman had not gone back to the factory. My mother went in and had a talk with both of them and made an excellent impression and then Mr. Berryman drove her home. She talked to them in the forthright and unemotional way she had, which was always agreeably surprising to people prepared to deal with a mother, and she told them that although I seemed to do well enough at school I was extremely backward—or perhaps eccentric—in my emotional development. I imagine that this analysis of my behaviour was especially effective with Mrs. Berryman, a great reader of Child Guidance books. Relations between them warmed to the point where my mother brought up a specific instance of my difficulties, and disarmingly related the whole story of Martin Collingwood.

Within a few days it was all over town and the school that I tried to commit suicide over Martin Collingwood. But it was already all over school and the town that the Berrymans had come home on Saturday night to find me drunk, staggering, wearing nothing but my slip, in a room with three boys, one of whom was Bill Kline. My mother had said that I was to pay for the bottle she had taken the Berrymans out of my baby-sitting earnings, but my clients melted away like the last April snow, and it would not be paid for yet if newcomers to town had not moved in across the street in July, and needed a baby sitter before they talked to any of their neighbors.

My mother also said that it had been a great mistake to let me go out with boys and that I would not be going out again until well after my sixteenth birthday, if then. This did not prove to be a concrete hardship at all, because it was at least that long before anybody asked me. If you think that news of the Berrymans adventure would put me in demand for whatever gambols[14] and orgies were on in and around that town, you could not be more mistaken. The extraordinary publicity which attended my first debauch[15] may have made me seem marked for a special kind of ill luck, like the girl whose illegitimate baby turns out to be triplets; nobody wants to have anything to do with her. At any rate I had at the same time one of the most silent telephones and positively the most sinful reputation in the whole High School. I had to put up with this until the next fall, when a fat blonde girl in grade ten ran away with a married man and was picked up two months later, living in sin—though not with the same man—in the city of Sault Ste. Marie. Then everybody forgot about me.

But there was a positive, a splendidly unexpected, result of this affair: I got completely over Martin Collingwood. It

14. *gambols:* playful running and jumping about

15. *debauch:* excessive indulgence in sensual pleasures

was not only that he at once said, publicly, that he had always thought I was a nut; where he was concerned I had no pride, and my tender fancy could have found a way around that, a month, a week, before. What was it that brought me back into the world again? It was the terrible and fascinating reality of my disaster; it was *the way things happened*. Not that I enjoyed it; I was a self-conscious girl and I suffered a good deal from all this exposure. But the development of events on that Saturday night—that fascinated me; I felt that I had had a glimpse of the shameless, marvellous, shattering absurdity with which the plots of life, though not of fiction, are improvised. I could not take my eyes off it.

And of course Martin Collingwood wrote his Senior Matric that June, and went away to the city to take a course at a school for Morticians,[16] as I think it is called, and when he came back he went into his uncle's undertaking business. We lived in the same town and we would hear most things that happened to each other but I do not think we met face to face or saw one another, except at a distance, for years. I went to a shower for the girl he married, but then everybody went to everybody else's showers. No, I do not think I really saw him again until I came home after I had been married several years, to attend a relative's funeral. Then I saw him; not quite Mr. Darcy but still very nice-looking in those black clothes. And I saw him looking over at me with an expression as close to a reminiscent° smile as the occasion would permit, and I knew that he had been surprised by a memory either of my devotion or my little buried catastrophe. I gave him a gentle uncomprehending look in return. I am a grown-up woman now; let him unbury his own catastrophes.

16. *Mortician:* an undertaker

---

follow-up

Discussing "An Ounce of Cure"

1. From whose point of view is this account written? What effect does this person's point of view have on the way you react to the narrator's situation?
2. What different points of view do the minor characters in the story adopt towards the heroine's "first debauch": the Berrymans, the mother, Martin Collingwood, Kay, the baby-sitting clients?
3. The title has been adapted from the sayings "An ounce of prevention is worth a pound of cure," and "The cure is worse than the disease." How does the author relate these "ounces" and "cure" to the story? From the title only, what point of view does the title recommend the reader to take?

4. As Alice Munro tells us her story, she also unfolds to us what she learned (besides temperance) from her first "lesser...disaster." Why, despite the public shame, was the scandal a relief for her and a cure from Martin Collingwood?

One Word: Several Meanings

You'd think that for efficiency sake each word in our English language would have only one meaning. Well, some do. But more don't. Take "last", for instance. On page 54 of "An Ounce of Cure" the story teller says that "in the last act they gave him a chance to embrace Elizabeth..." She is using "last" to mean "final".

(1) What do you mean by that last remark? (*last* = "immediately preceding")
(2) He spent his last quarter on ice cream. (*last* = "only remaining")
(3) The sick animal won't last through the night. (*last* = "endure")
(4) The shoemaker was using his last. (*last* = "wooden or metal form which is shaped like the human foot, and over which a shoe is made or repaired")

Six different meanings for the same word? That's right! *Last,* you see, is a MULTIPLE-MEANING word.

The meaning that a multiple-meaning word has at a particular time depends on how it's used. Consequently, when you come upon a multiple-meaning word, you have to let the context tell you which of the word's meanings fit. If the context doesn't help, you'll probably need to consult a dictionary.

Practice 1. Writing/Discussion
Three groups of words follow on page 65.
The ten words in Group A are multiple-meaning words that appear in "An Ounce of Cure." (pages 53-63)
In Group B you'll find the meanings for the Group A words as they were used in the selection. But those meanings are all mixed up.
In Group C you'll find *another* common meaning of each Group A word. But again the meanings are mixed up.
For you to do:
At the left side of your paper, list the ten Group A words.
Match each meaning in Group B with the appropriate word in Group A. Write the meaning in the centre of the appropriate line on your paper.

Match each meaning in Group C with the appropriate word in Group A. Write that meaning on the right side of the appropriate line on your paper.

Example
last—final—endure

Group A
1. rest (p. 53)
2. nature (p. 53)
3. like (p. 54)
4. will (p. 54)
5. time (p. 54)
6. iron (p. 55)
7. show (p. 55)
8. plant (p. 55)
9. opening (p. 55)
10. formal (p. 55)

Group B
a. personality
b. wish
c. moment
d. movie
e. a mineral
f. others
g. desires
h. long gown
i. introduction
j. industry

Group C
aa. demonstrate
bb. similar to
cc. stylized
dd. press
ee. a kind of measurement
ff. start growth
gg. is going to
hh. gap
ii. untouched outdoors
jj. relax

Practice 2. Writing/Discussion
On your paper, list the five multiple-meaning words below. For each one, supply at least two everyday meanings. Write those meanings on your paper. (If you need help, consult a dictionary.)

1. body   2. air   3. like   4. class   5. strike

With the class, discuss the meanings you've supplied for all the multiple-meaning words.

Practice 3. Writing
From Practice 2, select two multiple-meaning words, together with the two meanings you supplied for each.

For the first of those two words, write two sentences of your own. In the first sentence, use the word to mean the first of the two meanings you supplied for it. In the second sentence, use the word to mean the second meaning you supplied.

Now write two sentences for the second word you've chosen.

You will write a total of four sentences. Be prepared to read at least two of your sentences aloud. Does everyone agree that you've used the multiple-meaning word to mean what you intended it to mean?

Bookshelf

Dance of the Happy Shades, by Alice Munro. McGraw-Hill, 1973.
"An Ounce of Cure" is taken from this book.
Lives of Girls and Women, by Alice Munro. McGraw-Hill, 1974.
"One's a Heifer," in *The Lamp at Noon and Other Stories,* by Sinclair Ross. McClelland and Stewart, 1968. Set in the prairies, this story is about a young boy who is given a man's job and undergoes an unpleasant adventure.
Sixteen by Twelve, by John Metcalf. McGraw-Hill, 1970. The theme is growing up.
Who Do You think You Are?, by Alice Munro. Macmillan, 1978.

SQ3R

Much of what you read contains information that's worth remembering or information you need in order to complete an assignment or a project. It's easy to get and remember information; but to do so efficiently, you need to read in a systematic, organized way. That's where SQ3R comes in. SQ3R—**S**urvey, **Q**uestion, **R**ead, **R**ecite, **R**eview—is a reading method that's designed to help you get maximum understanding out of what you read when you are reading for information.

Suppose that you have been asked to read the short article "Behind the Price Tag" (page 69) for your social studies class and report on it. If you're going to share the article's important points with your classmates and help them and yourself save money when you shop, you know that you'll need to read the article carefully.

Step 1: **S**urvey

The purpose of the Survey step is to help you pick out main ideas and so gain a general impression of what the article is all about. The Survey step can be a big time-saver. Surveying the article can tell you quickly what's relevant—what's important.

When you Survey, you look for clues about the content of the article. Often the best clues are *titles* and *headings*. If there are no headings, or if the headings provide little help, read the *first paragraph or two* quickly and then the *topic sentences* of other paragraphs. Also look at tables, charts, and pictures—if any—to see what and how they add to the text.

Remember that in the Survey step you are *skimming*. Right now, for practice, look at the article "Behind the Price Tag" (page 69) and skim it to get a general idea of its content.

Did you find that the headings were useful? Did you find a major clue about the contents in the last sentence of paragraph 2? Were the topic sentences helpful?

Adaptation of "The SQ3R Method of Studying" in EFFECTIVE STUDY, 4th Edition by Francis P. Robinson. Copyright, 1941, 1946 by Harper & Row, Publishers, Inc. Copyright © 1961, 1970 by Francis P. Robinson. By permission of Harper & Row, Publishers, Inc.

Sometimes the informational materials you read will end with a summary. Did you happen to skim the last paragraph of "Behind the Price Tag" and find a useful clue?

Step 2: **Q**uestion

The second step involves *asking a question or two*—and writing each question down on your paper—about each heading, topic sentence, or other main idea that you discovered in your survey. Some of your questions should be about the meaning of any unfamiliar words that you have spotted in your survey.

The purpose of the Question step is to start you thinking. You are getting ready to follow the author's train of thought and to look for the answers to your questions.

You can practice this step with "Behind the Price Tag," starting with the title. Here are examples of the kinds of questions you might ask:

1. What price tag should you look behind? What *is* behind it?
2. What are "hidden costs"? (paragraph 2)
3. Why are some merchants' costs higher than those of others? How can "discount stores" underprice "smart shops"?
4. How do labor costs differ from store to store?
5. What is a store's "image" and how does it affect costs?

Now, on a piece of paper write down those five questions, together with at least *five more* questions, about points that you uncovered in your survey of "Behind the Price Tag."

Once you have asked your questions, you will be ready to read the article carefully in an effort to answer those questions. Step 3, then, is to *Read*.

Step 3: **R**ead; *Step 4:* **R**ecite

In Step 3 you read the article or lesson from beginning to end. While reading, you search actively for answers to the questions you raised in Step 2.

While you are reading for details, you should also *Recite*. The *read* and *recite* steps generally go together. To *recite* means to *answer* the questions you raised in Step 2. Reciting also involves asking additional questions about the material as you read it carefully. Perhaps you will ask some questions that the article or lesson does not answer. If you do raise such questions, it is a good sign that you are actively thinking.

Usually a good procedure is to read a section and then stop to answer the questions that you asked about that section. Then go on to the next section. What if the material has no clearly defined "sections" set off by headings? In that case, read a few paragraphs and recite. Topic sentences should tell you when the writer is introducing a new idea.

Now, for practice, turn again to "Behind the Price Tag." Read the article, section by section. When you finish a section, stop and recite, answering the questions you listed in Step 2, plus any additional questions you may have jotted down.

Step 5: **R**eview

The final step is to review what you have read. Reviewing should be easy if you have raised relevant questions in Step 2 and if you answered them to your own satisfaction in Steps 3 and 4.

If the article you're reading has headings and subheadings, you can review those headings by providing a few facts for each one. Another review method is to make an <u>outline</u> (in your mind or on paper) of the writer's main points. Include subpoints under each main point. Try to do this step without looking back at the article or lesson. If you can't readily complete the outline, go back to the *Read* and *Recite* steps. Then *Review* once more.

Behind the Price Tag

You've just bought a shirt at that new store, and you're pleased with your purchase. Then some friends walk up to you wearing the very same shirt. They tell you they paid half the price somewhere else. Now you're angry.

Sound familiar? Maybe you forgot to check the "hidden cost" in your sales slip. In these days of rising prices, people who can spot hidden costs know how to stretch their dollars.

You Choose

Hidden costs are the costs most people don't see when they make a purchase. The two stores shown on page 70 represent two types of places where you might buy some clothing. In which store would you expect to pay a higher price for the same item?

Most people would guess that The Smart Shop would carry higher price tags. But why shouldn't the same clothes cost the same amount? Is one owner more greedy than another? Perhaps, but hidden costs are more likely to make the difference.

Look at the two stores again. In order to stay in business, each owner must make enough money to cover all the expenses of operating the store. Can you see some of those costs? Can you identify some costs one owner has that the other does not have? On a sheet of paper jot down some of the differences you can see.

You probably noted that each owner has to pay for the stock

Abridged from OPT, The Magazine On People and Things, November, 1974, Vol. 1, No. 2. Copyright © 1974 Xerox Corporation. Reprinted by permission of the publisher, Ginn and Company (Xerox Corporation).

The Smart Shop

Bo's Discount

sold in the store. Did you also count the sales people? The price tag includes the cost of their labor.

Expensive Images

Did you notice each store's surroundings? Atmosphere is a hidden cost. Attractive window displays, thick carpets, and special lighting often require thousands of dollars. A store's image, created by advertising, sharp looking shopping bags, or an interesting front door, costs money, too. The owner passes that cost along to you.

Does the store have hundreds of sales each day or just a dozen or so? Stores with many sales can usually charge lower prices per item. Stores with fewer customers must charge higher prices to pay for their hidden costs.

Extras

Are alterations free? Will the store gift wrap your selections, or deliver them to your home, or provide other similar customer services? None of these extras come as free as you think. Some-one has to pay the tailor and the delivery person. That someone is the customer.

When clothing stores feature sales to get rid of slow-moving items, some stock never gets sold. Add soiled items and goods taken by shoplifters and dishonest em-ployees. This waste and "slip-page" doesn't disappear. The customer pays for it, too.

Everything you buy has a hid-den charge. Many extra expenses vary from store to store. Would you rather shop at fancy shops instead of sifting through piles of garments on discount store tables? Then you'll have to accept a higher hidden cost.

Eating Out

Think about the hidden costs you pay when you eat out. The check at the end of the meal covers much more than just the food you eat. Let's examine three places to eat: a fast food store, a table service restaurant, and the school cafeteria.

Fast-food chains cut down on labor costs by increasing the efficiency of their workers. The next time you order that 'burger, check how the people behind the counter organize their work. Notice the tools they use. That portion-sized french fry scoop and the pre-printed order blank save valuable time and money.

Some table service restaurants have begun to ask their customers to serve more of the meal to themselves. The "help yourself" bread and salad bar is not just a big giveaway. When you serve yourself, you're saving one more trip for your waiter.

Many schools and restaurants now offer fewer menu choices than before. By concentrating on fewer selections, chefs can standardize meal preparation. This also cuts down on unpopular items which go to waste.

Fast-food shops and restaurants must include all of their expenses in the prices they charge. School cafeterias don't have to charge the total meal cost because they receive government funds to keep prices low.

Hidden costs are not something to be scared about. All of us pay them. But understanding what the hidden costs amount to can help you make better decisions when you spend.

interlude

Canadians All

John Robert Colombo

So let it be with British America—
let every national distinction cease from among us—
let not the native Canadian
look upon his Irish or Scottish neighbor
as an intruder,
nor the native of the British Isles
taunt the other about stupidity and incapacity.
Rather let them become as one race,
and may the only strife among us
be a praiseworthy emulation
as to who shall attain the honor of conferring
the greatest benefits on the country of our birth—
or the land of our choice.

From ABRACADABRA by John Robert Colombo, 1967.
Reprinted by permission of the author.

Canada

Walter Bauer

This earth does not bestow
The wisdom of Plato.
Aristotle did not live here.
Nor did Dante pass here through the inferno
In the fellowship of Virgil.
And Rembrandt? Not here the glamor of great lords
And then the drunken unknown king in exile.

Here you receive another kind of wisdom,
Bitter and icy and not to everybody's taste.
This earth says:
I was here long before you and the likes of you came;
Unmolested I conversed with wind and rivers,
Don't forget that, my friend.
The wind blows cold from Labrador:
I have a message for you from the ice age,
But I shall not decode it for you.
The forests of the north surge like waves:
We shall last longer than you.
The Yukon and the Mackenzie flow with quiet patience:
Son, don't make things too hard for yourself;
Different times will come when you are gone, stranger.
The arctic expresses the sum total of all wisdom:
Silence. Nothing but silence. The end of time.

Henry Beissel, (translator)

From NOTES FOR A NATIVE LAND. Reprinted by permission
of Oberon Press.

5

If I Lived Through It

forestudy

Characters in Action

A novelist has the length of a book in which to write a story. He/she is like an artist modeling with clay: the medium is pliable. There is space for character analysis, background narration, subplots, and various digressions.

Unlike the novelist, the short-story writer has severe space restrictions. He/she must develop the story within a limited space. His/her art is like chiseling a small statue in granite. The short-story writer must chip and cut until every remaining word is essential to the single theme, the emotional effect, or the character image he/she wishes to emphasize.

Because a short story is short, the writer is likely to put it in motion at the start. The story has no time to stand still and view the scenery. "If I Lived Through It" (the selection beginning on page 78) introduces you to the main character ("I") at the very beginning. He is on stage and under the spotlight in the first two paragraphs. You start to know him—and to see human nature revealed—immediately, as you see him in action:

> When Father knocked, I should have known it wasn't Joe and said "Stop!," but I called out "Come in," and down came the bucket and clipped him on the head. There he stood, streaming blood and water, the letter in his hand soaking wet. Thank God it was the little bucket; the big one would have killed him. I had a string on it to keep it from falling as far as Joe's head, so it would just dump the water, but Father is 15 cm taller than Joe.
>
> I had the mop there already, so I could get the water up fast and not wreck the ceiling below. The whole thing had been planned so nicely. Well, that's how it goes.

Practice 1. Discussion

If you have read the two paragraphs thoughtfully, you have observed that the author has accomplished much in a short space.

1. The author does not use up words to explain the main character. Instead, he implies something important about that character. What kind of person do you think would play the old water-bucket practical joke on someone?
2. What three precautions has the main character taken? What do they reveal about the way his mind works and the way he feels about others?
3. Though the author does not explain, what do you assume is probably the relationship between the main character and Joe? How do you arrive at your assumption?
4. In the first paragraph there is already an unexpected development which suggests a conflict to follow.
   a. What is that unexpected development?
   b. What do you imagine it might lead to? (Not knowing for sure, but being curious to find out, is a matter of *suspense*.)
5. What is the boy's attitude, or mood, just after the joke misfires? How can you tell?
6. Discuss the second sentence in the first paragraph.
   a. What is the general base statement? What two phrases are added details?
   b. Which detail arouses your curiosity?

Practice 2. Writing

Up to this point in the lesson you have been finding out how a writer makes language work. Put your discoveries into practice by reversing your role from reader to writer: Begin a short original story with an emphasis on character.

Perhaps you yourself or someone you know has played a practical joke that backfired. If so, use the incident as a basis for your narrative. If you prefer, use a brief anecdote you have read or heard so long as it has a beginning, middle, and end, and also has a main character modeled on someone you know well. Whichever you use as the basis for your narrative, you probably would be wise to use fictitious names for your characters.

At this time, write only the opening of your narrative—that is, the first couple of paragraphs. Try to use the following aids, which are suggested in question form:

1. What is going to be the chief trait of your main character (Is he/she mischievous, awkward, rowdy, or what?) What will your character be doing (so that you can begin showing this trait immediately, without explaining it)?
2. What story-telling techniques in the opening of "If I Lived Through It" could you use? Reread the two paragraphs.
    a. The first sentence shows the setting and the opening situation. The "stage" is already set. The writer brings the reader face to face with all of the characters in the scene: The main character in the scene has planned the water-bucket prank for his brother, but his father opens the door instead. Then, the unexpected happens.
    b. The second sentence shows the result. Here is the sentence, with the added details italicized: "There he stood, *streaming blood and water, the letter in his hand soaking wet.*" In both sentences the reader sees every detail closely, as though he/she were in the room.
3. For your own story, pick a setting or a character and write a base statement about either.
4. What details can you add to your general base statement so that your reader can visualize the action completely?

Perhaps you'll find the following aid to be the most practical of all: The best way to get started writing is simply to apply pencil to paper and see what happens. Sometimes an opening sentence that pictures the middle of an action leads naturally to a second sentence, a third, and so on. "Once begun is half done."

Here is an example of the kind of two-paragraph opener you might compose. It starts with the setting and opening situation and then quotes the words of a speaker. Notice the importance of the detail-phrases added to the general base statements in the first paragraph.

> The little open-air cable car sat poised on the rails at the end of San Francisco's Powell Street, ready to retrace the run it had just completed. The conductor-gripman quietly placed his right knee on the seat nearest to him as the passengers boarded, blocking it to any occupant. The car was crowded, with late arrivals in the aisle.
>
> "What are we waiting for?" a woman's raspy voice complained, "Why aren't we going?"

You'll have a chance to complete your sketch after you read "If I Lived Through It."

If I Lived Through It

Ames Rowe Quentin

When Father knocked, I should have known it wasn't Joe and said "Stop!," but I called out "Come in," and down came the bucket and clipped him on the head. There he stood, streaming blood and water, the letter in his hand soaking wet. Thank God it was the little bucket; the big one would have killed him. I had a string on it to keep it from falling as far as Joe's head, so it would just dump the water, but Father is 15 cm taller than Joe.

I had the mop there already, so I could get the water up fast and not wreck the ceiling below. The whole thing had been planned so nicely. Well, that's how it goes.

I brought Father a towel and cleaned up the floor, but he didn't say anything, and I didn't either. We just worked in deadly silence. The cut was about 2 cm long. It would have to be sewed up. He looked at it in my mirror, still not saying anything. He seemed dazed. Then he went slowly downstairs and asked Mother to drive him to the doctor's.

The car had just come back from the body shop, with the big rust-colored spots of undercoat on the side facing the house, so, of course, that was right in front of him as he walked down the path. I watched out the window, feeling sick. I remembered that I hadn't even said I was sorry. I should have. He wouldn't necessarily have known it.

I could hear the motor roar and fade as Mother tested it before she headed out—an old flier's trick. I tell her engine failure isn't too serious in cars, you don't fall far; but she can't help it. I had the motor sounding pretty for her, though I don't suppose she noticed that except absentmindedly. They drove off, and I went downstairs, looking for something to do, like washing some dishes, to start making up for the accident.

Father had left the letter on the table, as if he meant me to see it or didn't care if I did; and when I saw the name at the bottom of the page, I had to read it. It was from my real father's mother. The spelling wasn't too good. The ink was smeared blue from the water bucket; it was on lined paper, so the lines were smeared too.

"Dear Reverend Page," it began. "You will be surprised to hear from me after all these years. I do not even know wether

Mrs. Page is still living. I saw in the church paper about your book, and I wrote to them for your address. If I knew Mrs. Page was alive I would write to her. When our house burned down eleven years ago the desk went too and none of us could remember your address. When Mrs. Page wrote both times she did not give the address so we could not answer. Anyhow we were having a lot of trouble then, needing a house but not able to build much because those were bad years for the stock and the apples weren't good either. My husband died about that time. There was a lot to worry over besides the wife and child of a son who had been dead for years, especially as we had never seen them and they were probably better off than we were. But now Henry's boy is sixteen and plenty old enough to take care of himself on the train. We have had four good years so we have a good big house for all of us. I would send him his ticket, if you would let him come to visit us. That is if he is still living. I hope you are all well, and that if Mrs. Page is still living she will write to us. Respectfully yours, Elda Crowe."

As I stood there looking at the letter, I heard Joe come in. I just waited, perfectly still, because he couldn't see me, and when he came around the corner I tackled him so fast he hardly saw me before he hit the floor. When I let him go, he looked up at me disgustedly and said, "I wish you wouldn't do things like that. I've got a headache. Help me pick up this mess." His books and papers were all over the rug, and the rug was wound up as if it were in a cement mixer. We got it all straight. He had some cornflakes and milk, and so did I; then I got out the cold roast beef from last night.

"I bet that's for supper," Joe said; but it looked good to him, too, so we both had some. When we had finished, there wasn't a lot left. He wouldn't have done it if it hadn't been for me.

Father had a big bandage; the doctor must have had to shave off a lot of hair. I said I was sorry. Father nodded. Then Mother asked which of us had lit into the roast. Joe said we both had. I said I'd started it. Father believed me; he gave me a mean look and walked out of the room. Mother believed me too.

"Well, you'd better not take any at supper, either of you," she said crossly.

I followed Father into the living room. "What about that letter?" I asked. I knew it was the wrong time, but I couldn't stop myself.

He gave me the sermon on Reading Other People's Mail. It took about ten minutes. I guess I was lucky it wasn't church length. Mother says he can't help it, it's an occupational disease.

"You'll have to change your plans and go," he finished off, pointing to the letter. "I've had just about all I can take from you. You don't study, you don't obey, there isn't anything your mother and I can teach you, because you won't learn from us—"

"Now, wait a minute," Mother said from the door; "what's going on here?"

"About his going to the Crowes'," Father said.

"He can't go to the Crowes'," Mother replied firmly. "He has to take the summer physics. He ought to, and he wants to, and it's preparation for his future. It's what he's good at."

"Look, I have something to say about this." Father sat down gingerly on the couch and folded his arms across his stomach. I knew his stomach was hurting him again; it hurts him when he argues. He glared at me from under the bandage. "I've helped you bring him up, and I'm fond of him, but I've come to my limit. It was one thing when I was younger and he was just a little boy. You expect idiocy from eight-year-olds. But I'm not young, I'm not well, and when you come down to it, I'm not his kind of person. Noise and horseplay distress me. I've asked him and asked him to control that horrible laugh, but he won't. I've asked him not to pound Joe all the time; he says he's careful, but Joe is only thirteen, and he's not very big. Henry doesn't know his own strength; he's going to break Joe's head next time, not just his arm—"

"That was four years ago, and it was an accident," Joe put in. "You shouldn't bring that up." But I could see that suddenly he was thinking it would be a relief to come home and not get jumped.

Mother looked upset. "That's as may be," she said, "but he can't go to the Crowes'. You don't know about them, or about that back country." Then she clammed up and just stood there. "Well," she started in again, "he's been waiting years to be eligible for that course. He'd be miserable at the Crowes', and he'd miss all the things he likes. All the summer things. His girls. His electrical equipment. The swimming."

"I don't care," Father said grimly. "They're his family. They have a right to see him. And I have a right to a restful summer. When he's in school, there are at least a few hours when he probably won't smash up the car, or take out the motor, or drop a bucket on my head. In summer, it's sixteen hours a day that he's in action. I deserve to be let off for a while. The Crowes can take their turn."

That kind of talk really makes you feel welcome. If I'd been Joe's age, I would have cried. Father had said that kind of thing before, but never so much or so hard. I guess it was the blow on the head. He'd lost control.

Mother hadn't. "I'm sorry," she said, perfectly cool and civil, "but I won't allow it. They're not our kind of people."

"Now, really," Father snapped, "you married one of them."

"In what way aren't they our kind of people?" Joe asked.

Mother didn't answer.

Always I've known I wasn't exactly "our kind" of person myself, but neither is she. She gets along with Joe and Father and the parish because they're her job and she likes them, and because she'd get along anywhere. But there's a funny streak in her. She stands there when I work on the car, because she doesn't want to get her dress dirty and then have to go all covered with oil to talk to someone at the door about the altar guild; but she watches me as if she were doing it herself. "That plug's still wrong," she'll say. "On the far side." When she drives she's usually slow and careful; but once, way out in the country with just me along, she forgot I was there and cut out like a race driver, cornering without touching the brake and gunning it coming out of the turn. I guess we were averaging 128 km/h.

"Who taught you to do that, Jimmy Dean?" I asked.

She slowed right down, but she gave me a dirty look. "In a real car I could make Jimmy Dean sit up in his grave," she said. "But don't you try anything like that, you hear me? You'd turn yourself over just the way he did. It takes a lot of fast driving before you can do that."

"You've done a lot of fast driving?" I said. "Like when? Taking us to nursery school?"

"During the war," she said vaguely. "And don't be sassy."

Another time, on the freeway, I said, "Hey, we're going to miss our turn," and she came out of whatever she was thinking about and hit the gas pedal and zig-zagged across four fast packed lanes in about 30 m and out the exit like a knife through mayonnaise. There was a siren screaming behind us; we would have starved to death if we'd had to pay that fine. She took the tail of a yellow light and weaseled us into a thick mess of trucks and slowpokes. The cop went past at about 80 km/h. Then she was all fussed about giving me a bad example.

I felt like telling the kids at school, but they would have thought that was a crazy way for a preacher's wife to act. And I certainly didn't tell Father.

When I asked her to teach me to drive, she said she couldn't stand to hear me or anybody else grinding her gears. So I learned in driver education at school, and of course I could brake and steer and shift gears and see things, but I couldn't believe how slow you had to go in fog, so that's how I got hit and messed up the car. I didn't see the other guy and he didn't see me.

Father never even goes as fast as a sick cow, and he shifts gears as if he were sawing a steel pipe, but he never hits anything. "Our kind of people" don't; they don't do anything but read and talk and write and telephone and drive like old ladies and fill the bottoms of their transmissions with broken gear teeth and get their cylinders and pistons all gummy because their poor motors never even get warm. But I notice when Father wants to get somewhere in a hurry, like to have a bleeding cut sewed up, he lets Mother drive. There's some use in people who aren't his kind.

But Mother didn't answer Joe's question about why the Crowes are different from us, and I wasn't about to say they're backwoodsmen who quit school about the eighth grade usually; and it was choir time anyhow, so that was the end of the argument for the moment.

I'm not a very good musician, but I'm not a bad one, either. It comes from Mother's side—Father can't sing—but it missed Joe. I have the choir, because we had a choir lady who was nervous, but she knew her job; she trained a lot of fifth- and sixth-graders to be so good they were asked to sing out of town sometimes. But then they kept getting bigger and meaner, and she kept getting more nervous, and when they were seventh- and eighth-grade kids, Father had to send me in to keep them in line for her. Kids that age are the worst. She and I handled them together or, rather, I handled them and she taught them—maybe four months, and then she had to go to the sanatorium. She thought people were after her.

When I walked in, they were all there, very quiet, and when I turned my back on them to sort the music, one of them let out a horrible whinnying laugh that was supposed to be just like mine. Then I spun around and they all whinnied. The church windows rattled.

"OK," I said, "who started that?"
They just snickered. So I made each one of them imitate my laugh, and only one of them got the sound wrong, and none of those kids ever gets a sound wrong except on purpose, so he was the guy, trying not to be recognized. So I made him do it over and over, good and loud, both my way and his wrong way; and then I made them all do it in exact unison. Then I picked up the music and told the one who started it to sing softly so he'd learn the pieces for Sunday but not so I could hear him. You have to protect these kids' voices, especially when they're changing, and I'd been pretty rough on his. I shouldn't be so touchy about that laugh; it does sound pretty bad, but when I forget myself, it just comes out.

They learned the pieces fast, and I turned them loose early. That was one reason the choir lady gave out. She kept them too long, and they got bored and didn't pay attention and got pulling each other's shirttails out, and then, of course, they didn't get the pieces right, so she kept them longer and they began trying to snatch things out of each other's pockets or do never mind what; and no guy can take that kind of treatment and not do something back. I'd go up and down the line behind them and sort of lean on them, but you really can't keep a bunch of guys in order for a person with no sense at all. Now she's gone, I bang the songs through hard and right, and the choir knows the faster it catches on, the faster it'll get loose. Father thinks I skimp the rehearsals because I want to get out myself.

When I got home, Joe was still asking what was wrong with the Crowes, and I could have hit him. Mother never met them, but she knew about them from my own father. He'd run away when he was about my age, after some kind of fight with my grandfather. They were just poor farmers, simple people. They even took snuff and chewed tobacco. My own father had always been crazy about motors, and especially planes, and he hadn't done anything in school that he didn't have to do to get into junior college, because that was where they did pilot training. In the war he was commissioned more because he was a terrific flier than because of his schooling. My mother is a mathematician and a clergyman's daughter, but she didn't want to do ladylike paper work in the war. So she learned enough at some airport to get into the women's ferry command, and my own father taught her to fly the bombers. Her family made a fuss at the time; but they got married quickly because he knew he'd be going overseas. He was killed over Germany, before I was born.

We lived with my mother's family till she married Father, when I was two. Joe was born when I was three. He always wants to know something bad about me, because I'm bigger than he is, and he gets sick of it. I wouldn't tell him my father's family made applejack and bootlegged it during the Depression because that was the only way they could make money for the groceries they had to buy. Father doesn't know this, and Mother told me privately. She never talked about my own father to Father; she says it's wrong for a widow who remarries to say anything that might make her second husband wonder if she loved the first better, but it's equally wrong to say anything against the first. She hasn't talked very much

about him even to me. In his pictures, which she gave me to keep, he doesn't look like me. I'm like her side.

Mother came to my room. "Father is dead set that you have to go to the Crowes'. Whenever he sees that bandage in the mirror he gets madder. I can't quite blame him; these practical jokes of yours are unpardonable."

"Oh, boy, you too," I said grimly.

"Well, how would you like to be Father and stand at the church door Sunday morning shaking hands, and have to answer maybe three hundred people asking what the bandage is for, and how you got cut? He can't wear a black cap like a rabbi's to cover it. And if you think ahead a little further, you'll realize that after the bandage comes off, the shaved patch on his head is going to show for weeks. He'll be cross at you every time he sees a mirror. I should think you'd want to get away. After all, the Crowes are your own people."

"*You* are my own people," I said. "Who's going to beat down the choir when I'm gone? Who'll keep the car running?"

"I will," Mother said. She looked sore. "And don't be too sure we're your own people. You're growing up. The day is coming soon when you'll be on your own. And I've had just about enough of you lately myself. You're getting big and mean and rebellious and lazy, you won't study anything but physics, you just chase one girl after another, and I wouldn't be surprised if you pick the ones you've heard are cooperative in cars."

"Now, look here," I said, "that was uncalled for."

"I guess so," she said, and burst into tears. "I'm sorry. I don't know what's what. I'm just caught between. I want you to have fun and I want you to be your own kind of person, only not get hurt, but I want Father to have some peace, and it isn't good for Joe to feel inferior."

"Now, look, Joe doesn't have any reason to feel inferior. When he's my age, he'll probably pound me down, the way I've trained him. And he gets the best grades."

"Try to tell Joe that," Mother said. "Henry, I'm afraid you've got to go. I'm not going to tell Father and Joe that the Crowes used to be bootleggers, just to keep you here. I loved your father, and I'm not going to run his family down. And I guess you can take care of yourself. But the way she wrote, about 'if Mrs. Page is still alive,' and 'if Henry is still alive,' means something. That's the way they think. It's dangerous country. One of your father's brothers was shot out hunting. The lumbermen get drunk Saturday night and fight; sometimes they kill each other. I wouldn't put it past you for a minute to get in those fights. There are bears and mountain lions. The people who live there understand the life, but newcomers always get in trouble. Especially city kids. And the Crowes will be embarrassed by your ways. They'll think you're stuck-up; you'll use words they don't know, you'll butter your bread differently—"

"Oh, great," I said, and sat down. "And I'll miss physics and swimming and all of my immoral girls." I gave Mother a bitter look.

"If the shoe fits, put it on," she said. She almost smiled. But then I laughed, and she winced and put her hands over her ears. "That noise you make drives me mad."

It was a fourteen-hour train ride, with a couple of changes. I took the workbook for the physics course along, but it was written to go with demonstrations and rough to follow. I'd forgotten my slide rule, so it took forever to work the problems by hand. I sat staring out at the empty mountain desert. I didn't talk to anybody. I felt too low. Even my mother couldn't stand me. I almost cried. Then I fell asleep. When I woke, it was late at night, and the conductor was shaking me. "This is your stop," he said. The car was empty; it was almost the end of the line.

I got my papers and things together and stumbled out. The train went on. The moon was about to rise, but it hadn't yet. I wondered if I'd have to spend the night there. At last car lights came down a winding steep hill toward me, and they were on a jeep. It bumped across the railroad tracks and stopped suddenly on the incline.

"You Henry Crowe?" a deep voice called out. "Henry Page?"

"Henry Page, usually," I said.

The man sat there; in the dimness I saw an angular rocky face. "I'm your Uncle Nick. Your father's brother. Can't get out; motor dies. Set your bag in back." I swung it up and climbed in. We shook hands. "Say Henry Crowe while you're up here," he told me, gunning the motor with his foot on the clutch. "Your grandmother would feel bad if you didn't. You're the one with your grandpa's and your dad's name. She doesn't know your stepfather, or why you call yourself Page."

"Just convenience," I said. "And my stepfather has been my father, really."

He didn't answer; in fact, he hardly

said a word till we got to the farm. If he had, I couldn't have heard him. That jeep was noisy, even for a jeep. We took off like a rabbit up the winding road. The lights would fade and come up again to show a narrow path through high brush and, later, woods. I had to watch the road ahead for bumps and shift position and hang on just to stay on my seat. He really drove, the way my mother did that time, shaving the corners and the trunks of trees, so that twice I thought we were going to hit one and got ready to jump. But he knew what he was doing. I didn't mind; I drive that way myself when I have the chance.

When we got to the house, he stopped on a grade and threw a log under one wheel. I got out. In the moonlight I saw that he had scars, claw marks, down one cheek.

The house was dark. He showed me my bed. I could tell that the room was big and that there were four bunks with guys asleep in them. There was a sort of bathroom next to that room—all the fixtures, but just raw-lumber roof and floor and log walls. They had electricity, but it wasn't very good. There was tubing that must have been part of a still stuck in one corner. I washed and sacked in. I can't say I wasn't a bit scared.

A strange bed always gets me up early, and I'd slept on the train. So when I woke up it was dawn. All the guys were still mostly under the covers, but they seemed to be different ages and have different colors of hair.

Outdoors it was mountains and big pine trees. Some kind of little yellow wild lily was all around. Nice air; cold. There were even patches of old icy snow. Nobody in sight, but smoke coming out of a chimney of the big log house.

Partly I wanted to do a good turn, to show Uncle Nick I was a good guy and could do something useful, but mostly I wanted to fix whatever was wrong with that jeep. I figured it could be the battery, but more likely it was in the wiring. Those lights had been running off the generator. I had a few things in my pocket that I always carry there and that I thought might be useful.

So I unlatched the hood and looked inside. Father would have been sick, if he'd understood it. Those lights sure *had* been running off the generator, because there wasn't any battery. And the reason Uncle Nick always parked on hills was that there wasn't any starter. That jeep was a rod, everything heavy gone, souped for the races. Mother would have laughed; anybody who'd do a thing like that to a jeep, and then take it out on a mountain road at night and get away with it, you had to respect, even if he was crazy. I slid underneath to see what else he'd done.

Then I heard footsteps and saw a pair of dirty boots walk up and kick the log block out from under the front wheel. A second later the jeep started rolling. I really doubled up fast. Lucky those things have clearance. It rolled about

1 m, so I wasn't underneath any more, and I got up, and then the guy with the boots leaned on the fender and threw the log under the wheel again and came around to look at me. I was kind of sore.

"Morning, Charlie," he said, grinning, and then his mouth fell open.

"I'm Henry," I said quietly, just looking at him. I was figuring whether to hit him or let it go. He was a big guy, about my age; bigger than me, and he looked tough, but I was too mad to let that bother me. Hitting him just didn't seem the right way to start getting along with my own father's family.

He threw his hands over his face. "Don't stwike me, pwease don't stwike me, I'm dust a wittle boy!" he squeaked, and let out an awful braying laugh and began to run. I went after him; I tackled him on the path and grabbed him by the belt and we went rolling over and over in the weeds. He was laughing fit to kill. He ended up sitting on my chest, with one of my arms pinned under his knee and my other arm caught under my head as if I were lying in a hammock looking up at the birds. "Had enough?" he asked.

"For now," I said. He let me up. I dusted myself off. "I'll get you later," I promised him.

"Oh, sure," he said, and started for the house.

"But not much later!" I yelled out, and went for him. This time I got a decent grip, and in a minute I had him on his face with his arms behind his back. Then all of a sudden there were about four guys on top of both of us, and a couple of little girls in there too, and by the time I got out from underneath I had dirt inside my clothes and dirt and weeds in my hair, and my hands and nose were bleeding, and it was a wonder I didn't have any broken bones.

There was a white-haired woman, brown like an Indian, standing there looking disgusted. I tried to clean myself up with my handkerchief. "Charlie," she said to me, "you sure had that coming. You should have got worse. You know better than messing around with your uncle's jeep. He's told you ten times. And I thought you knew better than to tangle with young Nick, after the bloody eye you got last week."

"I'm not Charlie" I said. "I'm Henry Crowe. I wasn't messing. I thought there was something wrong I could fix."

She looked at me and then at the guys. There were two of them enough like me to mistake. One was exact, and he was the one who'd got the bloody eye last week. He was holding his stomach, laughing like a hyena.

The woman quit glowering and smiled, and then she looked as if she were beginning to cry. "Well, welcome, Henry," she said, and reached out and shook my hand, dirty as I was. Then she turned me around and led me up to the house. The other guys went off somewhere.

There was a picture on the kitchen wall of my own father in a racing car. Mother had never told me that about him; I guess I was giving her enough trouble without her asking for more. But I might have known. Another picture showed a boy who could have been me, or Charlie, with three others. They all had banjos. "That was your dad when he was your age. You wouldn't think it was the same person"— she pointed at the race driver—"men's faces change so much from the way they looked as boys. Do you sing?"

I nodded. She told me about the quartet while she fixed bacon and eggs and pancakes. When the platters were almost full, she sent me to wash up. "But, look out," she whispered. "I think they've put a wire across the door to trip you up. Don't get sore. Just fall over it."

"Thanks," I said uneasily. But I still had one more thing on my mind. I wanted to know whether my father and grandfather had had that fight about racing, and whether that was why my father had left home.

"Oh, maybe," she said. "I kind of forget. It could have been anything. You boys get bigetty; sometimes we have to throw you out for everybody's peace. But you come back later. Nick did. Your father would have." She looked sad. Then she smiled. "Well, it's nice to have *you* here," she said, and poked a stick in the stove. The smoke smelled good. She burned apple prunings mostly, and everything in that kitchen smelled good—the food, and the mountain air coming in the window, and my grandmother too.

"It's nice to be here," I said. I meant that. I felt as if it was going to be the greatest summer of my life. If I lived through it.

There wasn't any wire for me to fall over, though. I started to wash up. I could hear some kind of scratching and squeaking, like rats in the walls. "I can't find a towel, Grandma," I called through the doorway. She came to help me. One of the guys jumped up, but she was ahead of him. I should have seen there was a cupboard with a sign saying "Towels."

The cat that was in there with the clean

linen shot out and clawed right up her dress and on over her shoulder. Then a big squawking brown chicken hit her face, and another whizzed past my ear. They landed on one side of the basin, but couldn't get a foothold there, and one fell in my wash water and the other pitched off and lit on a chair. The air was full of feathers. They'd been dosed with some kind of liquor to keep them quiet; mixed with the smell of hens, it was awful. The cat lurched across the floor and threw up.

"Whoever did this, I'll kill him," my grandmother said quietly, clutching her shoulder. The guys just stood there with their mouths open, not saying a word. But I figured it was that Nick; he made the first move to catch the chickens. Or if it wasn't, I still thought he needed attention. If I'd been home, I could have arranged an electric shock when he put on those dirty boots.

Those maniacs knew from my face what I was thinking. One of them snickered, which was too much for the rest of them. It was worse than the choir. You could have been deafened for life.

---

follow-up

Discussing "If I Lived Through It"

1. Considering all the things that happen in the story, do you think that Henry's mischievousness is good or bad? Why?
2. What useful activities is Henry definitely good at?
3. In what ways would you say Henry's mother is like him? In what ways is she different?
4. What difference does it make that Henry's first name does not come out until well along in the story?

Details That Add Interest

Like other competent authors, Ames Rowe Quentin completes a sentence picture by adding details to base statements—but just not any details. He is careful to choose DETAILS THAT ADD INTEREST to a base statement. For example:

He was holding his stomach, *laughing like a hyena*.

Note that two actions were going on at the same time. Note, too, that the italicized detail suggests *under what circumstances* "he" was holding his stomach. Notice that that added detail begins with *laughing*—a form of the verb *laugh*. *Laughing* is part verb and part adjective. It is part verb because it suggests action. What's more, it is itself modified by the adverbial prepositional phrase *like a hyena*, which tells *how* the laughing was done. *Laughing* is also part adjective because it modifies the pronoun *boy*. You see, when he was holding his stomach, he was a "laughing" person. Because *laughing* is partly a verb and partly an adjective, it is a PARTICIPLE. It begins the participial phrase *laughing like a hyena*—a participial phrase that adds an interesting, colorful detail to the idea expressed in the base sentence.

You can usually spot a participle (and a participial phrase) because it appears either as an *-ing* verb form or an *-ed* (or other past participial) verb form that modifies a noun. Here are some other example sentences containing participles and participial phrases. Note that each participial phrase adds an interesting detail to the base sentence picture:

> I watched out the window, *feeling sick*.
> He looked at it [the cut] in my mirror, *still not saying anything*. (*Saying* is the participle and is the important word in the phrase.)
> That jeep was a rod . . . , *souped for the races*.
> He ended up, *sitting on my chest*. . . .

Practice 1. Writing

Here are four general base statements about "If I Lived Through It." Copy each one, add a comma, and then add an interesting, colorful detail that begins with a participle.

Example
Henry's father stood in the doorway, *looking dazed*.

1. Henry planned a practical joke for Joe.
2. Henry assisted the choir director.
3. Henry's Uncle Nick drove the old jeep skilfully.
4. Henry's grandmother looked at him and then at the other boys.

Be prepared to read at least one of your sentences aloud. (You may also want to write it on the chalkboard.) Do your classmates agree that the participial phrase you've written adds interest to the last statement?

Double Details

In Practice 1, you added only one detail to each sentence. But does a writer ever need to add more than one detail to a base sentence? The answer is a definite yes. For example:

> Johnny banged away at the bag for a while, *not saying anything,* and *doing an awful job of it.*

Johnny banged away quietly (*not saying anything*). But that wasn't all; he also banged away poorly (doing an *awful job of it.*) In that sentence, the writer needs both participial phrases to add information to the base statement and to complete the picture. Each detail explains *how* Johnny performed.

Practice 2. Writing/Discussion

In the narrative that you began in Practice 2 of the FORESTUDY (page 76), you can no doubt find a sentence to which you can add two details to your general base statement. But right now, for practice, write one such sentence that's similar to the one above about Johnny.

First, write a base statement showing your character in a general action. Then add two details—each in the form of a participial phrase—to complete the picture of the action and to show *how* or *why*. Later, you might actually find a place for the sentence in your narrative.

To see whether your sentence presents a sharp picture, test it by reading it aloud to the class or to a group of classmates. Read the base statement only, and ask your classmates what they *see*. Their replies will no doubt vary. Then read your first participial-phrase detail, pause, and then read the second. Do your details sharpen what your classmates see now?

Details about Details

To give added information about a general base statement, a writer can effectively use two details in the same sentence. But sometimes when authors add details, they need to give *more information about that very detail*. They do so by adding a second detail *about the first detail*.

Right after the accident to Henry's unfortunate stepfather, Henry watches his parents drive off for the doctor's office. He says:

I went downstairs, *looking for something to do, like washing some dishes.*

I went downstairs is the base statement. *Why* did Henry go downstairs? The author answers that question by adding a detail: *looking for something to do.* But a reader might still ask, "Looking for something to do *like what?*" In order to make the sentence picture even clearer, the author adds an example of "something": *like washing dishes.* This example gives added information about the first detail, not about the base statement. It is called a *third-level addition,* and can be analysed like this:

    1 I went downstairs, (Base Statement)
      2 looking for something do do,
        3 like washing some dishes.

Here is another sentence which contains a detail about a detail, or a *third-level addition*:

Mary stood on the windy street corner, *waiting for her boyfriend with his friendly grin.*

Mary stood on the windy street corner is the base statement. *Why* did she stand there? The first added detail gives us the answer: she was *waiting for her boyfriend.* As the reader tries to picture the scene, an additional question might arise: what was Mary's boyfriend like? The second detail adds information about Mary's boyfriend: he has a *friendly grin.* Thus, the second detail gives added information about the first detail, not about the general base statement. The sentence could be analysed like this:

    1 Mary stood on the windy street corner, (Base Statement)
      2 waiting for her boyfriend
        3 with his friendly grin.

Here is a third sentence that contains a detail about a detail, or a *third-level addition*:

He struggled up the stairs, *tugging his heavy suitcase, almost losing his grip on it at every step.*

He struggled up the stairs is the base statement. *Why* did he struggle up the stairs? The first detail presents added information to answer that question: He struggled because he was *tugging his* **91** *heavy suitcase*. When trying to picture the scene, one of the things the reader might want to know is how well the person was doing in tugging the suitcase up the stairs. The second detail tells *how* he was tugging it: he was *almost losing his grip on it at every step*. In this sentence, as in the two preceding sentence examples, the second detail gives the reader added information about the first detail, not about the base statement. The sentence could be analysed like this:

    1 He struggled up the stairs, (Base Statement)
        2 tugging his heavy suitcase,
           3 almost losing his grip on it at every step.

Practice 3. Writing and Discussion

Somewhere in the narrative that you began for Practice 2 of the FORESTUDY (p. 76), you might find it useful to write a sentence with two added details, the second detail giving more information about the first. For practice, try to write one such sentence now.

First write a base statement showing your character in a certain general action. Then add a detail about the base statement. Finally, add a detail about your first detail. Use the preceding sentence examples with third-level additions as models for your sentence. You may want to use this sentence in your narrative.

Compare your sentence with those of other students.

Practice 4. Writing

Now complete the narrative character sketch that you began in Practice 2. Here are aids to help you:

1. Keep in mind that your purpose is to reveal a main character trait indirectly, by showing the character in action.
2. Use cumulative sentences wherever they are useful in developing a clear and effective picture in the reader's mind. Remember that a cumulative sentence gradually adds layers of meaning, accumulating details to describe either the base statement or the other details. Don't forget to use your sentences from Practices 1, 2, and 3 of this FOLLOW-UP lesson, if they fit in logically.
3. Experiment with some dialogue, but put different speakers in separate paragraphs. (Review the paragraphing in Quentin's story.)

4. After you complete your first draft, reread it, making corrections and changes. Perhaps you will need to combine certain sentences or reconstruct some of them to make them read smoothly and clearly. You may find that you need to add to some sentences for pictorial completeness, but cut out every word not really essential to your desired total effect.

A two-paragraph narrative opener was given as an example at the end of Practice 2 of the FORESTUDY (p. 76). Here is the example completed. You might wish to complete your own sketch in a way similar to this one.

The Case of the Stubborn Conductor

The little open-air cable car sat poised on its rails at the end of San Francisco's Powell Street, ready to retrace the run it had just completed. The conductor-gripman quietly placed

his right knee on the seat nearest to him as the passengers boarded, blocking it to any occupant. The car was crowded, with late arrivals standing in the aisle.

"What are we waiting for?" a woman's raspy voice complained. "Why aren't we going?"

The conductor stood, with one knee up, his face expressionless, as if he had not heard.

The voice sounded again, this time more plaintive than the last, almost whining. "He has a seat blocked. Why does he do that when so many of us are standing?"

"Some people show no respect," a companion voice observed. "Look at his badge. Get his number. He ought to be reported."

The conductor continued to ignore the passengers, his posture rigid, his eyes looking forward up the street, his hands resting on the grip-lever, a faint smile now crossing his face.

And there was a sudden hush, as a small hobbling figure approached from up the street, her shoulders bent with age, a gnarled hand picking at the concrete with a cane, in an ineffectual but desperate hurry.

As she lumbered aboard, the conductor reached down gently to take her arm. Then, as she dropped breathlessly into the "reserved" seat near him, he pulled the bell cord, a quick, businesslike jerk, engaged the cable grip, and the car began to move.

Bookshelf

Home Is the Hunter, by Helen MacInnes. Harcourt, 1964. A comedy about another homecoming—the story of Ulysses' return to Ithaca after 20 years.

A Mother's Kisses, by Bruce Jay Friedman. Pocket Books, 1970. While Henry's mother was willing to let him make it on his own, Joseph, the hero of Friedman's comedy, finds that his mother's constant efforts to help aren't always helpful.

Travels with My Aunt, by Graham Greene. Bantam, 1971. Henry's unpredictable aunt leads him on a series of wild adventures through Europe.

Zach, by John Craig. Coward, 1972. Zach, who discovers that he is the last of the Agawa tribe, undertakes a long journey to find out about his ancestors.

6

Scent of Apples

forestudy

Details, Details

A physician's diagnosis of a patient's condition must be clear and direct:

> The patient is suffering from a sore throat, fever, watery eyes, and respiratory congestion including sneezing. The patient has a bad cold.

Likewise, an intelligent service-station manager provides simple, logical directions for new employees whose job it is to change flat tires:

> To change a tire, first raise the car on the jack. Remove the lug nuts with wrench. Pull off the wheel with the flat tire; replace it with the spare. Replace the lug nuts; tighten them evenly. Check the spare tire for proper air pressure. Finally, lower the car and remove the jack.

But what must a writer do when there is no simple term—no simple way—to describe a situation or a person's feelings? What can a writer do when there is no neat, precise sequence of steps to follow in order to help the reader understand something? How does a writer convey a complex emotion, a feeling resulting from experiences over many years? For example, how can a writer convey the feelings of homesickness in a man who has been separated from his native land for twenty years or more? Simply to say "the man is homesick" won't do at all. Merely *stating* or *telling* that fact doesn't really get at the emotion. Perhaps in a general way we all know what it means to be homesick. But we may not know what homesickness actually is for someone in a story unless the author SHOWS us how it feels to be homesick.

A writer, then, who is dealing with any complex emotion—such as homesickness—must do essentially the same thing as the physician and the service-station manager did. He/she must supply the reader with precise details. Those details, however, cannot simply be listed. Instead, they must be presented in clearly written sentences that SHOW, *not* tell, the reader what it is to experience the emotion firsthand.

In "Scent of Apples," for example, Mr. Santos, the writer, wants us to know that Mr. Fabia still looks back on his birthplace with affection. And so, rather than just tell us that fact, Mr. Santos *shows* us. He describes the night as cold and icy. And then he writes:

> "It was the same night I met Celestino Fabia, "just a Filipino farmer," as he called himself, who had a farm about 50 km east of Kalamazoo.
>
> "You came all that way on a night like this just to hear me talk?" I asked.
>
> "I've seen no Filipino for so many years now," he answered quickly. "So when I saw your name in the papers where it says you come from the islands and that you're going to talk, I come right away."

Mr. Fabia, in short, will travel 50 km in freezing weather just to see and hear another Filipino. And so in these few precise details we understand how Mr. Fabia feels about the country of his birth. And then as the author describes his visit to Mr. Fabia's home, other important, relevant details accumulate, giving us an accurate understanding of precisely how Mr. Fabia feels—an understanding too complex to be communicated in the single word *homesickness*.

It's in carefully providing precise, relevant details, you see, that a writer shows you (the reader) exactly what it's like to experience something. It is through details that a writer makes you see and feel exactly what he/she sees and feels.

**Who'd drive 50 km just to hear a countryman talk?
Celestino Fabia. That's who.**

Scent of Apples

Bienvenido N. Santos

When I arrived in Kalamazoo, it was October and the war[1] was still on. Gold and silver stars hung on pennants above silent windows of white and brick-red cottages. In a back yard an old man burned leaves and twigs while a gray-haired woman sat on the porch, her red hands quiet on her lap, watching the smoke rising above the elms, both of them thinking the same thought, perhaps, about a tall, grinning boy with blue eyes and flying hair who went out to war; where could he be now this month when leaves were turning into gold and the fragrance of gathered apples was in the wind?

It was a cold night when I left my room at the hotel for a usual speaking engagement. I walked but a little way. A heavy wind coming up from Lake Michigan was icy on the face. It felt like winter straying early in the northern woodlands. Under the lampposts the leaves shone like bronze. And they rolled on the pavements like the ghost feet of a thousand autumns long dead, long before the boys left for faraway lands without great icy winds and promise of winter early in the air, lands without apple trees, *the singing and the gold*!

It was the same night I met Celestino Fabia, "just a Filipino farmer," as he called himself, who had a farm about 50 km east of Kalamazoo.

"You came all that way on a night like this just to hear me talk?" I asked.

"I've seen no Filipino for so many years now," he answered quickly. "So when I saw your name in the papers where it says you come from the islands and that you're going to talk, I come right away."

Earlier that night I had addressed a college crowd, mostly women. It appeared that they wanted me to talk about my country; they wanted me to tell them things about it because my country had become a lost country. Everywhere in the land the enemy stalked.[2] Over it a great silence hung; and their boys were there, unheard from, or they were on their way to some little-known island in the Pacific, young boys all, hardly men, thinking of harvest moons and smell of forest fire.

1. *the war:* World War II (1939–1945)

From *You Lovely People* by Bienvenido N. Santos. Reprinted by permission of the author.

2. *everywhere ... stalked:* the Philippines were occupied by Japanese troops

97

It was not hard talking about our own people. I knew them well and I loved them. And they seemed so far away during those terrible years that I must have spoken of them with a little fervor, a little nostalgia.°

In the open forum that followed, the audience wanted to know whether there was much difference between our women and the American women. I tried to answer the question as best as I could, saying, among other things, that I did not know much about American women except that they looked friendly, but differences or similarities in inner qualities such as naturally belonged to the heart or to the mind, I could only speak about with vagueness.

While I was trying to explain away the fact that it was not easy to make comparisons, a man rose from the rear of the hall, wanting to say something. In the distance, he looked slight and old and very brown. Even before he spoke, I knew that he was, like me, a Filipino.

"I'm a Filipino," he began, loud and clear, in a voice that seemed used to wide open spaces. "I'm just a Filipino farmer out in the country." He waved his hand towards the door. "I left the Philippines more than twenty years ago and have never been back. Never will, perhaps. I want to find out, sir, are our Filipino women the same like they were twenty years ago?"

As he sat down, the hall filled with voices, hushed and intrigued. I weighed my answer carefully. I did not want to tell a lie, yet I did not want to say anything that would seem platitudinous,° insincere. But more important than these considerations, it seemed to me that moment as I looked towards my countryman, I must give him an answer that would not make him so unhappy. Surely, all these years, he must have held on to certain ideals, certain beliefs, even illusions peculiar to the exile.

"First," I said as the voices gradually died down and every eye seemed upon me. "First, tell me what our women were like twenty years ago."

The man stood to answer. "Yes," he said, "you're too young. . . . Twenty years ago our women were nice, they were modest, they wore their hair long, they dressed proper and went for no monkey business. They were natural, they went to church regular, and they were faithful." He had spoken slowly, and now, in what seemed like an afterthought, added, "It's the men who ain't."

Now I knew what I was going to say.

"Well," I began, "it will interest you to know that our women have changed— but definitely! The change, however, has been on the outside only. Inside, here," pointing to the heart, "they are the same as they were twenty years ago, God-fearing, faithful, modest, and *nice*."

The man was visibly moved. "I'm very happy, sir," he said, in the manner of one who, having stakes on the land, had found no cause to regret one's sentimental investment.

After this, everything that was said and done in that hall that night seemed like an anticlimax;° and later, as we walked outside, he gave me his name and told me of his farm 50 km east of the city.

We had stopped at the main entrance of the hotel lobby. We had not talked very much on the way. As a matter of fact, we were never alone. Kindly American friends talked to us, asked us questions, said good night. So now I asked him whether he cared to step into the lobby with me and talk shop.

"No, thank you," he said, "you are tired. And I don't want to stay out too late."

"Yes, you live very far."

"I got a car," he said; "besides. . . . "

Now he smiled, he truly smiled. All night I had been watching his face, and I wondered when he was going to smile.

"Will you do me a favor, please," he continued, smiling almost sweetly. "I want you to have dinner with my family out in the country. I'd call for you tomorrow afternoon, then drive you back. Will that be all right?"

"Of course," I said. "I'd love to meet your family." I was leaving Kalamazoo for Muncie, Indiana, in two days. There was plenty of time.

"You will make my wife very happy," he said.

"You flatter me."

"Honest. She'll be very happy. Ruth is a country girl and hasn't met many Filipinos. I mean Filipinos younger than I, cleaner-looking. We're just poor farmer folks, you know, and we don't get to town very often. Roger, that's my boy, he goes to school in town. A bus takes him early in the morning and he's back in the afternoon. He's a nice boy."

"I bet he is. I've seen the children of some of the boys by their American wives, and the boys are tall, taller than the father, and very good looking."

"Roger, he'd be tall. You'll like him." **99**

Then he said good-bye, and I waved to him as he disappeared in the darkness.

The next day he came, at about three in the afternoon. There was a mild, ineffectual sun shining; and it was not too cold. He was wearing an old brown tweed jacket and worsted trousers to match. His shoes were polished, and although the green of his tie seemed faded, a colored shirt hardly accentuated it. He looked younger than he appeared the night before, now that he was clean-shaven and seemed ready to go to a party. He was grinning as we met.

"Oh, Ruth can't believe it. She can't believe it," he kept repeating as he led me to his car—a nondescript thing in faded black that had known better days and many hands. "I says to her, I'm bringing you a first-class Filipino, and she says, aw, go away, quit kidding, there's no such thing as first-class Filipino. But Roger, that's my boy, he believed me immediately. What's he like, daddy, he asks. Oh, you will see, I says, he's first-class. Like you, daddy? No, no, I laugh at him, your daddy ain't first-class. Aw, but you are, daddy, he says. So you can see what a nice boy he is, so innocent. Then Ruth starts griping about the house, but the house is a mess, she says. True it's a mess, it's always a mess, but you don't mind, do you? We're poor folks, you know."

The trip seemed interminable. We passed through narrow lanes and disappeared into thickets, and came out on barren land overgrown with weeds in places. All around were dead leaves and dry earth. In the distance were apple trees.

"Aren't those apple trees?" I asked, wanting to be sure.

"Yes, those are apple trees," he replied. "Do you like apples? I got lots of 'em. I got an apple orchard. I'll show you."

All the beauty of the afternoon seemed in the distance, on the hills, in the dull soft sky.

"Those trees are beautiful on the hills," I said.

"Autumn's a lovely season. The trees are getting ready to die, and they show their color, proud-like."

"No such thing in our own country," I said.

That remark seemed unkind, I realized later. It touched him off on a long deserted tangent,° but ever there, perhaps. How many times did the lonely mind take unpleasant detours away from the familiar winding lanes towards home for fear of this, the remembered hurt, the long-lost youth, the grim shadows of the years; how many times indeed, only the exile knows.

It was a rugged road we were travelling, and the car made so much noise that I could not hear everything he said, but I understood him. He was telling his story for the first time in many years. He was remembering his own youth. He was thinking of home. In these odd moments there seemed no cause for fear, no cause at all, no pain. That would come later. In the night perhaps. Or lonely on the farm under the apple trees.

In this old Visayan[3] town, the streets are narrow and dirty and strewn with coral shells. You have been there? You could not have missed our house; it was the biggest in town, one of the oldest; ours was a big family. The

---

3. *Visayan* (vē sä′ yən): a group of islands of the Philippines, located between the islands of Luzon and Mindanao

house stood right on the edge of the street. A door opened heavily and you enter a dark hall leading to the stairs. There is the smell of chickens roosting on the low-topped walls; there is the familiar sound they make, and you grope your way up a massive staircase, the banisters smooth upon the trembling hand. Such nights, they are no better than the days; windows are closed against the sun; they close heavily.

Mother sits in her corner looking very white and sick. This was her world, her domain. In all these years I cannot remember the sound of her voice. Father was different. He moved about. He shouted. He ranted. He lived in the past and talked of honor as though it were the only thing.

I was born in that house. I grew up there into a pampered brat. I was mean. One day I broke their hearts. I saw mother cry wordlessly as father heaped his curses upon me and drove me out of the house, the gate closing heavily after me. And my brothers and sisters took up my father's hate for me and multiplied it numberless times in their own broken hearts. I was no good.

But sometimes, you know, I miss that house, the roosting chickens on the low-topped walls. I miss my brothers and sisters. Mother sitting in her chair, looking like a pale ghost in a corner of the room. I would remember the great live posts, massive tree trunks from the forests. Leafy plants grow on the sides, buds pointing downwards, wilted and died before they could become flowers. As they fell on the floor, father bent to pick them and throw them out into the coral streets. His hands were strong; I have kissed those hands . . . many times, many times . . . .

101

Finally, we rounded a deep curve and suddenly came upon a shanty, all but ready to crumble in a heap on the ground; its plastered walls were rotting away, the floor was hardly 30 cm from the ground. I thought of the cottages of the poor colored folk in the South, the hovels of the poor everywhere in the land. This one stood all by itself as though by common consent all the folk that used to live here had decided to stay away, despising it, ashamed of it. Even the lovely season could not color it with beauty.

A dog barked loudly as we approached. A fat blonde woman stood at the door with a little boy by her side. Roger seemed newly scrubbed. He hardly took his eyes off me. Ruth had a clean apron around her shapeless waist. Now, as she shook my hands in sincere delight, I noticed shamefacedly (that I should notice) how rough her hands, how coarse and red with labor, how ugly! She was no longer young and her smile was pathetic.

As we stepped inside and the door closed behind us, immediately I was aware of the familiar scent of apples. The room was bare except for a few ancient pieces of secondhand furniture. In the middle of the room stood a stove to keep the family warm in winter. The walls were bare. Over the dining table hung a lamp yet unlighted.

Ruth got busy with the drinks. She kept coming in and out of a rear room that must have been the kitchen, and soon the table was heavy with food, fried chicken legs and rice, and green peas and corn on the ear. Even as we ate, Ruth kept standing and going to the kitchen for more food. Roger ate like a little gentleman.

"Isn't he nice looking?" his father asked.

"You are a handsome boy, Roger," I said.

The boy smiled at me. "You look like daddy," he said.

Afterwards I noticed an old picture leaning on the top of a dresser and stood to pick it up. It was yellow and soiled with many fingerings. The faded figure of a woman in Philippine dress could yet be distinguished, although the face had become a blur.

"Your . . . " I began.

"I don't know who she is," Fabia hastened to say. "I picked that picture many years ago in a room on La Salle Street in Chicago. I have often wondered who she is."

"The face wasn't a blur in the beginning?"

"Oh, no. It was a young face and good."

Ruth came in with a plate full of apples.

"Ah," I cried, picking out a ripe one, "I've been thinking where all the scent of apples came from. The room is full of it."

"I'll show you," said Fabia.

He showed me a back room, not very big. It was half full of apples.

"Every day," he explained, "I take some of them to town to sell to the groceries. Prices have been low. I've been losing on the trips."

"These apples will spoil," I said.

"We'll feed them to the pigs."

Then he showed me around the farm. It was twilight now, and the apple trees stood bare against a glowing western sky. In apple-blossom time it must be lovely here, I thought. But what about winter time?

103

One day, according to Fabia, a few years ago, before Roger was born, he had an attack of acute appendicitis. It was deep winter. The snow lay heavy everywhere. Ruth was pregnant and none too well herself. At first she did not know what to do. She bundled him in warm clothing and put him on a cot near the stove. She shovelled the snow from their front door and practically carried the suffering man on her shoulders, dragging him through the newly made path towards the road, where they waited for the U.S. Mail car to pass. Meanwhile snowflakes poured all over them, and she kept rubbing the man's arms and legs as she herself nearly froze to death.

"Go back to the house, Ruth!" her husband cried, "you'll freeze to death."

But she clung to him wordlessly. Even as she massaged his arms and legs, her tears rolled down her cheeks. "I won't leave you, I won't leave you," she repeated.

Finally the U.S. Mail car arrived. The mailman, who knew them well, helped them board the car, and without stopping on his usual route, took the sick man and his wife direct to the nearest hospital.

Ruth stayed in the hospital with Fabia. She slept in a corridor outside the patients' ward and in the daytime helped in scrubbing the floor and washing the dishes and cleaning the men's things. They didn't have enough money, and Ruth was willing to work like a slave.

"Ruth's a nice girl," said Fabia. "Like our own Filipino women."

Before nightfall, he took me back to the hotel. Ruth and Roger stood at the door holding hands and smiling at me. From inside the room of the shanty, a low light flickered. I had a last glimpse of the apple trees in the orchard under the darkened sky as Fabia backed up the car. And soon we were on our way back to town. The dog had started barking. We could hear it for some time, until finally we could not hear it any more, and all was darkness around us, except where the headlamps revealed a stretch of road leading somewhere.

Fabia did not talk this time. I didn't seem to have anything to say myself. But when finally we came to the hotel and I got down, Fabia said, "Well, I guess I won't be seeing you again."

It was dimly lighted in front of the hotel and I could hardly see Fabia's face. Without getting off the car, he moved to where I had sat, and I saw him extend his hand. I gripped it.

"Tell Ruth and Roger," I said, "I love them."

He dropped my hand quickly. "They'll be waiting for me now," he said.

"Look," I said, not knowing why I said it, "one of these days, very soon, I hope, I'll be going home. I could go to your town."

"No," he said softly, sounding very much defeated but brave. "Thanks a lot. But you see, nobody would remember me now."

Then he started the car, and as it moved away, he waved his hand.

"Good-bye," I said, waving back into the darkness. And suddenly the night was cold like winter straying early in these northern woodlands.

I hurried inside. There was a train the next morning that left for Muncie, Indiana, at a quarter after eight.

follow-up

Discussing "Scent of Apples"

1. What do you think the writer is suggesting when he says at the end of the story, that the night suddenly turned cold?
2. Why, in your opinion, is the image of Filipino women so important to Fabia—and to the impact of the essay itself?

Narrative: Sequence of Events

No matter whether it is imagined or real, NARRATIVE is an account of events—an account of things that happened. As a rule, narrative unfolds gradually. That is, the events are recounted in sequence from beginning to end. Each event leads naturally to another event, giving the narrative continuity. What's more, each event works to create mental images which, when read in their *proper sequence*, go together to produce an understandable story.

Practice 1. Writing/Discussion

Listed below in no particular order are ten events from "Scent of Apples." On your paper, list those events in their proper order, starting with the event that occurred first.

A. Celestino Fabia introduces the narrator to his family.
B. The narrator meets Celestino Fabia.
C. The narrator sends his love to Ruth and Roger.
D. The narrator goes to his hotel room because he has an early train to catch.
E. Celestino Fabia invites the narrator to his home for dinner.
F. Celestino Fabia questions the narrator about Filipino women.
G. The narrator eats dinner with the Fabia family.
H. The narrator arrives in Kalamazoo, Michigan.
I. Celestino Fabia and the narrator drive to Kalamazoo without talking very much.

J. The narrator discovers the source of the scent of apples in the Fabia house.

Be prepared to share your ordering of the ten events with your classmates. Is there general agreement on that order of events?

Arranging narrative events in order helps you see the logical progression of these events and reinforces your understanding and enjoyment of the narrative itself.

Flashbacks

But not all narratives move steadily from beginning to end. Sometimes an author feels it necessary to interrupt the story in order to show you *why* events happened as they did. That is, the author goes back in time and tells about important things that happened *before* the events of the main narrative happened. In "Scent of Apples" Bienvenido Santos incorporated several such FLASHBACKS into his narrative. The first FLASHBACK occurs when Santos explains how he happened to meet Celestino Fabia. It starts on page 97 with the sentence "Earlier that night I had addressed a college crowd, mostly women." It ends on page 99 with the words ". . . and later as we walked outside, he gave me his name and told me of his farm 50 km east of the city."

Perhaps you noticed that none of the ten events you re-arranged in Practice 1 above had to do with the account of Celestino Fabia's leaving his home in the Philippines (pages 100-101). Why not?

What other FLASHBACK can you find in "Scent of Apples"?

Practice 2. Writing

On your paper, draw a horizontal line. At regular intervals on that line, draw ten short vertical lines, one for each of the ten events you arranged in Practice 1. Label each vertical line with its proper letter—A, B, C, etc.

Example

A	B	C	D	E	F	G	H	I	J

Whenever a FLASHBACK occurs in "Scent of Apples," indicate by *1, 2, 3*, etc., its proper placement on the narrative line.

When you have completed your narrative line, compare your work with what your classmates have done. Did you detect all the FLASHBACKS Santos used? How valuable are these FLASH- BACKS to your total understanding of the events and the people in "Scent of Apples"?

Bookshelf

From the Belly of the Shark, ed. by Walter Lowenfels. Vintage, 1973. Poems expressing the perceptions and experiences of writers from several cultures—Chicano, Black, Native North American, and Inuit, among others.

Hot Land, Cold Season, by Pedro J. Soto. Dell, 1973. The story of a young man's life in Puerto Rico and the United States, Jacinto's divided loyalties leave him uncertain about where he belongs.

House Made of Dawn, by N. Scott Momaday. New American Library, 1969. After World War II, Abel finds that he no longer shares the values of his Kiowa tribe. After spending time in prison he finally returns to the reservation, with greater insight into his past.

My Enemy, My Brother, by James Forman. Scholastic Book Services, 1972. A young boy—survivor of a Nazi concentration camp—travels to Israel at the end of the war and suf- fers many hardships in rediscovering his heritage.

7

The Kid in the Stove

forestudy

Figurative Language

> Sally looks like her father.
> Sally sings like a meadow lark.

Two comparisons. But though each comparison is made up of five words and though each comparison is a statement, the second is not the same kind of comparison as the first. Look at them again. In the first, two human beings are compared insofar as their facial characteristics are concerned. The comparison is a LITERAL comparison. That is, the words mean exactly what they say.

But does Sally warble *exactly* as a meadow lark warbles? Hardly. That second comparison means that Sally's singing and the meadow lark's singing have *something in common*—namely, the pleasing quality of the sounds that make up that singing. The comparison, you see, creates a sensory impression—a sensory image. That is, in your mind, you tend to hear pleasant sounds. Of course, you could simply say, "Sally sings beautifully (sweetly)." But that statement sounds pretty flat in comparison to "Sally sings like a meadow lark." Why? Because the comparison appeals to one of your five senses—hearing.

Comparisons like "Sally sings like a meadow lark," are FIGURATIVE comparisons. Competent writers use figurative comparisons frequently to give their writing impact.

"Sally sings like a meadow lark" is a special kind of figurative comparison called a SIMILE (sim′ə lē). The term SIMILE simply means that the writer/speaker uses the words *like* or *as* to compare two different things that are alike in some way.

You use similes every day. For instance, when you say something like "That song has as much bounce as a lead pipe," you're using a simile. Or when you say something like "My room looks like a disaster area," you're using a simile.

Practice 1. Discussion

In paragraph two of "The Kid in the Stove", you'll find the following two similes. In examining each one, you have three jobs to do:

Explain why it is a *figurative comparison*—a simile.
Tell what two different things are being compared.
Tell in what way those two things are alike.

1. Joseph, he talk like the wind-up record player when it not cranked up good enough.
2. "... he grin and shake, happy a little, like a dog that know he gonna be petted."

The Kid In The Stove

W. P. Kinsella

"Tell us a story, Silas," the kids say to me a lot of evenings. I tell them lots of stories about our legends of how the Great Spirit made the land and us, and even a few that I made up myself. But no matter how many I tell, just about when it be time for bed they say, "Tell us about the kid in the stove."

For that one they all gather around close to me. Minnie and Thomas, Delores and Hiram, my little brothers and sisters. And there is Joseph too, my big brother. He is 22 already, but when he just a baby he catch the scarlet fever and his mind is never grow up like his body do. Joseph, he talk like the wind-up record player when it not cranked up good enough. "I ... be ... the ... kid ... that ... hid ... in ... the ... stove ..." and he grin and shake, happy a little, like a dog that know he gonna be petted.

So I tell them the story. Ma, she used to tell it to me and Illianna and Joseph when we was little, and she say her mother used to tell it to her. It kind of our own private scary story about how Lazarus Bobtail and all but one of his kids was murdered by a white man named Donald Henry Ditesman. It happened a long time ago when there was hardly any town at Wetaskiwin, and the reserve here at Hobbema was new. Mrs. Bobtail was away someplace is how she didn't die too. Afterward, they say she married with a Blood Indian from down south, moved away, and nobody ever heard of her or the kid in the stove no more.

I don't know why kids like scary stories but they do. I make everybody be quiet and turn the lamp down low and then I tell about this crazy white man come creep around the Bobtail cabin, peek in the window, and try the door real careful.

"You guys think you hear something?" I say. And they always do. They move in

Reprinted by permission of Oberon Press.

109

closer to me, and Delores, the littlest one, hold on to Joseph's neck real tight. Then I finish the story about how that Ditesman guy is shoot Lazarus Bobtail and four of his kids, but how the fifth kid crawl right up inside the big old cookstove in the cabin, and he get to live to tell all about it.

Once, some of us went up to the spot where them children died, and it make us feel all creepy. It ain't on the reserve no more; the Government, it take away land whenever it feel like it, and our reserve get smaller as it get older. The place was lonely even in the daytime. All we could find was a few logs people say was part of Lazarus Bobtail's cabin. Just being there at the place where it really happen make us think a lot about the story. I remember how when I first hear it, I figure that if something like that ever happened at our place, I'd of been the smart kid that hid in the stove and got to live. And I bet everybody who hear it think the same way.

For such a sad story it almost make a happy ending when you hear at the end that one child got away. Most anybody in these parts, Indian or white, can tell you about that escape. They're real certain about it, as certain as they are that we live on the Ermineskin Reserve and that the town down at the highway is called Hobbema. Yet it never happen at all.

I like to know about Indian history in Alberta, and I've read the couple of books in the Wetaskiwin library that are about Indians, maybe three-four times. I get to thinking about how I would like to know the history-book story of the Bobtail Massacre.

Mr. Nichols, my English instructor down at the Tech School in Wetaskiwin, the guy who is fix up the spelling in my stories, says maybe I could find out from the RCMP or maybe from the Glenbow Foundation in Calgary, who are people keep records of Indian history in Alberta.

The RCMP guys don't help much. They all young guys and I think they come maybe from places where they don't have no Indians. They make fun on me when I ask, want to know where my tomahawk, and how come an Indian kid like me want to be bothered worry about something that happen so long ago. They say maybe they get what I want for me if I tell them who's got a still on the reserve and where it's at. So I go away.

Next time I go to Calgary, I leave my girlfriend Sadie One-wound look around in the Goodwill Store, while I take the bus out to the Glenbow place. I meet with a real nice man called Mr. Hugh Dempsey.[1] He is white but he got Indian wife, and he have a picture of her right up on his desk to show he not ashamed to have her. He talk soft on me and make me feel calm, cause I sure not used to big fancy buildings and people run around dressed up all the time.

Mr. Dempsey is look in his books and things and he give me a paper to read and I copy some of it down.

On the night of July 14, 1907, an itinerant railroad worker named Donald Henry Deutchmann had a dispute, in the town of Wetaskiwin, with some Indians from the Ermineskin Reserve which is located at Hobbema, some 18 km distant. The nature of this dispute is not clear, but late that night, Deutchmann apparently walked from Wetaskiwin to the reserve, stopped at the first Indian residence that he came to, that of Lazarus Bobtail, entered and shot

---

1. *Hugh Dempsey:* Mr. Dempsey works at the Glenbow-Alberta Institute in Calgary. He is a writer and an expert on the Native tribes in Alberta. His wife is a Blood Indian, the daughter of Senator James Gladstone.

to death Bobtail and his four children. The bodies were discovered the next day by Bobtail's wife, White Sky. Deutchmann was arrested the same day by the Mounties, but was judged insane and the case never came to trial.

Mr. Dempsey he find me another book with a little chapter about Deutchmann, but the story is the same, not near as scary written down in history as when told at night in a cabin with a coal-oil lamp make shadow all over.

I feel kind of sad that there ain't nothing nowhere about the kid that got away. When I ask Mr. Dempsey about it he say that maybe part of the story is taken from some other story that happened here or maybe someplace else. He say that lots of time people get things mixed up like that when a story been told for a lot of years like that one has.

Mr. Dempsey, he point out another little paragraph in the book and say that maybe it explain a whole lot. That paragraph is say that a month or so after the murders, before Mrs. Bobtail move away, she is have a baby. Just a baby, the book don't say if it was a boy or a girl.

I think about that real hard, and when I hear Mr. Dempsey explain it, I have to agree with him. I know when I was little and hear the story, when they get to the part where everybody been shot, I always ask, "And did all the children die?" and I know the kids I tell the story to do the same.

What Mr. Dempsey suggest is that, way back, somebody, in the way big people like to make fun on kids and make a joke for themselves at the same time, say, "They all died but the one in the oven." Everybody growed up knows that that's a way for saying a lady is gonna have a baby.

Saying that would make the kids feel better about a sad story, and the big people could laugh and wink their eyes at each other. It seem to me that that is likely the way it happened and little by little the story got changed over the years until everybody is believe there really was a kid in the stove.

Boy, I can hardly wait to get back and tell everybody what I found out. All these years everybody is have the story all wrong, but, boy, I sure gonna fix that up in a hurry. I guess we going to have to get us a new scary story to tell, cause it is the kid in the stove part that make the Bobtail Massacre not just another murder story.

I feel kind of tingly all over and I'm almost as excited as the time I knew I was going to Edmonton to buy my new pair of cowboy boots. Yet when I meet with Sadie, I tell her don't bother me about what I found out at Glenbow.

On the bus on the way home I start to think about how much I liked that story, and how the kids I tell it to sure get a bang out of it.

Sadie want to talk to me but I tell her I got something to think about. She say maybe she wishes she was going to marry a bronc-buster like Eathen Firstrider instead of a guy like me, who sneak around all the time write down what people say. Finally, she just run her knee up against mine and look at her *Country Music Song Book* that she bought in Calgary with a picture of Donna Fargo on the cover.

That story like we been telling, is not really the truth, but it sure make a lot of kids happy for a lot of years, and I wonder who it gonna make feel good, besides me, if I tell what I found out. It seem to me that it kind of like... well, the reasons you don't shoot songbirds is that they don't do nobody no harm.

I look sideways at Sadie, and she look at me and then she put her head on my shoulder. I reach down and put my hand on the leg of her jeans.

"You finished thinking, Silas?" she asks.

"Yeah," I say.

follow-up

Discussing "The Kid In The Stove"

1. Why was Silas, the narrator, happy to discover the truth about "the kid in the stove"? Why, on the other hand, did he decide to keep telling the story in the old way?
2. In the story as a whole, what impression is conveyed of relationships between Native North Americans and non-Indians?
3. The story-teller is skilled in the use of figurative language. What do the images add to the story?

Native North American Borrowings

Though our English language is basically of German origin, the present-day English vocabulary—more than 600 000 words—contains words borrowed from almost every major language on earth. The languages spoken by Native North American tribes are no exception. Perhaps you recognized *tomahawk* as a Native North American word. Specifically, *tomahawk* is an Algonquin word.

Practice 1. Investigation/Discussion

Many words which we are familiar with are of Native North American origin. Using a dictionary that gives word origins, look up the following words to find the specific tribe from which each was borrowed. Share your findings with the class.

1. muskeg
2. moccasin
3. toboggan

Practice 2. Investigation/Discussion

Native North American words are all around us.

Cities, provinces, rivers, lakes, mountain ranges bear Native North American names. In groups, select one category—names of cities and towns, for example—and draw up a list of as many Native North American words as you can find. If possible, indicate the tribal origin of each name you list. Add your list to a much more extensive class list of Native North American words.

Recital of The Priest Chilan

from the Mayan chronicle, Chilan Balan

Eat, eat, while there is bread,
Drink, drink, while there is water;
A day comes when dust shall darken the air,
When a blight shall wither the land,
When a cloud shall arise,
When a mountain shall be lifted up,
When a strong man shall seize the city,
When ruin shall fall upon all things,
When the tender leaf shall be destroyed,
When eyes shall be closed in death;
When there shall be three signs on a tree,
Father, son, and grandson hanging dead on
the same tree;
When the battle flag shall be raised,
And the people scattered abroad in the forests.

Bookshelf

Dance Me Outside, by W. P. Kinsella. Oberon, 1977. "The Kid in the Stove" appears in this collection of stories. They tell of various adventures on the Hobbema Indian Reserve.

Half Breed, by Maria Campbell. McClelland & Stewart, 1973. The author's autobiography.

"One, Two, Three Little Indians," in *Hugh Garner's Best Stories,* by Hugh Garner. Ryerson Press, 1963. A beautiful story pinpointing the stereotypes in the conflicts between Natives and whites.

Shoeless Joe Jackson, by W. P. Kinsella. Oberon, 1980. The most recent collection of Kinsella's hilarious short stories.

Touch the Earth, by T. C. McLuhan. New Press, 1971. Excerpts from speeches given by various Native Chiefs.

8

Gaston

forestudy

Inferences

You walk into a crowded room. Almost immediately you begin to notice things about many of the people there—the dress one girl is wearing, the tie a boy has on, someone else's hairdo, and so on. From what you notice about various persons, you begin to make assumptions about them: You like the appearance of one; you don't like the appearance of another; someone seems to talk too loud; someone else seems to be shy because he/she isn't saying much. In making assumptions like that, you are engaged in the process of INFERENCE. That is, you are drawing conclusions based on the facts you have.

In writing a short story, an author must rely on words to create characters and to establish the relationships among those characters. Because the short story writer doesn't have unlimited space, he/she can't very well explain in great detail what kind of person each character is; and there simply isn't room to describe in detail the kinds of relationships existing among the characters. As a result the short story writer chooses words carefully—words that SUGGEST character traits and relationships.

When you—the reader—read the short story, you have to "read between the lines." That is, from the author's words—from the facts given and from what is suggested—you put two and two together and make some assumptions about the characters and their relationships. In other words, you have to INFER character traits and relationships.

Practice 1. Discussion
Here are five passages from "Gaston." In each case, what inferences can you make about the relationship between the

115

characters mentioned? Be prepared to give reasons for the inferences you make. (That is, on what do you base your assumptions?)

1. "She sat across from the man who would have been a total stranger except that he was in fact her father."

2. "He placed the biggest and best-looking peach on the small plate in front of the girl and then took the flawed peach [for himself to eat]."

3. "The man studied the seed dweller, and so, of course, did the girl."

4. "'If the phone rings, what shall I say?'
'I don't think it will ring, but if it does, say hello and see who it is.'
'If it's my mother, what shall I say?'
'Tell her I've gone to get you a bad peach, and anything else you want to tell her.'"

5. "You haven't been with your father two days, and already you sound like him."

A bit strange—isn't it—living in a peach seed?

Gaston

William Saroyan

They were to eat peaches, as planned, after her nap, and now she sat across from the man who would have been a total stranger except that he was in fact her father. They had been together again (although she couldn't quite remember when they had been together before) for almost a hundred years now, or was it only since day before yesterday? Anyhow, they were together again, and he was kind of funny. First, he had the biggest mustache she had ever seen on anybody, although to her it was not a mustache at all; it was a lot of red and brown hair under his nose and around the ends of his mouth. Second, he wore a blue-and-white striped jersey instead of a shirt and tie, and no coat. His arms were covered with the same hair, only it was a little lighter and thinner. He wore blue slacks, but no shoes and socks. He was barefoot, and so was she, of course.

He was at home. She was with him in his home in Paris, if you could call it a home. He was very old, especially for a young man—thirty-six, he had told her; and she was six, just up from sleep on a very hot afternoon in August.

That morning, on a little walk in the neighborhood, she had seen peaches in a box outside a small store and she had stopped to look at them, so he had bought a kilo.[1]

Now, the peaches were on a large plate on the card table at which they sat.

There were seven of them, but one of them was flawed. It *looked* as good as the others, almost the size of a tennis ball, nice red fading to light green, but where the stem had been there was now a break that went straight down into the heart of the seed.

He placed the biggest and best-looking peach on the small plate in front of the girl, and then took the flawed peach and began to remove the skin. When he had half the skin off the peach he ate that side, neither of them talking, both of them just being there, and not being excited or anything—no plans, that is.

The man held the half-eaten peach in his fingers and looked down into the cav-ity, into the open seed. The girl looked, too.

While they were looking, two feelers poked out from the cavity. They were attached to a kind of brown knob-head, which followed the feelers, and then two large legs took a strong grip on the edge of the cavity and hoisted some of the rest of whatever it was out of the seed, and stopped there a moment, as if to look around.

The man studied the seed dweller, and so, of course, did the girl.

The creature paused only a fraction of a second, and then continued to come out of the seed, to walk down the eaten side of the peach to wherever it was going.

The girl had never seen anything like it—a whole big thing made out of brown color, a knob-head, feelers, and a great many legs. It was very active, too. Almost businesslike, you might say. The man placed the peach back on the plate. The creature moved off the peach onto the surface of the white plate. There it came to a thoughtful stop.

"Who is it?" the girl said.

"Gaston."

"Where does he live?"

"Well, he *used* to live in this peach seed, but now that the peach has been harvested and sold, and I have eaten half of it, it looks as if he's out of house and home."

"Aren't you going to squash him?"

"No, of course not, why should I?"

"He's a bug. He's *ugh*."

"Not at all. He's Gaston the grand boulevardier."[1]

---

1. *kilo* (kĭl' ō, kē' lō): kilogram—a unit of mass and weight in the Metric System of measurement

1. *boulevardier* (bo͞o' lə vär dyā'): a man about town (*French*, a man who frequents boulevards)

"Everybody hollers when a bug comes out of an apple, but you don't holler or *anything*."

"Of course not. How would we like it if somebody hollered every time we came out of our house?"

"Why *would* they?"

"Precisely. So why should we holler at Gaston?"

"He's not the same as us."

"Well, not exactly, but he's the same as a lot of other occupants of peach seeds. Now, the poor fellow hasn't got a home, and there he is with all that pure design and handsome form, and nowhere to go."

"Handsome?"

"Gaston is just about the handsomest of his kind I've ever seen."

"What's he saying?"

"Well, he's a little confused. Now, inside that house of his he had everything in order. Bed here, porch there, and so forth."

"Show me."

The man picked up the peach, leaving Gaston entirely alone on the white plate. He removed the peeling and ate the rest of the peach.

"Nobody else I know would do that," the girl said. "They'd throw it away."

"I can't imagine why. It's a perfectly good peach."

He opened the seed and placed the two sides not far from Gaston. The girl studied the open halves.

"Is *that* where he lives?"

"It's where he used to live. Gaston is out in the world and on his own now. You can see for yourself how comfortable he was in there. He had everything."

"Now what has he got?"

"Not very much, I'm afraid."

"What's he going to do?"

"What are *we* going to do?"

"Well, we're not going to squash him, that's one thing we're *not* going to do," the girl said.

"What *are* we going to do, then?"

"Put him back?"

"Oh, *that* house is finished."

"Well, he can't live in our house, can he?"

"Not happily."

"Can he live in our house *at all*?"

"Well, he could *try*, I suppose. Don't you want to eat a peach?"

"Only if it's a peach with somebody in the seed."

"Well, see if you can find a peach that has an opening at the top, because if you can, that'll be a peach in which you're likeliest to find somebody."

The girl examined each of the peaches on the big plate.

"They're all shut," she said.

"Well, eat one, then."

"No. I want the same kind that you ate, with somebody in the seed."

"Well, to tell you the truth, the peach I ate would be considered a bad peach, so of course stores don't like to sell them. I was sold that one by mistake, most likely. And so now Gaston is without a home, and we've got six perfect peaches to eat."

"I don't want a perfect peach. I want a peach with people."

"Well, I'll go out and see if I can find one."

"Where will I go?"

"You'll go with me, unless you'd rather stay. I'll only be five minutes."

"If the phone rings, what shall I say?"

"I don't think it'll ring, but if it does, say hello and see who it is."

"If it's my mother, what shall I say?"

"Tell her I've gone to get you a bad peach, and anything else you want to tell her."

"If she wants me to go back, what shall I say?"

"Say yes if you want to go back."

"Do you want me to?"

"Of course not, but the important thing is what you want, not what I want."

"Why is *that* the important thing?"

"Because I want you to be where you want to be."

"I want to be here."

"I'll be right back."

He put on socks and shoes, and a jacket, and went out. She watched Gaston trying to find out what to do next. Gaston wandered around the plate, but everything seemed wrong and he didn't know what to do or where to go.

The telephone rang and her mother said she was sending the chauffeur to pick her up because there was a little party for somebody's daughter who was also six, and then tomorrow they would fly back to New York.

"Let me speak to your father," she said.

"He's gone to get a peach."

"*One* peach?"

"One with people."

"You haven't been with your father two days and already you *sound* like him."

"There *are* peaches with people in them. I know. I saw one of them come out."

"A *bug*?"

"Not a bug. Gaston."

"*Who*?"

"Gaston the grand something."

"Somebody else gets a peach with a bug in it, and throws it away, but not him. He makes up a lot of foolishness about it."

"It's not foolishness."

"All right, all right, don't get angry at me about a horrible peach bug of some kind."

"Gaston is right here, just outside his broken house, and I'm not angry at you."

"You'll have a lot of fun at the party."

"OK."

"We'll have fun flying back to New York, too."

"OK."

"Are you glad you saw your father?"

"Of course I am."

"Is he funny?"

"Yes."

"Is he crazy?"

"Yes. I mean, no. He just doesn't holler when he sees a bug crawling out of a peach seed or anything. He just looks at it carefully. But it *is* just a bug, isn't it, *really*?"

"That's all it is."

"And we'll *have* to squash it?"

"That's right. I can't wait to see you, darling. These two days have been like two years to me. Good-bye."

The girl watched Gaston on the plate, and she actually didn't like him. He was all *ugh*, as he had been in the first place. He didn't have a home anymore and he was wandering around on the white plate and he was silly and wrong and ridiculous and useless and all sorts of other things. She cried a little, but only inside, because long ago she had decided she didn't like crying because if you ever started to cry it seemed as if there was so much to cry about you almost couldn't stop, and she didn't like that at all. The open halves of the peach seed were wrong, too. They were ugly or something. They weren't clean.

The man bought a kilo of peaches but found no flawed peaches among them, so he bought a kilo at another store, and this time his luck was better, and there were *two* that were flawed. He hurried back to his flat and let himself in.

His daughter was in her room, in her best dress.

"My mother phoned," she said, "and she's sending the chauffeur for me because there's another birthday party."

"Another?"

"I mean, there's *always* a lot of them in New York."

"Will the chauffeur bring you back?"

"No. We're flying back to New York tomorrow."

"Oh."

"I liked being in your house."

"I liked having you here."

"Why do you live here?"

"This is my home."

"It's nice, but it's a lot different from our home."

"Yes, I suppose it is."

"It's kind of like Gaston's house."

"Where *is* Gaston?"

"I squashed him."

"Really? Why?"

"Everybody squashes bugs and worms."

"Oh. Well. I found you a peach."

"I don't want a peach anymore."

"OK."

He got her dressed, and he was packing her stuff when the chauffeur arrived. He went down the three flights of stairs with his daughter and the chauffeur, and in the street he was about to hug the girl

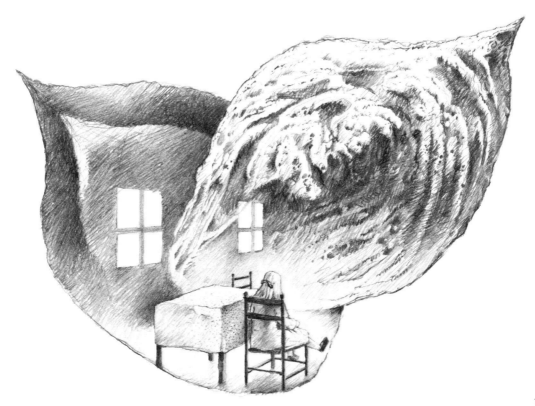

when he decided he had better not. They shook hands instead, as if they were strangers.

He watched the huge car drive off, and then he went around the corner where he took his coffee every morning, feeling a little, he thought, like Gaston on the white plate.

follow-up

Discussing "Gaston"

1. What do you think of the father? Is he crazy or perhaps just a little unusual? Explain.
2. Would you say that the girl changed in her attitude and/or behavior? If so, how? If not, why not?
3. Why do you suppose the peach is called "Gaston's broken house"?

Signs and Symbols

Here are the names of three companies, plus two designs that might be used by each on stationery or in advertising. What is the difference between the designs on the left and those on the right?

What sort of a business do you think Brown and Company might be in? What kind of machine do you suppose Gray's Machines sells or manufactures? What does Capp's Store sell? Which of the two designs for each company give you the most information? Why?

Although either design might be used by the company as labels on its property or as identifying trademarks in its advertising, the designs on the right clearly suggest more about the company than the designs on the left. Either design could be considered a sign, a mark that represents or stands for the company. But the designs on the right do a bit more than just represent the company's name. They also tell you something about the company. They give some extra meaning to the name. That extra meaning is a suggestion about what the company does.

When a sign carries additional meaning, as these do, it becomes a SYMBOL. The designs to the right are symbols. Not only do they identify the company, but they also tell something about it—something that the name alone does not tell.

Practice 1. Discussing/Writing

Who are you? What are you like? What do you want to do, or become? Reflect for a few minutes, and then try to design a symbol that represents you. If you wish, try to incorporate your name in the design. The symbol might suggest something about your character or your interests or your plans for the future.

When you have designed the symbol, write a brief paragraph explaining what it is intended to suggest about you.

Literary Symbols

Symbols in literary works operate in much the same way as they do in business. That is, they suggest meaning. When a writer seems to invite you to make comparisons between two things—or two situations—that seem to be very different, then you may suspect that one is to serve as a symbol for the other. In reading "Gaston," for instance, you may have noticed that Gaston's peach is called a "broken house."

That is a strange way to describe a half-eaten peach, and so you might naturally wonder why the writer chose those words. But in wondering about that phrase, you may recall that the man, too, is from a "broken house." He is divorced or separated and living in Paris, while his wife and child live in New York. Is the writer suggesting that there is some similarity between Gaston and the man?

And then you can look further to see whether the writer has done anything else to suggest a comparison between Gaston and the man. In doing so, you find the man saying:

> "Gaston is out in the world and on his own now. You can see for yourself how comfortable he was in there. He had everything."
> "Now what has he got?"
> "Not very much, I'm afraid."

It sounds almost as though the man is talking about himself. He, too, is out on his own. He, too, had once been comfortable, had once had everything. And apparently he, too, now has very little—just a small third-floor apartment. It is unlikely that so many comparisons between the man and Gaston could happen by chance. And so you can feel fairly confident that the writer *wants* you to see the similarities between the two, that he wants to show you something about the man's situation by comparing it to Gaston's situation. Gaston, in other words, might be viewed as a symbol for the man—representing the man, and telling you something about him.

Practice 2. Discussion

In groups of four or five, glance quickly through the story to see what other implied comparisons you can find between the man and Gaston. Discuss them briefly with the other members of your group. What does each comparison suggest about the man's situation?

Practice 3. Writing

Near the end of the story, the little girl squashes Gaston. If Gaston is a symbol for the man, then the squashing should tell you something about him. Write a brief essay explaining what that final incident means to you—that is, what it tells you about the man and his situation.

Bookshelf

The Fractured Family, by Leontine Young. McGraw, 1974. Young analyzes the modern family, examining the problems faced by both parents and children, and explaining why families sometimes fall apart.

It's Not the End of the World, by Judy Blume. Bradbury Press, 1972. The story of the impact of their parents' separation on three children.

My Dad Lives in a Downtown Hotel, by Peggy Mann. Doubleday, 1973. Joey assumes that he is responsible for his parents' divorce and believes that he will be able to bring them back together.

The Runaway's Diary, by Marilyn Harris. Pocket Books, 1974. The fights between her parents compel Catherine to set out on her own for Canada—and disaster.

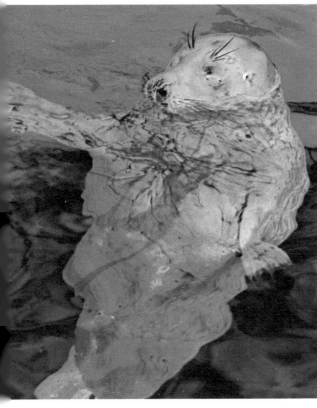

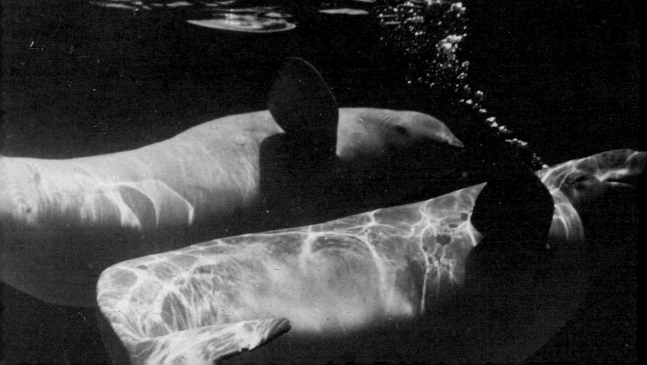

9

The Collecting Team

forestudy

Word Parts

"The Collecting Team," the story that begins on page 132, takes you to an unexplored planet. Your travelling companions are Gus, the spaceship pilot, and Clyde Holdreth and Lee Davison, two zoologists. To prepare yourself for the journey, you probably would like to be briefed on some of the terms Gus and Clyde and Lee will use.

The spaceship's *logbook*, or *log*, is a book in which an official record is kept of the events of the expedition. Compound words like *logbook* are common in science. And, Gus refers to a *thermocouple*, an instrument on the spaceship for measuring the temperature on the unexplored planet. The combining form *thermo-* means "heat," and *couple* means that two different metals are connected electrically to help determine temperature differences.

Also common in science are words having prefixes and suffixes. When the ship *decelerates* for landing, the prefix *de-*, "down," is joined with the Latin root *celerate* (from *celerare*, "to hasten"); thus *decelerate* means "to slow down the speed." The opposite is *accelerate* (from the Latin *ad*, "to" + *celerare*). In the logbook Holdreth writes down the *coordinates* (from the Latin *co*, "together," + *ordinare*, "to set in order") of the planet, and the various other items of information he observes.

You and the others are likely to find *extraterrestrial* wildlife on the planet. The prefix *extra-* means "beyond or outside the scope, area, or limits" of something. *Terrestrial* refers to earth or land (from the Latin *terra*, "land"). Hence, *extraterrestrial* means "beyond the earth."

Animals that eat plants are *herbivorous* (from the Latin *herba*, "grass" + *-vorous*, "to devour"). *Carnivorous* (from the Latin *carnis*, "flesh") animals are flesh eaters, and *omnivorous* (from the Latin *omnis*, "all") animals eat both plants and flesh. The combining form *pseudo-* (from the Greek *pseudes*, "false") means "not genuine, only apparent." On the planet there are *pseudogiraffes*, animals which resemble giraffes but which are really something else. *Ecology* (from the Greek *oikos*, "home" + the suffix *-logy*, "the study of") is a branch of biology that studies the relationship of animals to their environment.

The natural surroundings in which the animals live make up their *habitat*. The scientific name of an organism or a group of organisms has two parts: first, the general classification, or *genus*; and second, the *species*. Thus, *Homo sapiens* (from the Latin *homo*, "man" + *sapiens*, "wise") is the scientific term for "human being." The *fauna* and *flora* of a region refer to the region's animal and plant life, respectively.

Practice 1. Writing

Number from one to ten in a column. Then read the following sentences. From the preceding section on scientific vocabulary, choose and write the words that best complete the sentences. (Note that you will need to write two words each for sentences 5 and 7.)

1. The _____ of the animals included a moderate climate, lakes, and an abundance of plant life.
2. The animals all seemed to be _____, eating only plant life.
3. The _____ indicated that the temperature was about 21°C on the planet below.
4. The giraffe-like animals had long, wobbly legs, but they had tentacles too; they were really only_____.
5. The planet seemed to have various classifications of _____ and _____, all living in a mysteriously friendly manner together.
6. The ship prepared to _____ for landing.
7. Holdreth was busy studying the _____ of the planet and writing his observations in the _____.
8. In "The Collecting Team," one of the scientists' purposes was to capture and bring back to earth the _____ wildlife they found on the planets they visited.

9. The fact that there should have been carnivores present but that apparently there were none didn't make sense to Gus as far as _____ was concerned.
10. The scientists would have been reluctant to leave their ship had they discovered _____ animals on the planet.

With your classmates, discuss the terms you used to fill the blanks. Try for class agreement on the correct term for each blank.

There was *something* strange about that unexplored planet. But what?

The Collecting Team

Robert Silverberg

From 80 000 km up, the situation looked promising. It was a middle-sized, brown-and-green, inviting-looking planet, with no sign of cities or any other such complications. Just a pleasant sort of place, the very sort we were looking for to redeem what had been a pretty futile expedition.

I turned to Clyde Holdreth, who was staring reflectively at the thermocouple.

"Well? What do you think?"

"Looks fine to me. Temperature's about 21°C down there—nice and warm, and plenty of air. I think it's worth a try."

Lee Davison came strolling out from the storage hold, smelling of animals, as usual. He was holding one of the blue monkeys we picked up on Alpheraz,[1] and the little beast was crawling up his arm. "Have we found something, gentlemen?"

"We've found a planet," I said. "How's the storage space in the hold?"

"Don't worry about that. We've got room for a whole zoofull more, before we get filled up. It hasn't been a very fruitful trip."

"No," I agreed. "It hasn't. Well? Shall we go down and see what's to be seen?"

"Might as well," Holdreth said. "We

"The Collecting Team" from TWO WORLDS BEYOND by Robert Silverberg. Copyright 1965 by the author. Reprinted with the permission of the publisher, Chilton Book Company, Radnor, PA.

1. *Alpheraz:* a star in the constellation Andromeda, visible to the naked eye from Earth. Other stars from other constellations mentioned later in the story include Rigel, Sirius and Mizar.

132

can't go back to Earth with just a couple of blue monkeys and some anteaters, you know."

"I'm in favor of a landing too," said Davison. "You?"

I nodded. "I'll set up the charts, and you get your animals comfortable for deceleration."

Davison disappeared back into the storage hold, while Holdreth scribbled furiously in the logbook, writing down the coordinates of the planet below, its general description, and so forth. Aside from being a collecting team for the zoological department of the Bureau of Interstellar Affairs, we also double as a survey ship, and the planet down below was listed as *unexplored* on our charts.

I glanced out at the mottled brown-and-green ball spinning slowly in the viewport, and felt the warning twinge of gloom that came to me every time we made a landing on a new and strange world. Repressing° it, I started to figure out a landing orbit. From behind me came the furious chatter of the blue monkeys as Davison strapped them into their acceleration cradles, and under that the deep, unmusical honking of the Rigelian anteaters, noisily bleating their displeasure.

The planet was inhabited, all right. We hadn't had the ship on the ground more than a minute before the local fauna began to congregate. We stood at the viewport and looked out in wonder. **133**

"This is one of those things you dream about," Davison said, stroking his little beard nervously. "Look at them! There must be a thousand different species out there."

"I've never seen anything like it," said Holdreth.

I computed how much storage space we had left and how many of the thronging creatures outside we would be able to bring back with us. "How are we going to decide what to take and what to leave behind?"

"Does it matter?" Holdreth said gaily. "This is what you call an embarrassment of riches, I guess. We just grab the dozen most bizarre° creatures and blast off—and save the rest for another trip. It's too bad we wasted all that time wandering around near Rigel."

"We *did* get the anteaters," Davison pointed out. They were his finds, and he was proud of them.

I smiled sourly. "Yeah. We got the anteaters there." The anteaters honked at that moment, loud and clear. "You know, that's one set of beasts I think I could do without."

"Bad attitude," Holdreth said. "Unprofessional."

"Whoever said I was a zoologist, anyway? I'm just a spaceship pilot, remember. And if I don't like the way those anteaters talk—and smell—I see no reason why I—"

"Say, look at that one," Davison said suddenly.

I glanced out the viewport and saw a new beast emerging from the thick-packed vegetation in the background. I've seen some fairly strange creatures since I was assigned to the zoological department, but this one took the grand prize.

It was about the size of a giraffe, moving on long, wobbly legs and with a tiny

134

head up at the end of a preposterous° neck. Only it had six legs and a bunch of writhing snakelike tentacles as well, and its eyes, great violet globes, stood out nakedly on the ends of two thick stalks. It must have been seven metres high. It moved with exaggerated grace through the swarm of beasts surrounding our ship, pushed its way smoothly toward the vessel, and peered gravely in at the viewport. One purple eye stared directly at me, the other at Davison. Oddly, it seemed to me as if it were trying to tell us something.

"Big one, isn't it?" Davison said finally.

"I'll bet you'd like to bring one back, too."

"Maybe we can fit a young one aboard," Davison said. "If we can find a young one." He turned to Holdreth. "How's that air analysis coming? I'd like to get out there and start collecting. That's a crazy-looking beast!"

The animal outside had apparently finished its inspection of us, for it pulled its head away and, gathering its legs under itself, squatted near the ship. A small doglike creature with stiff spines running along its back began to bark at the big creature, which took no notice. The other animals, which came in all shapes and sizes, continued to mill around the ship, evidently very curious about the newcomer to their world. I could see Davison's eyes thirsty with the desire to take the whole kit and caboodle back to Earth with him. I knew what was running through his mind. He was dreaming of the umpteen thousand species of extraterrestrial wildlife roaming around out there, and to each one he was attaching a neat little tag: *Something-or-other davisoni*.

"The air's fine," Holdreth announced abruptly, looking up from his test-tubes. "Get your butterfly nets and let's see what we can catch."

There was something I didn't like about the place. It was just too good to be true, and I learned long ago that nothing ever is. There's always a catch someplace.

Only this seemed to be on the level. The planet was a bonanza for zoologists, and Davison and Holdreth were having the time of their lives, hipdeep in obliging specimens.

"I've never seen anything like it," Davison said for at least the fiftieth time, as he scooped up a small purplish squirrel-like creature and examined it curiously. The squirrel stared back, examining Davison just as curiously.

"Let's take some of these," Davison said. "I like them."

"Carry 'em on in, then," I said, shrugging. I didn't care which specimens they chose, so long as they filled up the storage hold quickly and let me blast off on schedule. I watched as Davison grabbed a pair of the squirrels and brought them into the ship.

Holdreth came over to me. He was carrying a sort of dog with insect-faceted[2] eyes and gleaming furless skin. "How's this one, Gus?"

"Fine," I said bleakly. "Wonderful."

He put the animal down—it didn't scamper away, just sat there smiling at us—and looked at me. He ran a hand through his fast-vanishing hair. "Listen, Gus, you've been gloomy all day. What's eating you?"

2. *insect-faceted:* Insect eyes are compound, having several flat surfaces, like a gem

"I don't like this place," I said.

"Why? Just on general principles?"

"It's too *easy*, Clyde. Much too easy. These animals just flock around here waiting to be picked up."

Holdreth chuckled. "And you're used to a struggle, aren't you? You're just angry at us because we have it so simple here!"

"When I think of the trouble we went through just to get a pair of miserable vile-smelling anteaters, and—"

"Come off it, Gus. We'll load up in a hurry, if you like. But this place is a zoological gold mine!"

I shook my head. "I don't like it, Clyde. Not at all."

Holdreth laughed again and picked up his faceted-eyed dog. "Say, know where I can find another of these, Gus?"

"Right over there," I said, pointing. "By that tree. With its tongue hanging out. It's just waiting to be carried away."

Holdreth looked and smiled. "What do you know about that!" He snared his specimen and carried both of them inside.

I walked away to survey the grounds. The planet was too flatly incredible° for me to accept on face value, without at least a look-see, despite the blithe way my two companions were snapping up specimens.

For one thing, animals just don't exist this way—in big miscellaneous quantities, living all together happily. I hadn't noticed more than a few of each kind, and there must have been five hundred different species, each one stranger-looking than the next. Nature doesn't work that way.

For another, they all seemed to be on friendly terms with one another, though they acknowledged the unofficial leadership of the giraffe-like creature. Nature doesn't work *that* way, either. I hadn't seen one quarrel between the animals yet. That argued that they were all herbivores, which didn't make sense ecologically.

I shrugged my shoulders and walked on.

Half an hour later, I knew a little more about the geography of our bonanza. We were on either an immense island or a peninsula of some sort, because I could see a huge body of water bordering the land some 15 km off. Our vicinity was fairly flat, except for a good-sized hill from which I could see the terrain.

There was a thick, heavily-wooded jungle not too far from the ship. The forest spread out all the way toward the water in one direction, but ended abruptly in the other. We had brought the ship down right at the edge of the clearing. Apparently most of the animals we saw lived in the jungle.

On the other side of our clearing was a low, broad plain that seemed to trail away into a desert in the distance; I could see an uninviting stretch of barren sand that contrasted strangely with the fertile jungle to my left. There was a small lake to the side. It was, I saw, the sort of country likely to attract a varied fauna, since there seemed to be every sort of habitat within a small area.

And the fauna! Although I'm a zoologist only by osmosis,° picking up both my interest and my knowledge second-hand from Holdreth and Davison, I couldn't help but be astonished by the wealth of strange animals. They came in all different shapes and sizes, colors and odors,

136

and the only thing they all had in common was their friendliness. During the course of my afternoon's wanderings a hundred animals must have come marching boldly right up to me, given me the once-over, and walked away. This included half a dozen kinds that I hadn't seen before, plus one of the eye-stalked, intelligent-looking giraffes and a furless dog. Again, I had the feeling that the giraffe seemed to be trying to communicate.

I didn't like it. I didn't like it at all.

I returned to our clearing and saw Holdreth and Davison still buzzing madly around, trying to cram as many animals as they could into our hold.

"How's it going?" I asked.

"Hold's all full," Davison said. "We're busy making our alternate selections now." I saw him carrying out Holdreth's two furless dogs and picking up instead a pair of eight-legged penguinish things that uncomplainingly allowed themselves to be carried in. Holdreth was frowning unhappily.

"What do you want *those* for, Lee? Those dog-like ones seem much more interesting, don't you think?"

"No," Davison said. "I'd rather bring along these two. They're curious beasts, aren't they? Look at the muscular network that connects the—"

"Hold it, fellows," I said. I peered at the animal in Davison's hands and glanced up. "This *is* a curious beast," I said. "It's got eight legs."

"You becoming a zoologist?" Holdreth asked, amused.

"No—but I am getting puzzled. Why should this one have eight legs, some of the others here six, and some of the others only four?"

They looked at me blankly, with the scorn of professionals.

"I mean, there ought to be some sort of logic to evolution here, shouldn't there? On Earth we've developed a four-legged pattern of animal life; on Venus, they usually run to six legs. But have you ever seen an evolutionary° hodgepodge like this place before?"

"There are stranger setups," Holdreth said. "The symbiotes[3] on Sirius Three, the burrowers of Mizar—but you're right, Gus. This *is* a peculiar evolutionary dispersal.[4] I think we ought to stay and investigate it fully."

Instantly I knew from the bright expression on Davison's face that I had blundered, had made things worse than ever. I decided to take a new tack.

"I don't agree," I said. "I think we ought to leave with what we've got, and come back with a larger expedition later."

Davison chuckled. "Come on, Gus, don't be silly! This is a chance of a lifetime for us—why should we call in the whole zoological department on it?"

I didn't want to tell them I was afraid of staying longer. I crossed my arms. "Lee, I'm the pilot of this ship, and you'll have to listen to me. The schedule calls for a brief stopover here, and we have to leave. Don't tell me I'm being silly."

"But you are, man! You're standing blindly in the path of scientific investigation, of—"

"Listen to me, Lee. Our food is calculated on a pretty narrow margin, to allow

3. *symbiotes:* dissimilar organisms living together in mutually advantageous partnership, as algae and fungi in lichens.

4. *evolutionary dispersal:* a way for the animals to have developed in structure and living habits.

you fellows more room for storage. And this is strictly a collecting team. There's no provision for extended stays on any one planet. Unless you want to wind up eating your own specimens, I suggest you allow us to get out of here."

They were silent for a moment. Then Holdreth said, "I guess we can't argue with that, Lee. Let's listen to Gus and go back now. There's plenty of time to investigate this place later when we can take longer."

"But—oh, all right," Davison said reluctantly. He picked up the eight-legged penguins. "Let me stash these things in the hold, and we can leave." He looked strangely at me, as if I had done something criminal.

As he started into the ship, I called him.

"What is it, Gus?"

"Look here, Lee. I don't *want* to pull you away from here. It's simply a matter of food," I lied, masking my nebulous° suspicions.

"I know how it is, Gus." He turned and entered the ship.

I stood there thinking about nothing at all for a moment, then went inside myself to begin setting up the blastoff orbit.

I got as far as calculating the fuel expenditure when I noticed something. Feedwires were dangling crazily down from the control cabinet. Somebody had wrecked our drive mechanism, but thoroughly.

For a long moment, I stared stiffly at the sabotaged° drive. Then I turned and headed into the storage hold.

"Davison?"

"What is it, Gus?"

"Come out here a second, will you?"

I waited, and a few minutes later he appeared, frowning impatiently. "What do you want, Gus? I'm busy and I—" His mouth dropped open. "*Look at the drive!*"

"You look at it," I snapped. "I'm sick. Go get Holdreth, on the double."

While he was gone I tinkered with the shattered mechanism. Once I had the cabinet panel off and could see the inside, I felt a little better; the drive wasn't damaged beyond repair, though it had been pretty well scrambled. Three or four days of hard work with a screwdriver and solderbeam might get the ship back into functioning order.

But that didn't make me any less angry. I heard Holdreth and Davison entering behind me, and I whirled to face them.

"All right, you idiots. Which one of you did this?"

They opened their mouths in protesting squawks at the same instant. I listened to them for a while, then said, "One at a time!"

"If you're implying that one of us deliberately sabotaged the ship," Holdreth said, "I want you to know—"

"I'm not implying anything. But the way it looks to me, you two decided you'd like to stay here a while longer to continue your investigations, and figured the easiest way of getting me to agree was to wreck the drive." I glared hotly at them. "Well, I've got news for you. I can fix this, and I can fix it in a couple of days. So go on—get about your business! Get all the zoologizing you can in, while you still have time. I—"

Davison laid a hand gently on my arm. "Gus," he said quietly, *"We didn't do it. Neither of us."*

Suddenly all the anger drained out of me and was replaced by raw fear. I could see that Davison meant it.

"If you didn't do it, and Holdreth didn't do it, and *I* didn't do it—then who did?"

Davison shrugged.

"Maybe it's one of us who doesn't know he's doing it," I suggested. "Maybe—" I stopped. "Oh, that's nonsense. Hand me that tool-kit, will you, Lee?"

They left to tend to the animals, and I set to work on the repair job, dismissing all further speculations and suspicions from my mind, concentrating solely on joining Lead A to Input A and Transistor F to Potentiometer K, as indicated. It was slow, nerve-harrowing work, and by mealtime I had accomplished only the barest preliminaries. My fingers were starting to quiver from the strain of small-scale work, and I decided to give up the job for the day and get back to it tomorrow.

I slept uneasily, my nightmares punctuated by the moaning of the accursed anteaters and the occasional squeals, chuckles, bleats, and hisses of the various other creatures in the hold. It must have been four in the morning before I dropped off into a really sound sleep, and what was left of the night passed swiftly. The next thing I knew, hands were shaking me, and I was looking up into the pale, tense faces of Holdreth and Davison.

I pushed my sleep-stuck eyes open and blinked. "Huh? What's going on?"

Holdreth leaned down and shook me savagely. "Get up, Gus!"

I struggled to my feet slowly. "What a thing to do, wake a fellow up in the middle of the—"

I found myself being propelled from my cabin and led down the corridor to

the control room. Blearily, I followed where Holdreth pointed, and then I woke up in a hurry.

The drive was battered again. Someone—or *something*—had completely undone my repair job of the night before.

If there had been bickering among us, it stopped. This was past the category of a joke now; it couldn't be laughed off, and we found ourselves working together as a tight unit again, trying desperately to solve the puzzle before it was too late.

"Let's review the situation," Holdreth said, pacing nervously up and down the control cabin. "The drive has been sabotaged twice. None of us knows who did it, and on a conscious level each of us is convinced *he* didn't do it."

He paused. "That leaves us with two possibilities. Either, as Gus suggested, one of us is doing it unaware of it even himself, or someone else is doing it while we're not looking. Neither possibility is a very cheerful one."

"We can stay on guard, though," I said. "Here's what I propose: first, have one of us awake at all times—sleep in shifts, that is, with somebody guarding the drive until I get it fixed. Two—jettison all the animals aboard ship."

"*What?*"

"He's right," Davison said. "We don't know what we may have brought aboard. They don't seem to be intelligent, but we can't be sure. That purple-eyed baby giraffe, for instance—suppose he's been hypnotizing us into damaging the drive ourselves? How can we tell?"

"Oh, but—" Holdreth started to protest, then stopped and frowned soberly. "I suppose we'll have to admit the possibility," he said, obviously unhappy about the prospect of freeing our captives. "We'll empty out the hold, and you see if you can get the drive fixed. Maybe later we'll recapture them all, if nothing further develops."

We agreed to that, and Holdreth and Davison cleared the ship of its animal cargo while I set to work determinedly at the drive mechanism. By nightfall, I had managed to accomplish as much as I had the day before.

I sat up as watch the first shift, aboard the strangely quiet ship. I paced around the drive cabin, fighting the great temptation to doze off, and managed to last through until the time Holdreth arrived to relieve me.

Only—when he showed up, he gasped and pointed at the drive. It had been ripped apart a third time.

Now we had no excuse, no explanation. The expedition had turned into a nightmare.

I could only protest that I had remained awake my entire spell on duty, and that I had seen no one and no thing approach the drive panel. But that was hardly a satisfactory explanation, since it either cast guilt on me as the saboteur or implied that some unseen external power was repeatedly wrecking the drive. Neither hypothesis° made sense, at least to me.

By now we had spent four days on the planet, and food was getting to be a major problem. My carefully budgeted flight schedule called for us to be two days out on our return journey to Earth by now. But we still were no closer to departure than we had been four days ago.

The animals continued to wander around outside, nosing up against the ship, examining it, almost fondling it,

140

with those ... pseudo-giraffes staring soulfully at us always. The beasts were as friendly as ever, little knowing how the tension was growing within the hull. The three of us walked around like zombies, eyes bright and lips clamped. We were scared—all of us.

Something was keeping us from fixing the drive.

Something didn't want us to leave this planet.

I looked at the bland face of the purple-eyed giraffe staring through the viewport, and it stared mildly back at me. Around it was grouped the rest of the local fauna, the same incredible hodgepodge of improbable genera and species.

That night, the three of us stood guard in the control-room together. The drive was smashed anyway. The wires were soldered in so many places by now that the control panel was a mass of shining alloy, and I knew that a few more such sabotagings and it would be impossible to patch it together any more—if it wasn't so already.

The next night, I just didn't knock off. I continued soldering right on after dinner (and a pretty skimpy dinner it was, now that we were on close rations) and far on into the night.

By morning, it was as if I hadn't done a thing.

"I give up," I announced, surveying the damage. "I don't see any sense in ruining my nerves trying to fix a thing that won't stay fixed."

Holdreth nodded. He looked terribly pale. "We'll have to find some new approach."

"Yeah. Some new approach."

I yanked open the food closet and ex-amined our stock. Even figuring in the synthetics° we would have fed to the animals if we hadn't released them, we were low on food. We had overstayed even the safety margin. It would be a hungry trip back—if we ever did get back.

I clambered through the hatch and sprawled down on a big rock near the ship. One of the furless dogs came over and nuzzled in my shirt. Davison stepped to the hatch and called down to me.

"What are you doing out there, Gus?"

"Just getting a little fresh air. I'm sick of living aboard that ship." I scratched the dog behind his pointed ears, and looked around.

The animals had lost most of their curiosity about us, and didn't congregate the way they used to. They were meandering all over the plain, nibbling at little deposits of a white doughy substance. It precipitated° every night. "Manna," we called it. All the animals seemed to live on it.

I folded my arms and leaned back.

We were getting to look awfully lean by the eighth day. I wasn't even trying to fix the ship any more; the hunger was starting to get to me. But I saw Davison puttering around with my solderbeam.

"What are you doing?"

"I'm going to repair the drive," he said. "You don't want to, but we can't just sit around, you know." His nose was deep in my repair guide, and he was fumbling with the release on the solderbeam.

I shrugged. "Go ahead, if you want to." I didn't care what he did. All I cared about was the gaping emptiness in my stomach, and about the dimly grasped fact that somehow we were stuck here for good.

141

"Gus?"

"Yeah?"

"I think it's time I told you something. I've been eating the manna for four days. It's good. It's nourishing stuff."

"You've been eating—the manna? Something that grows on an alien world? You crazy?"

"What else can we do? Starve?"

I smiled feebly, admitting that he was right. From somewhere in the back of the ship came the sounds of Holdreth moving around. Holdreth had taken this thing worse than any of us. He had a family back on Earth, and he was beginning to realize that he wasn't ever going to see them again.

"Why don't you get Holdreth?" Davison suggested. "Go out there and stuff yourselves with the manna. You've got to eat something."

"Yeah. What can I lose?" Moving like a mechanical man, I headed toward Holdreth's cabin. We would go out and eat the manna and cease being hungry, one way or another.

"Clyde?" I called. "Clyde?"

I entered his cabin. He was sitting at his desk, shaking convulsively, staring at the two streams of blood that trickled in red spurts from his slashed wrists.

"Clyde!"

He made no protest as I dragged him toward the infirmary° cabin and got tourniquets around his arms, cutting off the bleeding. He just stared dully ahead, sobbing.

I slapped him and he came around. He shook his head dizzily, as if he didn't know where he was.

"I—I—"

"Easy, Clyde. Everything's all right."

"It's *not* all right," he said hollowly.

"I'm still alive. Why didn't you let me die? Why didn't you—"

Davison entered the cabin. "What's been happening, Gus?"

"It's Clyde. The pressure's getting to him. He tried to kill himself, but I think he's all right now. Get him something to eat, will you?"

We had Holdreth straightened around by evening. Davison gathered as much of the manna as he could find, and we held a feast.

"I wish we had nerve enough to kill some of the local fauna," Davison said. "Then we'd have a feast—steaks and everything!"

"The bacteria," Holdreth pointed out quietly "We don't dare."

"I know. But it's a thought."

"No more thoughts," I said sharply. "Tomorrow morning we start work on the drive panel again. Maybe with some food in our bellies we'll be able to keep awake and see what's happening here."

Holdreth smiled. "Good. I can't wait to get out of this ship and back to a normal existence. . . . I just can't wait!"

"Let's get some sleep," I said. "Tomorrow we'll give it another try. We'll get back," I said with a confidence I didn't feel.

The following morning I rose early and got my tool-kit. My head was clear, and I was trying to put the pieces together without much luck. I started toward the control cabin.

And stopped.

And looked out the viewport.

I went back and awoke Holdreth and Davison. "Take a look out the port," I said hoarsely.

They looked. They gaped.

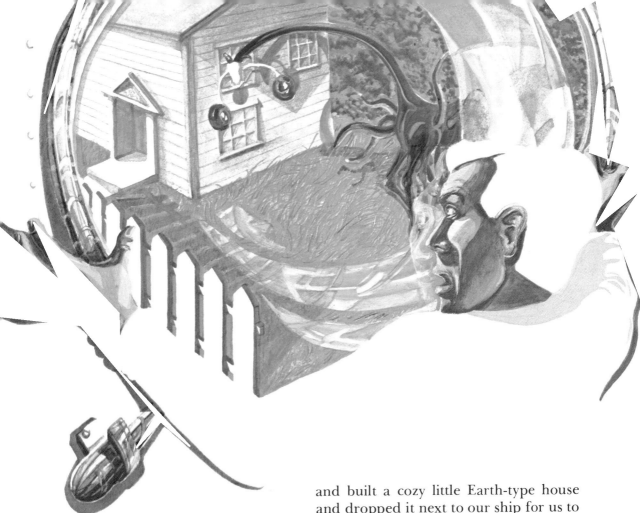

"It looks just like my house," Holdreth said. "My house on Earth."

"With all the comforts of home inside, I'll bet." I walked forward uneasily and lowered myself through the hatch. "Let's go look at it."

We approached it, while the animals frolicked around us. The big giraffe came near and shook its head gravely. The house stood in the middle of the clearing, small and neat and freshly-painted.

I saw it now. During the night, invisible hands had put it there. Had assembled and built a cozy little Earth-type house and dropped it next to our ship for us to live in.

"Just like my house," Holdreth repeated in wonderment.

"It should be," I said. "They grabbed the model from your mind, as soon as they found out we couldn't live on the ship indefinitely."

Holdreth and Davison asked as one, "What do you mean?"

"You mean you haven't figured this place out yet?" I licked my lips, getting myself used to the fact that I was going to spend the rest of my life here. "You mean you don't realize what this house is intended to be?"

They shook their heads, baffled. I **143**

glanced around, from the house to the useless ship to the jungle to the plain to the little pond. It all made sense now.

"They want to keep us happy," I said. "They knew we weren't thriving aboard the ship, so they—they built us something a little more like home."

"*They?* The giraffes?"

"Forget the giraffes. They tried to warn us, but it's too late. They're intelligent beings, but they're prisoners just like us. I'm talking about the ones who run this place. The super-aliens who make us sabotage our own ship and not even know we're doing it, who stand someplace up there and gape at us. The ones who dredged together this motley° assortment of beasts from all over the galaxy. Now we've been collected too. This whole . . . place is just a zoo—a zoo for aliens so far ahead of us we don't dare dream what they're like."

I looked up at the shimmering blue-green sky, where invisible bars seemed to restrain us, and sank down dismally on the porch of our new home. I was resigned. There wasn't any sense in struggling against *them*.

I could see the neat little placard now: EARTHMEN. Native Habitat, Sol III.[5]

5. *Sol III:* Sun Three.

---

follow-up

Discussing "The Collecting Team"

1. How are you affected early in the story by the word *unexplored*, which describes the planet the men are approaching?
2. Why, do you think, does Gus feel uneasy about the behavior of the animals and about the illogical differences in their appearances?
3. A well-written short story has unity in that all details should be closely related. Reread the first and final paragraphs of the story. How are they related?
4. Do we human beings tend to think of ourselves as the ultimate masters of nature—even of interplanetary space? Depending upon your answer, what irony do you find in the title of the story?
5. Do you think that other planets might have intelligent beings that are investigating us? Why? Why not?

Building Sentences: Embedding and Generating Details

In "The Collecting Team," Robert Silverberg could have written this:

> It was a middle-sized planet.
> It was a brown and green planet.
> It was an inviting-looking planet.
> It had no sign of cities or any other such complications.

Instead, he wrote this:

> It was a middle-sized, brown-and-green, inviting-looking planet, with no sign of cities or any other such complications.

In other words, he put into one sentence what it might have taken a less gifted writer four sentences to say.

Rather than writing this:	Silverberg wrote this:
1. Davison disappeared back into the storage hold. At the same time Holdreth scribbled furiously in the logbook. He wrote down the coordinates of the planet below. He described the planet, and so forth.	Davison disappeared back into the storage hold, while Holdreth scribbled furiously in the logbook, writing down the coordinates of the planet below, its general description, and so forth.
2. The animal outside had apparently finished its inspection of us. It pulled its head away. It gathered its legs under itself. It squatted near the ship.	The animal outside had apparently finished its inspection of us, for it pulled its head away and, gathering its legs under itself, squatted near the ship.

There are basically two ways of building effective sentences with details. Here is an example of one method:

Separate Details	*Combined Details—One Sentence*
1. It was a middle-sized planet. 2. The planet was brown and green. 3. The planet was inviting-looking.	It was a middle-sized, brown-and-green, inviting-looking planet.

Notice that the details were inserted between the LV (*was*) and the SC (*planet*). When details added to a sentence are *inserted within the basic sentence pattern*, the details are said to be EMBEDDED.

Practice 1. Discussion

See whether you can combine the following pairs of sentences into one sentence, by embedding the details of the second sentence into the first sentence.

```
       S        V
```
1. The spaceship landed on Mars.
   The spaceship was silver.

```
      S       V        IO      DO
```
2. The captain handed the creature a present of friendship.
   The captain moved slowly and carefully.

In addition to *embedding*, you can *add* details to a basic sentence, instead of inserting them between sentence elements:

Details	*Details Added to Make One Sentence*
1. It was a middle-sized planet.	It was a planet, middle-sized, brown-and-green, and inviting-looking.
2. The planet was brown and green.	
3. The planet was inviting-looking.	

When details are *added* to the basic sentence pattern, the process is called GENERATING. Both EMBEDDING and GENERATING are effective ways of making your sentences interesting. Here are some other comparative examples:

Details	*Embedded Details*	*Generated Details*
S V	S	S V
1a. The old man stroked	The old man *slowly*	The old man stroked
DO	*and mechanically*	DO
his beard.	V DO	his beard *slowly*
	stroked his beard.	*and mechanically*.
b. His hand moved slowly and mechanically.		

Details	Embedded Details	Generated Details
S V	S	
2a. The old man stroked	The old man,	*Shaking with palsy,*
DO	*shaking with*	S V
his beard.	V	the old man stroked
	palsy, stroked	DO
b. The old man was	DO	his beard.
shaking with	his beard.	
palsy.		

Practice 2. Writing

Combine each group of sentences into one sentence by embedding the details now in the starred sentences into the unstarred sentence. Underline the details you embed.

Example

    0a. His father owns the gas station.
    *b. His father is an experienced mechanic.
    *c. His father is hard-working.

Embedded Sentence

    0. His <u>hard-working</u> father, an <u>experienced mechanic</u>, owns the gas station.

    1a. The flood ravaged the city.
    *b. The flood moved quickly and frighteningly.
    *c. Ths city was old and vulnerable.

    2a. Disneyland is an exciting place for children of all ages.
    *b. Disneyland is in Anaheim, California.
    *c. People who go there are fun-loving.

    3a. Tap dancers twirled down the ramp.
    *b. The dancers wore bright flowing costumes.
    *c. The dancers moved quickly and rhythmically.

Practice 3. Writing

Combine each group of sentences into one sentence by generating the details now in the starred sentences into the unstarred sentence. Add those details at the appropriate places. Underline the details you generate.

Example
>0a. His father owns the gas station.
>*b. The station is a new building.
>*c. The station is located right on the bay.

Generated Sentence

>0. His father owns the gas station, <u>a new building,</u> <u>located right on the bay.</u>

>1a. The flood ravaged the city.
>*b. The city was the site of a medieval village.
>*c. The village was said to be the home of Charlemagne.

>2a. Disneyland is an exciting place for children of all ages.
>*b. Disneyland is huge and sprawling.
>*c. Disneyland is famous for its good food and enjoyable rides.

>3a. Tap dancers twirled down the ramp.
>*b. The ramp was a creaky, wooden structure.
>*c. The ramp was a permanent part of the old theatre.

>4a. A fire gutted a town landmark.
>*b. The fire was in the early morning; the structure was the old depot.

Another Look at Silverberg's Writing

Like all competent writers, Silverberg uses both embedding and generating, sometimes within the same sentence. Consider the sentence with which this lesson starts:

S   V   (embedded details . . . .)
It was a middle-sized, brown-and-green, inviting-looking

SC (noun) (generated details . . . .)
planet, with no sign of cities or any other complications.

Practice 4. Discussion/Writing
For each of the following sentences from "The Collecting Team," indicate, if you can, the basic sentence pattern. Then tell which lettered details are <u>embedded</u> and which are <u>generated</u>.

$$\overset{\text{A}}{}$$

1. It was about the size of a giraffe, *moving on long, wobbly*

$$\overset{\text{B}}{}$$

legs and **with a tiny head up at the end of a preposterous neck**.

$$\overset{\text{A}}{}$$

2. The other animals, *which came in all shapes and sizes,* continued to mill around the ship, **evidently very**

$$\overset{\text{B}}{}$$

curious about the newcomer to their world.

$$\overset{\text{A}}{}$$

3. I slept uneasily, *my nightmares punctuated by the moaning of the accursed anteaters* and **the occasional squeals,**

$$\overset{\text{B}}{}$$

chuckles, bleats and hisses of the various other creatures in the hold.

Practice 5. Writing

See, now, whether you can build your own effective sentences by *embedding* details where they are called for.

                     S   V   DO

1. My _____ and _____ dog _____ pushed the jar of jam _____.
    (two adjectives)   (tell how)   (where)

         S   V

2. George's sister, who _____, handed
                     (tell something about her)

                 IO   DO

the _____ butler her _____ umbrella and
   (describe him)   (describe)

_____ raincoat.
(describe)

                     S

3. The small monkey, while _____-ing _____,
                    (describe what the monkey was doing)

     V

stopped _____ to pick up the _____ coin the _____
     (how)   (describe)   (describe)

boy _____ thrown to it.
   (how)

Be prepared to read at least one of your sentences aloud. Point out the embedded details.

Practice 6. Writing

Try, now, to build effective sentences by <u>generating</u> details where they are called for.

        S   V

1. My dog jumped up onto the table, _____-ing _____,
                                      (moving a part of its body)

    _____-ing _____.
    (creating some sort of mischief)

                 S   LV   SC

2. The old hotel looked pitiful, its _____ _____-ing
                                    (part of building) (verb)

    _____, and its _____ _____-ing
     (how or where)   (another part) (verb)

    _____.
    (how or where)

                 S   V DO

3. The rhinoceros fixed me with its stare, _____, and _____,
                                         (describe its eyes)

    its _____ _____ and _____,
      (part of body)   (describe that part of body)
    as if it wanted to _____.
                 (describe what it might want to do)

Be prepared to read at least one sentence aloud. Point out the generated details.

Practice 7. Writing

In each sentence below, a basic sentence pattern is marked. Expand each basic pattern into a well-built sentence by <u>embedding</u> and <u>generating</u> details. If you wish, refer to other sentences you have written in this lesson.

          S   V

1. The rocket lunged.

             S   V   DO

2. The quarterback charged the defense.

          S   LV   SC (adj)

3. The hermit appeared frightened.

         S   LV   SC (noun)

4. The castle was a ruin.

         S   V   IO   DO

150
5. The general handed the saboteur his orders.

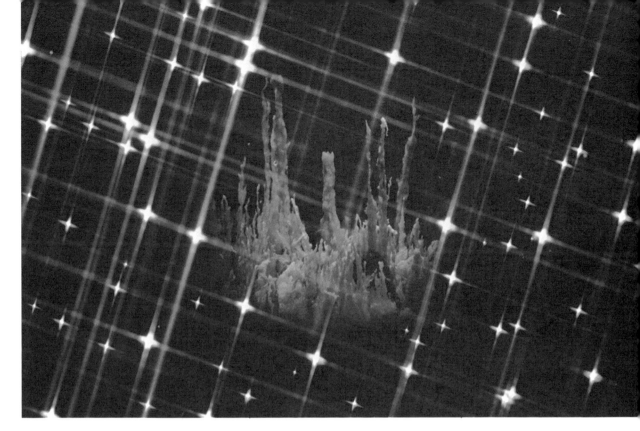

        S   V   DO OC (adj)
6. My teacher painted her house pink.

        S   V   DO   OC (noun)
7. The PTA elected Twila President.

Bookshelf

Asimov's Mysteries, by Isaac Asimov. Dell, 1969. A collection of science-fiction mystery stories.

Icepick: A Novel about Life and Death in a Maximum Security Prison, by Bruce Dobler. Little, Brown, 1974. This is a story about life in a federal penitentiary. The difficulties of life in prison are vividly presented.

Ross Macdonald Selects Great Stories of Suspense, ed. by Ross Macdonald. Knopf, 1974. An anthology of novels and short stories of mystery and suspense.

We Are Not Alone, by Walter Sullivan. McGraw, 1966. Sullivan has collected the information that suggests that there might be other intelligent life in the universe and discusses the implications of that knowledge.

focus

Reading—Relating Ideas

Connector Words and Phrases

When you read—especially when you read assignments—it is often important to read in detail. In order to understand and discuss a piece of writing, you have to be able to spot key ideas and key relationships. You have to see relationships within sentences, between sentences, and from paragraph to paragraph.

Connectors: Keys to Relationships

When reading for ideas, you will generally meet only a few types of ways a writer develops ideas. Writers may *list* details as supporting evidence. They may make a *comparison* to show similarities. They may *contrast* ideas to point out differences. They may set up a sequence to emphasize a *time* relationship. Or, they may talk in terms of *cause and effect*—that is, in terms of how something causes something else to happen or fail to happen. Each of these five general kinds of idea development can be spotted by recognizing specific CONNECTOR WORDS and PHRASES. The lists below show some of the most common examples of each type of connector.

1. *Listing* connectors indicate equal ideas or the addition of details:

> *and*
> *also, but also, and also*
> *including*
> *excluding*
> *following, the following*
> *moreover*
> *in addition*
> *what's more*
> *furthermore*

152

Examples

> Don't forget your lunch money, your raincoat, *and* your books. We had a great time at the picnic. We ate, we sang, *and* we played ball. *What's more*, I won the potato race.

2. *Comparison* connectors show similar or equal ideas:

> *or*
> *either . . . or*
> *neither . . . nor*
> *both . . . and*
> *like*
> *as . . . as*

Examples

> You have a choice of *either* marshmallow or whipped cream.
> May I have *as* much marshmallow *as* I can eat?
> I want a sundae *like* hers, with *both* chocolate *and* peanut butter.

3. *Contrast* connectors alert you to expect differences and/or exceptions:

> *but*
> *than, more than, better than, less than*
> *despite*
> *in spite of*
> *regardless*

Examples

> The longest earthworm on record is considerably longer *than* the world's tallest person!
> *Despite* having been crippled in childhood, Wilma Rudolph won three gold medals in running at the 1960 Olympic Games in Rome.

Reminder: It's easy to confuse *than* and *then*. The two words are spelled differently, and they signal different ideas. Try to remember them this way: TH<u>A</u>N, with an <u>A</u>, signals CONTR<u>A</u>ST. TH<u>E</u>N, like TIM<u>E</u> and S<u>E</u>QU<u>E</u>NC<u>E</u> and ORD<u>E</u>R, has an <u>E</u> in it.

4. *Time and sequence* connectors put things and events in order:

then	*first, second, etc.*
until	*after, shortly after, long after*
before	*meanwhile*

Examples

Don't start *until* you hear the gun.

Widespread sickness set in *after* famine began.

First I'll watch TV; *then* I'll do my homework.

5. *Cause-and-effect* connectors explain why something happened; they can also show what is necessary to cause something to happen:

> *because, because of*
> *for* (meaning *because*)
> *in order to*
> *due to*
> *consequently*
> *since* (meaning *because*)

Examples

Fires burn *because* of the oxygen in the air.

Joe's absence is *due to* illness.

Since he had only two cents, he couldn't buy a candy bar.

Practice 1. Writing/Discussion

Number your paper to 10. Read the sentences below for connectors. Write each connector word or phrase beside its appropriate number on your work sheet. Then, compare and discuss your answers with your classmates' answers.

1. Poverty is the parent of revolution and crime.
2. The mob has many heads but no brains.
3. Buy not what you want, but what you need.
4. It is better to live rich than to die rich.
5. Neither a borrower nor a lender be.
6. Sink or swim.
7. The whole is no greater than the sum of its parts.
8. Nothing succeeds like success.
9. It is difficult to argue with the belly, since it has no ears.
10. The young man who has not wept is a savage; and the old man who will not laugh is a fool.

Practice 2.

In this practice you are to supply connectors. Supply a connector that makes sense and that matches the idea in the parentheses at the end of each sentence.

Some sentences will require a word; some will need a phrase of two words. Choose words to fill the blanks from the list at the top of page 155. There will be one word left over.

like	also	due to
both . . . and	than	in order to
until	then	because
but	either . . . or	

1. Mocha is a flavor that tastes _____ chocolate. (COMPARISON)
2. And mocha _____ tastes like coffee. (LISTING—addition)
3. Mocha tastes like _____ coffee _____ chocolate. (COMPARISON)
4. Birds fly, _____ snakes crawl. (CONTRAST)
5. Words can be sharper _____ knives. (CONTRAST)
6. First sift the flour; _____ measure it. (TIME)
7. The runner did not pull ahead of the pack _____ the last 200 meters. (TIME)
8. The cancellation of school was _____ the record snowfall. (CAUSE-AND-EFFECT)
9. _____ get good seats, some of the rock fans showed up ten hours before the tickets went on sale. (CAUSE-AND-EFFECT)
10. You may elect _____ home economics _____ shop. (LISTING—equal ideas)

Practice 3. Writing /Discussion

In this practice you are to look for connectors and to identify the type of relationship signalled by each connector word or phrase. Number your paper to 10; then, for each sentence, jot down the connector word or phrase it contains. Next, label the kind of connector each is: list, comparison, contrast, time, cause-and-effect.

1. First we went to a movie; then we went out for pizza.
2. Both the movie and the pizza cost too much.
3. I enjoyed the pizza more than the movie.
4. Because the movie was a double feature, I didn't have enough time to finish my English assignment.
5. Four hikers began the ascent, but only two made it to the top of the mountain.
6. Shortly after we saw the lightning strike the tree, we heard an explosion of thunder.
7. Despite the fierce weather conditions, the construction workers completed the building on schedule.
8. New drugs insure longer life. Consequently, they contribute to the world's overpopulation problem.
9. The hummingbird's rapidly vibrating wings enable it to hover over a flower as well as to dart quickly away from danger.

10. Not until all passengers and crew were safely aboard lifeboats did the captain abandon ship.

Discuss the connectors and labels you've identified with those your classmates have identified.

Connectors: Keys to Main Ideas and Supporting Details

Perhaps you are one of the many students who gets along fine in a conversation or a discussion but feels lost when faced with a page instead of a person. If so, think of reading as a conversation in which you have the advantage. The writer cannot stop to ask "Do you follow me?" But you can always stop and "replay" the writer's exact words. This is basically what you do when you skim something for the main idea and then go back to read for important details.

One of the most important things to do when reading for details is to focus on those words that signal a change in the writer's train of thought. Many of these key signals are those same connector words and phrases you met on pages 152–154.

Practice 1. Reading / Writing / Discussion

Skim the article "Where *Could* We Go?", taken from the American journal *Family Health Magazine*. Then answer the questions that follow the article.

Where *Could* We Go?

Henry A. Dymsza

1. Today, when you go food shopping, you can choose from a total of about 8 000 products—from abalone, bread, and chocolate all the way to zucchini. Who determines the range of your choice?

2. We know about the farmers, fishermen, and ranchers who provide the raw materials; the food manufacturers that process, package, and distribute them; the government agencies that set guidelines for safety and quality; the consumer groups that keep a sharp eye on costs and food value. But behind the scenes—and almost never making the headlines—

are 14 000 men and women who play a key role in deciding what we eat today and what we'll have to choose from tomorrow.

3. These are the nation's food technologists, who not only design individual "new" foods but also explore the outer limits of food possibilities. Let's take a look at some of the more dramatic developments that these technologists are working on and see where they might lead.

4. Processing for preservation and convenience reached some kind of peak in the food systems designed for the Mercury, Gemini, and Apollo space flights. The astronauts' menus included such items as freeze-dried, bite-sized foods; dehydrated entrees in plastic pouches, to which water could be added; normal-moisture foods in pouches; and partly dried fruits.

5. Although some of these processing techniques are familiar to earthbound consumers (in the form of freeze-dried coffee, for example), it seems unlikely that spacecraft meals are the wave of the future. Economic conditions have encouraged a "back to basics" movement among homemakers, who are shunning the higher-priced convenience, pre-prepared, and frozen products and doing more food preparation from scratch. There has also been a reaction against the idea that increased processing stands for progress, and a growing interest in more "natural" foods.

6. This reaction may have some impact in certain areas of agriculture. Conventional farming, with its emphasis on standardization, mechanical harvesting, and large-scale storage, uses vast amounts of oil, gas, and electricity. Moreover, conventionally grown fruits and vegetables have been developed more for handsome appearance and ease of handling than for taste and nutritional content. What, for example, happened to the small, tender tomato of the past? It has been replaced by the big, tough tomato that will withstand lengthy storage and transportation.

7. So-called organic farming—which dispenses with chemical fertilizers and pesticides and relies on natural manures and pest predators—uses far less energy than conventional farming. Unfortunately it has so far been much more costly and less efficient. However, a recent small-scale study of organic farming, sponsored by the National Science Foundation in the Corn Belt, showed economic yields close to those of conventional farming methods. It's possible that organic

farming may have a larger future, at least in the growing of fruits and vegetables.

8. Organic produce often comes with bumps, blemishes, and blotches. If consumers—that is, you—will accept foods that taste better than they look, then you may be ready for some even odder appearances. Would you, for example, buy a tomato the color of a carrot? That may be one of your choices in the future if some of the following developments get under way.

9. Twenty years ago, food scientist Norman Borlaug, working in Mexico with the support of the Rockefeller Foundation, made the first breakthrough in what became known as the "Green Revolution." Borlaug . . . developed new strains of wheat that could produce twice as much grain per hectare as ordinary strains. Later a new high-yield rice was developed.

10. The new cereal crops require careful tending, fertilizing, and irrigation. Nevertheless they have caught on in many developing countries, and they postponed mammoth food shortages for many years. The recent severe droughts in India and Central Africa, along with fertilizer shortages, blunted their impact, but the crisis would have been worse without them.

11. In addition to crops with higher yields, technologists have also been developing new crops with higher nutritional value. Opaque-2 is a new type of corn with improved protein content. The first synthetic cereal, triticale, derived from a cross of wheat and rye, has higher nutritional value than either of its parents . . . .

12. If you are a science-fiction buff, you may wonder what is happening in "hydroponics"—the growing of crops in laboratory tanks of nutrient-rich solutions instead of in soil. Hydroponics is perfectly feasible, but it also extremely costly. The United States has 148 million hectares under cultivation, and, if needed, these could be expanded to about 300 million hectares. So long as arable land is available, it does not make economic sense to grow food crops hydroponically. . . .

1. There is a list in the first paragraph. What products are listed? What word or phrase in the question at the end of the paragraph describes the list?

2. What things are listed in paragraph 2? Jot them down.

3. Paragraph 2 states that there are "14 000 men and women who play a key role in deciding what we eat." Paragraph 3 names these 14 000. Who are they?
4. What are the two functions of the technologists in paragraph 3? What connector phrase indicates a double role for these persons?
5. How many lists can you find in paragraph 4? What is the purpose of each list (what information does it add)?
6. How many "listing" words do you find in paragraphs 5 and 6? (You may want to refer to the "listing" words and phrases on page 152.)
7. What important comparison is being made at the beginning of paragraph 7? (Spot the comparison phrase; then look for the two things being compared. You may want to refer to the list of comparison connectors on page 153.)
8. In paragraph 8 what contrast must consumers be prepared to accept if they want the "organic food" of the future? (What contrast phrase tips you off to the answer?)

Practice 2. Reading for Detail / Taking Notes

In answering the questions below, you will be taking notes. (You will use these notes in Practice 3.) Pay close attention to connector words and phrases.

1. What is the "Green Revolution"? (Paragraph 9)
2. How do the "new cereal crops" differ from those of "twenty years ago" or more? (Paragraph 10)
3. How is the cereal "triticale" different from natural cereals? (Paragraph 11)
4. Although "hydroponics" is feasible (likely because we have know-how) why aren't more laboratories experimenting with it? (Hint: Look for a common contrast word and a phrase of comparison.) (Paragraph 12)

Practice 3. Writing

Using your notes from Practice 2, write a brief paragraph that answers these two questions: What is the "Green Revolution"? Why is it important?

10

You Need to Go Upstairs

forestudy

Walking in Another's Shoes

At a movie, have you ever cheered—maybe with the rest of the audience—when a particularly hateful character got what was coming to him/her?

And have you ever shed a tear—well, at least felt a lump in your throat—at the death of the hero or the heroine?

Why?

Coming to like or dislike a character—whether it's a character in a story or in a movie or in a TV drama—is a matter over which you have little control. You come to like or dislike a character mainly because of what the author of the story (and the writer of the movie script or the TV script) does deliberately to influence your attitude. The author (1) emphasizes personality traits that you either admire or dislike and (2) has the character behave in a way that results in your admiration or your disapproval. The author's intent is to make it possible for you to know a character—usually the hero or the heroine—so well that you feel exactly what that character feels. You want him/her to win the prize or meet success just as you want those same things for yourself.

And so when you sit breathlessly on the edge of your seat, feeling what that character is feeling and desperately wanting success and victory for that character, we say you are WALKING IN THAT CHARACTER'S SHOES. We say that you have IDENTIFIED with him/her.

You Need to Go Upstairs

Rumer Godden

And just when everything is comfortably settled you need to go upstairs.

You are sitting in the garden for the first time this year, sitting on a cushion on the grass by Mother. The feel of the grass is good; when you press it down and lift your hand the blades spring up again at once as strong as ever; they will not be kept lying down.

You sit with your legs straight in front of you; they have come out from their winter stockings and are very thin and knobbly, but the sun is beginning to warm them gently as if it were glad to see them again.

Your back is against Mother's chair and occasionally she puts her finger between your collar and your skin, to feel if you are warm; you are warm and you pick up your knitting because you can knit; with your finger you follow the wool along the big wooden pins and you say, "Knit one—knit another"; with the slow puffs of wind. The wind brings the garden scents and the sounds to you; sounds of birds and neighbors and the street.

"I like it, Mother."

"So do I."

From GONE: A THREAD OF STORIES by Rumer Godden. Copyright 1944, © 1972 by Rumer Godden. Reprinted by permission of The Viking Press and Curtis Brown Ltd., London.

Then Doreen, who comes in the afternoons to help, brings out a visitor; voices and footsteps; Mother has to get up but you hang your head and go on knitting. Voices creaking and rustling and a sigh. The visitor has sat down. Presently she whispers to Mother, "What is her name?"

"Her name is Alice," says Mother loudly and clearly to blot out the whisper. "We call her Ally. Ally, stand up and say how do you do."

"Ah, don't!" says the visitor and you do not stand up; you press the grass down flat with your hand. It is then that you know you need to go upstairs. The cloakroom is out of order; you have to go upstairs.

The visitor's voice falls from high up, almost into your lap, cutting off the wind and the birds, cutting off Mother, so that you have to stand up.

"Yes, Ally?"

"Mother, I need to go upstairs," and you hurry to say, "I can go by myself, Mother."

Mother is looking at your face—you cannot look yourself, yet you can always feel Mother's look; now she is doubtful, but she is proud, and after a moment she says, "Very well, dear." You understand what she does not say, *"Be careful! Be careful!"*

"Alone?" breathes the visitor, and prickles seem to rise up all over you. You have said you will do it alone, and you will. You turn your back on the visitor.

From the chairs to the poplars is easy; you can hear them straining and moving their branches just enough to tell you where they are. There are two, and when you are up to them, you separate your hands the distance apart you think they will be and you do not hit them, you find them; their trunks are under your hands and you stay to feel those trunks; they are rough and smooth together; they are like people, they are alive.

On the other side of the trees is a smell of cinders where, last winter, ashes were thrown down on the snow. The smell warns you. Move your feet along the grass, don't lift them, because the path is there and it has a little brick-edge hidden in the grass. You fell over it last summer;

suddenly you were down on the grass and you have a fright about falling. You won't fall, the cinder smell has warned you. You find the path. Lift your feet—one—two. The cinders are crunching, now you can go along the path to where the flowers are.

"It's wonderful," says the visitor and her voice sounds like tears. "Her . . . little blue . . . jacket."

"It's a nice jacket, isn't it?" says Mother. "We got it at Pollard's bargain counter. Ally feels it's warm and gay."

That visitor there would be surprised if you picked the flowers, one by one, and took them to her and told her what they were. "I see no reason why you should not know your flowers," Mother has often told you. "Flowers have shapes and smells as well as colors." This is the hyacinth bed; hyacinths are easy, strong in scent and shaped like little pagodas—"Remember, I told you about pagodas"—and these are crocuses and these are aconites—but Mother is not close and you remember that Schiff may be out on the path.

Schiff! You stop. Schiff is so small that you might easily step on him, but Schiff is large enough for you to fall over. Mother . . . but you must not call, you must go on. You think of falling, you can't help thinking of falling—down—into nothing until you get hit. Mother! Schiff! Mother! But you have not called and Mother is saying in what seems an ordinary voice to the visitor, but is her special loud voice for you. "How strange! With all this sun, our tortoise has not come out on the path today."

At the end of the path are two orange bushes with bitter-smelling leaves; they are bad little bushes, with twigs that catch on your coat; you don't like them and you think you will hurry past. There are two bushes in two tubs, and there are four steps; you can remember that, twice two are four. One—two—three—four, and your foot is on the last step, but you catch at the air, catch at the door with a sharp pain ringing in your shin, catch your breath and catch the door and save yourself.

Someone, somebody, has left the scraper on the step. It has been pulled right out. You stand there shaking, boiling with anger, the pain hurting in your leg, but there is no sound from the garden; the visitor has not seen.

Now you are in the house. At first it is always curiously still; and then always out of the stillness you find it. This is the hall and in it are the smells and sounds of all the rooms: furniture cream and hot pipes: carpet and dried roses from the drawing-room, tobacco and a little of pickles from the dining-room: mint and hot cake from the kitchen, and down the stairs comes soap from the bathroom. The loo is up, next door to the bathroom—it has a piece of pine-smelling brick in a wire holder on the wall.

With the smells come the house sounds, all so familiar: Doreen's footsteps in the kitchen: a whirring like insects from the refrigerator and the clocks: a curtain flapping in the wind and a tapping, a tiny rustle from the canary. You know all these things better than anyone else.

Now you let go of the door—like this— and you go across the hall. Of course you could have gone round by the wall to the stairs, feeling around the hat rack and the chest, but you would not do that any more than you would go up the stairs on

your hands and knees. No, you go across—like this—like this—and the big round knob at the bottom of the stair is in your hands. Dear knob. You put your cheek against the wood; it is smooth and firm. Now you can go upstairs.

You are not at all afraid of the stairs. Why? Because Mother has put signals there for you, under the rail where no one can find them, and they guide you all the way up; now your legs go up the stairs as quickly as notes up a piano—almost. At the top is a small wooden heart for you to feel with your fingers; when you reach it, it is like a message and your own heart gets steady. It was not quite steady up the stairs.

"Ally, always, always be careful of the landing." Mother has said that so many times. The landing feels the same to you as the hall but it isn't. Once you dropped a ball over, and the sound came from far away down; if you tripped on the landing you might drop like the ball.

Now? Or not now? Are you facing the right way? That is an old fright. Did you turn round without noticing? You feel the stairs behind you with your foot and they are still there but now you are afraid to let go in case you can't step away. It is steep—steep behind you. Suppose you don't move away? Suppose you hit something—like the chair—and pitch down backwards? Little stickers come out along your back and neck; the back of your neck is cold, your fingers are sticky too, holding the heart signal. Suddenly you can't move away from the stairs. Mother. Mother, but you bite your lips. You must not call out.

Through the window you hear voices—voices from the path.

Drops of water burst out on your neck and under your hair, and you leave the rail and step out on to the carpet and walk very boldly towards the verbena and warm towelling and the hot-metal-from-the-bath-taps smell.

"Is she all right? Is she?"

"Ally, are you managing?" calls Mother.

"Perfectly," you answer, and you shut the loo door.

follow-up

Discussing "You Need to Go Upstairs"

1. Can you maintain your balance on ice skates? Can you do a back flip? Can you perform a handstand? Can you drive a car? Perhaps you can perform all of these tasks—and probably many more—without so much as a second thought. But when you performed the task *alone for the first time*, did you have the self-confidence then that you have now? Why? Why not?
2. What evidence is there at the beginning of the story that Ally depends heavily on her mother?
3. At what points on her way upstairs does Ally come close to panic? Had she panicked, what would she have done? Why didn't she?
4. "You Need to Go Upstairs" is simply the account of a blind girl's walk to the upstairs bathroom. Do you AGREE or DISAGREE? Why?
5. PROVE or DISPROVE: In reading "You Need to Go Upstairs," you can't help walking in another person's shoes.

Transforming Sentences

"I like it, Mother."

"So do I."

Then Doreen, who comes in the afternoons to help, brings out a visitor; voices and footsteps; Mother has to get up but you hang your head and go on knitting. Voices creaking and rustling and a sigh. The visitor has sat down. Presently she whispers to Mother, "What is her name?"

"Her name is Alice," says Mother loudly and clearly to blot out the whisper. "We call her Ally. Ally, stand up and say how do you do."

Nothing unusual about the passage from "You Need to Go Upstairs," is there? Yes, there *is*—insofar as sentence structure is concerned. Close examination will reveal that the passage contains sentences that have at least three different forms:

Statements
"I like it, Mother."
"So do I."
"Her name is Alice."
"We call her Ally."

Question
"What is her name?"

Command/request
"Ally, stand up and say how do you do."

These different sentence forms represent TRANSFORMATIONS—or changes in the ways sentences are put together.

Take that simple sentence "Her name is Alice." It can be TRANSFORMED in at least seven ways, all of which retain the same basic idea:

Is her name Alice? (a question)
Her name is not Alice. (a negative)
Isn't her name Alice? (a negative question)
Name her Alice! (a command)
Don't name her Alice! (a negative command)
She is named Alice. (a passive)
She is not named Alice. (a negative passive)

So far, then, you see that *questions, commands, negatives*, and *passives* are some ways to transform (change) sentence structure. But right now, let's concentrate on question transformations.

Question Transformations

Look again at that question "Is her name Alice?" What's the answer? Obviously, it's either "yes" or "no."

Practice 1. Discussion
Transform each of the following sentences into a yes-no question.

1. Jose and Robert are going clam-digging later tonight.
2. Tammy can be Miss Universe if she tries.
3. The *Lyric* is showing a horror film late tonight.
4. Chocolate frosting is good on chocolate cake.
5. Mildred and Toby get along well.

But yes-no questions aren't the only kind we can ask. In fact, the more interesting kind of questions are those that seek information. Compare the following pairs of questions:

Is her name Alice?
Why is her name Alice?

Are you going to the hockey game?
When are you going to the hockey game?

Do you have reasons for withdrawing your money?
What are your reasons for withdrawing your money?

Did you sprain your ankle?
How did you sprain your ankle?

You can see that the questions that begin with *why, when, what,* and *how* seek information, not a simple "yes" or "no" answer. Other words that ask information-seeking questions are *who (whom), which,* and *where.*

Practice 2. Discussion

Transform each of the following yes-no questions into an information-seeking question.

1. Did that black cat frighten you?
2. Is it time to leave?
3. Were the police setting up a road block?
4. Did you see anyone you know?

Practice 3. Writing

Below are six statements. First, transform each one into a yes-no question. Then transform the yes-no question into an information-seeking question.

1. We're going.
2. You're late.
3. It's time to change the oil.
4. The Edmonton Eskimos lead their division by two games.
5. You can strip that bike down and make it a first-class racer.
6. The ski tracks go between trees only 30 cm apart!

Choose one pair of your sentences and read them aloud. Is there general agreement that you've written two kinds of questions? Are there other acceptable ways of asking your two kinds of questions?

167

Behind the Word

Maybe you wondered about that word *loo*, which Ally used in "You Need to Go Upstairs." *Loo* is a common British term for our "bathroom." Interestingly enough, *loo* is a clipped form of the French *lieux d'aisance* (lyōō də SANS), meaning "places of ease."

Fear Not the Night's Darkness

Tina Morris

Fear not the night's darkness
but see beyond it the rhythms
of shapes & colors
which echo back upon
the music of your thoughts.
Follow
into the exquisite world
where thoughts are born
of Silence.

Take the hand
which reaches so gently
from the reflection of water.
It is your own
leading you beyond your Self
into the region
where there is no Self or Other.

There linger
among the flowers
of Love and Peace.

From *Children of Albion: Poetry of the Underground in Britain*, published by Penguin Books, © 1969. Reprinted by permission of the author.

Bookshelf

Bird on the Wing, by Winifred Madison. Dell, 1975. Elizabeth's conflicts with her stepmother force her to assume responsibility for herself before she is ready to do so. The result: a catastrophe that leads her toward maturity.

May I Cross Your Golden River? by Paige Dixon. Atheneum, 1975. Learning that he is near death with an incurable disease, Jordan resolves to experience as much of life as possible with the few months he has left.

Of Human Bondage, by W. Somerset Maugham. Pocket Books, 1971 (originally, 1915). Philip's physical deformity increases his difficulties in finding a direction for his life.

The Son of Someone Famous, by M. E. Kerr. Ballantine, 1975. Both Adam and Brenda, two friends, face the difficulties of dealing with their parents' expectations and of finding their own goals for their lives.

11

With an Eye to "I"

It's only natural that every human being should seek his or her rightful place in the world—should try to figure out just who he or she is—should determine just what it is that will bring happiness, contentment, satisfaction. Some people seem to need the approval and the applause of others. Some people seem to need to be famous. Some seem to need privacy. Some—well, see for yourself:

"I'm Nobody! Who are you?"

Emily Dickinson

I'm Nobody! Who are you?
Are you—Nobody—Too?
Then there's a pair of us?
Don't tell! they'd advertise—you know!

How dreary—to be—Somebody!
How public—like a Frog—
To tell one's name—the livelong June—
To an admiring Bog!

A: Sour grapes! Nobody!
B: Are you kidding? Just look at the pressures put on public figures. Those people have to be very careful about everything they say and do. Their every mistake makes the papers. They live in a goldfish bowl. That's not for me!
A: But can't you be a somebody and still live your own life? If you call yourself a nobody, aren't you really indulging in self-pity?

Well, maybe. Many people do want to be special or accomplish something special. And they take pride in their special abilities. For instance, consider the subject of the next poem:

Our Boy in Blue

Raymond Souster

"Edward Hanlan, the most renowned oarsman of any age, whose victorious career has no parallel in the annals of sport"—engraved on the statue to Ned Hanlan, CNE Grounds, Toronto.

Heroes are usually forgotten
so quickly it says much
for our shallow, fickle minds.

Take Ned Hanlan,
Toronto boy, five-foot-eight,
one hundred fifty pounds,
world-champion oarsman at 25 (1880),
finished at 30, and still
the fastest sculler ever.
Loser of only six races
out of three hundred fifty,
so good he made fools
of nearly all his opponents,
his rowing so smooth,
his sliding so methodical
and free from effort, man and boat
at one with the water.

And yet after five years
he could hardly win a race,
his challenges drew no takers,
and he became hotel-keeper,
then City alderman,
dying young in 1908.

From HANGING IN by Raymond Souster. Reprinted by permission of Oberon Press.

But 20 000 people
filed past his coffin,
and years later they built him
a twenty-foot statue,
where he still stands today,
gazing over Lake Ontario
(where he grew up as a boy,
learned to row
almost as soon as he walked),

perhaps waiting there to see
if some young hopeful
in a single scull will show
inside the breakwater,
stroking hard in dark blue
singlet and vest,
the early-morning sun
glinting back from his oars—

another Boy in Blue?

Not everyone makes the kind of outstanding achievement in a
sport that Ned Hanlan did. But many try. And it's because many *do*
try that a few become outstanding. The winners of gold medals in
the Olympic Games are good examples. But what becomes of them?
Are they nobodies—like the nobody in Emily Dickinson's poem?

Warren Pryor

Alden Nowlan

When every pencil meant a sacrifice
his parents boarded him at school in town,
slaving to free him from the stony fields,
the meagre acreage that bore them down.

They blushed with pride when, at his graduation,
they watched him picking up the slender scroll,
his passport from the years of brutal toil
and lonely patience in a barren hole.

When he went in the Bank their cups ran over.
They marvelled how he wore a milk-white shirt
work days and jeans on Sundays. He was saved
from their thistle-strewn farm and its red dirt.

And he said nothing. Hard and serious
like a young bear inside his teller's cage,
his axe-hewn hands upon the paper bills
aching with empty strength and throttled rage.

> X: Wow! That has to be a horrible thing—doing work that
> you hate.
> Y: Especially when your parents have scrimped and saved to get
> you there.
> Z: Well—did they ever ask him what he wanted to do? Did he
> ever tell them he hated what he was doing? How is he ever
> going to find out who he is if he can't get out and do what *he*
> wants to do?

Most people need to belong—to feel that they're part of
something. Few of us are self-contained enough to be happy without
acceptance by *some* group. And so we try to earn it—by outstanding
achievement as Ned Hanlan did. Or we force ourselves to do
something we dislike in order to gain others' approval, as Warren
Pryor did. Regardless of how we gain acceptance, however, most of
us soon feel the pressures of the group—pressures to conform, to fit
into the pattern the group has set for itself. And so sometimes we
feel ambivalent—uncertain—about what to do. Should we conform
and simply become members of the group? Or should we use our
own imaginations and express ourselves as individuals? Well, here's
how one person feels:

Ambivalence

Mark Greenspan

i like me as i am
  and here i will stay
until i find good reason
  to change,
such as you.

but who are you
  that i should become
a pebble in a stream
  or, better yet,
what am i that i should remain an island?

From *Social Education*, November, 1971. Reprinted by permission of the National Council for the Social Studies, and the
author.

X: Gee, he doesn't see any reason to change, and he doesn't see any reason not to change. What's he going to do?

Y: Exactly! He sure doesn't help me settle the problem.

Z: Well, at least he can say that he likes himself as he is. That's better than nothing.

X: Maybe that's it! Maybe it's deciding what pleases you and then letting everyone else learn to live with your decision. Maybe?

An island stands alone, isolated. Is being independent like being an island? Is the independent person—the free spirit—someone who stands alone like an island? Or is an independent person someone who recognizes his/her ties with others but who avoids being dominated by them?

The Song My Paddle Sings

E. Pauline Johnson

West wind, blow from your prairie nest,
Blow from the mountains, blow from the west,
The sail is idle, the sailor too;
Oh! wind of the west, we wait for you.
Blow, blow!
I have wooed you so,
But never a favor you bestow,
You rock your cradle the hills between,—
But scorn to notice my white lateen.[1]

I stow the sail and unship the mast;
I wooed you long, but my wooing's past;
My paddle will lull you into rest;
O drowsy wind of the drowsy west,
Sleep, sleep!
By your mountains steep,
Or down where the prairie grasses sweep,
Now fold in slumber your laggard wings,
For soft is the song my paddle sings.

August is laughing across the sky,
Laughing while paddle, canoe and I
Drift, drift,
Where the hills uplift
On either side of the current swift.

1. *lateen:* a sail with a short mast

From FLINT AND FEATHERS by E. Pauline Johnson Reprinted by permission of Hodder and Stoughton Canada.

The river rolls in its rocky bed,
My paddle is plying its way ahead,
Dip, dip,
When the waters flip
In foam as over their breast we slip.

And oh, the river runs swifter now;
The eddies circle about my bow;
Swirl, swirl,
How the ripples curl
In many a dangerous pool awhirl!

And far to forward the rapids roar,
Fretting their margin for evermore;
Dash, dash,
With a mighty crash,
They seethe and boil and bound and splash.

Be strong, O Paddle; be brave, Canoe!
The reckless waves you must plunge into.
Reel, reel,
On your trembling keel,
But never a fear my craft will feel.

We've raced the rapids; we're far ahead;
The river slips through its silent bed.
Sway, sway,
As the bubbles spray
And fall in tinkling tunes away.
And up on the hills against the sky,
A fir-tree rocking its lullaby
Swings, swings,
Its emerald wings,
Swelling the song that my paddle sings.

> A: The poet really likes nature.
> B: It's like a song—"the song my paddle sings."

Discussing "With an Eye to I"

1. To what extent does your group—your gang—your crowd—
   determine what you think and do? Have you ever found
   yourself following the crowd even though you felt your ideas
   were better or made more sense? What did you do?

2. Consider the speaker in each of the poems in this cluster. How do you think each feels about the importance of the group in a person's life? about the importance of approval by the group?

3. Why not write your own "I" poem—one that expresses you? Use one of the "I" poems in this cluster as a model. Make a personal statement about yourself from your point of view. You may want to follow the pattern used in "The Song My Paddle Sings." Like Pauline Johnson, tell who you are by describing your world. Use words that will make your world come alive for the reader or listener. You may wish to follow the example of Pauline Johnson and Emily Dickinson and write lines that rhyme, but it isn't necessary. Or, as in the poem "Our Boy in Blue," you might write about a skill of yours, something you do well. Or you might want to write about how you have spent your life up till now and whether or not you are satisfied with it, as in "Warren Pryor."

Be prepared to share your poem with your classmates. The class may want to select a number of poems to include in a class magazine.

interlude

Horrifying Clichés

Paul Coker, Jr. (artist)   May Sakami & E. Nelson Bridwell (writers)

"Splitting an INFINITIVE"

"Initiating A PROGRAM"

"Driving A MEAN BARGAIN"

"Ushering In an ERA"

"Chalking up A VICTORY"

"Reviving an OLD CUSTOM"

"Redressing A WRONG"

"Dangling A PARTICIPLE"

"Catching FORTY WINKS"

"Hurling An INVECTIVE"

179

12

Especially Worthy

forestudy

Synonyms—Word Power

Sure! Synonyms are words that mean approximately the same thing. And so maybe you're thinking that synonyms are always interchangeable. Not so. Very few synonyms, in fact, have exactly the *same* meaning. Take *flourish* (page 182), for instance. Flourish differs from its synonyms *brandish* and *wave* in its precise meaning of "make a showy display." *Brandish,* on the other hand, simply means "wave or shake threateningly." And *wave* means "a waving of something as a signal."

John Patrick Gillese, the author of "Especially Worthy," used *flourish* instead of either of its synonyms because *flourish* best expresses the precise meaning he wished to get across.

It's knowing which synonym to use at a given time that builds your vocabulary and your word power. When you use a collegiate or unabridged dictionary to find synonyms for a given word, watch for the abbreviation *syn.* The word you're looking up may be compared with its synonyms right there. Or you may be referred to one of its synonyms. For example, if you were looking up *flourish,* you'd find "syn. *v.* brandish." And then, when you look up *brandish,* you'd find an entry like this: "syn. *v.* flourish." (followed by a comparison of the precise meaning of each of the synonyms—*flourish, brandish* and *wave.*)

Practice 1. Writing/Discussion

Below are passages that appear in "Especially Worthy." In each there is an italicized word for you to look up to see how it differs in meaning from its synonyms. (Remember to watch for the abbreviation *syn.*)

On your paper, list each italicized word and its synonyms. Then to the right of each word, explain its precise meaning. Use your own words as much as possible. (The number in parentheses after each passage indicates the number of synonyms you'll find for the italicized word. Altogether, there are 10 words to be listed.)

1. At the station cream cans were *stacked* in the shade of the long stucco walls. (3)
2. Dad seldom used the buggy whip but he *flourished* it now. (2)
3. There were a few people *clustered* on the platform. (5)

Practice 2. Writing

Select one group of synonyms from Practice 1. From that group, choose three synonyms, and use each one accurately in an original sentence.

Be prepared to read your three sentences aloud. Does everyone agree that you've used each synonym precisely?

Especially Worthy

John Patrick Gillese

It was something of a sensation in our part of the world the morning we went to Edmonton for my brother Jim's graduation. Jim was the first one from our part of the country ever to go to college—an event that was a thing of both pride and doubt to my father—and that was back in the days when the Depression was at its worst and the Alberta bushland seemed to be the toughest place in the world to make a living.

There was still dew on the June roses as Dad drove to the station. My mother sat stiffly in the front seat of the buggy, and I had the sinking sensation that she was more scared than she'd ever been in her life before. That was saying something, for all her life Mother had been afraid of school teachers and even of refined° visitors, and only because Dad refused to leave the last of his seeding did she consent to go to the city at all. My father wore his

From *The Family Herald*. Reprinted by permission of the author.

overalls tucked inside his knee-rubber boots, which were colorfully patched with red strips from an older inner tube. I had on my good cap, with tissue paper in the lining—and in my pocket was a whole dollar to spend on anything I liked.

The night before, Dad had slipped it to me in the barn, unbeknownst to Mother or my kid sisters. All I could do was gawk. "Where'd you get that?"

"I borrowed it from the storekeeper," my father said, "and you don't have to shout it from the rooftops." He looked around, to make sure no one was within hearing. "Nipper, I want you to look after Mother at the speaking in there. Take her up where there's a good seat. And if Jim gets too rushed to take her to supper—or something—you remind him, eh?"

I knew what Dad meant. Sometimes I figured that was why he was always making fun of Jim's learning. Maybe Jim figured he wasn't one of us any more. Maybe he was ashamed of us—ashamed of the farm and all the hard work and the poorness. Sometimes I figured the way he studied maybe he had forgotten that when we were poorest of all, we had the most fun of all.

"You know tomorrow means a lot to your mother," Dad said. "It could break her heart, Nipper."

The way he was talking to Mother now, though, you'd never have thought he was worried.

"Well, old girl," he said, "be sure to take care of yourself in front of that grandeur."

My mother gave him a look. She never could tell when he was teasing.

"You might tell them," my dad went on, "that any brains he has he got from his old man."

My mother was so nervous she could hardly stand his talk. It was only a desper-ate hunger to share in Jim's day of glory that took her to Edmonton at all. In that shining world of his, so removed from the farm, she felt she did not belong and that somehow it was a sin even to intrude. Education, as Mother said, is a wonderful thing. But in her mind, the riches of it belonged only to great people who were especially clever, especially worthy.

"I suppose now," my father muttered, "he'll be too good to pick up a manure fork...."

It was the kind of talk that could have precipitated another bitter battle between the two of them, and I was relieved, as we went over Sam Mead's hill, to hear the train blowing as it left the village 16 km west of us.

Dad seldom used the buggy whip but he flourished it now, and the surprised team leaped down Mead's hill so fast that I almost fell backwards out of the buggy and horse hair flew all over my good suit.

At the station cream cans were stacked in the shade of the long stucco walls and the station agent had his long wagon piled high with egg crates. There were a few people clustered on the platform—neighbors who'd brought in cream or blacksmithing work. They all lifted their hat to my mother and asked Dad if he was going to the city, too.

"Nope," said my father, "can't take time off from seeding." The way he said it, you'd have thought money was of no consideration.

"What's this I hear about Jim giving some kind of speech?" Charlie Porter, the elevator agent, asked.

"Oh, you mean his "valediction"° address?" Father said. (He had spent half of one night trying to find out the meaning of the word.)

"What's he gonna do now he's educated?"

My father looked unconcerned. "Well, that's up to him. I wanted him to be able to do something more than shovel manure all his life."

I could tell my mother was scandalized by such talk from Dad, for in the first place he had been opposed to Jim's going to college at all and his favorite pastime, in winter, was to write letters to agricultural experts commending them on their various ideas for improving the farm and asking if they had any alternative plans, where you used haywire instead of cash.

There was no time for further talk, though, for the train was bearing down on us—a black, hissing monster that made the platform tremble as it passed.

It was my first train ride and, for a while, I hoped it would last for days. After a while, however, it grew a bit monotonous. I was tired drinking water in little paper cups, tired staring out of the windows at the sloughs, with their brown musked waters and wild ducks rising off them as the train clattered by. In every little field, carved out of the shining green poplars and the gay scrub willow, farmers were seeding, standing erect behind the levers, the old wooden drills raising dust clouds behind them.

Finally I went back and sat beside Mother. She had a seat by herself, so she wouldn't be obliged to talk to strangers. She was reading the invitation again, the little card with the green-and-gold crest that invited my parents to the graduation exercises in Convocation Hall and announced the valedictory address would be by James Hugh Kelly. That was Jim.

Suddenly it seemed to me a long time since Jim went away. For two years he'd hardly been home at all, except for the odd weekend. The summer before, he'd spent all the holidays freighting on the Mackenzie waterways. I could hardly remember what he looked like.

"Why didn't he help us on the farm, instead of working on a sternwheeler?"[1] I asked Mother.

"It was to earn the money to put him through," my mother said severely. "If you're ever going to be something, you have to have an education."

Somehow, in the way she said it I could sense her praying that she would conduct herself properly—that now that Jim was somebody, he wouldn't need to be ashamed because of his family.

It took about four hours to get to Edmonton. We went down the platform between dizzying lines of track, and I had never seen so many people in my life before. I was so busy gawking I lost sight of Mother, and a man's suitcase sent me sprawling.

"Watch where you're going!" Mother scolded me. "And look at your suit, we haven't money to be buying you clothes every year."

I was kind of thankful when Jim met us in the station itself. What I noticed most about him was his haircut and his pressed suit. He grabbed me, as if he didn't know whether just to shake hands or swing me up the way he used to in the old days.

"Well, Nipper!" he laughed. "You and your pants sure have a hard time staying the same size!"

Then he looked at Mother; and for a moment, before he kissed her, I thought I saw a worry in his eyes. He was looking at her vividly-colored print dress that had

1. *sternwheeler:* a steamboat driven by a paddle wheel at the stern or rear

184

been washed—by hand—too many times now to look new.

Then he laughed again and took us to a café. We thought he'd have dinner with us, but it turned out he still hadn't got his speech right and he wanted to spend more time on it.

I could see the disappointment in Mother's eyes. Then, surreptitiously° she fumbled with the catch of her old purse. "Here, Jim, you'll want a few cents to treat your friends afterwards."

"Aw, Mother—" I could see the bleakness back in Jim's eyes . . . as if, I thought suddenly, her money wasn't as good as other people's. But he took the two dollars she gave him, anyway, his face tight and different.

"I'll pay you back every cent," he said.

I wanted to say to him: "The only time you can ever pay her back, Jim, is right now." I wanted to desperately; but I was just too dumb to say anything. I knew at that minute Mother would have given everything just to have him eat with her for the last time before the mysterious evening ritual when he would pass forever from her hard world and become a man of learning. I could see the tears standing in her tired eyes as he walked away.

Mother and I ate alone. Then, for two hours, we trudged from one store to another, trying to pick a present for Jim. Nothing seemed practical enough for Mother, or else she couldn't afford it with the few dollars she had left. She priced a pair of slippers and turned away because they were too dear. The salesgirl gave a short, brittle laugh, and I felt embarrassed because everybody could tell we were from the country and were either amused or annoyed by us.

Finally we took a street-car for the South Side, and we went back to shopping. Mother bought a twenty-five-cent pipe for Dad, giving it a couple of experimental pulls to make sure the hole wasn't plugged up. She got some cloth to make dresses for the girls. Finally she bought Jim a striped shirt with a stiff collar, which cost more than all the other things together.

Jim told where we could get the room. It was near the University. It was hot and stuffy, and Mother let me take my coat off. She started fixing her hair with old-fashioned hairpins, all the while talking about how grand Jim had looked and how hard he had worked to be "something." I kicked my heels on the lumpy old bed and knew she was getting more scared, and this talk was only to bolster courage. I was getting scared, too—I didn't know why.

There was a knock at the door that made me jump. The hotel manager told Mother she was wanted on the telephone. Plain as day I could hear Jim's voice at the other end. He was explaining to Mother that his speech still wasn't satisfactory . . . that we were to have supper alone . . . that he'd pick us up in time to get to Convocation Hall.

I don't know when I have ever spent a more miserable afternoon. I didn't even feel like going out and spending the dollar. It was as if I was in a strange land where everybody rushed, nobody knew anyone else—and nobody cared. I wished I was back snaring gophers in the school grounds, or riding on the dusty, screeching old seeder with Dad.

My mother talked over the days since Jim had gone away. "Many a time," she reflected, "I never knew where the money was coming from. But we got him through, thank God. Now he won't need me no more."

To her, I guess, those words were a

triumph: they meant that, through her, Jim had got somewhere. But to me, they seemed the saddest words I had ever heard.

Convocation Hall took my breath away. The college colors—green and gold—were everywhere. The place was packed. The men all wore dark suits; the women had beautiful corsages. The great velvet curtains up on the stage were billowing softly, like something from a story-book. Dignified men—some fat and clean-shaven, some thin with little dark goatees, all of them preoccupied and seemingly oblivious of the soft buzzing of the crowd—disappeared towards the stage, reappeared again, walking soundlessly as if they didn't want to be seen and yet were quite conscious of the scrutiny.°

"The profs," Jim said absently, when I asked who they were.

A couple of fellows about Jim's age came by, showing each other graduation gifts from "the folks." One had a gold watch and the other was waving a cheque, and both were laughing.

"I didn't know what to get ye," Mother said, in an aside to Jim. "So I bought you a shirt."

"Oh—yeah—thanks, Mother," Jim whispered back. "You should not have bothered."

Somehow I was glad I had made Mother leave the shirt in the hotel room. I told her Jim would have no place to put it while he was making the speech.

Now, as he led us to a seat in the shadows near the back, I wanted to tell him what Dad had said, only Mother would have heard. I was beginning to feel as if I had stolen the dollar.

Jim was a bit pale, smiling vacantly at
people who spoke to him. Either he was

looking for somebody—or else he didn't want anybody to know we were his people.

Mother was staring at the beautiful gowns and hair-do's of the women next to her. Then she looked at their hands and buried her own below her handbag. Her fingers were twisted and bent from the hard years on the farm.

"Well—I have to go now!" Jim smiled

shakily at us. "It'll start in a minute. I'll see you right afterwards."

He was a few metres away, and I hollered at him.

"Jim! Wait a minute!"

Jim stopped, and I felt as if everybody in the hall was staring in our direction.

"Don't be tormenting him now! And him with his speech to give!" Mother warned angrily. But she wasn't quick enough to get hold of me before I was out of the seat and darting down the aisle.

I didn't say anything more to Jim until we were outside. Even then, it seemed crazy what I was saying and I was scared Jim would be mad at me for the rest of his life. But I had to tell him.

"Jim," I said, "didn't you want us to come?"

The breath hissed through Jim's teeth. "You're crazy, kid!"

"No, I'm not," I said. "I thought this was going to be fun. Mother looked forward so long for this—but you've forgotten."

"Forgotten what, Nipper?" Jim said, and his eyes looked as if he had a headache.

"The last time you needed money," I said. "Mother dug senega root in summer to get that. Every minute she wasn't doing her own work, she was out there digging. You've forgotten how hard it is to dig snake-root. The mosquitoes were so bad that when she'd come home, her clothes would be covered with blood."

"What are you trying to say, kid?" Jim seemed to yell at me, but it was only a whisper.

"She did it so you could have an education," I told him.

And all of a sudden, remembering her pleadings with Dad, remembering her keeping baby lambs in the kitchen all winter, going without eggs so she could sell them, getting headaches in the heat of August from picking berries to peddle to the townspeople—all of a sudden I could hardly see.

"I don't even know how Dad rustled the money so we could come," I said. "But I know he did it because he wanted her to have something for all she'd done. Jim, she doesn't know what to do or say—"

But I couldn't tell Jim any more.

I couldn't upset him on the biggest night of his life. That would have broken Mother's heart. The way he looked at me—like somebody who's known all along that what he was hearing was true, but that, maybe, if somebody didn't tell him he wouldn't have to face it—I was so scared maybe I'd put his speech right out of his mind. I ran indoors and left him there.

There was a lot I missed, in between "O Canada" and the appearance of a distinguished-looking man, in formal black clothes, who bowed against the backdrop of the brilliantly-lighted stage. He spoke briefly of the events that had gone before, then said he would call on James Hugh Kelly, the University's outstanding honor scholar of the year, to deliver the valedictory address.

Off-stage in the wings, the band began to play softly, the haunting theme song of the college. Then Jim stepped lightly across the stage, to a tiny table with a water pitcher on it. The drums sounded a deep roll and died. Applause came from the packed auditorium. The lights were off, but I could see the tears slipping down my mother's cheeks. She was so proud of him that nothing could spoil that moment for her.

"He's something at last," she was thinking.

Jim opened his address, and I could tell **187**

he was nervous. He said none of us gathered there that night would ever forget the memorable occasion. For the students, Jim said, it was both an ending and a beginning. He talked about the student year and the Tuck Shop and there was laughter, and that seemed to relax him.

With a sort of easy confidence now, he talked; and it didn't seem possible that once he had pitched hay and hauled firewood with Dad through the deep drifts of winter in the bush country.

Then, after more bursts of laughter and words that were just words to me, Jim paused. The smile left his face; and I think everybody suddenly realized that the next part of Jim's speech was going to be different.

"Ladies and gentlemen," Jim said, "when we—your sons and daughters—receive our diplomas tonight, we are supposed to be worthy of them." You could have heard the silence then, thick and fixed and pregnant.° "It means," said Jim, "that into our hands you have passed a great trust. When people come to our doctors, they will come, believing that we have not only the skill and knowledge—but the sacred regard for their bodies, to make them well. When you pass your children to our teachers, you will be conferring on us a tremendous—almost a terrible trust." Jim touched a strand of his hair that had fallen across his face. "I once heard a Divinity student say that the greatest prayer was: 'Lord, that I may be worthy.' Now, I know I at least understand."

Somewhere in the student gallery, somebody snickered. But for the rest of that hall, it was as if even breathing had stopped.

188   "So," Jim went on, "if we are to be worthy, it must mean that we set forth now with a realization of what others have done for us. There should be no room left for false pride. There should be only gratitude for the sacrifices, hidden and open, of all those who have made our education possible . . . who have given us, as it were, to the service of humanity."

Said Jim: "From the bottom of my heart, I want say to all tonight that whatever I am, I owe to others. To my professors, who have preserved and handed into my keeping the best knowledge of all the generations. To my classmates, who have shown me and shared with me a beautiful friendship. But most of all . . ."

And here Jim paused.

". . . most of all," he said, "I want to thank my mother, who is down there in the audience with you. With her permission, ladies and gentlemen—and yours—I'd like to tell you what she has given over the years, for my sake and, I hope, for mankind."

All of a sudden, listening to Jim's voice, I couldn't see. For Jim was up there, not pretending any longer, telling those people who knew the value of education, what it meant to be so poor in worldly goods that she'd never owned a washing machine or a toaster or one really lovely dress. She was so unlettered herself she was afraid to speak before strangers. . . . He went on and on, telling them about the lambs and the mosquitoes, till everywhere I looked, I could see women daubing at their eyes and men staring so straight ahead that you knew what it was like with them, too.

When Jim was done, the silence followed him off the stage. Then the applause began. It swept in waves through the auditorium, till at last the distinguished-looking man stepped back and lifted his hands for silence.

"This," he said, "is an occasion of which memories are made—a graduation I shall always remember with pride. May I just say how sincerely honored we are to have the mothers of our students with us. They, it seems, are behind the 'somebodies' of the world." For a moment, the distinguished-looking man seemed caught up in memories of his own. Then he smiled. "Perhaps it is a good thing for all our graduates to remember," he concluded, "that the riches of education are not meant for the educated alone. They should be given generously to all—but especially to all the unknowns who made our education possible."

Mother was lost completely in admiration of him. In him, she saw a reflection of what Jim would be some day.

At that, I guess it turned out to be the most wonderful trip she'd ever had. On the train going home, she wanted to sit and remember. For her, the years of sacrifice were forgotten; perhaps they had never been. I suppose she thought the only reason Jim's friends and associates had sought her out was because they were so proud of Jim. And when Jim brought up the distinguished-looking man and introduced him as the Dean of his faculty, Mother actually loosened up under his spell. The Dean bowed when he left her, and for years afterwards Mother referred to him with pride, as "a lovely man." It was the one subject she could comment on with a certain assurance, especially when Dad would begin talking to people of the constructive correspondence he used to carry on with some of the best professors in Alberta, in his earlier years on the farm.

Yes, for Mother it was a wonderful train ride home. For me, I thought it would never end. Mother was still in such a daze the day after graduation that I stuffed myself on banana splits, ice cream, green apples and candy. I could hardly remember to tell Dad that Jim was counting on coming back to the farm for at least a couple of months before he decided what to do with his education, now that he'd got it.

Dad said it was good value for a dollar, all the way.

---

follow-up

Discussing "Especially Worthy"

1. This story was written about the days of the Depression in Alberta. In what way does this setting and time period play an important role in the story?
2. Why do you feel Jim's brother brought up the mother's sacrifices to Jim?
3. How do you think Jim was feeling throughout the story? Give evidence from the story to back up your answer.

189

4. Explain what you feel is the importance of the last sentence: "Dad said it was good value for a dollar, all the way."

5. Do you feel parents have unreasonable expectations for their children? Why do you suppose they feel this way? Jim expressed his feelings in one way. How might you have responded to the same situation? What sort of parent do you think you would be with your son or daughter?

Editing

Have you ever said something that came out all wrong? As soon as you heard what you said, you realized that you didn't get your meaning across. Most people, at one time or another, make language blunders—sometimes humorous ones, as you will see in the following practices. Nobody is perfect. But blunders in writing can always be caught and corrected before the reader sees them. To prevent being misunderstood, you will want to re-read and edit your written drafts carefully. Make sure your written words say what you mean. After your words leave your pen, you will rarely have a chance to explain to your reader what you really meant to say.

Proofreading for Punctuation

Are those little dots, squiggles, and lines that we call punctuation marks really important in writing? Will your meaning come through without them? Well, read on!

Practice 1. Writing
Number your paper to ten. Then write the letter—A or B—of the sentence which is so punctuated that it best answers each of the following questions. (You may want to refer to the Handbook (pages 418-454) for an explanation of the use of particular punctuation marks.) Discuss your answers with the class.

1. Which sentence suggests that Eldon is in for some unkind words from the coach? Why?
   A. Eldon, the fullback, ran the wrong way.
   B. Eldon, the fullback ran the wrong way.
2. Which sentence tells you that the coach is probably angry? Why?
   A. The coach called the players' names.
   B. The coach called the players names.
3. Which sentence indicates that the boys, not the girls, will run? Why?

A. Only the boys, who have track shoes, will be allowed to run.

B. Only the boys who have track shoes will be allowed to run.

4. In which sentence does the dog rule the household? Why?

A. The dog knows its master.

B. The dog knows it's master.

5. Which of the following actions might prove painful? Why?

A. Shall I drive the nail in myself?

B. Shall I drive the nail—in myself?

6. In which sentence are the Edmonton Eskimos picked to win? Why?

A. The Edmonton Eskimos, say the Toronto Argos, are going to win the Grey Cup.

B. The Edmonton Eskimos say the Toronto Argos are going to win the Grey Cup.

7. In which sentence is the patient's pulse probably beating faster? Why?

A. A pretty young nurse took the patient's pulse.

B. A pretty, young nurse took the patient's pulse.

8. Which sentence would no doubt create a laundry problem? Why?

A. Dunk your donut, and roll in your coffee.

B. Dunk your donut and roll in your coffee.

9. In which sentence is your friend somewhat strange looking?

A. "He was a cute dog," said my friend with a curly tail and pointed ears.

B. "He was a cute dog," said my friend, "with a curly tail and pointed ears."

10. In which sentence is the young bride accusing her husband of cowardice? Why?

A. Why don't you try my roast chicken?

B. Why don't you try my roast, chicken?

Proofreading for Sense

Sometimes sentences may be punctuated correctly but still may contain language problems that mislead or confuse the reader. Such sentences often make for unintended humor.

Practice 2. Writing/Discussion

Read each sentence below to discover the humorous flub involved. Then rewrite each sentence so that it communicates clearly the meaning you think was intended. You may need to substitute words, **191** change the position of words, or make more than one sentence. Discuss your answers with the class. There may be more than one "correct" version of each sentence.

1. Anyone caught driving a car under sixteen years of age will be prosecuted.
2. The wealthy matron entertained fifteen children of six city police officers who were killed last year at a Christmas party in her home.
3. Mrs. Jones, who went deer hunting with her husband, was proud that she was able to shoot a deer as well as her husband.
4. Kim fed her dog biscuits.
5. When he was in Germany he looked up his family tree and found his grandfather.
6. The unfortunate man was killed while cooking his wife's breakfast in a horrible manner.
7. A manslaughter sentence carries a penalty of one to ten years in California.
8. Bill Hayes acquired a new sedan as well as a new wife, having traded in the old one for a liberal allowance.

Bookshelf

Growing pains: the autobiography of Emily Carr, by Emily Carr. Clarke, Irwin, 1946. A humorous account of Canada's famous artist and her struggles to assert and live by her own values, rather than those of her family and society.

Raisins and Almonds, by Fredelle B. Maynard. Paperjacks, 1973. The story of a Jewish girl in the Prairies who is forbidden by her father's strong cultural values to attend Christian festivals.

"The First Born Son," in *The Rebellion of Young David and Other Stories,* by Ernest Buckler. McClelland and Stewart, 1975. A father's values conflict with those of his son, Dave, who wants to move to the city instead of staying on the farm with his father.

Under the Ribs of Death, by John Marlyn. McClelland and Stewart, New Canadian Library, 1964. The book examines a poor Hungarian boy's conflict between his loyalty to his origins, and his need to be accepted by his Anglo-Saxon peers.

focus

Detecting Propaganda

"Go to your phone right now and let us know how much you will donate to help keep Channel 2—your educational TV station—on the air."

"Join the Pepsi generation."

"INVESTING IN VENEZUELA IS A GUARANTEE OF PROGRESS . . . No other country offers so many opportunities to the foreign investor and so many guarantees of their safety."

"Tired of recession with inflation? Elect Osgood for a change!"

What do all those quotations have in common? They are all attempts to influence people to think or act in a particular way. All of them are attempts to "sell" something—an idea, a program, a product, a course of action. All of them, therefore, are examples of PROPAGANDA.

Let the Buyer Beware

As a consumer, you are the target of advertising. Whenever you open a newspaper or magazine, turn on the TV or radio, or merely drive down the street, you are likely to be bombarded by numerous advertisements, all prepared by experts eagerly seeking your money or your vote.

What is advertising? Why does it have such a powerful effect in our society? Literally, *advertise* means "turn to"; an ad tries to catch your attention, causing you to "turn to" its suggestion—to buy a certain product or vote for a certain candidate.

Advertising is a form of PROPAGANDA. Its aim is to persuade you. The Romans, who gave us the words *advertise* and *propaganda*, also **193** provided a warning to the potential buyer: *Caveat emptor* (kā′ vē ăt ĕmp′ tôr), "Let the buyer beware."

People often use the word *propaganda* to disparage, or run down, efforts to influence or persuade. Have you ever said, "Oh, that's just a lot of propaganda"? But if you liked what you read or heard, you may have said, "That's a good sales pitch." Look again, however, at the opening examples in this lesson. Notice that propaganda can be used to support worthy causes just as much as ones that may seem to you selfish or undesirable.

Skilful persuaders—advertisers, public-relations experts, sales representatives, politicians, ministers, and others—use a variety of appeals to get their messages across. At times, their methods are so subtle that you may not realize they are attempting to persuade you. Learning to detect propaganda can make you a better "buyer" of ideas as well as commercial products and services.

Practice 1. Discussion

1. Newspapers, magazines, television, and radio are the most common means used by advertisers to spread their ideas. What are some other means that advertisers use? (*Hint*: Look around you; you will see advertisements on some very common objects.)
2. Name some ads you have seen that publicize a good cause or present important information to the public. What is your reaction to this type of advertising?
3. Name some ads that are particularly entertaining. Describe them to the class. What makes them interesting?

What's the Good Word?

Words are the stock in trade of advertisers and other persuaders. Words can have powerful effects on people. "Snarl" words can produce fear or anger. "Purr" words can produce a positive feeling.

"Purr" words are most commonly used in advertising because companies want to create pleasant images for their products. Even typically unpleasant subjects are given pleasant-sounding names. This type of sugar-coated word is called a *euphemism*.

People often want to sugar-coat unpleasant ideas by substituting euphemisms which sound less unpleasant. Perhaps some people want to believe that all they have to do to get rid of something evil or ugly is to invent a pleasant word for it.

In our own culture, there have been certain taboos associated with parts of the body. Many years ago when the sight of a woman's ankle was considered shocking, some people used the term *limb* as a euphemism for *leg*.

In some cases, euphemisms are created to make a common object or idea seem more important. This is particularly true with names of occupations. For example, the old term *barmaid* has been replaced by *cocktail waitress*. Cooks prefer to be *chefs*. Janitors prefer to be called *custodians*. Garbage collectors are now termed *sanitation engineers*, and undertakers are called *morticians*.

Practice 2. Discussion

1. From each of the following pairs of terms, select the term that seems to be a euphemism, the "nicer" term of the pair.

   foundation garment/girdle armpit/underarm
   hair dye/color rinse   senior citizen/old person
   die/pass away   false teeth/dentures
   fat person/weight watcher blemishes/pimples

2. For each of the following euphemisms, name at least one common but "less pleasant" word.

   Example
   memorial park: graveyard, cemetery

    1. secret agent 3. intoxicated 5. perspire
    2. fib   4. tavern   6. police officer

3. For each of the following common terms see how many euphemisms you can think of which have a more pleasant sound.

    1. guts 3. beggar 5. underwear 7. skinny
    2. to die 4. insane 6. jail   8. corpse

Labels That "Purr"

To be effective, advertisers must understand human nature. They must be able to describe their product or service in "purr" words that will appeal to their intended customers. The names of many products are carefully chosen to attract a particular segment of the population. The manufacturer prefers a name which is a natural "purr" for men or for women, or for executives or construction workers, and so forth.

Another technique that advertisers use to "purr up" their products is the size marking on the labels. This is particularly true of such items as soap and toothpaste, which do not come in "small" sizes—only "large," "extra large," "super large," "giant," "family size," "jumbo size," or "large economy size."

Obviously, advertisers rarely admit to any shortcomings in their products. They try to build up their products' strengths and perhaps inexpensiveness. Instead of "cheap," they call their products "bargains" that can save you money.

Practice 3. Discussion

1. Some products are given masculine-sounding brand names to appeal particularly to men and boys. What are some of these products? Why do these names appeal to men?
2. Some products are aimed specifically toward the female buyer; their brand names have a feminine sound. What are some of these products? Why do these names appeal to women?
3. The intended use and effectiveness of some products and services is suggested by their names. List a few of these, and discuss their particular appeal.

Slogans, Repetition, Glittering Generalities, and Name-Calling

Listen to a few ads on radio or TV this evening. Notice the number of times the name of the product is repeated. Pay attention to the simple slogans and catchwords repeated over and over. Why is repetition an effective persuader?

Words and phrases which can mean different things to different people are sometimes called *glittering generalities*. They are one of the most subtle propaganda devices. A candidate claims that he/she stands for "social justice and equality of opportunity." A promoter calls for a "clean environment." We all want social justice and a clean environment. But we need to ask, "How do these people propose to bring about social justice or to fight pollution? What are some costs and how will they affect me?"

The glittering generality is used to give a person, an idea, a cause, or a product a good name. Using words to give someone or something a bad name is the propaganda device known as *name-calling*.

Suppose, for instance, that the premier calls for an increase in spending for programs to protect consumers. Opponents label the proposal "reckless spending" and "anti-business." Others who want an even stronger program describe the plan as "penny-pinching." Other common name-calling terms are "socialistic," "reactionary," "radical," and "undemocratic." Such labels may be accurate, but you need to look for evidence. For example, what basis is there for calling a candidate "anti-labor" or tagging a proposal as "inflationary."

Practice 4. Discussion

1. At times in advertising, a product name or slogan is repeated so often that it becomes irritating. Yet the advertiser finds this technique effective. How would you explain this discrepancy?
2. A city council announces plans for a new public facility (swimming pool, skating rink, or other). Suggest some glittering generalities that might be used to "sell" the plan to the voters. What name-calling terms might opponents use to defeat the plan?

Bandwagon, Plain Folks, and Testimonials

Skilful persuaders appeal to the very human desires to be accepted and to be recognized. The *bandwagon* technique suggests that "Everyone is doing it. Why not you?" What young person hasn't used this trick: "But, Mom, everyone else is doing it!" A political candidate uses a favorable public opinion poll to show that voters are running to jump on his/her bandwagon. A person circulating a petition spends more time telling how many other citizens have signed than in explaining the merits of the petition. **197**

In the *plain folks* technique, persuaders link themselves or their product with the common people. "Elect me. I'm just one of you folks." During election campaigns many politicians walk along the street and shake hands with passers-by. This is a use of the *plain folks* technique.

The *testimonial* is the endorsement of a product or idea by some noted person. In effect, the persuader is saying, "This important person is on my side—and you ought to be there too." Many advertisers today make very effective use of testimonials from ordinary people: "I've used this product and found it to be superior to others. You ought to try it too."

Debaters make much use of the testimonial. They point out that their argument has the support of this leading economist, scientist, or statesman. But here are questions the reader or listener should ask: Is the endorser an authority really qualified to express an opinion? Was the testimony paid for? Has the person been quoted fully and correctly?

Practice 5. Discussion

1. When have you used, or been influenced by, the *bandwagon* technique?
2. Imagine that you are an adviser for a candidate in a federal election. In front of which of these audiences would you want your candidate to present a "plain folks" image: Chamber of Commerce; Federation of Agriculture; factory workers? Why?
3. Find examples of testimonials in commercial advertising and in materials prepared by special-interest groups. Do you think the testimonials are used effectively? Explain.

Stacking the Cards

If you wanted to sell your car, would you advertise its defects? If you were running for mayor, would you warn the voters about your weak points? Most advertisers and other persuaders use the device called *card stacking*. It means selecting favorable facts and arguments and omitting, or playing down, unfavorable ones.

In buying goods you can protect yourself to a degree against card stacking by reading the claims made by competitors. Sometimes you can find the good and bad features of particular products by reading consumer magazines.

In election campaigns and in making decisions on public issues you can detect card stacking by actively searching for opposing viewpoints on candidates and issues.

Practice 6. Writing

1. Find an ad for some brand-name product that is rated in a consumer magazine or its annual buying guide. In a paragraph or two, compare the claims in the ad with the product analysis in the buying guide. What card stacking, if any, do you find in the ad?
2. Find an article or editorial that clearly takes a stand on some public issue. In one or more paragraphs, identify some propaganda techniques used by the writer.

Persuading with Facts and Careful Analysis

Sometimes people use persuasion tricks when an appeal to common sense and reason would be more effective. Suppose that parents want to persuade the school board to support an addition to the local high school. A sound approach would be a clear presentation of the facts. Graphs and tables could show present class size, estimated future enrolments, and probable costs. The testimony of experts could show that an up-to-date school program requires new facilities. The presentation could even bring out into the open opposing views—and then try to respond to them.

Such an informative approach calls for organizing the facts and expert opinions around the main issues of the proposal. In this case the issues seem to be (1) the need for added space and new facilities and (2) the cost. Finally, the presentation should be made in an appealing and forceful manner.

Practice 7. Detecting Propaganda

For many years in the United States, a few states have had so-called right-to-work laws. These laws forbid the common practice of *requiring* an employee in a unionized shop to join the union (or be forced to pay union dues). Following is *one* American's *point of view* arguing that such laws should *not* be repealed.

Find examples of the persuasion techniques you've studied in this FOCUS lesson. Divide a sheet of paper into six "boxes," labelling them with the following terms: Glittering Generality, Name-Calling, Testimonial, Bandwagon, Plain Folks, Card Stacking. **199**

Then in the appropriate box, write examples (phrases or sentences) that you find in the paragraphs below. In the box labelled "Card Stacking," explain how the speaker uses that device.

The basic issue in the debate over right-to-work laws is individual freedom. The issue is whether or not a person should be forced to pay tribute to a private association in order to get and hold a job. For two centuries our nation has been dedicated to the idea of individual liberty. Compulsory unionism conflicts with the God-given right of freedom of choice.

Untold thousands of hard-working, common people resent the power of labor barons to shut the factory gates by calling strikes. They want no part in paying dues to unions that in turn make political donations to fuzzy-minded political candidates who jump at the beck and call of the union leaders. With the great Supreme Court Justice Louis D. Brandeis, they say, "We gain nothing by trading the tyranny of capital for the tyranny of labor."

Thousands of workers are joining in our fight to keep right-to-work laws. Come join this worthwhile cause.

13

Ruben

forestudy

Stream of Consciousness—Internal Monologue

Imagine trying to follow your thoughts during a conversation with a group of friends—a conversation that almost, but not quite, holds your attention. What happens? Well, for a few minutes you're there all right, listening to the conversation and even contributing to it. But then, before you realize it, your thoughts wander to something else—your plans for the evening, perhaps, or a remark a friend made sometime back, or something you saw on TV. Then suddenly you pull your mind back to the discussion in progress—until, once again, you find that your thoughts have wandered and that the others are waiting for you to answer a question you didn't even hear.

If you were to write down both the discussion and your wandering thoughts, you'd probably have to use different techniques. For the "discussion" parts of the experience—that is, the remarks each of your friends made and the remarks you contributed to the discussion—you might well use dialogue—the kind used in writing direct quotations. Then every time your thoughts wandered away from the discussion, you'd need to interrupt the dialogue and record your thoughts as you would in a letter or a diary.

In thus recording your thoughts, you are writing INTERNAL MONOLOGUE words you are, in effect, saying to ONE person, namely yourself. The transition from dialogue to monologue and back must necessarily be abrupt because you don't have the time to explain to your reader that you are shifting from one to the other.

Consider for a moment what the INTERNAL MONOLOGUE would be like. Instead of being a clear, orderly, logical presentation of ideas, it's more likely to jump from thought to thought as one idea triggers another.

> How could I forget that book two days in a row? I must have left it on the kitchen table when I took out—oh, no! I forgot to take out the garbage again. Dad is going to shoot me. He gets mad so easily these days; I wonder if things aren't going well at the office for him. He probably should have stayed with that other job. . . .

And so on, rambling, jumping, stumbling from one point to the next, confused perhaps, but nonetheless interesting, at least to the person in whose mind it spins itself out.

Practice 1. Writing

One way to hold your thoughts still for a moment, so that you can look at them and see where they take you, is to write them down.

Have pencil and paper handy. Try to relax as much as possible. Forget your surroundings, your problems, your plans for the weekend. Take your pencil, make a few lazy scrawls across the top line to limber your hand, and then begin to write. Write down whatever comes to mind, even if it is only, "I can't think of anything to say." Force yourself to keep writing, without pause, for ten minutes. If necessary, write the same sentence several times over, until a new thought creeps in. It may be difficult for a few minutes, but keep with it and you'll find that the thoughts start to flow. Don't worry about spelling, handwriting, or anything else.

When the ten minutes are up, look over your notes. What's on your mind? Does the paper tell you anything about your thoughts or your worries?

Authors sometimes portray an event by *telling you the thoughts of a character as he/she lives through an event.* In other words, the author "becomes" that character and records that character's thoughts through INTERNAL MONOLOGUE. In reading the story, you have to be particularly attentive so that you'll know when you are reading dialogue and when you are peering into a character's mind via INTERNAL MONOLOGUE.

In this brief passage from "Ruben," note how quickly the author moves from narration to dialogue to Ruben's thinking out loud.

> Ruben spent all of his waking hours wearing a skullcap. I don't know why. I asked him once but he did not know why either. "Why?" he said, questioning my question. His voice rose in

playful impudence. "Why? Why do we eat food? Why do you sleep? I don't know why." Then turning to a possible third listener in the room, "Why, he asks me."

"Liechtenstein was a very small country. My parents grew potatoes."

Practice 2. Discussion

It's easy to identify the dialogue in the passage above. But:

1. What sentence or sentences constitute straight narration?
2. Where does Ruben's thinking out loud begin? Where does it end? How do you know?

"Ruben in the mirror was really looking very closely at each thread, really seeing it with his eyes not just his fingers."

Ruben

Lesley Choyce

The first room to clean was Ruben's. My bucket rolled into the room, through the doorway like a poorly controlled bumping car.

"Hello, is that you?" Ruben said this to everyone who walked in. It made you feel expected, half recognized. Ruben, like the other four men in this wing of the building, was blind.

"Yeh, it's me." No one ever actually said their name. That would have betrayed faith in Ruben. Instead, he would recognize your voice and continue the game.

"You, you are the young man who comes to mop the floor?" It was both a question and an answer. Ruben preferred not to know my real name it seemed. I was just the young man who mops the floor.

He always smiled when he talked. It helped to keep the verbal volley going. "You have not been in here yet today? I thought I saw you here once already. Perhaps that was yesterday. I don't know." He'd pause and smile like he was leading me into some new territory. "Are you sure it was not today you were here?"

"Nope, Ruben, musta been yesterday. How are you today?" It was incredible the way I could keep asking that question over and over to dozens of people every day, people who were in pain, some were dying. All would provide me with very real answers, not like the outside world where the question elicits a response of no value.

"Ehhhh," he would begin, the sound falling slowly out of his mouth like a kitchen faucet turned slowly on. The hands began to move, creating a portrait in the air in front of him. How he felt. "Eh," he continued, smiling the buoyant unattached

From CHEZZETCOOK by Lesley Choyce. Reprinted by permission of Wooden Anchor Press.

203

smile that only a blind man can make. The smile was far outside of himself, in a visible world that was not his own. He had no part in it. The smile could well belong to someone else as far as Ruben was concerned. He claimed no responsibility for it. "I am feeling. I am feeling. How am I feeling?" It was important for him to establish himself with the question. I would lean on my mop handle patiently, looking into the mirror that framed Ruben and me like we were the characters in a Norman Rockwell painting. I smiled into the mirror, I could make weird faces into it if I liked. Ruben wouldn't notice. I took strange pleasure knowing I could do a number of things— yawn, wave my hands, suppress a belch —without Ruben being concerned why. Ruben too seemed to be smiling right into the mirror, completing our picture. Like it was a joke. He always looked like he could see; acted like he enjoyed sitting in front of the mirror. Shalom Aleichem[1], he seemed to say, the joke is on you, world. I am only pretending to be blind.

But he was blind. "How do I feel? You are asking me how I am feeling?" This topic of conversation went a long way. Even just the question. "I am feeling (pause) no worse, no better. I have been this way for, eh, years. I cannot see. I can do nothing." He holds up his hands to show me that he is doing nothing. The hands look enormous in the mirror. "With these hands I have made coats. I stitched and sewed. I put lapels and collars on many coats in the city. Now these hands do nothing. I cannot see, my eyes are old."

By now the real stories had begun. I could begin to mop the floor at this point but often lingered a long while before

working. No more questions were necessary. He would speak for perhaps a half hour, all in response to the how-are-you question. It was the only question that anyone would ever ask him during the day. This was part of his art; to learn how to make good out of that one question. He knew how to fill the listener with as much of his life as possible. It was important perhaps for his audience to know that the way he felt today was the end result of many years. "It is not the way you feel today," he had once explained to me, "It is the way you feel about your life."

"These hands," again holding them up for the world to see the two large boney white hands, "these hands have sewed on over four hundred thousand collars. Collars and lapels. Lapels for ladies' coats and dresses. Ladies' dresses don't have no more lapels. I don't know. They did when I worked. I worked for Mr. Rothman for fifty years. 'Ruben,' he said to me, 'You have sewed on over four hundred thousand of these things. You have worked for me for many good years. You are the best person we have.' I felt very important. I felt good. I had come over on the boat you know. From Liechtenstein."

He said the "cht" in Liechtenstein like he was clearing his throat. I found that very interesting. It was a sound we didn't use anymore.

"Liechtenstein," I asked, "where's that?" I wasn't looking at him. I was looking out the window at a robin pulling at a worm in the ground. I could do that in his presence. It's not that I wasn't interested. But when I didn't pay too close attention to him, he could speak at his own pace, rather than be pressured into confusion as I had seen the nurses do to him.

"Hello Ruben," they'd say to him. "How

1. *Shalom Aleichem:* a Jewish expression, meaning "peace be with you."

205

are you, Ruben?" The needle would be in his arm and the woman gone before Ruben had a chance to start, "Ehh...Who is that? Is that you?" But the needle had already been put back on the tray and the nurse was way down the hall. If I happened to be in the hall to catch the scene, I would have heard Ruben go on, "I don't know who that was. She didn't answer my question. She put something in my arm and now she is gone." Ruben spoke to his unseen reflection in the mirror. Ruben could speak quite coherently to himself. I admired him for it. Maybe it was because he was unsure if someone might actually be there to listen. "I don't know who that was," Ruben continued. "I know it was a woman. It smelled like a woman. Did you see who it was? Your eyes must be better than mine." If I was outside of the door, I would lean in and tell him it had been the nurse. I didn't always answer though. Sometimes I would just listen to his speech fade, knowing that an answer was not a necessity but a courtesy. Ruben expected no one to answer. There might not be anyone around.

"Liechtenstein. It was a very small country. I came over on the boat from there. I was a boy, a teenager." He adjusted his skullcap. He sometimes took it down to feel all of the stitches, make sure it was not coming apart. Ruben spent all of his waking hours wearing a skullcap. I don't know why. I asked him once but he did not know why either. "Why?" he said, questioning my question. His voice rose in playful impudence. "Why? Why do we eat food? Why do you sleep? I don't know why." Then turning to a possible third listener in the room, "Why, he asks me."

"Liechtenstein was a very small country. My parents grew potatoes." He shaped the potatoes in front of him with his hands. They grew quite large between Ruben's palms. "It is no longer a country, I think. The Germans. The Russians. I don't know who else. My parents put me on a boat. I was just a boy. 'Shalom Aleichem,' they said. 'Goodbye, go. Too many people want our little country. Get out.' They pushed me up the plank of the boat. I don't know why. They wanted me to leave, I guess."

"When Hanna died, she was only fifty-five." Ruben had switched scenes automatically to a different period of his life. I had learned to understand such erratic transitions. "I didn't know what to do, she was dying. Doctor Ackerman said, 'No, there is nothing you can do. If the fever gets worse take her to the hospital.' I would have stayed home but Hanna said, 'You fool, you go to work. I will be all right.' She showed me she was all right, she walked across the room like this....." Ruben got up and walked along the length of his bed. He was bent over, clutching the bedcovers for support and direction. Then he went back to his chair and sat down. "See," she said, "see how good I am. I am ok." Ruben adjusted the black skullcap. It perched on his bald, boney head like a small blackbird sitting on a large pale egg.

"At work, Moey Bilstein who sat at the machine beside me, asked me, 'Ruben, what if you make love to all of the women who wear coats and dresses to which you have sewn lapels? What then, Ruben?' I told him, 'Moey, so what? So I would have made love to a lot of women. Where would it get me? Would I be the world's greatest lover? No. But I might be the world's greatest garment maker just by sitting here and doing my work. I can use my hands good.' Moey says, 'Oh boy, could you use your hands good on all those women. How many, Ruben, ten thousand, twenty thousand?'

"It would have been more like a hundred and fifty thousand then, but who's counting. I didn't say this to Moey. He was just trying to cheer me up. I worried about Hanna. I ran home, ten blocks, during our twenty minute lunch break. I took my cheese sandwich home with me. I was gonna share it with Ḥanna but Hanna was dead. I called Doctor Ackerman at his office. I didn't know if there was something he could do. I don't understand doctors, I thought maybe some trick, that Hanna would still have a chance. He could do nothing. 'You should have stayed home with her,' Doctor Ackerman told me. I sat down and held Hanna's hand for a long time."

Ruben wiped a tear from one eye, very slowly, as if he was savoring the tear, as if it was a gift from Hanna. He seemed to look at the drop of dampness on his finger, letting it dry there rather than wiping it on his pants.

"It would have been four hundred thousand women by the time I retired. I worked piece work, you know, that's how I know. They paid me by the piece. I liked the old machines the best, they did what you wanted them to do."

I would at this point actually begin to mop the floors, which was my job. I figured I could get away with a half hour in each room. I'd sit for a while and listen to people talk, people like Ruben. They liked to talk. Or I'd lean on my mop handle and daydream, wishing I'd find some girl that night, a girl I had never met yet who would fall in love with me. I was still a kid but I was tired of waiting.

Sometimes I would look at all of the family pictures on a dresser. The nursing home limited the amount of personal possessions a client was allowed to keep in his room. It was easier to clean up when they died. Ruben had no personal belongings except for two pairs of incredibly baggy pants, two white starchy shirts, his skullcap

207

and some underwear. And one metal tin full of cookies under his bed. No pictures of his family.

"Here. Eat one. I can't eat that many." He held the can up in the air as if offering it to God. Instead, I walked over from the window, leaned my mop on the mirror and took one. Some kind of Jewish cookie. I don't know too much about them. It was a good cookie though. "Thanks."

The nurse came in. I jumped and went back to the mop, pushing it under the bed, cleaning a floor that had already been cleaned too often. Every day in fact. I didn't see the need of it. I cleaned it good once a week and the other days I just faked it.

"Who is that? Is that you?" The nurse would of course be already gone.

"Yes, Ruben, it's me. Who did you think it was?" She had a semi-polite, tolerant voice, but a fading one, lost in the noises of the hall.

"I didn't know who I thought it was. I thought it might be her but I didn't know. Did you see who it was?"

I made a point of moving back across the room to be in the place where Ruben thought I was, so my voice would come from where he expected it. I told him who it was. He was pleased, having solved one small mystery of his life.

Ruben removed his skullcap again and studied the seams with his fingers. I watched him in the mirror. Everything as usual was backwards, but I could swear that the Ruben in the mirror was really looking very closely at each thread, really seeing it with his eyes not just his fingers. He was still smiling, almost giggling now. There was a long quiet.

"Are you still there? Is that you, the boy who mops the floor?" He heard me moving my bucket toward the door. "You did a good job," he said. "I wish I could have done it as good as you. Shalom Aleichem. I am glad to see you. But I think you already did the floor today. Or was that yesterday? That's all right with me if you want to do the floor again today . . ."

After saying good-bye several times and shaking his hand, I made a point of banging the mop bucket against the metal door frame to make sure Ruben would know I was gone and not continue talking to me.

follow-up

Discussing "Ruben"

1. What indications are there from the story that Ruben is lonely?
2. What sort of work did Ruben do? How do you think he felt towards his work?

208

3. Ruben says:

   "It is not the way you feel today.

   It is the way you feel about your life."

   Explain in your own words what you feel Ruben means by this statement. Do you agree or disagree?
4. Think about Ruben's past life as revealed in his internal monologues about his parents, his native Liechtenstein, Moey Bilstein and his job, and his wife, Hanna. What sort of life do you think he has led? What aspects of his personality can you spot through these monologues?
5. Do you feel it is important to hold onto past memories? What are some of the ways we can preserve our past?

Word Parts—Clues to Meaning

Chances are that the word *coherently* (page 206) caused you to pause in your reading of "Ruben." Maybe you knew that it means "consistent in structure and thought." But if you didn't, you might still have figured out its meaning from its various parts.

A general knowledge of how words are put together can often help you get at the meaning of an unfamiliar term. One-syllable words, many two-syllable words, and even some three-syllable words consist only of the ROOT—the basic element that gives the word its meaning.

Many words, however, are made up of a PREFIX and a *root*. **Remove** is a good example. Other words are made up of a *root* and a SUFFIX. Example: *downward*. Still other words consist of a *root* and two SUFFIXES. Example: *carefully*. And still other words are made up of all three word parts. Example: *inactivity*.

A PREFIX precedes the *root* and changes the root's meaning somewhat. The following are commonly used prefixes:

1. *com-* (also *con-*): with, together
2. *dis-*: reversal of, opposite of
3. *ex-*: out of, former
4. *in-* (also *im-*, *en-*): in, into
5. *in-* (also *im-*, *ir-*): not
6. *mis-*: badly, wrongly, not
7. *pre-*: before
8. *re-*: back, again
9. *sub-*: under, below
10. *un-*: not

A SUFFIX follows the *root* and makes it possible for the root to function as a noun or a verb or an adjective or an adverb. The following are commonly used suffixes:

1. *-able* (also *-ible*): adjective suffix meaning "capable of, tending to"
2. *-ful*: adjective suffix meaning "characterized by, having the qualities of"
3. *-ion*: noun suffix meaning "act of, process of"
4. *-ity*: noun suffix meaning "state or condition of"
5. *-ive*: adjective suffix meaning "having the nature of"
6. *-ize*: verb suffix meaning "cause to become like"
7. *-ly*: adverb suffix meaning "in a _____ manner"
8. *-ment*: noun suffix meaning "action of, condition resulting from"
9. *-ness*: noun suffix meaning "condition, degree"
10. *-ward*: adverb suffix meaning "in a _____ direction"

Practice 1. Discussion

Use the prefixes and suffixes you've studied in this lesson to figure out the meaning of each word below. Then, in each case, explain how you arrived at that meaning.

1. actually (page 203)
2. unseen (page 206)
3. slowly (page 203)
4. attention (page 205)
5. impudence (page 206)
6. confusion (page 205)
7. retired (page 207)
8. dampness (page 207)
9. backwards (page 208)
10. playful (page 206)

Practice 2. Writing

Eight words appear below. The roots in some of the words may be unfamiliar to you. For you to do:

If the root *is* unfamiliar, look it up in the dictionary.

In each case, using the prefix and/or suffix in the word, explain briefly what the word means.

In each case, explain briefly how you arrived at the meaning you gave.

1. conversation (page 205)
2. question (page 205)
3. transition (page 206)
4. patiently (page 205)
5. incredible (page 207)
6. apart (page 206)
7. reflection (page 206)
8. possessions (page 207)

For at least one of the words, be prepared to read your definition and your explanation aloud. Is there general class agreement that your definition and your explanation are accurate?

Bookshelf

The Mending Man, by David M. Collins. Coach House, 1972. The sensitive story of a young man who learns to become whole in spite of being crippled.

The Stone Angel, by Margaret Laurence. McClelland and Stewart, 1968. A woman decides to live her old age in her own way, in spite of pressures from her daughter to conform to society's expectations.

Trapped, by Betty Banister. Western Producer Prairie Books, 1975. A polio victim tells the story of her struggle to overcome her handicap.

14

Raymond's Run

forestudy

Points of View

If you've read "An Ounce of Cure" and the FORESTUDY with it—page 49—you know that your POINT OF VIEW determines much of what you do and much of what you say.

The same is true for the writer of narrative—the story-teller. The point of view from which he/she decides to tell a story makes all the difference in the world. For instance, the story-teller can stand outside the story and assume a god-like view. In this case, the story-teller sees and knows all. He/she tells you not only what the characters say and do, but also what they think. In adopting this point of view, the story-teller is somewhat like a puppeteer, pulling the strings to make the characters say and act as he/she wants them to. Because the writer/narrator sees and knows all, we say that he/she is telling the story from the OMNISCIENT point of view. Telling a story from the OMNISCIENT point of view permits the writer to control events and so create suspense. So far in this book "Night Drive" (page 11), "Gaston" (page 116), and "The Collecting Team" (page 132) are stories told from the OMNISCIENT point of view.

But suppose that a narrator feels that his/her story will have greater impact if it's told from a *personal* point of view. In this case, the story is told as if seen through the eyes of a person taking part in the action. The narrator, in short, becomes the "I" in the story. Of course, the "I" can tell you what he/she thinks. But no longer can the narrator (the "I") tell you what others are thinking. He/she can tell you only what he/she sees and how the action affects him/her. Of course, you know that the narrator survives whatever happens in the story. Otherwise, there would be no story. When a story has "I" as the narrator, we say that it is written from a first-person PARTICIPANT point of view. So far in this book "An Ounce of Cure" (page 53), "If I Lived Through It" (page 78). "You Need to Go Upstairs" (page 161), "Especially Worthy" (page 181), and "Ruben" (page 203) are examples of stories written from the first-person PARTICIPANT point of view.

Practice 1. Discussion

1. What advantages do you think a writer has in telling his/her story from the OMNISCIENT point of view?
2. What advantages do you think a writer has in telling his/her story from the first-person PARTICIPANT point of view?

"We stand there with this big smile of respect between us." And all because of . . .

Raymond's Run

Toni Cade Bambara

I don't have much work to do around the house like some girls. My mother does that. And I don't have to earn my pocket money . . . . George runs errands for the big boys and sells Christmas cards. And anything else that's got to get done, my father does. All I have to do in life is mind my brother Raymond, which is enough.

Sometimes I slip and say my little brother Raymond. But as any fool can see he's much bigger and he's older too. But a lot of people call him my little brother cause he needs looking after cause he's not quite right. And a lot of smart mouths got lots to say about that too, especially when George was minding him. But now, if anybody has anything to say to Raymond, anything to say about his big head, they have to come by me. And I don't play the dozens or believe in standing around with somebody in my face doing a lot of talking. I much rather

just knock you down and take my chances even if I am a little girl with skinny arms and a squeaky voice, which is how I got the name Squeaky. And if things get too rough, I run. And as anybody can tell you, I'm the fastest thing on two feet.

There is no track meet that I don't win the first place medal. I used to win the 20 m dash when I was a little kid in kindergarten. Nowadays, it's the 50 m dash. And tomorrow I'm subject to run the 400 m relay all by myself and come in first, second, and third. The big kids call me Mercury cause I'm the swiftest thing in the neighborhood. Everybody knows that—except two people who know better, my father and me. He can beat me to Amsterdam Avenue with me having a two fire-hydrant headstart and him running with his hands in his pockets and whistling. But that's private information. Cause can you imagine some thirty-five-year-old man stuffing himself into PAL[1] shorts to race little kids? So as far as everyone's concerned, I'm the fastest and that goes for Gretchen, too, who has put out the tale that she is going to win the first-place medal this year. Ridiculous. In the second place, she's got short legs. In the third place, she's got freckles. In the first place, no one can beat me and that's all there is to it.

I'm standing on the corner admiring the weather and about to take a stroll down Broadway so I can practise my breathing exercises, and I've got Raymond walking on the inside close to the buildings, cause he's subject to fits of fantasy and starts thinking he's a circus per-

1. *PAL:* Police Athletic League

former and that the curb is a tightrope strung high in the air. And sometimes after a rain he likes to step down off his tightrope right into the gutter and slosh around getting his shoes and cuffs wet. Then I get hit when I get home. Or sometimes if you don't watch him he'll dash across traffic to the island in the middle of Broadway and give the pigeons a fit. Then I have to go behind him apologizing to all the old people sitting around trying to get some sun and getting all upset with the pigeons fluttering around them, scattering their newspapers, and upsetting the waxpaper lunches in their laps. So I keep Raymond on the inside of me, and he plays like he's driving a stage coach which is O.K. by me so long as he doesn't run me over or interrupt my breathing exercises, which I have to do on account of I'm serious about my running, and I don't care who knows it.

Now some people like to act like things come easy to them, won't let on that they practise. Not me. I'll high-prance down 34th Street like a rodeo pony to keep my knees strong even if it does get my mother uptight so that she walks ahead like she's not with me, don't know me, is all by herself on a shopping trip, and I am somebody else's crazy child. Now you take Cynthia Procter, for instance. She's just the opposite. If there's a test tomorrow, she'll say something like, "Oh, I guess I'll play handball this afternoon and watch television tonight," just to let you know she ain't thinking about the test. Or like last week when she won the spelling bee for the millionth time, "A good thing you got 'receive,' Squeaky, cause I would have got it wrong. I completely forgot about the spelling bee." And she'll clutch the lace on her blouse like it was a narrow escape. Oh, brother. But of course when I pass her house on my early morning trots around the block, she is practising the scales on the piano over and over and over and over. Then in music class she always lets herself get bumped around so she falls accidently on purpose onto the piano stool and is so surprised to find herself sitting there that she decides just for fun to try out the ole keys. And what do you know—Chopin's waltzes just spring out of her fingertips and she's the most surprised thing in the world. A regular prodigy. I could kill people like that. I stay up all night studying the words for the spelling bee. And you can see me any time of day practising running. I never walk if I can trot, and shame on Raymond if he can't keep up. But of course he does, cause if he hangs back someone's liable to walk up to him and get smart, or take his allowance from him, or ask him where he got that great big pumpkin head. People are so stupid sometimes.

So I'm strolling down Broadway breathing out and breathing in on counts of seven, which is my lucky number, and here comes Gretchen and her sidekicks: Mary Louise, who used to be a friend of mine when she first moved to Harlem from Baltimore and got beat up by everybody till I took up for her on account of her mother and my mother used to sing in the same choir when they were young girls, but people ain't grateful, so now she hangs out with the new girl Gretchen and talks about me like a dog; and Rosie, who is as fat as I am skinny and has a big mouth where Raymond is concerned and is too stupid to know that there is not a big deal of difference between herself and Raymond and that she can't afford to throw stones. So they are steady coming up Broadway and I see right away that it's going to be one of those Dodge City[2] scenes cause the street ain't that big and they're close to the buildings just as we are. First I think I'll step into the candy store and look over the new comics and let them pass. But that's chicken and I've got a reputation to consider. So then I think I'll just walk straight on through them or even over them if necessary. But as they get to me, they slow down. I'm ready to fight, cause like I said I don't feature a whole lot of chit-chat. I much prefer to just knock you down right from the jump and save everybody a lotta precious time.

"You signing up for the May Day races?" smiles Mary Louise, only it's not a smile at all. A dumb question like that doesn't deserve an answer. Besides, there's just me and Gretchen standing there really, so no use wasting my breath talking to shadows.

"I don't think you're going to win this time," says Rosie, trying to signify with her hands on her hips all salty, completely forgetting that I have whupped her behind many times for less salt than that.

"I always win cause I'm the best," I say straight at Gretchen who is, as far as I'm concerned, the only one talking in this ventriloquist-dummy routine. Gretchen smiles, but it's not a smile, and I'm thinking that girls never really smile at each other because they don't know how and don't want to know how and there's probably no one to teach us how, cause grown-up girls don't know either. Then they all look at Raymond who has just brought his mule team to a standstill. And they're about to see what trouble they can get into through him.

"What grade you in now, Raymond?"

"You got anything to say to my brother, you say it to me, Mary Louise Williams of Raggedy Town, Baltimore."

"What are you, his mother?" sasses Rosie.

"That's right, Fatso. And the next word out of anybody and I'll be *their* mother too." So they just stand there and Gretchen shifts from one leg to the other and so do they. Then Gretchen puts her hands on her hips and is about to say something with her freckle-face self but doesn't. Then she walks around me looking me up and down but keeps walking up Broadway, and her sidekicks follow her. So me and Raymond smile at each other and he says, "Gidyap" to his team and I continue with my breathing exercises, strolling down Broadway toward the ice man on 145th with not a care in the world cause I am Miss Quicksilver herself.

I take my time getting to the park on May Day because the track meet is the last thing on the program. The biggest thing on the program is the May Pole dancing, which I can do without, thank you, even if my mother thinks it's a shame I don't take part and act like a girl for a change. You'd think my mother'd be grateful not to have to make me a white organdy dress with a big satin sash and buy me new white baby-doll shoes that can't be taken out of the box till the big day. You'd think she'd be glad her daughter ain't out there prancing around a May Pole getting the new clothes all dirty and sweaty and trying to act like a fairy or a flower or whatever you're sup-

2. *Dodge City:* a frontier town in southwest Kansas often depicted in Western movies

posed to be when you should be trying to be yourself, whatever that is, which is, as far as I am concerned, a poor Black girl who really can't afford to buy shoes and a new dress you only wear once in a lifetime cause it won't fit next year.

I was once a strawberry in a Hansel and Gretel pageant when I was in nursery school and didn't have no better sense than to dance on tiptoe with my arms in a circle over my head doing umbrella steps and being a perfect fool just **217** so my mother and father could come dressed up and clap. You'd think they'd know better than to encourage that kind of nonsense. I am not a strawberry. I do not dance on my toes. I run. That is what I am all about. So I always come late to the May Day program, just in time to get my number pinned on and lay in the grass till they announce the 50 m dash.

I put Raymond in the little swings, which is a tight squeeze this year and will be impossible next year. Then I look around for Mr. Pearson, who pins the numbers on. I'm really looking for Gretchen if you want to know the truth, but she's not around. The park is jampacked. Parents in hats and corsages and breast-pocket handkerchiefs peeking up. Kids in white dresses and light-blue suits. The parkees unfolding chairs and chasing the rowdy kids from Lenox[3] as if they had no right to be there. The big guys with their caps on backwards, leaning against the fence swirling the basketballs on the tips of their fingers, waiting for all these crazy people to clear out of the park so they can play. Most of the kids in my class are carrying brass drums and glockenspiels[4] and flutes. You'd think they'd put in a few bongos or something for real like that.

Then here comes Mr. Pearson with his clipboard and his cards and pencils and whistles and safety pins and fifty million other things he's always dropping all over the place with his clumsy self. He sticks out in a crowd because he's on stilts. We used to call him Jack and the Beanstalk to get him mad. But I'm the only one that can outrun him and get away, and I'm too grown for that silliness now.

"Well, Squeaky," he says, checking my name off the list and handing me number seven and two pins. And I'm thinking he's got no right to call me Squeaky, if I can't call him Beanstalk.

"Hazel Elizabeth Deborah Parker," I correct him and tell him to write it down on his board.

"Well, Hazel Elizabeth Deborah Parker, going to give someone else a break this year?" I squint at him real hard to see if he is seriously thinking I should lose the race on purpose just to give someone else a break. "Only six girls running this time," he continues, shaking his head sadly like it's my fault all of New York didn't turn out in sneakers. "That new girl should give you a run for your money." He looks around the park for Gretchen like a periscope in a submarine movie. "Wouldn't it be a nice gesture if you were . . . to ahhh . . . "

I give him such a look he couldn't finish putting that idea into words. Grownups got a lot of nerve sometimes. I pin number seven to myself and stomp away, I'm so burnt. And I go straight for the track and stretch out on the grass while the band winds up with "Oh, the Monkey Wrapped His Tail Around the Flagpole," which my teacher calls by some other name. The man on the loudspeaker is calling everyone over to the track and I'm on my back looking at the sky, trying to pretend I'm in the country, but I can't, because even grass in the city feels hard as sidewalk, and there's just no pretending you are anywhere but in a "concrete jungle" as my grandfather says.

3. *Lenox:* one of the principal streets in Harlem

4. *glockenspiels* (glŏk′ ən spēlz′): a set of steel bars mounted in a frame and struck with hammers, used by marching bands

The 20 m dash takes all of two minutes cause most of the little kids don't know no better than to run off the track or run the wrong way or run smack into the fence and fall down and cry. One little kid, though, has got the good sense to run straight for the white ribbon up ahead so he wins. Then the second-graders line up for the 30 m dash and I don't even bother to turn my head to watch cause Raphael Perez always wins. He wins before he even begins by psyching the runners, telling them they're going to trip on their shoelaces and fall on their faces or lose their shorts or something, which he doesn't really have to do since he is very fast, almost as fast as I am. After that is the 40 m dash which I use to run when I was in first grade. Raymond is hollering from the swings cause he knows I'm about to do my thing cause the man on the loudspeaker has just announced the 50 m dash, although he might just as well be giving a recipe for angel food cake cause you can hardly make out what he's sayin for the static. I get up and slip off my sweat pants and then I see Gretchen standing at the starting line, kicking her legs out like a pro. Then as I get into place I see that ole Raymond is on line on the other side of the fence, bending down with his fingers on the ground just like he knew what he was doing. I was going to yell at him but then I didn't. It burns up your energy to holler.

Every time, just before I take off in a race, I always feel like I'm in a dream, the kind of dream you have when you're sick with fever and feel all hot and weightless. I dream I'm flying over a sandy beach in the early morning sun, kissing the leaves of the trees as I fly by. And there's always the smell of apples, just like in the country when I was little and used to think I was a choo-choo train, running through the fields of corn and chugging up the hill to the orchard. And all the time I'm dreaming this, I get lighter and lighter until I'm flying over the beach again, getting blown through the sky like a feather that weighs nothing at all. But once I spread my fingers in the dirt and crouch over the Get on Your Mark, the dream goes and I am solid again and am telling myself, Squeaky, you must win, you must win, you are the fastest thing in the world, you can even beat your father up Amsterdam if you really try. And then I feel my weight coming back just behind my knees then down to my feet then into the earth and the pistol shot explodes in my blood and I am off and weightless again, flying past the other runners, my arms pumping up and down and the whole world is quiet except for the crunch as I zoom over the gravel in the track. I glance to my left and there is no one. To the right, a blurred Gretchen, who's got her chin jutting out as if it would win the race all by itself. And on the other side of the fence is Raymond with his arms down to his side and the palms tucked up behind him, running in his very own style, and it's the first time I ever saw that and I almost stop to watch my brother Raymond on his first run. But the white ribbon is bouncing toward me and I tear past it, racing into the distance till my feet with a mind of their own start digging up footfuls of dirt and brake me short. Then all the kids standing on the side pile on me, banging me on the back and slapping my head with their May Day programs, for I have won again and everybody on 151st Street can walk tall for another year.

"In first place ... " the man on the loudspeaker is clear as a bell now. But then he pauses and the loudspeaker starts to whine. Then static. And I lean down to catch my breath and here comes Gretchen walking back, for she's over-shot the finish line too, huffing and puffing with her hands on her hips taking it slow, breathing in steady time like a real pro and I sort of like her a little for the first time. "In first place ... " and then three or four voices get all mixed up on the loudspeaker and I dig my sneaker into the grass and stare at Gretchen who's staring back, we both wondering just who did win. I can hear old Beanstalk arguing with the man on the loudspeaker and then a few others running their mouths about what the stopwatches say. Then I hear Raymond yanking at the fence to call me and I wave to shush him, but he keeps rattling the fence like a gorilla in a cage like in them gorilla movies, but then like a dancer or something he starts climbing up nice and easy but very fast. And it occurs to me, watching how smoothly he climbs hand over hand and remembering how he looked running with his arms down to his side and with the wind pulling his mouth back and his teeth showing and all, it occurred to me that Raymond would make a very fine runner. Doesn't he always keep up with me on my trots? And he surely knows how to breathe in counts of seven cause he's always doing it at the dinner table, which drives my brother George up the wall. And I'm smiling to beat the band cause if I've lost this race, or if me and Gretchen tied, or even if I've won, I can always retire as a runner and begin a whole new career as a coach with Raymond as my champion. After all, with a little more study I can beat Cynthia and her phony self at the spelling bee. And if I bugged my mother, I could get piano lessons and become a star. And I have a big rep as the baddest thing around. And I've got a roomful of ribbons and medals and awards. But what has Raymond got to call his own?

So I stand there with my new plans, laughing out loud by this time as Raymond jumps down from the fence and runs over with his teeth showing and his arms down to the side, which no one before him has quite mastered as a running style. And by the time he comes over I'm jumping up and down so glad to see him—my brother Raymond, a great runner in the family tradition. But of course everyone thinks I'm jumping up and down because the men on the loud-speaker have finally gotten themselves together and compared notes and are an-nouncing "In first place—Miss Hazel Elizabeth Deborah Parker." (Dig that.) "In second place—Miss Gretchen P. Lew-is." And I look over at Gretchen wonder-ing what the "P" stands for. And I smile. Cause she's good, no doubt about it. May-be she'd like to help me coach Raymond; she obviously is serious about running, as any fool can see. And she nods to con-gratulate me and then she smiles. And I smile. We stand there with this big smile of respect between us. It's about as real a smile as girls can do for each other, con-sidering we don't practice real smiling every day, you know, cause maybe we too busy being flowers or fairies or strawber-ries instead of something honest and worthy of respect ... you know ... like being people.

follow-up

Discussing "Raymond's Run"

1. By the end of the story how has the relationship between Squeaky and Raymond changed? Why has it changed?
2. What's your impression of Squeaky?
3. Was "Raymond's Run" written from the omniscient point of view or from the first-person participant point of view? Why, do you think, did Toni Cade Bambara take the point of view she did take?

Punctuating Informal Writing

Toni Cade Bambara begins her story in a friendly, informal way:

> I don't have much work to do around the house like some girls. My mother does that. And I don't have to earn my pocket money. . . .

Had she wanted to be formal, Bambara might have started this way:

> Unlike most small young women my age, I do not have an abundance of employment opportunities at home. My mother efficiently handles all chores that require attention. In addition, it appears that I do not have to acquire funds by actively seeking employment outside the house.

Practice 1. Discussion

1. Why, do you think, did the author choose to write her story informally rather than formally?
2. What specific punctuation mark do you see frequently in the informal version above?

The Apostrophe for Contraction: A Review

In informal writing and in most speech, we tend to run our words together. It's not that we are being careless; it's just that we try to sound friendly and natural. Here are a few examples from "Raymond's Run":

1. Or sometimes if you don't watch him he'll dash across traffic to the island in the middle of Broadway. . . .
2. So as far as everyone's concerned, I'm the fastest. . . .
3. You'd think she'd be glad her daughter ain't out there prancing around a May Pole. . . .

Practice 2. Discussion

1. In the three sentences above, which words are run together or *contracted*.
2. In each case, what are the two original words that were run together?
3. In each case, which letter or letters does the apostrophe replace?

When words are run together, or *contracted*, the apostrophe (') is placed where the letters were left out. For example, *do* plus *not* becomes don't; *would* plus *have* becomes *would've*.

Practice 3. Writing

Punctuate the following paragraph of informal writing by inserting apostrophes where needed:

> "Sos your old man," hed yell at me every time hed think I was getting the better of him. He wouldve been nicer to me as a kid, but Im sure now that itd been different if hed not been thinking Id always try to get the best of him.

Comma for Direct Address

Besides using contractions to advantage, informal writing frequently uses direct address. Here are a few examples from "Raymond's Run":

1. What grade you in now, *Raymond?*
2. That's right, *Fatso.*

222

3. Well, *Hazel Elizabeth Deborah Parker*, going to give someone else a break this year?

Practice 4. Discussion

1. If *Raymond*, *Fatso*, and *Hazel . . . Parker*, are examples of *direct address*, what, in your own words, is a good definition of *direct address*?
2. When the direct address occurs in the middle of the sentence, how do you show it? When it occurs at the end of a sentence, how do you show it? When it occurs at the beginning of a sentence?

Practice 5. Writing

Write three sentences in which you use direct address. In one sentence, have the direct address appear at the beginning of the sentence. In the second sentence, have the direct address appear in the middle. In the third sentence, the direct address should appear at the end. Be prepared to write at least one of your sentences on the chalkboard.

Quotation Marks for Dialogue: A Review

Toni Cade Bambara enlivens her informal telling of a story with dialogue—the exact words her characters used. Examples:

1 "What grade you in now, Raymond?"
2 "You got anything to say to my brother, you say it
3 to me, Mary Louise Williams of Raggedy Town, Baltimore."
4 "What are you, his mother?" sasses Rosie.
5 "That's right, Fatso. And the next word out of
6 anybody and I'll be *their* mother too."

Practice 6. Discussion

1. What punctuation marks set off the exact words the characters use?
2. In lines 1 and 4, why do the quotation marks follow the question marks?
3. In line 4, why isn't "sasses" capitalized?
4. How do writers let you know when a "new" character speaks?

Practice 7. Writing

See whether you can punctuate and paragraph the following dialogue:

Where are you going his mother asked. Out he said. Thats not enough. I want to know exactly where youre going. Down to the arcade he said insolently. Oh no youre not she said. You clean out the garage. If Id told you I was going to the library would youve let me go. Im not answering that one.

Using the Dash for Emphasis

Toward the end of "Raymond's Run," Bambara wrote:

And by the time he comes over I'm jumping up and down so glad to see him—my brother Raymond, a great runner in the family tradition.

To emphasize Hazel's excitement over seeing her brother, the author used a dash to set off that part of the sentence explaining the reason for the excitement. Later when the winning runners are announced, the dash appears again—for emphasis:

1. In first place—Miss Hazel Elizabeth Deborah Parker.
2. In second place—Miss Gretchen P. Lewis.

Practice 8. Writing

Insert dashes in each of the following sentences where you feel they are appropriate.

1. And there she stood my Aunt Agnes carrying a birdcage with a parrot.
2. And the winning marathon dance couple Phyllis and Jack Kirkbridge.
3. All right, class, I want you to are you listening to me open your text to page 12.
4. Tim brought home his newest purchase a 1937 Hudson.

Summary

"Raymond's Run" is an entertaining story, mostly because of its informal style. In this lesson, you have studied only one way in which Toni Cade Bambara achieved an informal style—that is, through punctuation. Contractions, direct address, dialog, and the use of dashes—all contributed to the story's informal conversational style.

Practice 9. Writing

By looking into your past, recall an occasion that might make an interesting story—a short, short, short story. Tell the story in the informal conversational way that Toni Cade Bambara did. Use contractions, direct address, dialogue, and dashes for emphasis. Be sure that you punctuate your story according to the conventions you have reviewed in this lesson.

Bookshelf

It Takes All Kinds, by Florence Means. Houghton, 1964. Florrie's family is beset by a great many serious problems, including mental retardation. But she works hard to overcome them all.

The Learning Tree, by Gordon Parks. Fawcett, 1974 (originally, 1963). A novel, based on Parks' experiences, about a young man's confrontations with racial prejudice.

The Skating Rink, by Mildred Lee. Dell, 1970, (originally 1969). A young man, ostracized because he stutters, finds a friend in the owner of a new skating rink and gradually finds that his life has become completely changed.

The Summer of the Swans, by Betsy Byars. Viking, 1970. Her retarded brother, Charlie, is mostly a nuisance for Sara until he is lost one day. Then Sara begins to realize that she has been somewhat self-centred.

15

Munro's First Cable After Dieppe

Comrades

Richard Hovey

Comrades, pour the wine to-night,
  For the parting is with dawn.
Oh, the clink of cups together,
  With the daylight coming on!
    Greet the morn
    With a double horn,
When strong men drink together!

Comrades, gird your swords to-night,
  For the battle is with dawn.
Oh, the clash of shields together,   10
  With the daylight coming on!
    Greet the foe
    And lay him low,
When strong men fight together.

Comrades, watch the tides to-night,
  For the sailing is with dawn.
Oh, to face the spray together,
  With the tempest coming on!
    Greet the sea
    With a shout of glee,   20
When strong men roam together.

Comrades, give a cheer to-night,
  For the dying is with dawn.
Oh, to meet the stars together,
  With the silence coming on!
    Greet the end
    As a friend a friend,
When strong men die together.

forestudy

There Transformations

As you know, the basic S-V pattern of the English sentence can be changed—TRANSFORMED—in several ways. (See page 166). One of the most common TRANSFORMATIONS—one that you see and use every day—is the *there* transformation.

In "Munro's First Cable After Dieppe," Ross Munro could have written:

> A furious attack was made by German E-boats...

> The lashing fire of machine gunning came from other Nazi aircraft...

Instead, he wrote:

> There was a furious attack by German E-boats...

> ...there was the spine-chilling experience of a dive-bombing attack by seven Stukas...

In short, what Ross Munro did was to use a THERE TRANSFORMATION to make his description more dramatic. To say "There was a furious attack..." and "...there was the spine-chilling experience..." helps put emphasis on the words *attack* and *spine-chilling experience*.

As pointed out above, you frequently use *there* transformations—perhaps like these:

Basic Sentence	*There transformation*
1. Two guys *unloaded* the truck.	1. There *were* two guys *unloading* the truck.
2. As usual John *sat* in the last row.	2. There *was* John *sitting* as usual in the last row.
3. Other clues *existed*.	3. There *were* other clues.

Practice 1. Discussion
1. Note that in each of the basic sentences the underlined word is a verb. What happens to the verb when the sentence is rephrased as a *there* transformation?

2. Why, in the third sentence, isn't the verb *existed* needed in the *there*-transformed sentence?

Practice 2. Discussion
Transform each sentence below so that it starts with *there*.

1. Three shadowy figures lurked in the dark cellar.
2. Only 50 000 sports fans showed up at the coliseum for the big game.
3. A few informers knew the whereabouts of the hostage.
4. Two tightrope-walkers lost their balance.
5. One metre of snow covers the ski trails.

In reading "Munro's First Cable After Dieppe," you'll have a chance to see the writer use *there* transformations.

from
Munro's First Cable After Dieppe

Ross Munro

The time: August 19, 1942. The Second Canadian Division in its first experience in action attacked the German forces on the coast of France.

The place: Dieppe

The result: Complete failure owing to the strength of the German defences and the inadequate artillery and aerial bombardment from the Allied side. Of the 4 963 Canadian soldiers embarked, 3 367 became casualties.

With the Canadian raiding force at

Dieppe, Aug. 19—For eight raging hours, under intense Nazi fire from dawn into a sweltering afternoon, I watched Canadian troops fight the blazing, bloody battle of Dieppe.

I saw them go through this biggest of the war's raiding operations in wild scenes that crowded helter-skelter one upon another in crazy sequence.

There was a furious attack by German E-boats while the Canadians moved in on Dieppe's beaches, landing by dawn's half-light.

When the Canadian battalions stormed

From The Canadian Press (CP), August 19, 1942.

through the flashing inferno of Nazi defences, belching guns of huge tanks rolling into the fight, I spent the grimmest 20 minutes of my life with one unit when a rain of German machine-gun fire wounded half the men in our boat and only a miracle saved us from annihilation.

A few hours later there was the spine-chilling experience of a dive-bombing attack by seven Stukas, the dreaded Nazi aircraft that spotted out the small assault landing craft waiting off-shore to re-embark the fighting men.

Our boat was thrown about like a toy by their seven screeching bombs that plunged into the water around us and exploded in gigantic cascades.

There was the lashing fire of machine-gunning from other Nazi aircraft and the thunder of anti-aircraft fire that sent them hustling off.

Over our heads in the blue, cloud-flecked French sky were fought the greatest air engagements since the Battle of Britain, dogfights carried on to the dizzy accompaniment of planes exploding in the air, diving down flaming, some plummeting into the sea from thousands of metres.

Hour after hour guns of the supporting warships growled salvos at targets ashore where by now our tanks also were in violent action.

Unearthly noises rumbled up and down the French coast, shrouded for kilometres in smoke screens covering the fleet.

There was heroism at sea and in the skies in those hours but the hell-spot was ashore, where the Canadians fought at close quarters with the Nazis. They fought to the end, where they had to, and showed courage and daring. They attacked the Dieppe arsenal of the coastal defence. They left Dieppe silent and afire, its ruins and its dead under a shroud of smoke.

follow-up

Discussing "Munro's First Cable After Dieppe"

1. In this introductory section Ross Munro provides you with an eye-witness account of what he experienced at Dieppe with the Canadian troops attempting to land there. Would you say his point of view is that of a participant or of a reporter? Why?
2. What do you understand by the phrase "a shroud of smoke"?
3. What organization—what order—do you find in the way Munro describes the battle of Dieppe?
4. What feelings—what reaction—do you have as a result of reading this short account? Do you suppose it's the feeling Ross Munro hoped you would have? Why? Why not?

Subject-Verb Agreement

Ross Munro, war correspondent, wanted to make his eye-witness account of Dieppe vivid and memorable for his readers. One way in which he did so was to point out incredible sights:

> Our boat was thrown about like a toy by their seven screeching bombs that plunged into the water around us and exploded in gigantic cascades.

> Over our heads in the blue, cloud-flecked French sky were fought the greatest air engagements since the Battle of Britain, dogfights carried on to the dizzy accompaniment of planes exploding in the air, diving down flaming, some plummetting into the sea from thousands of metres.

To write like Ross Munro a person needs years of disciplined training in the techniques of close observation. To write sentences like the above would take, among other things, knowledge of subject-verb agreement.

There Sentences

> There were tanks that only just made the beach before being knocked out.
> There was another—and more human—litter.
> There was a dog still on the beach.
> There were torn pistol belts and canvas water buckets.

Practice 1. Discussion
All four of the above sentences begin with *there* . Yet how is it that the first and the fourth sentences use the verb *were,* while the second and the third use *was*?

When a sentence begins with *there* (and *here*), the subject of the sentence *follows* the verb, and the verb agrees with that subject, NOT with *there.* In the first sentence, *were* agrees with the plural subject *tanks*; in the fourth, *were* agrees with the plural subject *belts* and *buckets*. However, in the second sentence, *was* agrees with the singular subject *litter*; in the third, *was* agrees with the singular subject *dog*.

Practice 2. Discussion

Read each of the following sentences, supplying *is*, *are*, *was*, or *were*, whichever is appropriate.

1. There _____ a few things I've been meaning to tell you.
2. There _____ a reason for the way things happen.
3. There _____ a cute puppy and a spunky cat in the pet store window.
4. There _____ damage done to the downstairs radiator during the storm.
5. There _____ one of many reasons why I don't want you to go.

Practice 3. Writing

Write five original sentences that begin with these expressions: "There is . . . ," "There are . . . ," There was . . . ," and "There were. . . ." Be sure to supply subjects that agree with your verbs. Be prepared to read at least one of your sentences.

Inverted Sentences

You can call "there sentences" INVERTED sentences, because the subject and verb "switch" places:

Examples

  S   V

Tanks were there. (regular order)

          V   S

There were tanks. (inverted order)

However, not all inverted sentences use "there." Note the example from "Munro's First Cable After Dieppe":

                                         V

Over our heads in the blue, cloud-flecked French sky were fought

               S

the greatest air engagements since the Battle of Britain. . . .

The verb *were* agrees with its plural subject *engagements*. Notice that *heads* is the object of the preposition *over*, *not the subject* of the sentence.

Practice 4. Discussion

In the following sentences, supply present-tense verbs that agree with their subjects.

1. Near the entrance to the theatre _____ four gentlemen in tuxedos.

2. Apart from the rest of the crowd's angry faces _____ a gentle smile.
3. With unprecedented force and violence _____ the tornado.
4. Emerging from the back of the auditorium _____ the guest speaker and her escort.

Separated Subjects and Verbs

Sometimes subjects and verbs become separated by phrases, even clauses. Examine this sentence:

<pre>
       S   LV
   Two of the most dominant items in the beach refuse were
     SC (noun)   SC (noun)
   cigarettes and writing paper.
</pre>

Practice 5. Discussion

For each of the following sentences, locate the subject. Next, see if it agrees with its verb. If it doesn't, correct the verb so that it does agree with its subject.

1. One of the major problems that this country faces with respect to local elections are the finances it takes to support the candidate.
2. Several of the vehicles wrecked on the freeway has received only minor damage.
3. Only one of the four candidates has the qualifications for success.
4. The lemon factory with all its unpleasant odors fill the country's shelves with fine fruit.

Plural Subjects, Singular in Meaning

Sometimes a subject can be plural in form but singular in meaning. For instance, note this sentence:

<pre>
                         S   LV   LV SC (noun)
   The awful <i>waste and destruction</i> of war...has always been one of
   its outstanding features to those who are in it.
</pre>

The writer considers *waste* and *destruction* to mean the same thing, not two separate things.

Practice 6. Discussion

Study each of the following pairs of items carefully. Determine whether the pair is singular in meaning or plural.

1. bread and butter
2. butter and bread
3. water and power
4. gas and electricity
5. love and honor
6. peanuts and popcorn
7. nuts and bolts
8. cream and sugar

Practice 7. Writing

Select five of the pairs of items in Practice 6. Make each the subject of an original sentence. Remember to make the verb agree with the intent of the subject. Use all present-tense verbs. Be prepared to read at least one of your sentences aloud for class reaction.

Bookshelf

And No Birds Sang, by Farley Mowat. McClelland and Stewart, 1979. Mowat's reminiscences of his experiences as a serviceman in World War II.

Assault in Norway, by Thomas Gallagher. Harcourt, 1975. The story of a small band of Norwegian guerrilla fighters, whose raid on a German plant prevented the Germans from developing the atomic bomb during World War II.

Canadiana Scrapbook 1939-45, by Donald Santor. Prentice-Hall, 1979. A pictorial account of individual Canadians' stories of the war years.

"First Blood," by R. J. Childerhose, in *Breakthrough: A Literary Reader,* by Mary Ashworth and L. F. Ashley. McClelland and Stewart, 1972. The story of a young Canadian pilot's first mission at the height of World War II.

focus

From Sentence to Paragraph to Composition

You probably have some strong opinions about the world you live in. For instance, you may get upset at some of the things you find wrong in our society—such as miscarriages of justice or lack of concern about environmental hazards. Or you may have strong feelings in favor of something—such as a specific social program for improving life for the elderly. Sometime you may want or need to express your opinions effectively by composing an argument or explanation. You can easily learn to do so!

From Sentence to Paragraph

First, you start with an opinion sentence that will be the basis for your argument. Here, for example, is an opinion sentence that is critical of adolescents:

> Teenagers are pampered.

Using the statement above as a base, you next generate specific details to add information (see the lesson on generating details—page 145) and so explain your opinion further:

> Teenagers are pampered, with free schooling, with entertainment provided by others, with clothes bought by parents, and with transportation financed by their elders.

The expanded sentence can be analysed on two levels in this way:

> 1. Teenagers are pampered,
>   2. with free schooling,
>   2. with entertainment provided by others,
>   2. with clothes bought by parents,
>   2. and with transportation financed by their elders.

Notice that each added phrase gives an example to explain the base sentence. Each phrase is at the second level because each is related in the same way to the base sentence. Each tells how teenagers are pampered.

Practice 1. Writing

Write an expanded opinion sentence of your own. If you disagree with the view stated in the sample sentence above, you may want to present an opposing opinion—from the teenager's point of view. Or you may want to state an opinion on another subject that you feel strongly about. Follow these steps:

1. Start with a simple sentence, stating your opinion.
2. Using your sentence as a base, add several specific detail-phrases to explain or support your opinion.

Here are some possible opinion sentences that you can choose from or adapt.

> Teenagers are treated like second-class citizens.
> Adults should practise what they preach.
> Teenagers should have more opportunities.
> Many adults live in the past.
> Native North Americans deserve justice.
> Males/Females have it easy in our society.

The next step is to convert the expanded sentence into a paragraph. In this process the base clause becomes the topic sentence (1) of the paragraph, and each detail-phrase becomes a detail sentence (2). In the sample paragraph below, note that words have been added to flesh out the detail sentences:

> (1) Teenagers are pampered. (2) They enjoy, without thought or gratitude, free public schooling. (2) They demand and receive entertainment provided by others. (2) They bleed their parents' pocketbooks for the most fashionable clothes. (2) They obtain costly transportation at their elders' expense.

Practice 2. Writing and Discussion

Write a paragraph, using your opinion sentence as the topic sentence. Then convert your detail-phrases into supporting detail sentences. Compare your paragraph with those your classmates have written. Save your paragraph for use later in this lesson.

From Paragraph to Composition

So far you have seen how a writer can expand a simple sentence into a unified paragraph. The idea in the sentence serves as a core around which layers of meaning are added, forming a full-bodied paragraph.

Now note how that same paragraph can be extended into a full-length composition of explanation or argument. In fact, the level analysis of the paragraph can serve as a basic outline for the unified multi-paragraph composition:

1. Teenagers are pampered.
   2. They enjoy, without thought or gratitude, free public schooling.
   2. They demand and receive entertainment provided by others.
   2. They bleed their parents' pocketbooks for the most fashionable clothes.
   2. They obtain costly transportation at their elders' expense.

Practice 3. Discussion

1. How is the paragraph analysis above similar to the sentence analysis on page 234? How is it different?
2. The four detail (level 2) sentences give specific information about the topic sentence (level 1). Now you are ready to expand the detail-sentences further, adding even more specific information at a third level. Even though you disagree with the statements, see whether you can supply added information by answering the following questions:
   a. What specific examples or details could the writer give to support the first detail-sentence: "They enjoy, without thought or gratitude, free public schooling"?
   b. What specific examples or details could the writer give to support the second detail-sentence: "They demand and receive entertainment provided by others"?
   c. What specific examples or details could the writer give to support the third detail-sentence: "They bleed their parents' pocketbooks for the most fashionable clothes"?
   d. What specific examples or details could the writer give to support the fourth detail-sentence: "They obtain costly transportation at their elders' expense"?

When the new information is added to the level analysis of the paragraph, you have the basic outline for a unified composition of opinion. Even though you may not agree with the ideas expressed, you can see that the outline has a focus and a logical structure. Below is the completed composition outline. Note that the topic sentence of the base paragraph has now become the *central idea* (or thesis) of the full-length composition outline. Also note that the level numbers have been converted to the traditional outline symbols—Roman numerals and letters. How many of the added third-level details correspond to the ones you came up with in answer to the questions (a–d) in Practice 3?

Central idea: Teenagers are pampered.

I. They enjoy, without thought or gratitude, free public schooling.
   A. Their books are given to them free of charge or at a minimal cost.
   B. School buses deliver them to the school door, without costing them a cent.
II. They demand and receive entertainment provided by others.
   A. In many communities youth centres and recreation halls are made available to young people free of charge.
   B. The family TV set is usually taken over by the teenage members of the family.
III. They bleed their parents' pocketbooks for the most fashionable clothes.
   A. Both boys and girls believe that they must wear the latest fashion, regardless of the cost.
   B. Most teenagers will not settle for less than the most expensive brand names on their clothes.
IV. They obtain costly transportation at their elders' expense.
   A. They drive powerful cars, usually furnished by their parents.
   B. They take part of their parents' income to buy gasoline to fuel their high-powered cars.
   C. Because of teenagers' reckless driving, their insurance rates are the highest in the nation, adding a further burden to the family funds.

Practice 4. Writing
   Make an outline for your opinion composition by adding specific third-level details to the paragraph you wrote for Practice 2. **237**

You may first want to make a two-level analysis of your paragraph, as in the sample shown earlier. Then add your third-level details. Finally, convert your three-level analysis into outline form, as in the sample above.

Writing the Composition

You have seen how one simple sentence ("Teenagers are pampered") can be developed into an expanded sentence, then into a paragraph, and then into a full composition outline. The final step in the sequence is to write the completed composition, using the outline as a blueprint.

In writing the completed composition, think of all the outline points (I–IV) and subpoints (lettered) as the composition body, supporting the central idea. Each major point and its details become a separate paragraph. Thus, the sample composition will have four body paragraphs.

The next step is to add an introduction, leading up to and ending with the central idea. This introductory paragraph should help interest the reader in the subject of the composition.

The final step is to add a conclusion. This concluding paragraph helps to "wrap up" the composition by summarizing or echoing the central idea.

Following is the completed sample composition in the right column, with the matching outline points in the left column. Notice that connecting words and phrases have been added to some of the sentences to make the ideas flow smoothly from sentence to sentence and from paragraph to paragraph.

Something for Nothing

Wake up, parents, before it is too late. This country is producing a generation that expects a free ride. Our young people between the ages of twelve and twenty, commonly known as teenagers, are getting out of control because they have come to expect something for nothing. This something-for-nothing attitude can be traced to one basic cause. Teenagers are pampered.

Introduction

Central Idea.
Teenagers are pampered.

Body

I. They enjoy, without thought or gratitude, free public schooling.
   A. Their books are given to them free of charge or at a minimal cost.
   B. School buses deliver them to the school door, without costing them a cent.
II. They demand and receive entertainment provided by others.
   A. Youth centres and recreation halls in most cities are made available to youths free of charge.
   B. The family TV set is usually taken over by the teenage members of the family.
III. They bleed their parents' pocketbooks for the most fashionable clothes.
   A. Both boys and girls believe that they must wear the latest fashions, regardless of the cost.
   B. Most teenagers will not settle for less than the most expensive brand names on their clothes.
IV. They obtain costly transportation at their elders' expense.
   A. They drive powerful cars, usually furnished them by their parents.
   B. They take part of their parents' income for gasoline to fuel their high-powered cars.
   C. Due to reckless driving, their insurance rates are the highest in the nation, adding a further burden to the family funds.

Conclusion

First of all, teenagers enjoy, without thought or gratitude, free public schooling. For example, their books are given to them free of charge or at a minimal cost. In addition, public-supported school buses deliver the students to the school door, without costing them a cent.

Aside from their free education, teenagers demand and receive entertainment provided by others. For this reason, youth centres and recreation halls in many communities are made available to youths free of charge. Then, at home, the family TV set is usually taken over by the teenage members of the family.

When it comes to shopping, teenagers bleed their parents' pocketbooks to buy the most fashionable clothes available. In fact, both boys and girls believe that they must wear the latest fashions, regardless of the cost. Furthermore, most teenagers will not settle for less than the most expensive brand names on their clothes.

Last, but hardly least, teenagers of driving age obtain costly transportation at their elders' expense. Often they drive powerful cars, usually furnished them by their parents. At the same time, part of their parents' income goes to fuel their high-powered cars. In addition, because of reckless teenage driving, their insurance rates are the highest in the nation, adding a further burden on the family funds.

It is understandable that parents want to give their sons and daughters everything "on a silver platter," to make it easy for them. However, if teenagers are to become useful citizens, they must learn to work for themselves, to get "something for *something*." This condition can come about only when parents stop pampering their teenagers.

239

Practice 5. Writing

Write a completed opinion composition based on your outline from Practice 4. Follow the procedure used with the sample composition above. Be prepared to share your finished composition with your classmates.

If you have built an effective argument, with a clear, logical development, you may convince your readers to agree with your ideas.

16

All the Years of Her Life

forestudy

The Power of Words

Maybe you've never stopped to think about it, but words are powerful things. They can influence your attitude and your feelings favorably or unfavorably *because of what they suggest.* People who make their living by using words—authors, politicians, advertising people—well understand that fact. When they want to influence you favorably, they choose words that will arouse pleasant feelings—words that you associate with things you approve of. On the other hand, when they seek to turn your mind against something, they select words that will arouse unpleasant feelings—feelings of anger or scorn or disgust. For example, if someone describes an animal as "a dog of mixed breed," what attitude/feeling does he/she want you to have? But suppose that same speaker describes the animal as "a mangy cur." Do you still have that same attitude/feeling?

Practice 1. Writing/Discussion
Listed below are 14 terms. For each one that creates a favorable reaction or pleasant feeling, write *P* on your paper after the appropriate item number. For each one that creates an unfavorable reaction or unpleasant feeling, write *U*.

1. cancer	8. slim and trim
2. smooth, refreshing taste	9. patriotism
3. home	10. coward
4. velvet	11. moonlight
5. racist	12. brat
6. rat	13. inexpensive
7. spit	14. snake

Compare your responses to those your classmates give. Is there general agreement on each term? If not, how do you account for any differences of opinion?

Practice 2. Discussion

Both Paragraph A and Paragraph B concern the same event. What purpose do you think each writer had in mind?

A

Pushing through a bunch of reporters third-rate wrestler Toe-Hold Kemp bawled, "No comment" and chomped sullenly on a smoldering cigar stump. Waiting in his office was Promotor Jack ("Lips") Jackson, ex-gangster and recent graduate of the federal penitentiary at New Westminster. The two gorillas slapped each other on the back. A mousy little man tiptoed in with some soggy pizza. "Get me a brew," grunted Toe-Hold. Then he lit another stogie, tossed the burning match to the unswept floor, and turned to "Lips."

B

As he entered the building and was surrounded by friends and admirers, Thomas Kemp, longtime favorite of the Westville Athletic Club, waved and smiled and dodged the reporters' questions. After five years in the wrestling circuit, Tom—affectionately known as "Toe-Hold"—entered the office of his capable manager and promoter, Jack Jackson. The two buddies greeted each other warmly. One of Tom's faithful employees brought in a plate of tempting sandwiches. "You know," said Tom, "I'd be eternally in your debt if you could find me something cold to wash these delicious sandwiches down." Then he turned to Jack to discuss a matter of mutual concern.

The impression you get from each paragraph stems from the words used and the details emphasized. Which words and phrases are designed to cause you to react favorably to Tom and Jack? Why? Which words and phrases cause you to react unfavorably? Why?

When, in reading a story, you spot words that appeal to your emotions, you know that the author is seeking to influence you one way or another.

> "Yeah, he's in trouble . . . Yeah, your boy works for me. You'd better come down in a hurry!"

All the Years of Her Life

Morley Callaghan

They were closing the drugstore, and Alfred Higgins, who had just taken off his white jacket, was putting on his coat and getting ready to go home. The little grey-haired man, Sam Carr, who owned the drugstore, was bending down behind the cash register, and when Alfred Higgins passed him he looked up and said softly, "Just a moment, Alfred. One moment before you go."

The soft, confident, quiet way in which Sam Carr spoke made Alfred start to button his coat nervously. He felt sure his face was white. Sam Carr usually said "Good night" brusquely, without looking up. In the six months he had been working in the drugstore Alfred had never heard his employer speak softly like that. His heart began to beat so loud it was hard for him to get his breath. "What is it, Mr. Carr?" he asked.

"Maybe you'd be good enough to take a few things out of your pocket and leave them here before you go," Sam Carr said.

"What things? What are you talking about?"

"You've got a compact and a lipstick and at least two tubes of toothpaste in your pockets, Alfred."

"What do you mean? Do you think I'm crazy?" Alfred blustered. His face got red and he knew he looked fierce with indignation.° But Sam Carr, standing by the door with his blue eyes shining bright behind his glasses and his lips moving underneath his grey mustache, only nodded his head a few times, and then Alfred grew very frightened and he didn't know what to say. Slowly he raised his hand and dipped it into his pocket, and with his eyes never meeting Sam Carr's eyes, he took out a blue compact and two tubes of toothpaste and a lipstick, and he laid them one by one on the counter.

"Petty thieving, eh, Alfred?" Sam Carr said. "And maybe you'd be good enough to tell me how long this has been going on."

"This is the first time I ever took anything."

"So now you think you'll tell me a lie, eh? What kind of a sap do I look like, huh? I don't know what goes on in my own store, eh? I tell you you've been doing this pretty steady," Sam Carr said as

243

he went over and stood behind the cash register.

Ever since Alfred had left school he had been getting into trouble wherever he worked. He lived at home with his mother and father, who was a printer. His two older brothers were married and his sister had got married last year, and it would have been all right for his parents now if Alfred had only been able to keep a job.

While Sam Carr smiled and stroked the side of his face very delicately with the tips of his fingers, Alfred began to feel that familiar terror growing in him that had been in him every time he had got into such trouble.

"I liked you," Sam Carr was saying. "I liked you and would have trusted you, and now look what I got to do." While Alfred watched with his alert, frightened blue eyes, Sam Carr drummed with his fingers on the counter. "I don't like to call a cop in point-blank," he was saying as he looked very worried. "You're a fool, and maybe I should call your father and tell him you're a fool. Maybe I should let them know I'm going to have you locked up."

"My father's not at home. He's a printer. He works nights," Alfred said.

"Who's at home?"

"My mother, I guess."

"Then we'll see what she says." Sam Carr went to the phone and dialled the number. Alfred was not so much ashamed, but there was that deep fright growing in him, and he blurted out arrogantly,° like a strong, full-grown man, "Just a minute. You don't need to draw anybody else in. You don't need to tell her." He wanted to sound like a swaggering, big guy who could look after himself,

yet the old, childish hope was in him, the longing that someone at home would come and help him. "Yeah, that's right, he's in trouble," Mr. Carr was saying. "Yeah, your boy works for me. You'd better come down in a hurry." When he was finished Mr. Carr went over to the door and looked out at the street and watched the people passing in the late summer night. "I'll keep my eye out for a cop," was all he said.

Alfred knew how his mother would come rushing in; she would rush in with her eyes blazing, or maybe she would be crying, and she would push him away, when he tried to talk to her, and make him feel her dreadful contempt;° yet he longed that she might come before Mr. Carr saw the cop on the beat passing the door.

While they waited—and it seemed a long time—they did not speak, and when at last they heard someone tapping on the closed door, Mr. Carr, turning the latch, said crisply, "Come in, Mrs. Higgins." He looked hard-faced and stern.

Mrs. Higgins must have been going to bed when he telephoned, for her hair was tucked in loosely under her hat, and her hand at her throat held her light coat tight across her chest so her dress would not show. She came in, large and plump, with a little smile on her friendly face. Most of the store lights had been turned out and at first she did not see Alfred, who was standing in the shadow at the end of the counter. Yet as soon as she saw him she did not look as Alfred thought she would look; she smiled, her blue eyes never wavered, and with a calmness and dignity that made them forget that her clothes seemed to have been thrown on her, she put out her hand to Mr. Carr and said politely, "I'm Mrs. Higgins. I'm Alfred's mother."

Mr. Carr was a bit embarrassed by her lack of terror and her simplicity, and he hardly knew what to say to her, so she asked, "Is Alfred in trouble?"

"He is. He's been taking things from the store. I caught him red-handed. Little things like compacts and toothpaste and lipsticks. Stuff he can sell easily," the proprietor said.

As she listened Mrs. Higgins looked at Alfred sometimes and nodded her head sadly, and when Sam Carr had finished she said gravely, "Is it so, Alfred?"

"Yes."

"Why have you been doing it?"

"I been spending money, I guess."

"On what?"

"Going around with the guys, I guess," Alfred said.

Mrs. Higgins put out her hand and touched Sam Carr's arm with understanding gentleness, and speaking as though afraid of disturbing him, she said, "If you would only listen to me before doing anything." Her simple earnestness made her shy; her humility made her falter and look away, but in a moment she was smiling gravely again, and she said with a kind of patient dignity, "What did you intend to do, Mr. Carr?"

"I was going to get a cop. That's what I ought to do."

"Yes, I suppose so. It's not for me to say, because he's my son. Yet I sometimes think a little good advice is the best thing for a boy when he's at a certain period in his life."

Alfred couldn't understand his mother's quiet composure, for if they had been at home and someone had suggested that he was going to be arrested, he knew she would be in a rage and would cry out against him. Yet now she was standing there with that gentle, pleading smile, saying, "I wonder if you don't think it would be better just to let him come home with me. He looks like a big fellow, doesn't he? It takes some of them a long time to get any sense," and they both stared at Alfred, who shifted away with a bit of light shining for a moment on his thin face and the tiny pimples over his cheekbone.

But even while he was turning away uneasily, Alfred was realizing that Mr. Carr had become aware that his mother was really a fine woman; he knew that Sam Carr was puzzled by his mother, as if he had expected her to come in and plead with him tearfully, and instead he was being made to feel a bit ashamed by her vast tolerance.° While there was only the sound of the mother's soft, assured voice in the store, Mr. Carr began to nod his head encouragingly at her. Without being alarmed, while being just large and still and simple and hopeful, she was becoming dominant there in the dimly lit store. "Of course, I don't want to be harsh," Mr. Carr was saying. "I'll tell you what I'll do. I'll just fire him and let it go at that. How's that?" and he got up and shook hands with Mrs. Higgins, bowing low to her in deep respect.

There was such warmth and gratitude in the way she said, "I'll never forget your kindness," that Mr. Carr began to feel warm and genial° himself.

"Sorry we had to meet this way," he said. "But, I'm glad I got in touch with you. Just wanted to do the right thing, that's all," he said.

"It's better to meet like this than never, isn't it?" she said. Suddenly they clasped hands as if they liked each other, as if they had known each other a long time. "Good night, sir," she said.

"Good night, Mrs. Higgins. I'm truly sorry," he said.

The mother and son walked along the street together, and the mother was taking a long, firm stride as she looked ahead with her stern face full of worry. Alfred was afraid to speak to her; he was afraid of the silence that was between them too, so he only looked ahead, for the excitement and relief were still pretty strong in him; but in a little while, going along like that in silence made him terribly aware of the strength and the sternness in her; he began to wonder what she was thinking of as she stared ahead so grimly; she seemed to have forgotten that he walked beside her; so when they were passing under the railway bridge and the rumble of the train seemed to break the silence, he said in his old, blustering way, "Thank God it turned out like that. I certainly won't get in a jam like that again."

"Be quiet. Don't speak to me. You've disgraced me again and again," she said bitterly.

"That's the last time. That's all I'm saying."

"Have the decency to be quiet," she snapped.

When they were at home and his mother took off her coat, Alfred saw that she was really only half-dressed, and she made him feel afraid again when she said, without even looking at him, "You're a bad lot. God forgive you. It's one thing after another and always has been. Why do you stand there stupidly? Go to bed, why don't you?" When he was going, she said, "I'm going to make myself a cup of tea. Mind, now, not a word about tonight to your father."

While Alfred was undressing in his bedroom, he heard his mother moving around the kitchen. She filled the kettle and put it on the stove. She moved a chair. As he listened there was no shame in him, just wonder and a kind of admiration of her strength and repose. He could still see Sam Carr nodding his head encouragingly to her; he could hear her talking simply and earnestly, and as he sat on his bed he felt a pride in her strength. "She certainly was smooth," he thought. "Gee, I'd like to tell her she sounded swell."

At last he got up and went along to the kitchen, and when he was at the door he saw his mother pouring herself a cup of tea. He watched and he didn't move. Her face, as she sat there, was a frightened, broken face utterly unlike the face of a woman who had been so assured a little while ago in the drugstore. When she reached out and lifted the kettle to pour hot water in her cup, her hand trembled and the water splashed on the stove. Leaning back in the chair, she sighed and lifted the cup to her lips, and her lips were groping loosely as if they would never reach the cup. She swallowed the hot tea eagerly, and then she straightened up in relief, though her hand holding the cup still trembled. She looked very old.

It seemed to Alfred that this was the way it had been every time he had been in trouble before, that this trembling had really been in her as she hurried out half-dressed to the drugstore. Now he felt all that his mother had been thinking of as

246

they walked along the street together a little while ago. He watched his mother, and he never spoke, but at that moment his youth seemed to be over; he knew all the years of her life by the way her hand trembled as she raised the cup to her lips. It seemed to him that this was the first time he had ever looked upon his mother.

247

The Man Who Finds His Son
Has Become a Thief

Raymond Souster

Coming into the store at first angry
at the accusation, believing
the word of his boy who has told him,
I didn't steal anything, honest. . . .

Then becoming calmer, seeing that anger
won't help in the business, listening patiently
as the other's evidence unfolds, so painfully slow.

Then seeing gradually that evidence
almost as if slowly tightening around the neck
of his son, at first circumstantial,° then gathering damage,
until there's present guilt's sure odor seeping
into the mind, laying its poison.

                        Suddenly feeling
sick and alone and afraid, as if
an unseen hand had slapped him in the face
for no reason whatsoever; wanting to get out
into the street, the night, the darkness, anywhere to hide
the pain that must show to these strangers, the fear.

It must be like this.
It could not be otherwise.

From THE COLOUR OF THE TIMES/TEN ELEPHANTS ON YONGE
STREET by Raymond Souster. Reprinted by permission of
McGraw-Hill Ryerson Limited.

follow-up

Discussing "All the Years of Her Life"

1. Do you think Mr. Carr was too lenient with Alfred? Why?
2. During her brief time at the drug store, Mrs. Higgins persuaded Mr. Carr to do no more than fire Alfred. Why, in your opinion, did she do that when she actually felt so bitter toward the boy?
3. When he was watching his mother in the kitchen, drinking tea, Alfred felt that "his youth seemed to be over; he knew all the years of her life by the way her hand trembled as she raised the cup to her lips" (text p. 247). What, in your opinion, do the words "he knew all the years of her life" mean as they are used here?
4. What evidence—if any—can you find in the story to lead you to think that Alfred never stole again? What evidence—if any—can you find to lead you to think that he did?
5. "So now you think you'll tell me a lie, eh?" Note the word *lie*. What emotional effect does it arouse? Why didn't Mr. Carr use *fib*, instead, or *story*?

   And then he asks, "What kind of a sap do I look like, huh?" Why *sap*? Why not *fool*?

   Later in the story, Mrs. Higgins says, "It's not for me to say, because he's my son." Why *son*? Why not *kid*? or *brat*? or *offspring*? What emotional effect does *son* have that the other words don't? What other words to you find that appeal to your emotions?

Clauses as Adjectives, Adverbs, and Nouns

Carefully examine the following pairs of sentences:

    1a. Old Mr. Carr was closing the drug store.
     b. Mr. Carr, *who was old*, was closing the drug store.
    2a. Alfred sneaked the money *quickly*.
     b. Alfred sneaked the money *while no one was looking*.
    3a. Sam Carr *asked a question*.
     b. Sam Carr asked, *"What do you think you're getting away with?"*

Though the two sentences in each pair mean approximately the same thing, the first sentence in each pair uses a *single word*; the second sentence uses a *clause*. Clauses, you see, can function as single words—that is, as adjectives, as adverbs, and as nouns.

Clauses as Adjectives

Take another look at the first pair of sentences above. In sentence 1a, *old* is an *adjective* used to describe Mr. Carr. In sentence 1b, *who was old*, a clause, also describes Mr. Carr. In other words, *who was old* is a clause used as an adjective—in short, an adjective clause. Here are a few other sentences from "All the Years of Her Life." Each sentence contains an *adjective clause*. See if you can spot it.

1. Alfred Higgins, who had just taken off his white jacket, was putting on his coat and getting ready to go home.
2. The soft, confident, quiet way in which Sam Carr spoke made Alfred start to button his coat.
3. She did not see Alfred, who was standing in the shadow at the end of the counter.

You can easily identify adjective clauses because they usually begin with *which, who (whom),* and *that.*

Practice 1. Writing

Replace each one of the following underlined adjectives with an adjective clause. If necessary, set off your adjective clauses with commas.

Example

The general wore a bullet-proof helmet.

—Revised with adjective clause—

The general wore a helmet, which was bullet-proof.

1. The six-weeks-old puppy chewed up Dad's slippers.
2. The light, fluffy cake won first prize.
3. The doctor was using an ancient scalpel.
4. The weathered-looking woman gestured toward the battered closet door.

Be prepared to read at least one of your revised sentences aloud. Do the others in the class agree that you've correctly used an adjective clause?

Clauses as Adverbs

Look again at the second pair of sentences at the beginning of this lesson. In sentence 2a, *quickly* tells "how" and so is an adverb modifying the verb *sneaked*. In sentence 2b, *while no one was looking* is a clause; it tells "when" and so it modifies the verb *sneaked* too. Because *while no one was looking* functions as an *adverb*, it is an *adverb clause*. Adverbs tell "how," "when," "where," and "why." So do adverb clauses. Here are two additional sentences from "All the Years of Her Life" that contain adverb clauses:

1. When he was at the door, he saw his mother pouring herself a cup of tea. (The clause tells "when" and modifies the verb *saw*.)
2. Her lips were groping loosely as if they would never reach the cup. (The clause tells "how" and modifies the verb *were groping*.)

Practice 2. Writing

Replace each of the underlined words or phrases with an adverb clause that says approximately the same thing.

Example

Clara darted carelessly out of the room.

—Revised with adverb clause—

Clara darted out of the room as if she didn't care about anything.

1. The old soldier became understandably angry. (Try *when*.)
2. The police sergeant filled out the report immediately. (Try *while, when, after*.)
3. The nine-year-old boy was to receive his allowance conditionally. (Try *if*.)
4. Angie lost the last tennis game. But she wants to play another. (Try *although*.)
5. Maybelle sang beautifully.
6. The train was pulling out of the station. At the same time we were racing down the platform.

Be prepared to read at least one of your sentences aloud. Do the others in the class agree that you've correctly used an adverb clause?

Clauses as Nouns

Now, look again at the third pair of sentences at the beginning of this lesson. In Sentence 3a, the noun *question* is the direct object of the verb *asked*. In Sentence 3b, "What do you think you're getting away with?" is a clause used as the direct object of the verb *asked*. In other words, it is a *noun clause* because it functions the same way a noun or pronoun does. Many direct quotations that have explainers are noun clauses. For example:

S   V   ⌐————DO————⌐
1. He said, "Please bring me that hammer."

⌐——— DO ———⌐   S   V
2. "Tomorrow is another day," she said reassuringly.

Many noun clauses begin with the word *that*:

S   V   ⌐——— DO ———⌐
1. He knew *that he would be late.* (What did he know?)

⌐———— S ————⌐   V   DO
2. *That she was to be Rose Queen* pleased Sally. (*What* pleased Sally?)

S   LV   ⌐——— SC (noun) ———⌐
3. The warning was *that he had to leave town.* (*What* was the warning?)

Other noun clauses omit the word *that*:

S   V   ⌐—— DO ——⌐
1. He knew *he looked fierce.* (*What* did he know?)

V   S   V   ⌐——DO——⌐
2. Do you think *(that) I'm crazy?* (*What* do you think?)

Occasionally, noun clauses begin with *how, when, where, what,* and forms of *who.*

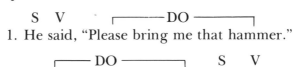

S   V

John never fully understood

                        DO
             how the machine worked.
             when he was supposed to go.
             where he was to meet Beth
             what he was supposed to say.
             who had called him.
             to whom he was to write the
                message.

Practice 3. Writing

In each of the following sentences, replace the underlined noun (or pronoun) with a noun clause.

> *Example*
>
>   S   V
>
> John always knew <u>it</u>.
>
> —Revised with noun clause—
>
> John always knew <u>that he would graduate one day</u>.

1. At the top of his lungs, Peter yelled <u>it</u>.
2. For the life of him, George could not figure <u>it</u> out.
3. The little boy had wanted to tell his mother <u>something</u>.
4. At the age of fifty, Mr. Bobbit saw his <u>dream</u>. (Try *what*.)

Be prepared to read at least one of your rewritten sentences aloud. Do the others in the class agree that you have correctly used a noun clause?

Bookshelf

The Car Thief, by Theodore Weesner. Dell, 1973 (originally, 1972). Stealing cars seems to be the only thing Alex can do well.

None of the Above, by Rosemary Wells. Dial, 1974. Marcia's new family is perfect. The trouble is that she is not! And the pressure to live up to their expectations is more than Marcia can bear.

A Separate Peace, by John Knowles. Bantam, 1969 (originally, 1960). When Gene's best friend is injured, Gene has to accept his own responsibility for the accident.

Through a Brief Darkness, by Richard Peck. Avon, 1974 (originally, 1973). Karen's kidnappers try to use her to exert pressure upon her father, an important figure in organized crime.

interlude

from "The Dictionary of Misinformation"

Tom Burnam

Drowning persons always rising three times. This is absolute and utter balderdash. Persons who are drowning may sink at once or may struggle their way to the surface. How many times depends on how much they struggle.

Everest as world's highest mountain. This is a fact that depends entirely on a convention: measuring the height of mountains from sea level. If they were measured in terms of how far they stick out into space from the center of the earth, Chimborazo, a peak in the Ecuadorian Andes, at 6 267 m, against Everest's 8 848 m, would be the "highest"; the earth is not round, but rather bulges out at the equator so that sea level there is some 22 km farther from the center of the earth than at the North Pole. As Robert L. Birch, a *Scientific American* reader, points out, Chimborazo is within two degrees of the equator; Everest is nearly twenty-eight degrees from it. On this basis, Chimborazo is some 3 km higher than Everest.

Leathernecks. This term for members of the United States Marine Corps did not originate recently, nor does it have any reference either to the sunburn that might conceivably result from duty on the shores of Tripoli, or the kind of stiff military bearing often associated with the Marine Corps. It was, in fact, first applied to the light infantry, who were the elite of George Washington's army and wore dashing leather helmets with horsehair crests.

Sideburns. Many people think that the term was coined to describe the location, but originally the word was *burnsides*, after the Civil War general who liked them, Ambrose E. Burnside. No doubt because the *side* in his name can indeed so easily be taken for the location of sideburns, the two elements got turned around.

SOS. The universal symbol requesting aid, contrary to what is often said, doesn't stand for "Save Our Ship," or "Save Our Souls." It doesn't, in fact, stand for anything. It was selected because it is very simple both to remember and to transmit—three dots, three dashes, three dots. It is not, by the way, an oral signal, but strictly a Morse code one. The oral signal is *mayday*, perhaps selected because it sounds like the French *m'aidez*, or "help me."

Suntan as a sign of good health. A suntan shows only that the skin has adopted a protective device against further damage by the ultraviolet rays of the sun, which are dangerous just like many other forms of radiation. It certainly is no indication of good health. In fact, during the Renaissance and Elizabethan eras it was a sign of the lower classes, who were constantly exposed to the sun in the outdoors. A suntan or sunburn, incidentally, can be acquired easily enough on a fairly cloudy day; thin clouds do not filter out ultraviolet rays.

Xmas. Often regarded as a newfangled and vulgar abbreviation, this word has its origin in very ancient times indeed. In the Anglo-Saxon Chronicle, written near the beginning of the twelfth century, the Old English word for Christmas begins with X. Whether or not the X in *Xmas* is meant to symbolize the Cross, as some say, it is true that the Greek word for "Christ," from which the English derived, begins with the Greek letter *chi*, or X. X is thus a quite proper abbreviation for "Christ."

"You can't fool Mother Nature." Unless one wishes to discard a vast amount of progress in the treatment and prevention of disease, one *must* fool Mother Nature. Vaccines against poliomyelitis, smallpox, and a host of other once-dreaded diseases work by deceit, in a sense; the body is "fooled" into producing the necessary defenses before the disease actually strikes.

255

17

Juan Romo

forestudy

From Character to Character

Are there two sides to every story? Yes, but that's true only of stories involving two people. When there are three persons involved, there are probably three sides to the story. If there are four people, there are four sides—and so on. Each individual, you see, has a unique perspective that determines his/her view of—his/her impression of—his/her attitude toward—the situation.

What different reactions, for example, might these individuals have to the same heavy snowstorm:

A ten-year-old child, tired of school and eager for a short vacation

A mail carrier who walks a long route in a hilly neighborhood

The weather forecaster who predicted sunshine and a light breeze

A ski enthusiast

The Minister of Transportation

Obviously, no two of those individuals would react to the snowstorm in the same way. The weather forecaster would no doubt be very much embarrassed, whereas the ski enthusiast would be delighted. If the weather forecaster were also a skier, he/she might be both embarrassed *and* elated.

In some stories the interest lies *not* in the events but in the different ways the various characters in the story view and react to those events. In writing such a story the author faces a real challenge. Unable simply to begin at the beginning and move steadily to the end of the story, the author must move back and forth from one character to another, showing how each one sees and reacts to the events. The trick, of course, is to make the shifts from character to character—from viewpoint to viewpoint—so smooth that the reader does not become confused.

In accomplishing this task, the author cannot be heavy-handed. That is, he/she can't come out and say, "Now let's look at this event again from Jane's point of view," only to say a few sentences later, "And now, let's go through it again from Oscar's point of view." If an author did that, you'd have every right to toss the story into the trash.

How, then, can an author let you know that he/she is revealing one particular character's point of view and taking you into the mind of that character? One technique is to tell you what that specific character is doing so that you have him/her clearly in mind. Then the author introduces the character's thoughts—as if the person were talking to himself/herself. As you continue to read, the only conclusion you can make is that you are involved with the thoughts of the character who has most recently been the centre of attention. For instance, in "Juan Romo" you find this passage:

> Imelda stared straight ahead, entranced, oblivious to the road, the traffic, Jake, and the funeral home director. Gabriel. Gabriel. The humming motor of the Cadillac said, "Gabriel, Gabriel."

In those words "Gabriel. Gabriel. The humming motor of the Cadillac said, 'Gabriel, Gabriel,'" the author isn't telling you anything about the action—the ride to the cemetery. Instead she is recording someone's thoughts. And inasmuch as Imelda is the character on whom your attention has just been centred, it is only logical that the thoughts are hers. And so for a while you know you'll be inside Imelda's mind, sharing her thoughts and feelings.

Another technique for shifting the point of view to another character and placing the reader inside that character's mind is more obvious. The author simply uses a different type face. You know then that as long as the words appear in that type face, you are involved with that particular character and with his/her thoughts. For instance, in the story "Juan Romo," a paragraph about Juan Romo concludes like this:

. . . Juan was in a movie audience, last row, watching a film he had dreaded.

Sorry I'm late, said Gabriel.

When the scene shifts abrubtly and when the words appear in a different type face—here they are in italics—you know right away that you are sharing Juan's memories. You know that must be so because, having read the story up to this point, you know that Gabriel is dead. Therefore, if he speaks, he is doing so only in the memory of the character most recently the focus of attention.

"Dad! Dad! I'm glad you waited!"

Juan Romo

Thelma T. Reyna

The hearse pulled to the curb, and the pallbearers carried the coffin into the open back doors, groaning and trying to ignore their red faces as they strained to push the coffin inside.

The mother was not watching. Her face was buried in the shoulder of a thin, tall, dark man—her eldest son. Her youngest, and dearest, of five doting boys was in the coffin. He'd been shot in the head a mere three weeks ago. He'd been shipped home in time for Mother's Day.

"All set now, Mrs. Deanda," the funeral director said to her softly. He'd been one of the pallbearers, the only blond head amongst the five dark-haired youths who'd strained so. He dusted his palms almost inconspicuously, but the mother would not have noticed anyway. He gestured discreetly to the pallbearers, and the six of them disappeared through the side door into the funeral home. Mrs. Deanda had stood motionless, stiff, her head inclined the slightest bit to hide her face.

"Mama, it's done now," said her son. He rested his large bony hands on her shoulders and waited a few seconds longer, in respect. "It's done now. Let's go." His voice was a gentle echo of the funeral director's.

Mrs. Deanda moved her head but left

it bowed. She dabbed at her eyes with a flowered handkerchief, sniffled, then sighed tiredly. "Yes," she murmured. "It's done, Jake. Let's go."

Her son supported her elbow and turned, head bowed in respect for her grief, walking alongside her but not quite even in step. She was half-a-step ahead of him. Again, for her grief.

At the door of the funeral home, the two paused. The dead boy's father stood there. He had watched the loading of the hearse in silence. The sun came through the slatted veranda in such a way that half his face was in shadow, but his eyes were hit by the late morning sunlight. They stood spotlighted now, a bandit mask of brightness across his wide face. They were empty eyes, dry, lined in the corners. They gazed back calmly at Jake and Mrs. Deanda.

She spoke first. "I'll say this only because I feel obligated." She paused. "I'm glad you came. Gabriel might have liked it, knowing you were here in the end."

The bandit eyes merely looked at her. The man did not shift posture, did not move his hands holding the beige Stetson before him. Jake lifted his mother's elbow gently, and the two went indoors,

where the rest of her family and dozens of Gabriel's friends awaited her.

Outside, the wide-faced man remained motionless. His hair was damp against his starched shirt collar, his thick mustache glistened with sweat. He gazed for long moments at the shiny, majestic hearse left unattended in the shade of the carport. He could see his son's coffin through the spaces between the window drapes. He looked up at the sun through the red-wood slats and said, as clearly as if he were speaking to someone: "He would have liked it. I know it." He walked to his old gray Pontiac parked a block and a half away and sat in the heat to wait for the procession to begin.

Mr. Romo, the salesgirl said brightly as she folded down the ends of the papersack. *I saw your boy's picture in the paper. He's so handsome. When do we meet?*

Juan Romo laughed the masculine giggle he was often teased for. *You'd like that, wouldn't you, maniosa?*[1]

She persisted. *Every girl in town is after him. Haven't you noticed?*

The salesgirl smiled at the stocky, balding man she'd bantered with for years. He was pensive for a moment. *No, no, I haven't noticed.* He took the sack, then asked slyly, *But is it so?*

Every girl, she repeated seriously.

Juan chuckled with delight. He walked away, then turned and said loudly, for the other salesgirls in the small store to hear: *My boy's got plans for when he gets out. I think they include Princess Caroline.*

Jake spoke in confidential tones to the funeral director. Mrs. Deanda sat in a padded folding chair in a glass hallway niche, a ruffled fern cascading from the ceiling to just inches above her head. She watched her eldest son and felt soothed by his efficiency, his calmness. The funeral director pointed to the list on the counter before him, spoke so softly, that had Mrs. Deanda not been a mere two metres away, she would not have heard. The other mourners stood silent, respect-ful, in the lobby of the funeral home. They all waited on her. On her, Jake, and the director.

"But Mr. Romo is here," said the blond man. "Where in the procession will he ride?"

Jake looked at him with polite incredu-lity. "Mr. Romo? We have no plans for him."

"But it's only proper that the father . . ."

"Not in this case," said Jake firmly. He glanced at his mother. She gazed at him calmly. "There are no plans for Mr. Romo. He can ride in his own car."

"Where?"

"Anywhere in the procession. As long as it's after family and friends." Jake looked at the funeral director as if to cas-tigate° him for having thought of the man. He stepped politely to his mother's side, offered her his arm.

His voice was a soothing murmur. "Come, Mama. We're all set now."

Juan Romo wiped his forehead. Laredo heat was unbeatable for discomfort. He saw Imelda Deanda emerge from the front door of the funeral home, a tiny black figure beneath the curved canvas canopy. Jake helped her into the dark Cadillac and slid in beside her. The fu-

260   1. *maniosa:* naughty girl

neral director got in behind the wheel. In four other funeral home Cadillacs lined up behind, the other Deanda sons, some with wives, some with a child or two, got in. Doors slammed silently. Juan watched a movie, it seemed, a movie he had often previewed in horror, the sound turned off. Tiny dusty figures a block and a half away, model cars pulling away from the curb without a whisper—Juan was in a movie audience, last row, watching a film he had dreaded.

Sorry I'm late, said Gabriel. His handsome, youthful face panted and huffed—and smiled tentatively. Juan had waited outside the west-end theatre for almost an hour. His son was late, but he was here. And that was something.

The two looked at each other, measuring, probing, uneasy. Neither was in a rush to go inside. The movie was just an excuse. This meeting was long overdue. It could have been anywhere: at Gabriel's school, at a grocery, anywhere. But Gabriel had chosen the theatre; he liked movies. He went each Saturday, over at the east-end, his end of town, and never with his father. But today they were together.

Juan Romo scanned the boy's face, the thick eyebrows, the broad jaw, the square white teeth, and saw himself at fifteen.

So this is who you are, he murmured. Gabriel seemed to hold his breath. *So this is who you are!* the father said

261

again, and clapped his hands on the boy's shoulders, laughing. They gazed eye-to-eye. Gabriel was grown! The boy exploded into laughter, joyous laughter, and the two were soon in each other's arms.

Dad! Dad! I'm glad you waited! The two laughed like idiots in the noonday sun.

You're . . . right I've waited, said Juan. He blinked against the brilliance of the day.

When Juan entered the church, most of the mourners were already seated. He saw Imelda, Jake, and the other Deanda boys in the front pew, left side. The roped-off pews stood dark, polished, well-filled with sniffing relatives, wrinkled aunts and uncles, plain and lovely wives, all youthful-looking, one with an infant on her shoulder. The child was fast asleep.

Juan slipped into a pew toward the middle of the huge church. Only an old woman he had never seen, probably a community mourner,[2] occupied that pew. The flag-draped coffin stood in the aisle by the altar banister. The little bald priest sprinkled holy water on the casket, walked around it solemnly, intoning words Juan knew well: Oh, Lord, we pray for our servicemen. . . .

The priest prayed earnestly, reverently, not like the absent-minded one who'd presided at the services of Juan's brother two years before. The priest then had glanced at his logbook periodically to check the name of the deceased. He had scratched his chin, looked critically at the giant chandeliers as he'd prayed for Roberto's soul. But this little priest seemed genuinely sad that an eighteen-year-old youth lay before him. He rested his white hands on the flag, touched his forehead to it, and began the keening. His soul was in it. His eyes, when he raised his head, were closed, clenched tightly, sorrowfully.

Juan was thankful to him for that.

Mr. Romo, am I going to have to furnish the little sacristy° for you? Father Romeo walked toward Juan with outstretched hand. *Mr. Romo—almost my namesake. You know I've adopted you, don't you?*

Juan was flattered but a little embarrassed. He held the little priest's hand. They stood on the red brick steps by the side of the church. The sun was a nonentity° here. Cottonwood trees, ruffled leaves shimmying gently in the spring wind, formed an archway above their heads. Juan noticed once more that Father Romeo's bald head was very freckled.

I was just leaving, Father.

What for? You'll be right back again. It's a good thing you're not married. Don't you know that even the saints get headaches from so much entreatying? Give them a rest.

The priest stepped closer to Juan, looked sincerely into his eyes. *You've been forgiven, Juan. The whole town has forgiven you.*

How can I ruin the reputation of Imelda Deanda and be forgiven? Juan said in mock levity.

Her? Widows are easy to forgive. You?

---

2. *community mourner:* a person, usually a woman, who attends funeral services of people she does not know, merely as atonement for her sins, or to unselfishly offer her prayers for the soul of the deceased

We understand love. Even priests do. Father Romeo still held Juan's hand. The heat and dust were light years away. Juan gazed at the priest's freckles, at the brick beneath their feet. This cool hand in his was the sweetest balm he'd had since the day Gabriel established regular contact with him.

Her family has forgiven her. They've long accepted Gabriel as one of them, said Father Romeo. Juan rested in the serenity of the deep-set eyes. Father Romeo's congregation was the largest, most faithful in Laredo. Juan understood why. But the little priest was wrong about his namesake.

I give thanks for Gabriel, said Juan. *I pray for him . . . and me.*

Imelda Deanda held Jake's hand as they rode in silence to the cemetery. She'd hardly seen Juan since this morning when she spoke to him on the veranda. She was a little glad that he'd thought enough of Gabriel to come, but there was a touch of hypocrisy° there that smelled quite ill to her. Juan had seen little of his son, although for that she was glad. That way the boy had been assimilated into the Deanda family much more easily. When Gabriel was born, her house was filled for days with a silent reproach, an accusation by her four adolescent sons that hung in the air and depressed her. It was a blow to them, as it was a shock to the town, that Imelda Deanda, respectable widow, had given birth.

Yet Gabriel was a delight, an uninhibited° child who'd returned raucous° family laughter to the cool, polished house with its walnut floors and marble halls. And he'd grown! The beautiful Imelda had forgotten her mirrors, her early preoccupation° with first gray hairs, and had raced forward with her son in a timeless vacuum.

Imelda stared straight ahead, entranced, oblivious to the road, the traffic, Jake, and the funeral home director. Gabriel. Gabriel. The humming motor of the Cadillac said, "Gabriel, Gabriel." Gabriel of the strong brown body and white, laughing teeth, the sweetheart of debutante balls and proms. Gabriel of books and shy poems and letters and thoughtful sentiments inscribed on birthday cards to her. Gabriel of the hard, blue uniform, the collar holding his neck straight as he leaned toward her to kiss her cheek. He was so grown!

And through it all, Juan Romo had never seen his son. At least, never seen him since that afternoon soon after the birth. He had come for the second consecutive week to see the child, to sit silently in the den with the infant in his arms, seemingly in awe of the wiggling bundle. Juan was clumsy in his solicitousness° toward Imelda. She'd sit in a leather chair across from him, regal in her quilted satin robe, watching Juan with the strong hands gaze in wonder at his child, their child, watching him look up at her occasionally, that hungry light in his eyes, that indefinable gentle, hungry light, asking daily in his quiet voice how she fared, never knowing what she planned.

She'd wanted her boy to grow up as a Deanda, not a Romo. Juan had sat stiffly in the wing chair by the hallway as she'd said this that day. He'd been unresponsive, obviously hurt, but he'd listened patiently to her—and afterward, already secure in her family's acceptance and forgiveness, she'd liked to think that Juan

263

Romo had been a character in a book, a fascinating role in one of her widow's dreams. He'd been easily brushed away. Thank God Gabriel had never spoken of his father, although he knew it was Juan Romo, and—Imelda recalled uncomfortably now—although Gabriel had mentioned once, when he was away, that he wrote to his father.

"Mama," said Jake. He'd hardly spoken above a whisper all day, but his soft voice now jarred Imelda from her reverie. He'd treated his mother with utmost delicacy, and now he was apologetic. "Mama, I don't think it was proper of you to acknowledge Mr. Romo." Jake regretted not deeming it proper, said his mien.°

Imelda was momentarily flustered. Jake seemed to have read her thoughts. She was pensive for a moment. "It was for Gabriel's sake. I told him that." She withdrew her hand from Jake's, but he retrieved it gently, his eyes moist.

"Forgive me, Mama," he murmured. "I say that only because he never did anything for Gabriel. You know that. We all know that."

"I know," she said, and sighed. She looked sadly out the tinted window, glad for the air-conditioning in the car.

The heat attacked the mourners without mercy. Even beneath the canvas shelter, the Deanda family wiped foreheads as regularly as they wiped cheeks and dabbed at eyes or blew noses. The little priest was at his station again, beside the flag-draped coffin, beside the ugly, gaping hole that soon would take the youth from the face of the earth permanently.

Imelda's body heaved. Jake buried his face in her hair and black veil, and the two were utterly helpless to one another. His bony hands clutched her arms, all delicacy gone. He was as shattered as she. The priest sprinkled and intoned, lined face no longer calm. He had planned to deliver his best elegy. He had finished the final draft of it at midnight last night. Instead, he stood silent now, in respect for Imelda's grief, in respect for the entire family, in personal respect for Juan.

His eyes searched the crowd as the family wept noisily. Wives, uncles, aunts, brothers all leaned on one another underneath the canvas shelter: a portrait in black. Father Romeo's eyes sifted through the modest throng around the shelter. He saw Juan Romo; their dry eyes held together. The priest remembered many encounters with Juan—inside the church, by the side of the church, in front of the church, in the parking lot. And always, morning or evening, once or twice a day, winter rain or summer madness, Juan alone, Juan brightening at the sight of Father Romeo, Juan raising a hand in greeting, open-palmed, sometimes calling out: "More headaches for the saints, Father."

The two gazed at each other above many bowed heads, and Father Romeo's heart at once felt the eighteen years' burden Juan had borne.

follow-up

Discussing "Juan Romo"

1. Would you say that Juan Romo was or was not a part of his son's family? Why? What family did Juan have?
2. What do the two flashbacks—one featuring the sales girls in the small store and the other in the movie theatre—tell you about the relationship between Juan Romo and his son Gabriel?
3. Why, do you suppose, were Juan Romo and Imelda Deanda never married?
4. To what extent do you share Jake's attitude toward Juan Romo? Why?
5. What do you understand by that last sentence: "The two gazed at each other above many bowed heads, and Father Romeo's heart at once felt the eighteen years' burden Juan Romo had borne"?
6. On page 260, the scene suddenly shifts from Juan Romo's sitting in his car to his talking to some sales girls in a store.

How do you know the scene has shifted? Is this shift a flash-back or a flash forward? How do you know?

Then suddenly the scene shifts back to the funeral again. What device did the author use to signal that shift?

In the story there are at least four additional shifts from character to character and from scene to scene. Spot at least three of those shifts and explain how you know that it is indeed such a shift.

The Passive Transformation: Passive Voice

"You've been forgiven, Juan."

"The boy had been assimilated into the Deanda family."

"He had been easily brushed away."

Though these sentences from "Juan Romo" *seem* to follow the standard S-V pattern of English sentences, they don't. Instead, they follow a different pattern. In the regular S-V sentence, it is the *subject* that acts. Example: "The hearse pulled to the curb." Obviously, it is the hearse (the subject) that did the pulling (*pulled* is the verb). The action, you see, goes to the right: →.

But look again at the three sentences above. In the first one, *you* is the subject, all right, and *have been forgiven* is the verb. But is it *you* who are doing the forgiving? Not at all. *Someone else (or others) have forgiven you.* In other words, *you* (the subject) RECEIVES the action. The direction of that action is back to the subject. The action goes to the left: ←

Look at the second sentence. True, *boy* is the subject of the sentence; *had been assimilated* is the verb. Yet is the boy doing the assimilating? No. Instead, the family assimilated him. And so in this sentence, too, the subject *boy* is the RECEIVER, not the DOER, of the action. Again, the action goes to the left ←, back to the subject.

Look, now, at the third sentence above. Does the action go to the right or to the left? How can you tell?

When the subject of a sentence *receives* the action of the verb—that is, when the subject is acted upon—the sentence pattern is changed, or transformed. It becomes a PASSIVE TRANSFORMATION.

Besides the fact that the subject in a passive transformation is passive, receiving the action, there is another characteristic you should be aware of. Examine the following pairs of sentences:

Standard S-V Pattern	*Passive Transformation*
We have forgiven you, Juan.	You've been forgiven, Juan.
The Deanda family had assimilated the boy.	The boy had been assimilated into the Deanda family.
They had easily brushed him away.	He had been easily brushed away (by them).

What difference do you notice in the verbs of each pair of sentences? In the first pair, the verb in the standard S-V sentence is *have forgiven*. But in the passive transformation, it is *have been forgiven*. In the S-V sentence of the second pair, the verb is *had assimilated*. But in the passive transformation, it is *had been assimilated*. Is this same variation true of the verbs in the third pair of sentences?

Notice, then, that in each passive transformation, these conditions are present:

The main verb appears in its past-participle form (*forgiven, assimilated, brushed*).

A form of the verb *be* is used as a helping verb. (In these three sentences, that form appears as *been*.)

Depending on the tense of the verb, there may or may not be another helping verb. (In the three sentences, *have* and *had* are used.)

In short, the verbs *have been forgiven, had been assimilated,* and *had been brushed* are in the PASSIVE VOICE.

All of this is simply another way of saying that in a passive transformation, the verb acts upon the subject, which is not active but passive.

Practice 1. Discussion

Decide whether or not the verb in each sentence below is in the passive voice. In each case, explain why you decided as you did.

1. The street was paved yesterday.
2. In the basketball game Pete tallied 20 points in five minutes.
3. The injured puppy was taken to the vet's office.
4. Marge hasn't been seen since yesterday.
5. I am being blackmailed.
6. The premier will visit the factory tomorrow.
7. Rome's Angels will be featured on the Mike Douglas show. **267**

8. We've all seen that picture three times.
9. Drink your coffee!
10. Those sheets were changed yesterday!
11. Sorry, this table was reserved by the manager.
12. "Bright Eyes" has been played ten times this evening by that band.

Practice 2. Discussion

Look again at the twelve sentences in Practice 1. If the sentence is in the passive voice, rephrase it so that it is in the active voice. If the sentence is now in the active voice, rephrase it to make it passive.

The passive voice is useful when you want to stress the *result*—the *outcome*—of an action or when the doer is not readily known.

> *Examples*
> *The ice has been cleared for skating.* (Here, your chief interest is in the result of the action—in the fact that the ice is ready for skating. You aren't concerned about who did the clearing.)
>
> *The astronaut was welcomed to the city.* (Here, the emphasis lies in the fact that the astronaut received proper treatment; you're not so much concerned in who it was that did the welcoming.)

But ordinarily the passive voice is a weaker form of expression than is the active voice. Because it emphasizes the result of an action, the passive voice is inappropriate when you want to emphasize action. What's more, the passive voice often leads to buck-passing.

> *Examples*
> 1. *It is thought that no one will wish to attend the play.*

Well, *who* thinks that nobody wants to see the play? You see, the passive voice can be used to dodge responsibility. (Note that we've just used the passive voice to emphasize *one result* of its use.)

> 2. *The touchdown was made by Juan Romero, the wide receiver.* (The passive voice makes this sentence flabby. How much more forceful it is to say: "Juan Romero, the wide receiver, made the touchdown"!)

268

Practice 3. Discussion

After examining each sentence below, decide whether the use of the passive voice is advisable. (There will no doubt be differences of opinion.)

1. The lights were turned on by the suspicious guard.
2. The time was checked by the referee.
3. The snow has finally been removed from the roof!
4. It is considered unwise to speak frankly.
5. Many are called; few are chosen.
6. The whistle was blown by the umpire.
7. "Stop, thief!" was yelled by the old man.
8. We have been given four tickets to the play by the theatre manager.
9. The leak was finally found and repaired.
10. Two stop signs were ignored by the speeding driver.

Practice 4. Writing

Look back at the ten sentences in Practice 3. In each case where you consider a sentence weak because of the ineffective use of the passive voice, rewrite the sentence, placing the emphasis where you think it belongs.

> *Example*
> *Weak passive*: The fire alarm was sounded by the night clerk.
> *More forceful*: The night clerk sounded the fire alarm.

Be prepared to read at least one of your rewritten sentences aloud. Do your classmates agree that you've written a more forceful sentence?

Bookshelf

The Dollar Man, by Harry Mazer. Delacorte, 1974. Marcus, who has never known his father, sets out—at the age of 14—to find him.

Mom, the Wolfman, and Me, by Norma Klein. Avon, 1974, (originally, 1972). Her mother's plans to get married upset Brett's comfortable life.

The Price, by Arthur Miller. Bantam, 1972 (originally, 1969). A play, in which the death of their father brings two brothers together to reconsider the directions their lives have taken.

Do Not Go Gentle into That Good Night

Dylan Thomas

Do not go gentle into that good night,
Old age should burn and rave at close of day;
Rage, rage against the dying of the light.

Though wise men at their end know dark is right,
Because their words had forked no lightning they
Do not go gentle into that good night.

Good men, the last wave by, crying how bright
Their frail deeds might have danced in a green bay,
Rage, rage against the dying of the light.

Wild men who caught and sang the sun in flight,
And learn, too late, they grieved it on its way,
Do not go gentle into that good night.

Grave men, near death, who see with blinding sight
Blind eyes could blaze like meteors and be gay,
Rage, rage against the dying of the light.

And you, my father, there on the sad height,
Curse, bless, me now with your fierce tears, I pray.
Do not go gentle into that good night.
Rage, rage against the dying of the light.

18

This Funny Thing Called Love

Just what is love? That's a question men and women have been asking for centuries. Of course, the question has taken many forms. One we like is this one: What is this funny thing called love? It would probably be fair to say that every human being who ever lived has sought an answer to that question. But we wouldn't hazard a guess about who has—or how many have—found a satisfactory answer. Do you think the speaker in this poem has?

Song of the Young Man Girls Cannot Resist

(Omaha)

It was the gods that made me as I am:
blame them,
if you will!
Hiiiiiiiiiiiiiiiiiiiiii . . . .

A: Now there's a guy with self-assurance, poise, charm, sex-appeal, wit . . .

B: . . . pride, vanity, appalling conceit . . . .

A: Aw, come off it. What would you give to have his self-confidence—the certainty that you were irresistible?

Love is indeed a funny thing. Few of us are so content with ourselves that we are convinced we have a devastating effect on the opposite sex. Like the fellow in the next poem, most of us probably suffer an occasional pang of uncertainty, wondering just how we stack up with a person of the opposite sex:

It's Raining in Love

Richard Brautigan

I don't know what it is,
but I distrust myself
when I start to like a girl
    a lot.

It makes me nervous.
I don't say the right things
or perhaps I start
    to examine,
        evaluate,
            compute
    what I am saying.

If I say, "Do you think it's going to rain?"
and she says, "I don't know,"
I start thinking: Does she really like me?

In other words
I get a little creepy.

A friend of mine once said,
"It's twenty times better to be friends
    with someone
than it is to be in love with them."

I think he's right and besides,
it's raining somewhere, programming flowers
and keeping snails happy.
    That's all taken care of.

Excerpted from THE PILL VERSUS THE SPRINGHILL MINE DISASTER by Richard Brautigan. Copyright © 1968 by Richard Brautigan. Reprinted by permission of DELACORTE PRESS/ SEYMOUR LAWRENCE.

BUT
if a girl likes me a lot
and starts getting real nervous
and suddenly begins asking me funny questions
and looks sad if I give the wrong answers
and she says things like,
"Do you think it's going to rain?"
and I say, "It beats me,"
and she says, "Oh,"
and looks a little sad
at the clear blue California sky,
I think: Thank God, it's you, baby, this time
    instead of me.

> X: Right on!
> Y: Yeah, if you're in love, you look for insinuations and
>   hidden messages and things that aren't said.
> Z: It's enough to drive you crazy. You can't really be sure
>   whether "It beats me" means "I love you" or "It's been
>   fun."

As Richard Brautigan suggests, being in love does involve taking risks. Of course, when the other person seems to be risking a bit more, it can give you a feeling that you're in control. Even then, however, there's a tendency to search for implications in this remark or that comment. We want to know how we stand, how the other person feels about us. Little things can be revealing. After all, isn't it the thought that counts?

273

Collection Harry Torczyner, New York

One Perfect Rose

Dorothy Parker

A single flow'r he sent me, since we met.
　All tenderly his messenger he chose;
Deep-hearted, pure, with scented dew still wet—
　One perfect rose.

I knew the language of the floweret;
　"My fragile leaves," it said, "his heart enclose."
Love long has taken for his amulet[1]
　One perfect rose.

Why is it no one ever sent me yet
　One perfect limousine, do you suppose?
Ah no, it's always just my luck to get
　One perfect rose.

1. *amulet* (ăm′ yə lĭt): a good luck piece

From THE PORTABLE DOROTHY PARKER. Copyright 1926, 1954 by Dorothy Parker. Reprinted by permission of The Viking Press.

274

A: Hey! Wait a minute! A limousine? She doesn't want much!
B: Well, maybe a limousine would be a more vivid expression of love than a rose. It's sure a *different* expression, anyway.
C: But isn't a limousine so big that it replaces the thought of love instead of symbolizing it?

How do *you* express love? The young woman in Dorothy Parker's poem sort of turned up her nose at the rose—that eternal symbol of love. Do you suppose she'd turn up her nose at the expression of love in this next poem, too?

Kidnap Poem

Nikki Giovanni

ever been kidnapped
by a poet
if i were a poet
i'd kidnap you
put you in my phrases and metre
you to jones beach
or maybe coney island,
or maybe just to my house
lyric you in lilacs
dash you in the rain
blend into the beach
to complement my see
play the lyre for you
ode you with my love song
anything to win you
wrap you in the red Black green
show you off to mama
yeah if i were a poet i'd kid
nap you

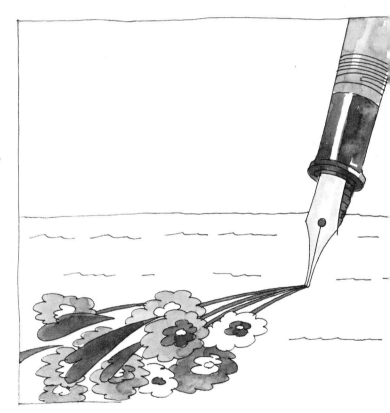

X: That's a thought. Maybe to express true love, you need to show it by your actions instead of buying something.
Y: Then I suppose you'd rather have a poem written for you than to get a limousine?

Roses—poems—even limousines—all are really symbols of love, not love itself. Love—true love—can exist without roses or poems or limousines. But what exactly *is* true love? Is it an indispensable part of life?

In All Men

Gordon Parks

In all men
Love or hate
Is inevitable.
Young men,
With fewer
Loves conceived,
With fewer
Hates defined,
Make more
Imprudent choices.
Old men,
With little time
Left to waste
Seldom choose—
Knowing that both,
Love and hate,
Are filled with pain.

A: But would anyone ever choose to reject love?
B: Well, I suppose being in love *does* make you vulnerable. There's always the chance that you'll be hurt.
C: And also the chance that you'll be happy. You have to take chances. Life's full of chances.

Whatever love is, maybe it was best summed up by these poetic words: "The greatest thing you'll ever learn is to love and be loved in return."

From WHISPERS OF INTIMATE THINGS by Gordon Parks. Copyright © 1971 by Gordon Parks. Reprinted by permission of The Viking Press.

Discussing "This Funny Thing Called Love"

1. In the poem "In All Men," Gordon Parks seems to say that
   love can be filled with pain. Which of the other poems in
   this cluster support that point of view? Which of the poems
   suggest the forms that pain might take?
2. Do you think that there are aspects of love that none of
   these poems consider? What might they be?
3. How do you feel about the idea in Parks's poem that love
   might be an "imprudent choice," that choosing to fall in love
   might be a waste of time?

focus

Generating Efficient Sentences

If you have read "The Collecting Team," by Robert Silverberg (page 132), you may recall this sentence:

> Davison disappeared back into the storage hold, while Holdreth scribbled furiously in the logbook, writing down the coordinates of the planet below, its general description and so forth.

By the end of this FOCUS lesson, believe it or not, you can be writing efficient sentences structured on the order of that one. First, however, you'll probably need to examine Silverberg's sentence to find out how it is built—what its elements are. Here is a level outline (or level analysis) of that sentence.

       S   V

1. Davison disappeared back into the storage hold,

              S   V

2. while Holdreth scribbled furiously in the logbook,

3. writing down the coordinates of the planet below, its general description and so forth.

That's right—three levels! The Level 1 element, as you can readily see, is an independent clause with the standard S-V pattern. (Note that it is the *only* independent clause in the entire sentence.)

You'll recognize the Level 2 element as a subordinate clause—an adverb clause modifying the verb *disappeared* in Level 1. (The clause tells "when" Davison disappeared.) The solid-line arrow from Level 2 to *disappeared* shows that the entire clause modifies that verb.

But the Level 3 element is something else. You guessed it! It's a
PARTICIPIAL PHRASE (an -*ing* phrase) that modifies the noun *Holdreth* in the Level 2 clause. The participle *writing* tells what kind
of person Holdreth was as he scribbled. (He was a "writing" person.) The solid-line arrow from Level 3 to *Holdreth* shows that the
entire participial phrase modifies that noun.

Practice 1. Writing

Here is a sentence similar in structure to the one we have just
analysed. See whether you can make a level outline for it. Label
the sentence pattern of the *Level 1* element and, if you can, draw
arrows to show which words the other elements modify. Use the
level outline above as a model.

> The magician sawed the woman in half, while the audi-
> ence was reacting with horror, gasping loudly and moving
> around in their seats.

Be prepared to write your level outlines on the chalkboard so that
the rest of the class can see how you've analysed the sentence. Is
there general agreement that your analysis is correct?

Generating Subordinate Clauses

Now that you've examined the Silverberg sentence as a whole,
take time out to examine its parts.

        S   V
1. Davison disappeared back into the storage hold.
                    S   V
2. while Holdreth scribbled furiously in the logbook.

Notice that even this two-level sentence is effective. It consists of
an independent clause and a subordinate clause. Yet other subordinate clauses could also fit:

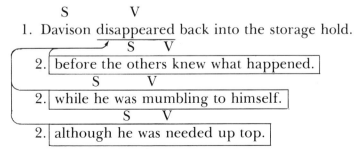

        S   V
1. Davison disappeared back into the storage hold.
             S V
2. before the others knew what happened.
          S   V
2. while he was mumbling to himself.
          S   V
2. although he was needed up top.

Practice 2. Writing

Below are five independent (Level 1) clauses. To each one, add a Level 2 subordinate clause. For the first two sentences, there are clues to help you out.

```
                  S       V
A. 1. Mrs. Mitchell tumbled down the cellar stairs,
      2. after _____.

               S          V        DO
B. 1. Mrs. Balow introduced us to the aging professor,
      2. who _____.

                    S        V
C. 1. The DC–10 was soaring across the sky,
      2. _____.

                   S          V
D. 1. The old bank building shook violently,
      2. _____.

                S           V
E. 1. The pickpocket moved quickly through the crowd,
      2. _____.
```

Be prepared to put at least one of your sentences on the chalkboard for others to discuss.

Generating Participial Phrases

Look again at Level 3 of Silverberg's sentence at the beginning of this lesson:

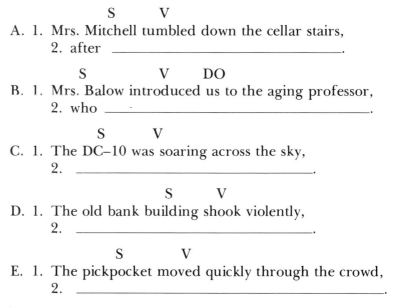

```
         S          V
1. Davison disappeared back into the storage hold,
                    S        V
   2. while Holdreth scribbled furiously in the logbook,
      3. writing down the coordinates of the planet below, its
         general description and so forth.
```

Notice the three-level structure: an independent clause (Level 1) a subordinate clause (Level 2), and a participial phrase (Level 3) that modifies the noun *Holdreth* in Level 2. Yet other participial phrases could also fit:

```
         S           V
1. Davison disappeared back into the storage hold,

                    S        V
  2. while Holdreth scribbled furiously in the logbook,

      3. | sliding his pencil carelessly across the page. |

      3. | shaking his head as he wrote. |

      3. | clenching his teeth in anger. |
```

Practice 3. Writing

Below are three independent clauses (Level 1). To each, add a Level 2 subordinate clause and a Level 3 participial phrase. Remember that what you write in Level 3 must describe a noun in Level 2.

```
           S      V    IO       DO
A. 1. Philip handed me the tickets,
       2. while _____,
       3. _____-ing _____.

         S      V
B. 1. Fred started through the revolving door
      2. when _____
      3. _____-ing _____.

          S                       V
C. 1. The racer unfortunately ran downhill out of control,
      2. after _____,
      3. _____-ing _____.
```

Be prepared to put at least one of your sentences on the chalkboard for the rest of the class to discuss.

Practice 4. Writing

Mix and match your own three-level sentences. Begin with any independent clause in Box A (on page 282). Add any subordinate clause from Box B. Top it off with any participial phrase from Box C. Write your five sentences in the level-outline form if you wish, or you can write them in regular form. **281**

Box A
1. Shopping was fun
2. My brother was strong,
3. English used to be my favorite subject,
4. The shadow disappeared,
5. The boxer knocked out his opponent,

Box B
1. before I had my accident
2. when enough money was available.
3. after the explosion rocked the city
4. until that embarrassing thing happened
5. although pieces were left behind as clues

Box C
1. causing sudden deafness
2. sprinkle litter everywhere
3. making everyone shake and shudder
4. turning all in the vicinity purple
5. transforming a quiet scene into a panic

Be prepared to write at least one of your sentences on the chalkboard for others to see and discuss.

Practice 5. Writing

Try your hand at composing one three-level sentence of your own. Write it in level-outline form first, and then write it out in regular form. For guidance, refer to other three-level sentences in this lesson.

1. _____,
   (independent clause)

   2. _____,
   (subordinate clause)

     3. _____.
   (participial phrase)

Be prepared to write your sentence on the chalkboard. Do the others in the class agree that your sentence is indeed a three-level sentence?

19

Say It with Flowers

forestudy

Standard Language *vs.* Nonstandard Language

Ordinarily when we talk with people we know, we tend be be ourselves—natural and relaxed. We use INFORMAL LANGUAGE— with contractions and clipped words and twenty-five cent words rather than the dollar to two-dollar variety. For example, in "Say It with Flowers," the narrator says:

"I guess in this weather they'll hold a day or two."

No two-dollar words there. Instead, *guess* and *they'll* and the expression *a day or two* sound conversational and natural.

Informal English is one variety of STANDARD English—English used by all the people who, though relaxed and natural, try to make sure that they say what they mean and mean what they say. Informal English often bends grammar rules, but it doesn't break them.

Practice 1. Discussion
Which of the following twelve sentences would you judge to be informal yet standard English? Discuss these sentences with your classmates.

1. Where's it at?
2. Mom couldn't go to the party because Dad was sick.
3. That guy he ain't about to come around here again.
4. So I up and says to her, I says, "What's wrong wit' youse?"
5. Sue, you'll just have to refer back to your dictionary.
6. It don't matter.
7. Mr. Clark built the model all by himself.
8. Sheila seen two lights on the shore.

9. Me and her was on our way to the show.
10. Them TV characters sure are funny.
11. They couldn't of done anything like that!
12. Don't nobody move!

How many sentences did you name as using standard English? If you said only two, you're right. Each of the other ten sentences have NONSTANDARD English—expressions that informed, educated persons avoid. Informed, educated people aren't all professors and doctors and lawyers and millionaires. Most of them are common ordinary folks who want to be sure that what they say can be clearly understood.

What, then, is NONSTANDARD about ten of the sentences above? Here's a rundown:

1. *At* is unnecessary. *Where* includes *at*. We say that *at*—in this case—is redundant.
2. OK.
3. The pronoun *he* is unnecessary. *Guy* is enough.
4. *I* and *says* don't agree in number. *Wit'* for *with* sounds like someone whose teeth are missing. And the plural of *you* is *you*, not *youse*.
5. *Back* is redundant. Where else can you refer but back?
6. *It* and *don't* don't agree in number.
7. OK.
8. *Seen* is a past participle used without a helping verb.
9. *Me* and *her* are incorrect forms to be used as subjects of sentences.
10. *Them* is a personal pronoun, not a demonstrative.
11. *Of* functions as a preposition, not as a helping verb.
12. *Don't* and *nobody* constitute a double negative.

Practice 2. Writing

Rewrite each of the nonstandard sentences above changing the nonstandard word or phrase into <u>standard</u> informal English.

Be prepared to read at least one of your rewritten sentences aloud. Do your classmates agree that your sentence uses only standard English?

There is a good deal of conversation in "Say It with Flowers." After you've read the story, you may want to comment on that conversation. Do the characters, for the most part, talk informally in standard English? Can you find any nonstandard expressions?

Say It with Flowers

Toshio Mori

He was a strange one to come to the shop and ask Mr. Sasaki for a job, but at the time I kept my mouth shut. There was something about this young man's appearance which I could not altogether harmonize with a job as a clerk in a flower shop. I was a delivery boy for Mr. Sasaki then. I had seen clerks come and go, and although they were of various sorts of temperaments and conducts, all of them had the technique of waiting on the customers or acquired one eventually. You could never tell about a new one, however, and to be on the safe side I said nothing and watched our boss readily take on this young man. Anyhow we were glad to have an extra hand because the busy season was coming around.

Mr. Sasaki undoubtedly remembered last year's rush when Tommy, Mr. Sasaki, and I had to do everything and had our hands tied behind our backs from having so many things to do at one time. He wanted to be ready this time. "Another clerk and we'll be all set for any kind of business," he used to tell us. When Teruo came around looking for a job, he got it, and Morning Glory Flower Shop was all set for the year as far as our boss was concerned.

When Teruo reported for work the following morning Mr. Sasaki left him in Tommy's hands. Tommy had been our number one clerk for a long time.

"Tommy, teach him all you can," Mr. Sasaki said. "Teruo's going to be with us from now on."

"Sure," Tommy said.

"Tommy's a good florist. You watch and listen to him," the boss told the young man.

"All right, Mr. Sasaki," the young man said. He turned to us and said, "My name is Teruo." We shook hands.

We got to know one another pretty well after that. He was a quiet fellow with very little words for anybody, but his smile disarmed a person. We soon learned that he knew nothing about the florist business. He could identify a rose when he saw one, and gardenias and carnations too; but other flowers and materials were new to him.

"You fellows teach me something about this business and I'll be grateful. I want to start from the bottom," Teruo said.

From *Yokohama, California* (Caxton Printers). Reprinted by permission of the author.

Tommy and I nodded. We were pretty sure by then he was all right. Tommy eagerly went about showing Teruo the florist game. Every morning for several days Tommy repeated the prices of the flowers for him. He told Teruo what to do on telephone orders; how to keep the greens fresh; how to make bouquets, corsages, and sprays. "You need a little more time to learn how to make big funeral pieces," Tommy said. "That'll come later."

In a couple of weeks Teruo was just as good a clerk as we had had in a long time. He was curious almost to a fault, and was a glutton for work. It was about this time our boss decided to move ahead his yearly business trip to Seattle. Undoubtedly he was satisfied with Teruo, and he knew we could get along without him for a while. He went off and left Tommy in full charge.

During Mr. Sasaki's absence I was often in the shop helping Tommy and Teruo with the customers and the orders. One day Teruo learned that I once worked in the nursery and had experience in flower-growing.

"How do you tell when a flower is fresh or old?" he asked me. "I can't tell one from the other. All I do is follow your instructions and sell the ones you tell me to sell first, but I can't tell one from the other."

I laughed. "You don't need to know that, Teruo," I told him. "When the customers ask you whether the flowers are fresh, say yes firmly. 'Our flowers are always fresh, madam.'"

Teruo picked up a vase of carnations. "These flowers came in four or five days ago, didn't they?" he asked me.

"You're right. Five days ago," I said.

"How long will they keep if a customer bought them today?" Teruo asked.

"I guess in this weather they'll hold a day or two," I said.

"Then they're old," Teruo almost

gasped. "Why, we have fresh ones that last a week or so in the shop."

"Sure, Teruo. And why should you worry about that?" Tommy said. "You talk right to the customers and they'll believe you. 'Our flowers are always fresh? You bet they are! Just came in a little while ago from the market.'"

Teruo looked at us calmly. "That's a hard thing to say when you know it isn't true."

"You've got to get it over with sooner or later," I told him. "Everybody has to do it. You too, unless you want to lose your job."

"I don't think I can say it convincingly again," Teruo said. "I must've said yes forty times already when I didn't know any better. It'll be harder next time."

"You've said it forty times already so why can't you say yes forty million times more? What's the difference? Remember, Teruo, it's your business to live," Tommy said.

"I don't like it," Teruo said.

"Do we like it? Do you think we're any different from you?" Tommy asked Teruo. "You're just a green kid. You don't know any better so I don't get sore, but you got to play the game when you're in it. You understand, don't you?"

Teruo nodded. For a moment he stood and looked curiously at us for the first time, and then went away to water the potted plants.

In the ensuing weeks we watched Teruo develop into a slick salesclerk but for one thing. If a customer forgot to ask about the condition of the flowers Teruo did splendidly. But if someone should mention about the freshness of the flowers he wilted right in front of the customers. Sometimes he would splutter. He

would stand gaping speechless on other occasions without a comeback. Sometimes, looking embarrassedly at us, he would take the customers to the fresh flowers in the rear and complete the sales.

"Don't do that any more, Teruo," Tommy warned him one afternoon after watching him repeatedly sell the fresh ones. "You know we got plenty of the old stuff in the front. We can't throw all that stuff away. First thing you know the boss'll start losing money and we'll all be thrown out."

287

"I wish . . . I could sell like you," Teruo said. "Whenever they ask me, 'Is this fresh?' 'How long will it keep?' I lose all sense about selling the stuff, and begin to think of the difference between the fresh and the old stuff. Then the trouble begins."

"Remember, the boss has to run the shop so he can keep it going," Tommy told him. "When he returns next week you better not let him see you touch the fresh flowers in the rear."

On the day Mr. Sasaki came back to the shop we saw something unusual. For the first time I watched Teruo sell some old stuff to a customer. I heard the man plainly ask him if the flowers would keep good, and very clearly I heard Teruo reply, "Yes, sir. These flowers'll keep good." I looked at Tommy, and he winked back. When Teruo came back to make it into a bouquet he looked as if he had a snail in his mouth. Mr. Sasaki came back to the rear and watched him make the bouquet. When Teruo went up front to complete the sale Mr. Sasaki looked at Tommy and nodded approvingly.

When I went out to the truck to make my last delivery for the day Teruo followed me. "Gee, I feel rotten," he said to me. "Those flowers I sold to the people, they won't last longer than tomorrow. I feel lousy. I'm lousy. The people'll get to know my word pretty soon."

"Forget it," I said. "Quit worrying. What's the matter with you?"

"I'm lousy," he said, and went back to the store.

Then one early morning the inevitable happened. While Teruo was selling the fresh flowers in the back to a customer Mr. Sasaki came in quietly and watched the transaction. The boss didn't say any-thing at the time. All day Teruo looked sick. He didn't know whether to explain to the boss or shut up.

While Teruo was out to lunch Mr. Sasaki called us aside. "How long has this been going on?" he asked us. He was pretty sore.

"He's been doing it off and on. We told him to quit it," Tommy said. "He says he feels rotten selling old flowers."

"Old flowers!" snorted Mr. Sasaki. "I'll tell him plenty when he comes back. Old flowers! Maybe you can call them old at the wholesale market but they're not old in a flower shop."

"He feels guilty fooling the customers," Tommy explained.

The boss laughed impatiently. "That's no reason for a businessman."

When Teruo came back he knew what was up. He looked at us for a moment and then went about cleaning the stems of the old flowers.

"Teruo," Mr. Sasaki called.

Teruo approached us as if steeled for an attack.

"You've been selling fresh flowers and leaving the old ones go to waste. I can't afford that, Teruo," Mr. Sasaki said. "Why don't you do as you're told? We all sell the flowers in the front. I tell you they're not old in a flower shop. Why can't you sell them?"

"I don't like it, Mr. Sasaki," Teruo said. "When the people ask me if they're fresh I hate to answer. I feel rotten after selling the old ones."

"Look here, Teruo," Mr. Sasaki said. "I don't want to fire you. You're a good boy, and I know you need a job, but you've got to be a good clerk here or you're going out. Do you get me?"

"I get you," Teruo said.

In the morning we were all at the shop early. I had an eight o'clock delivery, and the others had to rush with a big funeral order. Teruo was there early. "Hello," he greeted us cheerfully as we came in. He was unusually high-spirited, and I couldn't account for it. He was there before us and had already filled out the eight o'clock package for me. He was almost through with the funeral frame, padding it with wet moss and covering all over with brake fern, when Tommy came in. When Mr. Sasaki arrived, Teruo waved his hand and cheerfully went about gathering the flowers for the funeral piece. As he flitted here and there he seemed as if he had forgotten our presence, even the boss. He looked at each vase, sized up the flowers, and then cocked his head at the next one. He did this with great deliberation, as if he were the boss and the last word in the shop. That was all right, but when a customer soon came in, he swiftly attended him as if he owned all the flowers in the world. When the man asked Teruo if he was getting fresh flowers Teruo without batting an eye escorted the customer into the rear and eventually showed and sold the fresh ones. He did it with so much grace, dignity and swiftness that we stood around like his stooges. However, Mr. Sasaki went on with his work as if nothing had happened.

Along toward noon Teruo attended his second customer. He fairly ran to greet an old lady who wanted a cheap bouquet around fifty cents for a dinner table. This time he not only went back to the rear for the fresh ones but added three or four extras. To make it more irritating for the boss, who was watching every move, Teruo used an extra lot of maidenhair[1] because the old lady was appreciative of his art of making bouquets. Tommy and I watched the boss fuming inside of his office.

When the old lady went out of the shop Mr. Sasaki came out furious. "You're a blockhead. You have no business sense. What are you doing here?" he said to Teruo. "Are you crazy?"

Teruo looked cheerful. "I'm not crazy, Mr. Sasaki," he said. "And I'm not dumb. I just like to do it that way, that's all."

The boss turned to Tommy and me. "That boy's a sap," he said. "He's got no head."

Teruo laughed and walked off to the front with a broom. Mr. Sasaki shook his head. "What's the matter with him? I can't understand him," he said.

While the boss was out to lunch Teruo went on a mad spree. He waited on three customers at one time, ignoring our presence. It was amazing how he did it. He hurriedly took one customer's order and had him write a birthday greeting for it; jumped to the second customer's side and persuaded her to buy Columbia roses because they were the freshest of the lot. She wanted them delivered so he jotted it down on the sales book, and leaped to the third customer.

"I want to buy that orchid in the window," she stated without deliberation.

"Do you have to have orchid, madam?" Teruo asked the lady.

"No," she said. "But I want something nice for tonight's ball, and I think the orchid will match my dress. Why do you ask?"

"If I were you I wouldn't buy that orchid," he told her. "It won't keep. I could

1. *maidenhair:* a fine delicate type of fern used by florists **289**

a little boy about eleven years old came in and wanted a twenty-five-cent bouquet for his mother's birthday. Teruo waited on the boy. He was out in the front, and we saw him pick out a dozen of the two-dollar-a-dozen roses and give them to the kid.

Tommy nudged me. "If he was the boss he couldn't do those things," he said.

"In the first place," I said, "I don't think he could be a boss."

"What do you think?" Tommy said. "Is he crazy? Is he trying to get himself fired?"

"I don't know," I said.

When Mr. Sasaki returned, Teruo was waiting on another customer, a young lady.

"Did Teruo eat yet?" Mr. Sasaki asked Tommy.

"No, he won't go. He says he's not hungry today," Tommy said.

We watched Teruo talking to the young lady. The boss shook his head. Then it came. Teruo came back to the rear and picked out a dozen of the very fresh white roses and took them out to the lady.

"Aren't they lovely?" we heard her exclaim.

We watched him come back, take down a box, place several maidenhairs and asparagus, place the roses neatly inside, sprinkle a few drops, and then give it to her. We watched him thank her, and we noticed her smile and thanks. The girl walked out.

Mr. Sasaki ran excitedly to the front. "Teruo! She forgot to pay!"

Teruo stopped the boss on the way out. "Wait, Mr. Sasaki," he said. "I gave it to her."

"What!" the boss cried indignantly.

sell it to you and make a profit but I don't want to do that and spoil your evening. Come to the back, madam, and I'll show you some of the nicest gardenias in the market today. We call them Belmont and they're fresh today."

He came to the rear with the lady. We watched him pick out three of the biggest gardenias and make them into a corsage. When the lady went out with her package

"She came in just to look around and see the flowers. She likes pretty roses. Don't you think she's wonderful?"

"What's the matter with you?" the boss said. "Are you crazy? What did she buy?"

"Nothing, I tell you," Teruo said. "I gave it to her because she admired it, and she's pretty enough to deserve beautiful things, and I liked her."

"You're fired! Get out!" Mr. Sasaki spluttered. "Don't come back to the store again."

"And I gave her fresh ones too," Teruo said.

Mr. Sasaki rolled out several bills from his pocketbook. "Here's your wages for this week. Now, get out," he said.

"I don't want it," Teruo said. "You keep it and buy some more flowers."

"Here, take it. Get out," Mr. Sasaki said.

Teruo took the bills and rang up the cash register. "All right, I'll go now. I feel fine. I'm happy. Thanks to you." He waved his hand to Mr. Sasaki. "No hard feelings."

On the way out Teruo remembered our presence. He looked back. "Good-bye. Good luck," he said cheerfully to Tommy and me.

He walked out of the shop with his shoulders straight, head high, and whistling. He did not come back to see us again.

---

follow-up

Discussing "Say It with Flowers"

1. Do you think Teruo did the right thing? Why? Why not?
2. Though there is no outright physical conflict in the story, there is conflict. In fact, there are two conflicts. What are the opposing forces in each?
3. Reread the last three short paragraphs of the story. Note the next-to-last sentence: *He walked out of the shop with his shoulders straight, head high, and whistling.*
   Teruo has just been fired. How do you explain his behavior?
4. Teruo *gave* an 11-year-old boy a dozen fresh roses, and he *gave* a young girl a dozen white roses. Why?
5. Would you characterize the dialogue in the story as informal or formal language? Why? What instances of nonstandard English—if any—did you spot?

Idioms

"Everybody has to . . . . "
"Pretty soon. . . . "
"Off and on. . . . "

Familiar expressions? Yes. But look at each one again. Does that first one mean that each person owns (is in possession of) something yet to be named? Not at all. You are quite aware that *"Everybody has to. . . . "* means that each person must (is obliged to) do something.

Take that second expression—*pretty soon*. Do you understand it to mean "pleasant looking short time lapse"? Hardly. It means "in a short space of time, before very much time has elapsed."

And what do you understand by *off and on*? Well, obviously the expression <u>doesn't</u> mean what the words—taken literally— would seem to mean. It's quite clear that the expression means "with interruptions," "intermittently."

Each of those three expressions is an IDIOM. That is, each one has a meaning different from what the literal meanings of the component words would seem to suggest.

Like every major language, English is full of these expressions—IDIOMS—that seem to say one thing but actually mean something different. Idioms make it possible for us to express ourselves simply and briefly. They are language shortcuts, and so they help make English a comfortable language to use.

As you might well suppose, idioms appear mostly in informal language. But some of them have become so useful that they appear in formal language, too.

Practice 1. Discussion

Listed below and on page 293 are twelve idioms from "Say It with Flowers." Imagine that you are with a friend from a foreign country—someone who doesn't know English too well. Explain what you'd say to your friend so that he/she would understand clearly what each idiom means.

1. "had our hands tied behind our backs from having so many things to do at one time"
2. "Mr. Sasaki left him in Tommy's hands"
3. "I want to start from the bottom"
4. "the florist game"
5. "They'll hold a day or two"

6. "You've got to get it over with."
7. "You're just a green kid"
8. "Don't get sore."
9. " . . . we'll all be thrown out."
10. "I feel lousy."
11. "Do you get me?"
12. "You're fired!"

Practice 2. Writing

Look back through "Say It with Flowers," and find at least five additional idioms. On your paper, write out a brief explanation of the meaning of each.

Be prepared to read one of the idioms and its explanation aloud. Is there general agreement that the expression you've spotted is indeed an idiom? Is there also general agreement that your explanation is valid?

Bookshelf

The Clock Winder, by Ann Tyler, Knopf, 1972. Elizabeth is an independent young woman who refuses to conform to the expectations of her friends.

Don't Play Dead before You Have To, by Maja Wojciechowska. Dell, 1971 (originally, 1970). Byron's understanding of himself and his world is deepened by his work at a home for the elderly and his job babysitting for a bright child.

Reaper: The Inside Story of a Gang Leader, by Gary Hoenig. Bobbs-Merrill, 1975. Georgie's desperate efforts to overcome the frustrations of life in an inner-city gang prove futile.

20

The Face Is Familiar, But—

forestudy

A Way-Out Tone: Slang

If you were the author of a serious or tragic story, you might possibly begin your story like this:

> One can never anticipate what the future will bring. Such prediction is impossible. I cite the weekend of May 18. All indications promised that it would be pleasant and exhilarating.

From such a formal opening your reader might expect a serious story, certainly not a funny one. But if you were a writer like Max Shulman, a specialist in comedy, you could cast a certain desperate experience into a humorous light and begin like this:

> You never can tell. Citizens, you never can tell. Take the weekend of May 18. From all indications it was going to be a dilly, a dreamboat.

The general difference between the two story openings is one of TONE. TONE has to do with the writer's feelings and attitude toward what he/she is writing about—as revealed in the language he/she uses. In this case, obviously, the two examples show different attitudes—different feelings—about a memorable weekend.

Practice 1. Discussion

1. How do the words *one* in the first example and *you* in the second suggest a difference in tone?
2. Which words in the first example seem especially serious or formal?

3. Which words in the second example seem informal?
4. What in Shulman's opening gives you the impression that his story will probably be humorous?

Dilly and *dreamboat*, the two most informal words of Shulman's opening paragraph are slang words. In 1945, when this story first appeared, a thoroughly pleasant experience was to many people a "dilly," a "dreamboat." Ten years later, such an experience was a "ball" or a "blast"—or, in descriptive terms, it was "crazy" or "real George."

Twenty years later, great fun was "groovy," "Boss," or "tough"—or, with more enthusiasm—"wild, man, wild." In the 1970s, the expression "real bad, man, bad" often indicated enthusiasm for something.

Back in the 1960s guys were still "guys," but the "broads" of the thirties and the "dolls" of the forties had become "chicks." Pre-teenage girls were "teeny-boppers." An apartment was a "pad." A "groovy" night on the town was probably "out of sight," and a favorite expression of disapproval may have been a sarcastic, "Oh wow!"

A person might leave the "scene" of a gathering with the words, "Sorry, but I gotta cut out." If a boy got into his "cool rod" and "blasted off" up the street, "burning rubber" or "laying scratch," he ran the risk of being apprehended by the police for "showing an excess of speed"—a much more formal expression!

Perhaps a dull class in school is still a "drag." Teenagers occasionally enjoy "soul" music, but mostly they go where the "action" is. They prefer dance music with "the big beat" loud enough from electronic amplifiers to scramble the brain and make the body quiver. When Louis Armstrong, the great trumpeter of jazz tradition, returned with his band from a European tour, it was not surprising to hear him comment on TV: "Those cats really dig us over there."

In the late forties a male who dressed well looked "sharp," and if he was otherwise up-to-date, he was "hep." In the fifties many hep cats began to dress and act quite differently from the "squares" in "the establishment." They had a sense of general social rebellion, and they became "hip." "Hipsters" of the fifties became the "hippies" of the next decade.

What slang terms do you use today to convey the idea of sophistication, of knowing how to handle almost any situation?   **295**

Young people obviously like to experiment with language, to play with words in fresh and colorful contexts. But *sophisticated* users of slang know the dangers. They know that only a Johnny One-Note uses a word like "terrific" for *everything*. They know that too much slang is like too much salt and can ruin the flavor of their language. They know that expressions come and go, that only a few remain to achieve dictionary status, and that old slang is as stale as old toast.

It takes as much imagination and skill to use slang effectively as it does to use other words effectively. Perhaps this hipster joke makes the point:

> A tourist in New York, pulling to the curb: "I beg your pardon, sir. How can I get to Carnegie Hall?"
>
> Hipster, whipping off his shades and snapping his fingers: "Practise, man, practise!"

Practice 2. Discussion

Attack or defend the following statements. In each case give examples or explain your answer.

1. Most slang expressions are no more than fads.
2. People who use slang lack imagination.
3. Habitual use of a slang word, such as *swell, terrific, neat,* or *groovy,* reveals mental fuzziness.
4. Though slang is often amusing, it actually fills no real need.
5. Slang never has the status of respectable language.
6. Neither students nor teachers should ever use slang in the classroom.

In "The Face Is Familiar, But—" informal language and slang suit Shulman's tone—his way of entertaining you through humor.

The Face Is Familiar, But—

Max Shulman

You never can tell. Citizens, you never can tell. Take the weekend of May 18. From all indications it was going to be a dilly, a dreamboat. Saturday night was the fraternity formal, and Sunday night Petey Burch was taking me to the Dr. Askit quiz broadcast. Every prospect pleased.

At 7:30 Saturday night I got into my rented tux and picked up my rented car. At 8:30 I called for my date and was told that she had come down with the measles at 7:30. So I shrugged my rented shoulders, got into my rented car, and went to the dance alone.

I had taken my place in the stag line when Petey Burch rushed up to me, his seventeen-year-old face flushed with excitement. He waved a letter at me. "I got it! I got it!" he cried. "Here's a letter from my parents saying I can join the Navy."

"That's swell, Petey," I said. "I got some news, too. My date got the measles."

"That's too bad," he said sympathetically. Then he suddenly got more exited than ever and hollered: "No! No, that's perfect. Listen, Henry. There's a bus leaving here tonight that will get me to Minneapolis in the morning. I can be at the Navy recruiting station as soon as it opens."

"But what about the dance? What about your date?"

"The Navy," said Petey, snapping to attention, "needs men *now*. Every minute counts. How can I think of staying at a dance when there's a war[1] to be won? I've got to get out of here, Henry. I owe it to the boys Over There."

"What are you going to tell your date?"

"That's where you come in, Henry. You take my girl; I go catch the bus. I won't tell her anything. I'll just disappear and you explain it to her later."

"Won't she mind?"

"I suppose she will. But this is the first date I've ever had with her. It doesn't matter. I'll probably never see her again." He set his jaw. "God knows when I'll be coming back from Over There."

"I understand," I said simply.

"Thanks, old man," he said simply.

We shook hands.

"By the way," I said, "what about those two tickets you've got for the Dr. Askit broadcast tomorrow night?"

"They're yours," he said, handing them to me.

"Thanks, old man," I said simply.

1. *a war:* World War II (1939–1945)

297

"Here comes my date now," Petey said, pointing at the powder-room door. I took one look at her and knew what a patriot he must be to run out on a smooth operator like that. She was strictly on the side of angels.

"Where'd you find her?" I drooled.

"Just met her the other night. She's new around here. Now I'll introduce you and you dance with her while I make my getaway."

"Solid," I agreed.

She walked over to us, making pink-taffeta noises. The timing was perfect. The orchestra was tuning up for the first number just as she reached us.

"Hi," said Petey. "I want you to meet a friend of mine. Henry Ladd, this is—"

At that instant the orchestra started to play and I didn't catch her name. And no wonder. The orchestra was led by a trumpeter who had a delusion° that good trumpeting and loud trumpeting are the same thing. Between him and Harry James[2], he figured, were only a few hundred decibels of volume. Every time he played he narrowed the gap.

"Excuse me," shouted Petey, and left.

"Dance?" I yelled.

"What?" she screamed.

I made dancing motions and she nodded. We moved out on the floor. I tried to tell her while we were dancing that I hadn't caught her name, but it was impossible. The trumpeter, feeling himself gaining on Harry James, was pursuing his advantage hard. And the kind of dancing we were doing, I was too far away from her to talk. She was a smooth dancer, all right. At last there came a

2. *Harry James:* a band leader and trumpet player in the "Big Band Era" of the 1940s

short trumpet break, and I made a determined stab at it.

"I don't like to seem dull," I said to the girl, "but when Petey introduced us, I didn't catch your—"

But the trumpeter was back on the job, stronger than ever after his little rest. The rest of the song made the "Anvil Chorus" sound like a lullaby. I gave up then, and we just danced. Any girl that could dance like that I had to know her name.

Came the intermission and I tried again. "I know this is going to sound silly, but when we were intro—"

"I wonder where Petey is," she interrupted. "He's been gone an awfully long time."

"Oh, not so long really. Well, as I was saying, it makes me feel foolish to ask, but I didn't—"

"It has, too, been a long time. I think that's an awfully funny way for a boy to act when he takes a girl out for the first time. Where do you suppose he is?"

"Oh, I don't know, Probably just—oh, well, I suppose I might as well tell you now." So I told her.

She bit her lip. "Henry," she quavered, "will you please take me home?"

"Home? It's so early."

"Please, Henry."

Seventeen years of experience had taught me not to argue with a woman whose eyes are full of tears. I went and got my Driv-Ur-Self limousine, packed her into it, and started off.

"I—live—at—2123—Fremont—Avenue," she wailed.

"There, there," I cooed. "Try to look at it this way. The Navy needs men *now*. The longer he stayed around the dance tonight, the longer the war would last.

Believe me, if my parents would sign a letter for me, I'd be Over There plenty quick, believe me."

"You mean," she wept, "that you would run off and stand up a girl at a formal affair?"

"Well," I said, "maybe not that. I mean I would hardly run out on a girl like you." I took her hand. "A girl so beautiful and lovely and pretty."

She smiled through tears. "You're sweet, Henry."

"Oh, pshaw," I pshawed. "Say, I've got a couple of tickets to the Dr. Askit quiz broadcast tomorrow night. How about it?"

"Oh, Henry, I'd love to. Only I don't know if Daddy will let me. He wants me to stay in and study tomorrow night. But I'll see what I can do. You call me."

"All right," I said, "but first there's something you have to tell me." I turned to her. "Now, please don't think that I'm a jerk, but it wasn't my fault. When Petey introduced us, I didn't—"

At this point I ran into the rear end of a bus. There followed a period of unpleasantness with the bus driver, during which I got a pithy° lecture on traffic regulations. I don't know what he had to be sore about. His bus wasn't even nicked. The radiator grille of my car, on the other hand, was a total loss.

And when I got back in the car, there was more grief. The sudden stop had thrown the girl against the windshield head first, and her hat, a little straw number with birds, bees, flowers, and a patch of real grass, was now a heap of rubble. She howled all the way home.

I'm afraid this evening hasn't been much fun," I said truly as I walked her to her door.

"I'm sorry, Henry," she sniffled. "I'm sorry all this had to happen to you. You've been so nice to me."

"Oh, it's nothing any young American wouldn't have done," I said.

"You've been very sweet," she repeated. "I hope we'll get to be very good friends."

"Oh, we will. We certainly will."

She was putting her key in the lock.

"Just one more thing," I said. "Before you go in, I have to know—"

"Of course," she said. "I asked you to call and didn't give you my number. It's Kenwood 6817."

"No," I said, "it's not that. I mean yes, I wanted that, too. But there's another thing."

"Certainly, Henry," she whispered and kissed me quickly. Then the door was closed behind her.

"Nuts," I mumbled, got into the car, returned it to the Driv-Ur-Self service, where I left a month's allowance to pay for the broken grille, and went back to the fraternity house.

A few of the guys were sitting in the living room. "Hi, Henry," called one. "How'd you come out with that smooth operator? Petey sure picked the right night to run off and join the Navy, eh?"

"Oh, she was fine," I answered. "Say, do any of you fellows know her name?"

"No, you lucky dog. She's all yours. Petey just met her this week and you're the only one he introduced her to. No competition. You lucky dog."

"Yeah, sure," I said. "Lucky dog." And I went upstairs to bed.

It was a troubled night, but I had a headful of plans when I got up in the

morning. After all, the problem wasn't so difficult. Finding out a girl's name should be no task for a college sophomore, a crossword-puzzle expert, and the senior-class poet (1942) of the Salmon P. Chase High School, Blue Earth, Minnesota.

First I picked up the phone and dialled the operator. "Hello," I said, "I'd like to find out the name of the people who live at 2123 Fremont Avenue. The number is Kenwood 6817."

"I'm sorry," replied the operator, "we are not allowed to give out that information."

"But this is an emergency."

"I'm sorry. We're not allowed to give out that information."

I hung up. Then I tried plan No. 2. I dialled Kenwood 6817. A gruff male voice answered, "Hello."

"Hello," I said. "Who is this?"

"Who is *this*?" he said.

"This is Henry Ladd. Who is this?"

"Who did you wish to speak to?"

Clearly, I was getting nowhere. I hung up.

Then I went and knocked on the door of Ed Beasley's room. Ed was a new pledge of the fraternity, and he was part of my third plan. He opened the door. "Enter, master," he said in the manner required of new pledges.

"Varlet," I said, "I have a task for you. Take yon telephone book and look through it until you find the name of the people who have telephone number, Kenwood 6817."

"But, master—" protested Ed.

"I have spoken," I said sharply and walked off briskly, rubbing my palms.

In ten minutes Ed was in my room with Roger Goodhue, the president of the fraternity. "Henry," said Roger, "you are acquainted with the university policy regarding the hazing of pledges."

"Hazing?"

"You know very well that hazing was outlawed this year by the Dean of Student Affairs. And yet you go right ahead and haze poor Ed. Do you think more of your own amusement than the good of the fraternity? Do you know that if Ed had gone to the Dean instead of me we would have had our charter taken away? I am going to insist on an apology right here and now."

Ed got his apology and walked off briskly, rubbing his palms.

"We'll have no more of that," said Roger, and he left, too.

I took the phone book myself and spent four blinding hours looking for Kenwood 6817. Then I remembered that Petey had said the girl was new around here. The phone book was six months old; obviously her number would not be listed until a new edition was out.

The only course left to me was to try calling the number again in the hope that she would answer the phone herself. This time I lucky. It was her voice.

"Hello," I cried, "who is this?"

"Why, it's Henry Ladd," she said. "Daddy said you called before. Why didn't you ask to talk to me?"

"We were cut off," I said.

"About tonight: I can go to the broadcast with you. I told Daddy we were going to the library to study. So be sure you tell the same story when you get here. I better hang up now. I hear Daddy coming downstairs. See you at eight.'Bye."

"Good-bye," I said.

And good-bye to some lovely ideas. But I was far from licked. When I drove up to her house at eight in a car I had borrowed from a fraternity brother (I wisely decided not to try the Driv-Ur-Self people again), I still had a few aces up my sleeve. It was now a matter of pride with me. I thought of the day I had recited the senior-class poem and I said to myself, "By George, a man who could do that can find out a simple girl's name, by George." And I wasn't going to be stupid about it either. I wasn't going to just ask her. After all this trouble, I was going to be sly about it. Sly, see?

I walked up to the porch, looking carefully for some marker with the family name on it. There was nothing. Even on the mailbox there was no name.

But in the mailbox was a letter! Quickly I scooped it out of the box, just in time to be confronted by a large, hostile man framed in a suddenly open doorway.

"And what, pray, are you doing in our mailbox?" he asked with dangerous calmness.

"I'm Henry Ladd," I squeaked. "I'm here to call on your daughter. I just saw the mail in the box and thought I'd bring it in to you." I gave him a greenish smile.

"So you're Henry Ladd. The one who hung up on me this afternoon." He placed a very firm hand on my shoulder. "Come inside, please, young man," he said.

The girl was sitting in the living room. "Do you know this fellow?" asked her father.

"Of course, Daddy. That's Henry Ladd, the boy who is going to take me over the the library to study tonight. Henry, this is my father."

"How do you do, Mr. zzzzm," I mumbled.

"What?" she said.

"Well, we better run along," I said, taking the girl's hand.

"Just a moment, young man. I'd like to ask you a few things," said her father.

"Can't wait," I chirped. "Every minute counts. Stitch in time saves nine. Starve a cold and stuff a fever. Spare the rod and spoil the child." Meanwhile I was pulling the girl closer and closer to the door. "A penny saved is a penny earned," I said and got her out on the porch.

"It's such a nice night," I cried. "Let's run to the car." I had her in the car and the car in low and picking up speed fast before she could say a word.

"Henry, you've been acting awfully strange tonight," she said with perfect justification. "I think I want to go home."

"Oh, no, no, no. Not that. I'm just excited about our first real date, that's all."

"Sometimes you're so strange, and then sometimes you're so sweet. I can't figure you out."

"I'm a complex type," I admitted. And then I went to work. "How do you spell your name?" I asked.

"Just the way it sounds. What did you think?"

"Oh, I thought so, I just was wondering." I rang up a "No sale" and started again. "Names are my hobby," I confessed. "Just before I came to get you tonight I was looking through a dictionary of names. Do you know, for instance, that *Dorothy* means 'gift of God'?"

"No. Really?"

"Yes. And *Beatrice* means 'making happy,' and *Gertrude* means 'spear maiden.'"

"Wonderful. Do you know any more?"

"Thousands," I said. "*Abigail* means 'my father's joy,' *Margaret* means 'a pearl,' *Phyllis* means 'a green bough,' and *Beulah* means 'she who is to be married.'" My eyes narrowed craftily; I was about to spring the trap. "Do you know what your name means?"

"Sure," she said. "It doesn't mean anything. I looked it up once, and it just said that it was from the Hebrew and didn't mean anything."

We were in front of the broadcasting studio. "Curses," I cursed and parked the car.

We went inside and were given tickets to hold. In a moment Dr. Askit took the stage and the broadcast began. "Everyone who came in here tonight was given a ticket," said Dr. Askit. "Each ticket has a number. I will now draw numbers out of this fishbowl here and call them off. If your number is called, please come up on the stage and be a contestant." He reached into the fishbowl. "The first number is 174. Will the person holding 174 please come up here?"

"That's you," said the girl excitedly.

I thought fast. If I went up on the stage, I had a chance to win $64. Not a very good chance, because I'm not very bright about these things. But if I gave the girl my ticket and had her go up, Dr. Askit would make her give him her name and I would know what it was and all this nonsense would be over. It was the answer to my problem.

"You go," I told her. "Take my ticket and go."

"But, Henry—"

"Go ahead." I pushed her out in the aisle.

"And here comes a charming young lady," said Dr. Askit. He helped her to the microphone. "A very lucky young lady, I might add. Miss, do you know what you are?"

"What?"

"You are the ten thousandth contestant that has appeared on the Dr. Askit quiz program. And do you know what I am going to do in honor of this occasion?"

"What?"

"I am going to pay you *ten* times as much as I ordinarily pay contestants. Instead of a $64 maximum, you have a chance to win $640!"

I may have to pay $640 to learn this girl's name, I thought, and waves of blackness passed before my eyes.

"Now," said Dr. Askit, "what would you like to talk about? Here is a list of subjects."

Without hesitation she said, "Number six. The meaning of names of girls."

I tore two handfuls of upholstery from my seat.

"The first one is Dorothy," said Dr. Askit.

"Gift of God," replied the girl.

"Right! You now have $10. Would you like to try for $20? All right? The next one is Beatrice."

Two real tears ran down my cheeks. The woman sitting next to me moved over one seat.

"Making happy," said the girl.

"Absolutely correct!" crowed Dr. Askit. "Now would you care to try for $40?"

"You'll be sorry!" sang someone.

"Like . . . . she will," I hollered.

"I'll try," she said.

"Gertrude," said Dr. Askit.

"Forty dollars," I mourned silently. A sports coat. A good rod and reel. A new radiator grille for a Driv-Ur-Self car.

"Spear maiden," said the girl.

"Wonderful! There's no stopping this young lady tonight. How about the $80 **303** question? Yes? All right. Abigail. Think now. This is a toughie."

"Oh, that's easy. My father's joy."

"Easy, she said. Easy. Go ahead," I wept, as I pommelled the arm of my seat, "rub it in. Easy!"

"You certainly know your names," said Dr. Askit admiringly. "What do you say to the $160 question? All right? Margaret."

"A pearl."

The usher came over to my seat and asked if anything was wrong. I shook my head mutely. "Are you sure?" he said. I nodded. He left, but kept looking at me.

"In all my years in radio," said Dr. Askit, "I have never known such a contestant. The next question, my dear, is for $320. Will you try?"

"Shoot," she said gaily.

"Phyllis."

"A green bough."

"Right! Correct! Absolutely correct!"

Two ushers were beside me now. "I seen them epileptics before," one whispered to the other. "We better get him out of here."

"Go away," I croaked, flecking everyone near me with light foam.

"Now," said Dr. Askit, "will you take the big chance? The $640 question?"

She gulped and nodded.

"For $640—Beulah."

"She who is to be married," she said.

The ushers were tugging at my sleeves.

"And the lady wins $640! Congratulations! And now, may I ask you your name?"

"Come quietly, Bud," said the ushers to me. "Please don't make us use no force."

"Great balls of fire, don't make me go now!" I cried. "Not now! I paid $640 to hear this."

"My name," she said, "is Mary Brown."

"You were sweet," she said to me as we drove home, "to let me go up there tonight instead of you."

"Think nothing of it, Mary Brown," I said bitterly.

She threw back her head and laughed. "You're so funny, Henry. I think I like you more than any boy I've ever met."

"Well, that's something to be thankful for, Mary Brown," I replied.

She laughed some more. Then she leaned over and kissed my cheek. "Oh, Henry, you're marvellous."

So Mary Brown kissed me and thought I was marvellous. Well, that was just dandy.

"Marvellous," she repeated and kissed me again.

"Thank you, Mary Brown," I said.

No use being bitter about it. After all, $640 wasn't all the money in the world. Not quite, anyhow. I had Mary Brown, now. Maybe I could learn to love her after a while. She looked easy enough to love. Maybe some day we would get married. Maybe there would even be a dowry. A large dowry. About $640.

I felt a little better. But just a little.

I parked in front of her house. "I'll never forget this evening as long as I live," she said as we walked to the porch.

"Nor I, Mary Brown," I said truthfully.

She giggled. She put her key in the front door. "Would you like to come in, Henry—dear?"

"No thanks, Mary Brown. I have a feeling your father doesn't care for me." Then it dawned on me. "Look!" I cried. "Your father. You told him you were at the library tonight. What if he was listening to the radio tonight and heard you on the Dr. Askit program?"

"Oh, don't worry. People's voices sound different over the radio."

"But the name! You gave your name."

She looked at me curiously. "Are you kiddin'? You know very well I didn't give my right name . . . . HENRY! WHY ARE YOU BEATING YOUR HEAD AGAINST THE WALL?"

follow-up

Discussing "The Face Is Familiar, But—"

1. In this story three elements are important: character, language style, and plot. How is each important in contributing to the humor of the story? Give examples.
2. In reading fiction the critical reader ordinarily expects the action to be believable.
   a. Which events in this story do you think are unbelievable?
   b. Which events are believable?
3. Where is the real ending of the story? Is it in the last sentence or in the next to the last? Why?
4. How did the ending affect you? Did you expect this kind of ending? Explain.
5. Explain whether or not you think this story could be effectively adapted for TV. What are some of the changes that would have to be made?

Clipped Words

Practice 1. Discussion

Slang words like *dilly* and *dreamboat* are outdated today. But *bus* (p. 299) is an example of old slang that not only has lasted but also has become a part of our everyday vocabulary. Short for *omnibus* (a Latin word meaning "for all"), it illustrates the tendency of North Americans to shorten—to CLIP—words. What are the CLIPPED forms of the following words?

1. gasoline	5. influenza	9. memorandum
2. telephone	6. airplane	10. zoological park
3. television	7. automobile	11. rattlesnake
4. taxicab	8. photograph	12. bridegroom

Varieties of Language

As illustrated in the first example on page 294, formal language is appropriate in formal speech situations and in most writing. Informal language, on the other hand, includes contractions (*don't, he's, where'd, etc.*) and common, long-lasting expressions such as "awfully funny." This informal language is appropriate in most conversation and in humorous writing. Slang expressions, such as "groovy" and "out of sight," can be effective in suitable situations but they go *out of style quickly*. What's more, they are boring when overused. A fourth variety of language includes such expressions as "I ain't," "it don't," "we seen," "he done," "them cars," and "haven't got no." Such language "errors" are considered nonstandard; educated people tend to avoid them.

Practice 2. Discussion

Neither Shulman nor the main characters in his story, who are obviously educated people, use nonstandard English. (Only the ushers use a few nonstandard expressions.) But the story does have sentences that represent slang, informal language, and formal language. Judge and label each of the following ten sentences from the story. That is, in each case, decide whether the sentence is made up basically of slang expressions, informal language, or formal language.

1. "Solid," I agreed.
2. The orchestra was led by a trumpeter who had a delusion that good trumpeting and loud trumpeting are the same thing.
3. "I'm afraid this evening hasn't been much fun," I said truly as I walked her to her door.
4. Quickly I scooped it out of the box, just in time to be confronted by a large, hostile man framed in a suddenly open doorway.
5. I think that's an awfully funny way for a boy to act when he takes a girl out for the first time.
6. Now, please don't think that I'm a jerk, but it wasn't my fault.
7. "That's swell, Petey," I said.
8. "You mean," she wept, "that you would run off and stand up a girl at a formal affair?"
9. I took one look at her and knew what a patriot he must be to run out on a smooth operator like that.
10. There followed a period of unpleasantness . . . during which I got a pithy lecture on traffic regulations.

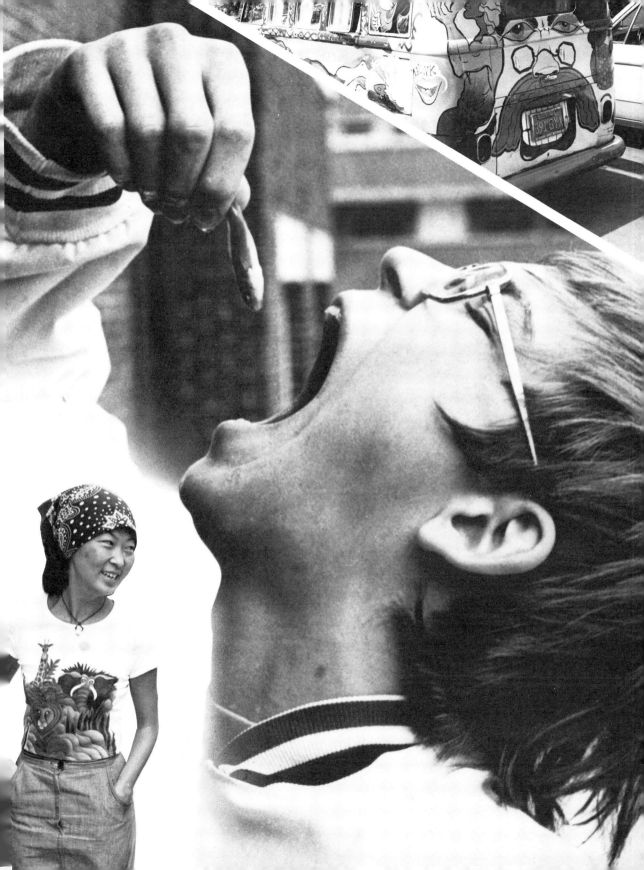

21

Cranes Fly South

forestudy

Let's Change the Subject! Let's Also Change the Object!

One of the things that makes the study of English fascinating is the variety of ways there are to say the same thing. Consider the following sentence:

		S	LV	SC (adj)
You can say		Panic	is	frightening.
You can also say	To panic	is	frightening.
	Panicking	is	frightening.
	That a person panics	is	frightening.

Notice that *panic, to panic, panicking,* and *that a person panics* all function as the subject of their respective sentences. *Panic*, of course, is a noun. What's more, *to panic, panicking,* and *that a person panics* perform the same job as the noun *panic*, but not one of those three expressions is actually a noun.

	S	V	DO
You can say	Albert Einstein	loved	knowledge.
You can also say	Albert Einstein	loved	to know.
	Albert Einstein	loved	knowing.
	Albert Einstein	loved	what he knew.

Notice that *knowledge, to know, knowing,* and *what he knew* all function as direct objects in their respective sentences. *Knowledge*, of course, is a noun. But though the other three expressions *act like nouns*, each of them is actually something else!

Infinitives

As you have seen above, *to panic* and *to know* function as nouns. Yet they are actually verb forms called INFINITIVES. Infinitives are formed by putting the word *to* in front of the present-tense form of a verb: *to panic, to know, to see,* and so on. (*To* is called the "sign of the infinitive.")

Practice 1. Discussion
In each of the following sentences, transform the underlined noun into an infinitive that functions as a noun.

Example
The establishment of a school was his highest dream.
To establish a school was his highest dream.

1. The painter's goal was the reflection of the trees in the water.
2. Modification of the building's exterior was the committee's purpose.
3. Above all he wanted avoidance of all dangerous roads.
4. Transportation of senior citizens was the purpose of the mini-bus organization.

Gerunds

Look back at the two groups of sentences which began this lesson. There you see the sentences, "Panicking is frightening" and "Albert Einstein loved knowing." What is frightening? *Panicking.* What did Albert Einstein love? *Knowing. Panicking* and *knowing,* then, are verb forms (*-ing* forms) used as nouns. (They answer the question "What?") They look exactly like participles, don't they? But participles, you'll recall, are *verbal adjectives. Panicking* and *knowing,* however, are *verbal nouns* called GERUNDS.

These sentences will help you spot the difference between participles and gerunds:

PARTICIPLES: Boyd looked up suddenly, *panicking* at the sound of footsteps. (What kind of person was Boyd as he looked up? He was a *panicking* person. *Panicking* functions as an adjective that modifies Boyd. Thus it's a participle.) **313**

GERUND: *Panicking* is a sign of unreasonable terror. (What is? *Panicking* is. *Panicking*, then, functions as a noun. Because it's a verb form acting as a noun, it's called a gerund.)

PARTICIPLE: *Knowing* the answer to the question, Tina raised her hand. (What kind of person was Tina when she raised her hand? She was a *knowing* person. Here, *knowing* describes Tina. *Knowing*, then, is a verb form used as an adjective. It's a participle.)

GERUND: *Knowing* the answer put Tina ahead by ten points. (What put Tina ahead? *Knowing* did. *Knowing*, then, acts as a noun—the subject of the sentence. As a verbal noun, *knowing* is a gerund.)

To review: A *gerund* is simply an *-ing* form of a verb used as a noun. You use gerunds every day. For example:

S LV SC
Seeing is *believing*.

     S   V   DO
My brother appreciates good *cooking*.

Practice 2. Discussion

In each of the following sentences, replace each underlined *noun* or *infinitive* with a *gerund*.

Example
My brother likes <u>to fish</u>.
My brother likes <u>fishing</u>.

1. <u>To err</u> is human; to <u>forgive</u>, divine.
2. <u>Manipulation</u> of money is the secret of financial success.
3. My English teacher actually likes <u>to correct</u> papers.
4. Every Halloween my brother loves <u>to scare</u> little children who come to the door.
5. <u>Appreciation</u> of life's finer experiences makes a person truly happy.

Noun Clauses

Looking again at the two groups of sentences at the beginning of this lesson, you'll notice the expressions *that a person panics* and *what he knew.* Both substitute for nouns—one for *panic,* the other for *knowledge.* Expressions like *that a person panics* and *what he knew* are *noun clauses.* Unlike infinitives and gerunds—but like adjectives and adverb clauses—noun clauses have subjects and verbs. However, as you have seen, the entire clause functions as a noun. Noun clauses often begin with such words as *that, when, why, how, what, where.* Here are a few examples of sentences that have noun clauses:

     S   V   DO

1. He didn't know *where he was going.*

               S   LV   SC

2. *What caused the explosion* was the first item on the council's agenda.

3. You can tell a person by *where he's been.* (The noun clause is the object of the preposition *by.*)

Practice 3. Discussion

In each of the sentences below, replace each underlined passage with a *noun clause.* You may want to refer to the list of noun clause "beginners."

1. Eva didn't understand her <u>vocational goal.</u>
   Eva didn't understand what ————————————————.

2. The inspector discovered the <u>gems' location.</u>
   The inspector discovered *where* ————————————.

3. She told her brother <u>the time of departure.</u>
   She told her brother when————————————————.

4. Toni couldn't explain <u>her reasons.</u>
   Toni couldn't explain ————————————————————.

5. Gina understood <u>the procedure</u> for building the dam.
   Gina understood ——————————————————————.

Practice 4. Writing

The sentence pattern—S-V-DO—appears on page 316. As specified, write original sentences that contain nouns, infinitives, gerunds, and noun clauses—both as subjects and as direct objects. You'll write eight sentences in all:

	S	V	DO
1.	(a noun)		
2.	(an infinitive)		
3.	(a gerund)		
4.	(a noun clause)		
5.			(a noun)
6.			(an infinitive)
7.			(a gerund)
8.			(a noun clause)

Be prepared to read at least two of your sentences aloud.

Practice 5. Discussion

Here are four sentences from "Cranes Fly South." See whether you can identify any gerunds or infinitives or noun clauses in these sentences.

1. Lee remembered what his mother had said.
2. He tried to pull the greatcoat close about his shrunken body.
3. The old man's voice lost its tone of loud authority, and dropped into feeble wheedling.
4. Her fingers touched his hair, to show that what he had done didn't matter any more.

Cranes Fly South

Edward McCourt

"They fly all night," the old man said. "First you hear a sound far off and you figger it's thunder—and it gits louder and nearer, and soon it's like a freight train passin' right over your head, and if there's a moon they fly across it and the night gits dark—"

"But I tell you I saw one!" Lee said.

"Honest, Grandpa. Out at Becker's slough.[1] I was looking for ducks—and all of a sudden—"

"Ain't no whoopin' cranes nowadays," the old man said disconsolately.

Lee spoke very slowly now, trying hard to be patient. "At Becker's slough. Honest.

1. *slough:* in the Prairie Provinces, a body of fresh water formed from rain or melted snow.

I saw the black tips of his wings just as clear!"

"And you feel like you want to go, too," Grandpa said. "Breaks your heart almost, you want to go that bad, when you hear the thunder right over your head—like a big, long freight train passin' in the nighttime."

His voice rose in an unexpected harsh croak. "At Becker's slough, you say? A whoopin' crane—a real, honest-to-gosh whooper? Boy, I ain't seen a whooper for forty years!"

"There's only twenty-eight whoopers left in the whole world," Lee said. "They fly south in the fall clear to Texas."

"Me, I'm going south, too," Grandpa said. "You can set in the sun all winter and see things besides flatness. Man gets mighty tired of flatness—after eighty years." His voice trailed off. He fell back in his chair and closed his eyes.

Lee remembered what his mother had said. "Grandpa is a very old man, Lee; he mustn't ever get excited." He knew a moment of paralysing fear. Maybe Grandpa was dying; maybe he was already dead! "Grandpa!" he shouted hoarsely. "Wake up, wake up!"

A convulsive shudder twisted the shrunken body in the chair. The old man stood up without laying a hand on the arm rest of the chair, and his voice was loud and strong. "Boy, I got to see it. I tell you I got to!"

Lee stared, fascinated and irresolute. "But Mum says—"

The old man's voice lost its tone of loud authority, dropped into feeble wheedling. "Aw, come on, boy. Ain't nobody goin' to see us. Your paw's workin' in the far quarter and Ellen she's off to a hen party somewheres. We can slip out and back just as easy."

"But it's three miles.[2] And Mum's got the car."

Grandpa wrinkled up his face. "We got a horse and buggy, ain't we?"

"But the buggy hasn't been used for years and years," Lee protested. "And the harness—"

The old man caught up his stick from beside the chair. Fury chased the cunning from his puckered face. "You git along, boy," he screamed, "or I'll welt the hide off you!"

Lee retreated to the door. "All right, Grandpa," he said placatingly. "I'll hitch Bessie up right now."

Grandpa had a hard time getting into the buggy. But the moment he reached the seat he snatched the lines from Lee's hands and slapped the old mare's rump with the ends of the lines. Bessie broke into a startled trot and Lee held his breath. But Bessie slowed almost at once to a shambling, reluctant walk, and Lee felt a little easier. Maybe the buggy wouldn't fall to pieces after all.

They drove along the road a little way and turned off to a trail that wound across bleak open prairie. Grandpa stared straight ahead, and his eyes were bright. "Like I say, boy, they go south. Figger they see the Mississippi from a mile up. Sure like to see it myself. Will, too, some day."

The old man's chin dropped toward his chest. The lines fell from his fingers, and Lee caught them just before they slipped over the dashboard.

"Thanks, boy, for takin' me out. Maybe we'd better go home now. I'm tired—awful tired."

The boy's throat tightened. "We're near there, Grandpa," he said. "You can see the slough now."

2. *three miles:* 4.827 km; 1 mile = 1.609 km

"Ain't no whoopers any more," the old man mumbled peevishly. "Gone south."

Lee swung Bessie out of the rutted trail into the shelter of a poplar grove. He eased the old man down from the buggy and slipped a hand under his arm. "Come on, Grandpa," he urged. "We'll make it all right."

They advanced slowly from behind the sheltering bluff into the tall grass that rimmed the borders of the slough. The sun dazzled their eyes, but the wind blew strong and cold across the slough, carrying with it the rank smell of stagnant water and alkali-encrusted mud. Grandpa huddled under his greatcoat.

"What are you doin' to me, boy?" he complained almost tearfully. "You know what Ellen said. I ain't supposed to go out without she's along."

"Down, Grandpa—down!"

The old man crumpled to hands and knees. "Where is it, boy? Where is it?" His voice rose in a shrill, frenzied squeak.

"Come on—I can see his head!"

Something moved in the long grass. For a shuddering moment the boy lay helpless, beyond the power of speech or movement. Then his body jerked convulsively to life and he leaped to his feet and his voice rang wild and shrill.

"Grandpa—look—look!"

He wheeled to clutch at Grandpa, but the old man already stood upright, staring out of dim, fierce eyes at the great white body flung against the pale sky. "Great God in heaven!" The words were a strange, harsh cry of ecstasy and pain. "A whooper, boy—a whooper!"

They stood together, man and boy, held by an enchantment that was no part of the drab, flat world about them. The great bird rose steadily higher, the black tips of his wings a blurred streak against the whiteness of his body. He swung in a wide arc, flew high about the heads of the watchers by the slough, then climbed fast and far into the remote pale sky. For a minute or more he seemed to hang immobile, suspended in a space beyond the limits of the world. Then the whiteness faded, blended with the pale of the sky, and was gone.

The old man's fingers were tight on the boy's arm. Again the harsh cry burst from his lips—"Great God in heaven!"—the cry that was at once a shout of exultation and a prayer. Then the light in his eyes faded and went out.

"He's gone south," Grandpa said. His shoulders sagged. He tried to pull the greatcoat close about his shrunken body. "They come in the night and you hear a sound like thunder and the sky gits dark—and there's the Mississippi below and the smell of the sea blown in from a hundred miles away . . ."

Lee's mother led the boy to the door. "He's raving," she said, and there were tears in her eyes and voice. "He's so sick. Oh, Lee, you should never—"

At once she checked herself. "The doctor should be here soon," she whispered. "Tell your father to send him up the minute he comes."

Lee fled downstairs, away from the dim-lit, shadow-flecked room where the only sounds to break the heavy silence were Grandpa's muttered words and his hard, unquiet breathing. Grandpa was sick—awful sick. He had no strength left to lift his head from the pillow, and his eyes didn't seem to see things any more. But he wasn't crazy; he knew all right what he was saying. Only no one except Lee understood what he meant. He did not regret what he had done. No matter what happened he was glad that Grandpa had seen the whooper.

"He just had to see it," he said stubbornly to his father. "He just had to."

His father nodded slowly from behind the paper he was pretending to read. "I know, son," he said. And he added, a queer, inexplicable note of pain in his voice, "Wish I'd been along."

Lee fell asleep on the couch after a while. When he awoke much later, he was alone in the living room and the oil lamp on the table was burning dimly. He sat up, instantly alert. The house seemed strange and lonely, and the noises which had troubled him even in sleep were still. Something had happened. You could tell.

His mother came downstairs, walking very quietly. Her face was set and calm. He knew at once what she had come to say. Her fingers touched his hair, to show that what he had done didn't matter any more.

"Grandpa is dead," she said.

Suddenly her voice choked and she turned away her head. A moment of anguish engulfed him. He couldn't bear to hear his mother cry. But when at last he spoke, the words sprang clear and triumphant from his throat.

"He's gone south," he said.

follow-up

Discussing "Cranes Fly South"

1. Why, in your opinion, are the whooping cranes so important to Grandpa?
2. Why do you think Lee's father wishes he had seen the whooping crane with Lee and Grandpa?
3. What impression do you get of Grandpa in this story?

Images

Think of one person—someone you can picture in your mind. It might be a friend, a rock star, an athlete. When you have a mental picture of that person, try to answer the following questions:

1. If that person were a vehicle, what kind would it be?
2. If that person were an animal, what would it be?
3. If that person were a musical instrument, what kind would it be? **319**

Now review your answers, and try to figure out why you chose the particular vehicle, the particular animal, the particular instrument you did. What traits of the person caused you to select the answers you gave? What characteristics of the vehicle, animal, and instrument seemed appropriate for the person you had in mind?

If the person you had in mind was small and delicate, then it is unlikely that you pictured him/her as a school bus, a buffalo, or a tuba. On the other hand, if you had in mind the tackle on the football team, then you probably did not imagine that person as a baby carriage, a gazelle, or a piccolo. Somehow, those IMAGES just don't fit. Instead, perhaps the football player might be imagined as a buffalo, since both are large and powerful. The small person might be visualized as the gazelle, since both are light and fragile. Those second comparisons are appropriate because it's easy to see that the person and the animal share certain characteristics.

In visualizing the football player as a buffalo and the small person as a gazelle, you are creating IMAGES that tell us something about the people you have in mind.

So far, we have been discussing images that tell us about a person's physical appearance, but images might also be used to give other information. For instance:

> "Although she was usually quiet and gentle, in club meetings she was a bulldozer."

We know that meetings do not call for great physical power, as football games do, and so the image of the bulldozer probably is not intended to describe size and strength. We know that meetings *do* sometimes demand persistence and a willingness to argue for a position or a course of action. Thus, it is likely that the image is intended to describe the person's drive and determination. If the person referred to in the sentence is a bulldozer in meetings, she probably pushes and fights until she overcomes all objections from other members.

Practice 1. Writing

Take the three questions you answered on page 319, and ask them about yourself. What vehicle, animal, and musical instrument would you be? You may think of yourself either as you are now or as the person you would like to be. Write a brief paragraph about each image, explaining why you chose it.

Symbols

Sometimes an image is used not only to describe the characteristics of a person or of something else, but also to represent—to stand for—that person or thing. The beaver, for instance, is an image often associated with Canada. The beaver was of prime importance in the fur trade which was responsible for much of the early settling of this country. It also came to represent the vast areas of forests and lakes which make up much of Canada, and has eventually become understood as representing Canada itself. Thus, for example, when we see a drawing of the beaver in a political cartoon, we know that it stands for Canada. It has, in other words, become a SYMBOL.

Symbols can also be more abstract. For example, the Canadian flag is a symbol of our country. The sign "+" is a symbol for the mathematical operation called addition. The mark "$" is a symbol for our dollar. All of these things have become symbols because a great many people in the course of history have agreed to use them as shorthand expressions of ideas. Thus the stylized red maple leaf which is the characteristic feature of our flag, has become the symbol of anything that is totally Canadian, and we see it on everything from library books to Canadian-made appliances to bumper stickers.

Practice 2. Discussion

What other symbols—religious, commercial, social—are you familiar with? Do you have anything that is so personal and unique that it has become a symbol of yourself—a particular hair style, a style of clothing, something that you own?

In "Cranes Fly South," the whooping crane becomes a symbol of Grandpa. When Lee says, "He's gone south," he is speaking symbolically of his grandfather. Do you think this is an effective ending for the story? Do you think it is appropriate for Lee to speak in a "clear and triumphant" way when he hears of Grandpa's death? Does the ending alter your feeling toward the crane incident and Grandpa's subsequent death?

The Bird

Patrick Lane

The bird you captured is dead.
I told you it would die
but you would not learn
from my telling. You wanted

to cage a bird in your hands
and learn to fly.

Listen again.
You must not handle birds.
They cannot fly through your fingers.
You are not a nest
and a feather is
not made of blood and bone.

Only words
can fly for you like birds
on the wall of the sun
A bird is a poem
that talks of the end of cages.

Bookshelf

"A Bird in the House," in *A Bird in the House,* by Margaret Laurence.
McClelland and Stewart New Canadian Library, 1974. Vanessa
comes to a new understanding of her father almost too late.

"A Cap for Steve," in *Morley Callaghan's Stories,* by Morley Callaghan.
Macmillan, 1967. A father and son come to a deeper
understanding of each other because of a stolen baseball cap.

Everybody Gets Something Here, by Ken Mitchell. Macmillan, 1977.
Hilarious stories with interesting, zany characters. The stories
are set in southern Saskatchewan.

"Privilege of the Limits," by E. W. Thomson, in *Selected Stories of
E. W. Thomson,* ed. by Lorraine McMullen. University of Ottawa
Press, 1973. The humorous story of how a clever father gets out
of jail to see his sick son.

"The Summer My Grandmother was Supposed to Die," by Mordecai
Richlcr, in *Modern Canadian Stories,* cd. by Giosc Rimanclli
and Roberto Roberts. Ryerson Press, 1966. Jewish family
relationships provide a humorous context for an old woman's
dying and eventual death.

From POEMS NEW & SELECTED by Patrick Lane. Reprinted by
permission of the author and Oxford University Press.

22

The Monkey's Paw

forestudy

Stage Directions

"What are you doing here?"

How would *you* ask that question? In what tone of voice *should* the question be asked? Obviously, there is no "right" tone of voice for asking that question or any other question. And the manner in which you'd ask the question depends on (1) the situation you're in and (2) the person you're asking.

Practice 1. Discussion

1. a. In a tone of voice that shows surprise, ask the question aloud: "What are you doing here?"
   b. Under what circumstances would you be likely to ask the question to show surprise?
   c. If you are surprised when you ask the question, what is likely to be your attitude toward the person you're addressing?
2. a. Ask the same question aloud so that your voice shows anger.
   b. Under what circumstances might the question be asked in an angry tone?
   c. What's likely to be your attitude toward the person you're addressing?
3. a. Ask the question again, letting your tone of voice show fear.
   b. Under what circumstances might the question be asked in such a way?
   c. What is your attitude toward the person you're asking?

323

Practice 2. Discussion

Here's a statement that almost anyone might make: "I don't want to go."

1. Be prepared to make that statement in any one of the following tones of voice:
   a. Bored
   b. Adamant, unyielding (you absolutely will not change your mind)
   c. Angry
   d. Annoyed
2. Under what circumstances would the speaker be likely to use each tone of voice specified above?

You can readily see that a statement can be made or a question asked in a number of ways, depending upon the situation in which the speaker finds himself/herself.

Authors of stories can tell you in so many words just exactly how a character says what he/she says. For example, in "Cranes Fly South," this passage appeared:

> "Ain't no whoopin' cranes nowadays," the old man said disconsolately.
> Lee spoke very slowly now, trying hard to be patient. "At Becker's slough. Honest. I saw the black tips of his wings just as clear!"

Playwrights, on the other hand, can't tell you how their characters say what they say. A playwright cannot come out on the stage during the performance of a play and tell you that a character is speaking angrily or sadly. Instead, the playwright writes suggestions and directions to show the actors how specific lines should be spoken. Those suggestions and directions are written right along with the dialogue—the words that the actors speak. But those suggestions and directions are enclosed in brackets ([ ]) or parentheses and printed in italics. Such suggestions and directions are called STAGE DIRECTIONS.

A writer of narrative can *tell* you what his characters are doing. A playwright can't. To indicate what the actors should do on stage, a playwright includes STAGE DIRECTIONS that help the actors perform as the playwright intended.

In addition to writing STAGE DIRECTIONS for dialogue and for action, the playwright also writes STAGE DIRECTIONS to describe how the stage should look when the curtain goes up.

In a play, STAGE DIRECTIONS are every bit as important as the dialogue—especially if you're reading the play. It's up to you to read all STAGE DIRECTIONS carefully so that you see in your mind what you'd see if you were watching an actual performance of the play.

The Monkey's Paw

W. W. Jacobs

SCENE—*The living-room of an old-fashioned cottage on the outskirts of Fulham.*[1] *Set corner-wise in the left angle at the back a deep window; further front, three or four steps lead up to a door. Further forward a dresser, with plates, glasses, etc. At back an alcove with the street door fully visible. On the inside of the street door, a wire letter-box. On the right a cupboard, then a fireplace. In the centre a round table. Against the wall, an old-fashioned piano. A comfortable armchair each side of the fireplace. Other chairs. On the mantelpiece a clock, old china figures, etc. An air of comfort pervades the room.*

1. *Fulham:* a district of London, England

SCENE ONE

At the rise of the curtain, MRS. WHITE, *a pleasant-looking old woman, is seated in the armchair below the fire, attending to a kettle which is steaming on the fire, and keeping a laughing eye on* MR. WHITE *and* HERBERT. *These two are seated at the right angle of the table nearest the fire with a chess-board between them.* MR. WHITE *is evidently losing. His hair is ruffled; his spectacles are high up on his forehead.* HERBERT, *a fine young fellow, is looking with satisfaction at the move he has just made.* MR. WHITE *makes several attempts to move, but thinks better of them. There is a shaded lamp on the table. The door is tightly shut. The curtains of the window are drawn; but every now and then the wind is heard whistling outside.*

MR. WHITE (*moving at last, and triumphant*): There, Herbert, my boy! Got you, I think.

HERBERT: Oh, you're a deep 'un, Dad, aren't you?

MRS. WHITE: Mean to say he's beaten you at last?

HERBERT: Lord, no! Why, he's overlooked——

MR. WHITE (*very excited*): I see it! Lemme have that back!

HERBERT: Not much. Rules of the game!

MR. WHITE (*disgusted*): I don't hold with them scientific rules. You turn what ought to be an innocent relaxation——

MRS. WHITE: Don't talk so much, Father. You put him off——

HERBERT (*laughing*): Not he!

MR. WHITE (*trying to distract his attention*): Hark at the wind.

HERBERT (*drily*): Ah! I'm listening. Check.

MR. WHITE (*still trying to distract him*): I should hardly think Sergeant-Major Morris'd come tonight.

HERBERT: Mate. (*Rises.*)

MR. WHITE (*with an outbreak of disgust and sweeping the chessmen off the board*): That's the worst of living so far out. Your friends can't come for a quiet chat, and you addle your brains over a confounded——

HERBERT: Now, Father! Morris'll turn up all right.

MR. WHITE (*still in a temper*): Lover's Lane, Fulham! Ho! Of all the beastly, slushy, out-o'-the-way places to live in ——! Pathway's a bog, and the road's a torrent. (*To* MRS. WHITE, *who has risen, and is at his side*) What's the County Council thinking of? That's what I want to know. Because this is the only house

in the road it doesn't matter if nobody can get near it, I s'pose.

MRS. WHITE: Never mind, dear. Perhaps you'll win tomorrow. (*She moves to back of table.*)

MR. WHITE: Perhaps I'll—perhaps I'll ——! What d'you mean? (*Bursts out laughing*) There! You always know what's going on inside o' me, don't you, Mother?

MRS. WHITE: Ought to, after thirty years, John. (*She goes to dresser, and busies herself wiping tumblers on tray there. He rises, goes to fireplace and lights pipe.*)

HERBERT: And it's not such a bad place, Dad, after all. One of the few old-fashioned houses left near London. None o' your stucco villas. Home-like, I call it. And so do you, or you wouldn't ha' bought it. (*Rolls a cigarette.*)

MR. WHITE (*growling*): Nice job I made o' that, too! With two hundred pounds owin' on it.

HERBERT (*on back of chair*): Why, I shall work that off in no time, Dad. Matter o' three years, with the rise promised me.

MR. WHITE: If you don't get married.

HERBERT: Not me. Not that sort.

MRS. WHITE: I wish you would, Herbert. A good, steady, lad—— (*She brings the tray with a bottle of whisky, glasses, a lemon, spoons, buns, and a knife to the table.*)

HERBERT: Lots o' time, Mother. Sufficient for the day—as the sayin' goes. Just now my dynamos don't leave me any time for love-making. Jealous they are, I tell you!

MR. WHITE (*chuckling*): I lay awake o' night often, and think: If Herbert took a nap, and let his what-d'you-call-ums—dynamos, run down, all Fulham would be in darkness. Lord! what a joke!

326

HERBERT: Joke! And me with the sack! Pretty idea of a joke you've got, I don't think. (*Knock at outer door*)

MRS. WHITE: Hark! (*Knock repeated, louder*)

MR. WHITE (*going toward door*): That's him. That's the Sergeant-Major. (*He unlocks door, back.*)

HERBERT (*removes chess-board*): Wonder what yarn he's got for us tonight. (*Places chess-board on piano*)

MRS. WHITE (*goes up right, busies herself putting the other armchair nearer fire, etc.*): Don't let the door slam, John! (MR. WHITE *opens the door a little, struggling with it. Wind.* SERGEANT-MAJOR MORRIS, *a veteran with a distinct military appearance—left arm gone—dressed as a commissionaire, is seen to enter.* MR. WHITE *helps him off with his coat, which he hangs up in the outer hall.*)

MR. WHITE (*at the door*): Slip in quick! It's as much as I can do to hold it against the wind.

SERGEANT: Awful! Awful! (*Busy taking off his cloak, etc.*) And a mile² up the road—by the cemetery—it's worse. Enough to blow the hair off your head.

MR. WHITE: Give me your stick.

SERGEANT: If 'twasn't I knew what a welcome I'd get——

MR. WHITE (*preceding him into the room*): Sergeant-Major Morris!

MRS. WHITE: Tut! tut! So cold you must be! Come to the fire; do'ee, now.

SERGEANT: How are you, marm? (*To* HERBERT) How's yourself, laddie? Not on duty, eh? Day-week, eh?

HERBERT: No sir. Night week. But there's half an hour yet.

SERGEANT (*sitting in the armchair above the fire, toward which* MRS. WHITE *is motioning him.* MR. WHITE *mixes grog for* MORRIS): Thank'ee kindly, marm. That's good—

2. *a mile:* 1.609 km

hah! That's a sight better than the trenches at Chitral. That's better than settin' in a puddle with the rain pourin' down in buckets, and the natives takin' pot-shots at you.

MRS. WHITE: Didn't you have no umbrellas? (*At corner below fire, kneels before it, stirs it, etc.*)

SERGEANT: Umbrell——? Ho! ho! That's good! Eh, White? That's good. Did ye hear what she said? Umbrellas!—— *And* goloshes! *And* hot-water bottles!——Ho, yes! No offense, marm, but it's easy to see you was never a soldier.

HERBERT (*rather hurt*): Mother spoke out o' kindness, sir.

SERGEANT: And well I know it; and no offense intended. No, marm, 'ardship, 'ardship is the soldier's lot. Starvation, fever, and get yourself shot. That's a bit o' my own.

MRS. WHITE: You don't look to've taken much harm—except—(*Indicates his empty sleeve. She takes kettle to table, then returns to fire.*)

SERGEANT (*showing a medal hidden under his coat*): And that I got this for. No, marm. Tough. Thomas Morris is tough. (MR. WHITE *is holding a glass of grog under the* SERGEANT'S *nose*) And sober. What's this now?

MR. WHITE: Put your nose in it; you'll see.

SERGEANT: Whisky? And hot? And sugar? And a slice o' lemon? No. I said I'd never—but seein' the sort o' night. Well! (*Waving the glass at them*) Here's another thousand a year!

MR. WHITE (*also with a glass*): Same to you, and many of 'em.

SERGEANT (*to* HERBERT, *who has no glass*): What? Not you?

HERBERT (*laughing and sitting across chair*): Oh! 'tisn't for want to being so- **327** ciable. But my work don't go with it. Not if 'twas ever so little. I've got to keep a cool head, a steady eye, and a still hand. The fly-wheel might gobble me up.

MRS. WHITE: Don't, Herbert. (*Sits in armchair below fire*)

HERBERT (*laughing*):   No fear, Mother.

SERGEANT: Ah! You electricians!—Sort o' magicians, you are. Light! says you—and light it is. And, power! says you—and the trams go whizzin'. And, knowledge! says you—and words go 'ummin' to the ends o' the world. It fair beats me—and I've seen a bit in my time, too.

HERBERT (*nudges his father*):   Your Indian magic? All a fake, Governor. The fakir's fake.

SERGEANT: Fake, you call it? I tell you, I've *seen* it.

HERBERT (*nudging his father with his foot*): Oh, come, now! Such as what? Come, now!

SERGEANT: I've seen a cove with no more clothes on than a babby (*to* MRS. WHITE) if you know what I mean—take an empty basket—empty, mind!—as empty as—as this here glass—

MR. WHITE: Hand it over, Morris. (*Hands it to* HERBERT, *who goes quickly behind table and fills it.*)

SERGEANT: Which was not my intentions, but used for illustration.

HERBERT (*while mixing*):   Oh, *I've* seen the basket trick; and I've read how it was done. Why, I could do it myself, with a bit o' practice. Ladle out something stronger. (HERBERT *brings him the glass.*)

SERGEANT: Stronger?—What do you say to an old fakir chuckin' a rope up in the air—in the *air*, mind you!—and swarming up it, same as if it was 'ooked on—and vanishing clean out o' sight?—I've seen *that*. (HERBERT *goes to table, plunges a knife into a bun and offers it to the* SERGEANT *with exaggerated politeness.*)

SERGEANT (*eyeing it with disgust*):   Bun—? What for?

HERBERT: That yarn takes it. (MR. *and* MRS. WHITE *delighted*)

SERGEANT: Mean to say you doubt my word?

MRS. WHITE: No, no! He's only taking you off.—You shouldn't, Herbert.

MR. WHITE: Herbert always was one for a bit o' fun! (HERBERT *puts bun back on table, comes round in front, and moving the chair out of the way, sits cross-legged on the floor at his father's side.*)

SERGEANT: But it's true. Why, if I chose, I could tell you things—But there! You don't get no more yarns out o' *me*.

MR. WHITE: Nonsense, old friend. (*Puts down his glass*) You're not going to get shirty about a bit o' fun. (*Moves his chair nearer* MORRIS'S) What was that you started telling me the other day about a monkey's paw, or something? (*Nudges* HERBERT, *and winks at* MRS. WHITE.)

SERGEANT (*gravely*):   Nothing. Leastways, nothing worth hearing.

MRS. WHITE (*with astonished curiosity*): Monkey's *paw*—?

MR. WHITE: Ah—you was tellin' me—

SERGEANT: Nothing. Don't go on about it. (*Puts his empty glass to his lips—then stares at it*) What? Empty again? There! When I begin thinkin' o' the paw, it makes me that absent-minded—

MR. WHITE (*rises and fills glass*):   You said you always carried it on you.

SERGEANT: So I do, for fear o' what might happen. (*Sunk in thought*) Ay! ay!

MR. WHITE (*handing him his glass refilled*): There. (*Sits again in same chair*)

MRS. WHITE: What's it for?

SERGEANT: You wouldn't believe me, if I was to tell you.

HERBERT: *I* will, every word.

SERGEANT: Magic, then! Don't you laugh!

HERBERT: I'm not. Got it on you now?

SERGEANT: Of course.

HERBERT: Let's see it. (*Seeing the* SER-GEANT *embarrassed with his glass,* MRS. WHITE *rises, takes it from him; places it on mantelpiece and remains standing.*)

SERGEANT: Oh, it's nothing to look at. (*Hunting in his pocket*) Just an ordinary—little paw—dried to a mummy. (*Produces it and holds it toward* MRS. WHITE) Here.

MRS. WHITE (*who has leant forward eagerly to see it, starts back with a little cry of disgust*): Oh!

HERBERT: Give us a look. (MORRIS *passes the paw to* MR. WHITE, *from whom* HERBERT *takes it*) Why, it's all dried up!

SERGEANT: I said so.

(*Wind.*)

MRS. WHITE (*with a slight shudder*): Hark at the wind! (*Sits again in her old place*)

MR. WHITE (*taking the paw from* HERBERT): And what might there be special about it?

SERGEANT (*impressively*): That there paw has had a spell put upon it!

MR. WHITE: No? (*In great alarm he thrusts the paw back into* MORRIS'S *hand.*)

SERGEANT (*pensively, holding the paw in the palm of his hand*): Ah! By an old fakir. He was a very holy man. He'd sat all doubled up in one spot, goin' on for fifteen year; thinkin' o' things. And he wanted to show that fate ruled people. That everything was cut and dried from the beginning, as you might say. That there warn't no gettin' away from it. And that, if you tried to, you caught it hot. (*Pauses solemnly*) So he put a spell on this bit of a paw. It might ha' been anything else, but he took the first thing that came handy. Ah! He put a spell on it, and made it so that three people (*looking at them and with deep meaning*) could each have three wishes.

(*All but* MRS. WHITE *laugh rather nervously*)

MRS. WHITE: Ssh! Don't!

329

SERGEANT (*more gravely*): But—! But, mark you, though the wishes was granted, those three people would have cause to wish they *hadn't* been.

MR. WHITE: But how *could* the wishes be granted?

SERGEANT: He didn't say. It would all happen so natural, you might think it a coincidence if so disposed.

HERBERT: Why haven't you tried it, sir?

SERGEANT (*gravely, after a pause*): I have.

HERBERT (*eagerly*): You've had your three wishes?

SERGEANT (*gravely*): Yes.

MRS. WHITE: Were they granted?

SERGEANT (*staring at the fire*): They were.

(*A pause.*)

MR. WHITE: Has anybody else wished?

SERGEANT: Yes. The first owner had his three wish—(*Lost in recollection*) Yes, oh, yes, he had his three wishes all right. I don't know what his first two were, (*very impressively*) but the third was for death. (*All shudder*) That's how I got the paw.

(*A pause.*)

HERBERT (*cheerfully*): Well! Seems to me you've only got to wish for things that *can't* have any bad luck about 'em— (*Rises*)

SERGEANT (*shaking his head*): Ah!

MR. WHITE (*tentatively*): Morris—if you've had your three wishes—it's no good to you, now—what do you keep it for?

SERGEANT (*still holding the paw; looking at it*): Fancy, I s'pose. I did have some idea of selling it, but I don't think I will. It's done mischief enough already. Besides, people won't buy. Some of 'em think it's a fairy tale. And some want to try it first, and pay after.

(*Nervous laugh from the others.*)

MRS. WHITE: If you could have another three wishes, would you?

SERGEANT (*slowly—weighing the paw in his hand and looking at it*): I don't know—I don't know—(*Suddenly, with violence, flinging it in the fire*) No!

(*Movement from all.*)

MR. WHITE (*rises and quickly snatches it out of the fire*): What are you doing? (WHITE *goes to the fireplace.*)

SERGEANT (*rising and following him and trying to prevent him*): Let it burn! Let the infernal thing burn!

MRS. WHITE (*rises*): Let it burn, Father!

MR. WHITE (*wiping it on his coatsleeve*): No. If you don't want it, give it to me.

SERGEANT (*violently*): I won't! I won't! My hands are clear of it. I threw it on the fire. If you keep it, don't blame me, whatever happens. Here! Pitch it back again.

MR. WHITE (*stubbornly*): I'm going to keep it. What do you say, Herbert?

HERBERT (*laughing*): I say, keep it if you want to. Stuff and nonsense, anyhow.

MR. WHITE (*looking at the paw thoughtfully*): Stuff and nonsense. Yes. I wonder—(*casually*) I wish—(*He was going to say some ordinary thing, like "I wish I were certain."*)

SERGEANT (*misunderstanding him; violently*): Stop! Mind what you're doing. That's not the way.

MR. WHITE: What *is* the way?

MRS. WHITE (*moving away to back of table, and beginning to put the tumblers straight, and the chairs in their places*): Oh, don't have anything to do with it, John. (*Takes glasses on tray to dresser, busies herself there,*

330

rinsing them in a bowl of water on the dresser, and wiping them with a cloth.)

SERGEANT: That's what I say, marm. But if I warn't to tell him, he might go wishing something he didn't mean to. You hold it in your right hand, and wish aloud. But I warn you! I warn you!

MRS. WHITE: Sounds like the Arabian Nights. Don't you think you might wish me four pair o' hands?

MR. WHITE (*laughing*): Right you are, Mother!—I wish—

SERGEANT (*pulling his arm down*): Stop it! If you must wish, wish for something sensible. Look here! I can't stand this. Gets on my nerves. Where's my coat? (*Goes into alcove*)

(MR. WHITE *crosses to fireplace and carefully puts the paw on mantelpiece. He is absorbed in it to the end of the tableau.*[3])

HERBERT: I'm coming your way, to the works, in a minute. Won't you wait? (*Helps* MORRIS *with his coat*)

SERGEANT (*putting on his coat*): No. I'm all shook up. I want fresh air. I don't want to be here when you wish. And wish you will as soon's my back's turned. I know. I know. But I've warned you, mind.

MR. WHITE (*helping him into his coat*): All right, Morris. Don't you fret about us. (*Gives him money*) Here.

SERGEANT (*refusing it*): No, I won't—

MR. WHITE (*forcing it into his hand*): Yes, you will. (*Opens door*)

SERGEANT (*turning to the room*): Well, good night all. (*To* WHITE) Put it in the fire.

ALL: Good night.

3. *tableau* (tăb′ lō, tă blō′): *French.* a striking scene

(*Exit* SERGEANT. MR. WHITE *closes door, comes toward fireplace, absorbed in the paw.*)

HERBERT: If there's no more in this than there is in his other stories, we shan't make much out of it.

MRS. WHITE (*to* WHITE): Did you give him anything for it, Father?

MR. WHITE: A trifle. He didn't want it, but I made him take it.

MRS. WHITE: There, now! You shouldn't. Throwing your money about.

MR. WHITE (*looking at the paw which he has picked up again*): I wonder—

HERBERT: What?

MR. WHITE: I wonder, whether we hadn't better chuck it on the fire?

HERBERT (*laughing*): Likely! Why, we're all going to be rich and famous, and happy.

MRS. WHITE: Throw it on the fire, indeed, when you've given money for it! So like you, Father.

HERBERT: Wish to be an Emperor, Father, to begin with. Then you can't be henpecked!

MRS. WHITE (*going for him front of table with a duster*): You young—! (*Follows him to back of table*)

HERBERT (*running away from her, hiding behind table*): Steady with that duster, Mother!

MR. WHITE: Be quiet, there! (HERBERT *catches* MRS. WHITE *in his arms and kisses her*) I wonder—(*He has the paw in his hand*) I don't know what to wish for, and that's a fact. (*He looks about him with a happy smile*) I seem to've got all I want.

HERBERT (*with his hands on the old man's shoulders*): Old Dad! If you'd only cleared the debt on the house, you'd be quite happy, wouldn't you? (*Laughing*) **331**

Well—go ahead!—wish for the two hundred pounds: that'll just do it.

MR. WHITE (*half laughing*): Shall I?

HERBERT: Go on! Here!—I'll play slow music. (*Goes to piano*)

MRS. WHITE Don't 'ee, John. Don't have nothing to do with it!

HERBERT: Now, Dad! (*Plays*)

MR. WHITE: I will! (*Holds up the paw, as if half ashamed*) I wish for two hundred pounds. (*Crash on the piano. At the same instant* MR. WHITE *utters a cry and lets the paw drop.*)

MRS. WHITE *and* HERBERT: What's the matter?

MR. WHITE (*gazing with horror at the paw*): It moved! As I wished, it twisted in my hand like a snake.

HERBERT (*goes down and picks the paw up*): Nonsense, Dad. Why, it's as stiff as a bone. (*Lays it on the mantelpiece*)

MRS. WHITE: Must have been your fancy, Father.

HERBERT (*laughing*): Well—? (*Looking round the room*) I don't see the money; and I bet I never shall.

MR. WHITE (*relieved*): Thank God, there's no harm done! But it gave me a shock.

HERBERT: Half-past eleven. I must get along. I'm on at midnight. (*Fetches his coat, etc.*) We've had quite a merry evening.

MRS. WHITE: I'm off to bed. Don't be late for breakfast, Herbert.

HERBERT: I shall walk home as usual. Does me good. I shall be with you about nine. Don't wait, though.

MRS. WHITE: You know your father never waits.

HERBERT: Good night, Mother. (*Kisses her. She lights candle on dresser, goes up stairs and exit.*)

332 HERBERT (*coming to his father, who is sunk in thought*): Good night, Dad. You'll find the cash tied up in the middle of the bed.

MR. WHITE (*staring, seizes* HERBERT'S *hand*): It moved, Herbert.

HERBERT: Ah! And a monkey hanging by his tail from the bed-post, watching you count the golden sovereigns.

MR. WHITE (*accompanying him to the door*): I wish you wouldn't joke, my boy.

HERBERT: All right, Dad. (*Opens door*) Lord! What weather! Good night. (*Exit*) (*The old man shakes his head, closes the door, locks it, puts the chain up, slips the lower bolt, has some difficulty with the upper bolt.*)

MR. WHITE: This bolt's stiff again! I must get Herbert to look to it in the morning. (*Comes into the room, puts out the lamp; crosses toward steps; but is irresistibly attracted toward fireplace. Sits down and stares into the fire. His expression changes: he sees something horrible.*)

MR. WHITE (*with an involuntary cry*): Mother! Mother!

MRS. WHITE (*appearing at the door at the top of the steps with candle*): What's the matter?

MR. WHITE (*mastering himself. Rises*): Nothing—I—haha!—I saw faces in the fire.

MRS. WHITE: Come along. (*She takes his arm and draws him toward the steps. He looks back frightened toward fireplace as they reach the first step.*)

TABLEAU CURTAIN

SCENE TWO

Bright sunshine. The table, which has been moved nearer the window, is laid for breakfast. MRS. WHITE *busy about the table.* MR. WHITE *standing in the window looking off. The inner door is open, showing the outer door.*

MR. WHITE: What a morning Herbert's got for walking home!

MRS. WHITE: What's o'clock? (*Looks at clock on mantelpiece*) Quarter to nine, I declare. He's off at eight. (*Crosses to fire*)

MR. WHITE: Takes him half an hour to change and wash. He's just by the cemetery now.

MRS. WHITE: He'll be here in ten minutes.

MR. WHITE (*coming to the table*): What's for breakfast?

MRS. WHITE: Sausages. (*At the mantelpiece*) Why, if here isn't that dirty monkey's paw! (*Picks it up, looks at it with disgust, puts it back. Takes sausages in dish from before fire and places them on table*) Silly thing! The idea of us listening to such nonsense!

MR. WHITE (*goes up to window again*): Ay—the Sergeant-Major and his yarns! I suppose all old soldiers are alike—

MRS. WHITE: Come on, Father. Herbert hates us to wait. (*They both sit and begin breakfast.*)

MRS. WHITE: How could wishes be granted, nowadays?

MR. WHITE: Ah! Been thinking about it all night, have you?

MRS. WHITE: You kept me awake, with your tossing and tumbling—

MR. WHITE: Ay, I had a bad night.

MRS. WHITE: It was the storm, I expect. How it blew!

MR. WHITE: I didn't hear it. I was asleep and not asleep, if you know what I mean.

MRS. WHITE: And all that rubbish about its making you unhappy if your wish *was* granted! How could two hundred pounds hurt you, eh, Father?

MR. WHITE: Might drop on my head in a lump. Don't see any other way. And I'd try to bear that. Though, mind you, Morris said it would all happen so naturally that you might take it for a coincidence, if so disposed.

MRS. WHITE: Well—it hasn't happened. That's all I know. And it isn't going to. (*A letter is seen to drop in the letter-box*) And how you can sit there and talk about it— (*Sharp postman's knock; she jumps to her feet*) What's that?

MR. WHITE: Postman, o' course.

MRS. WHITE (*seeing the letter from a distance; in an awed whisper*): He's brought a letter, John!

MR. WHITE (*laughing*): What did you think he'd bring? Ton[4] o' coals?

MRS. WHITE: John—! John—! Suppose—?

MR. WHITE: Suppose what?

MRS. WHITE: Suppose it was two hundred pounds!

4. *ton:* 1.016 t

MR. WHITE (*suppressing his excitement*): Eh!—Here! Don't talk nonsense. Why don't you fetch it?

MRS. WHITE (*crosses and takes letter out of the box*): It's thick, John—(*feels it*)—and—and it's got something crisp inside it. (*Takes letter to* WHITE.)

MR. WHITE: Who—who's it for?

MRS. WHITE: You.

MR. WHITE: Hand it over, then. (*Feeling and examining it with ill-concealed excitement*) The idea! What a superstitious old woman you are! Where are my specs?

MRS. WHITE: Let me open it.

MR. WHITE: Don't you touch it. Where are my specs?

MRS. WHITE: Don't let sudden wealth sour your temper, John.

MR. WHITE: *Will* you find my specs?

MRS. WHITE (*taking them off mantelpiece*): Here, John, here. (*As he opens the letter*) Take care! Don't tear it!

MR. WHITE: Tear what?

MRS. WHITE: If it was banknotes, John!

MR. WHITE (*taking a thick, formal document out of the envelope and a crisp-looking slip*):[5] You've gone dotty.[5]—You've made me nervous. (*Reads*) "Sir,—Enclosed please find receipt for interest on the mortgage of £200 on your house, duly received." (*They look at each other.* MR. WHITE *sits down to finish his breakfast silently.* MRS. WHITE *goes to the window.*)

MRS. WHITE: That comes of listening to tipsy old soldiers.

MR. WHITE (*pettish*): What does?

MRS. WHITE: You thought there was banknotes in it.

MR. WHITE (*injured*): I didn't! I said all along—

MRS. WHITE: How Herbert will laugh, when I tell him!

MR. WHITE (*with gruff good-humor*): You're not going to tell him. You're going to keep your mouth shut. That's what you're going to do. Why, I should never hear the last of it.

MRS. WHITE: Serve you right. I shall tell him. You know you like his fun. See how he joked you last night when you said the paw moved. (*She is looking through the window.*)

MR. WHITE: So it did. It did move. That I'll swear to.

MRS. WHITE (*abstractedly; she is watching something outside*): You thought it did.

MR. WHITE: I say it did. There was no thinking about it. You saw how it upset me, didn't you? (*She doesn't answer*) Didn't you?—Why don't you listen? (*Turns round*) What is it?

MRS. WHITE: Nothing.

MR. WHITE (*turns back to his breakfast*): Do you see Herbert coming?

MRS. WHITE: No.

MR. WHITE: He's about due. What *is* it?

MRS. WHITE: Nothing. Only a man. Looks like a gentleman. Leastways, he's in black, and he's got a top-hat on.

MR. WHITE: What about him? (*He is not interested; goes on eating.*)

MRS. WHITE: He stood at the garden-gate as if he wanted to come in. But he couldn't seem to make up his mind.

MR. WHITE: Oh, go on! You're full o' fancies.

MRS. WHITE: He's going—no; he's coming back.

MR. WHITE: Don't let him see you peeping.

MRS. WHITE (*with increasing excitement*): He's looking at the house. He's got his hand on the latch. No. He turns away again. (*Eagerly*) John! He looks like a sort of a lawyer.

334

5. *dotty* (dŏt′ĭ): *British colloquialism.* crazy

MR. WHITE: What of it?

MRS. WHITE: Oh, you'll only laugh again. But suppose—suppose he's coming about the two hundred—

MR. WHITE: You're not to mention it again! You're a foolish old woman. Come and eat your breakfast. (*Eagerly*) Where is he now?

MRS. WHITE: Gone down the road. He has turned back. He seems to've made up his mind. Here he comes! Oh, John, and me all untidy! (*Crosses to fire. There is a knock.*)

MR. WHITE (*to* MRS. WHITE *who is hastily smoothing her hair*):   What's it matter? He's made a mistake. Come to the wrong house.

(*Goes to fireplace.* MRS. WHITE *opens the door.* MR. SAMPSON, *dressed from head to foot in solemn black, with a top-hat, stands in the doorway.*)

SAMPSON (*outside*):   Is this Mr. White's?

MRS. WHITE: Come in, sir. Please step in. (*She shows him into the room. He is awkward and nervous*) You must overlook our being so untidy; and the room all any-how; and John in his garden-coat. (*To* MR. WHITE, *reproachfully*) Oh, John.

SAMPSON (*to* MR. WHITE):   Morning. My name is Sampson.

MRS. WHITE (*offering a chair*):   Won't you please be seated?

(SAMPSON *stands quite still.*)

SAMPSON: Ah—thank you—no, I think not—I think not. (*Pause*)

MR. WHITE (*awkwardly, trying to help him*): Fine weather for the time o' year.

SAMPSON: Ah — yes — yes — (*Pause; he makes a renewed effort*) My name is Sampson—I've come—

MRS. WHITE: Perhaps you was wishful to see Herbert; he'll be home in a minute. (*Pointing*) Here's his breakfast waiting—

SAMPSON (*interrupting her hastily*): No, no! (*Pause*) I've come from the electrical works—

MRS. WHITE: Why, you might have come *with* him. (MR. WHITE *sees something is wrong, tenderly puts his hand on her arm.*)

SAMPSON: No—no—I've come—*alone.*

MRS. WHITE (*with a little anxiety*): Is anything the matter?

SAMPSON: I was asked to call—

MRS. WHITE (*abruptly*): Herbert! Has anything happened? Is he hurt? Is he hurt?

MR. WHITE (*soothing her*): There, there, Mother. Don't you jump to conclusions. Let the gentleman speak. You've not brought bad news, I'm sure, sir.

SAMPSON: I'm—sorry—

MRS. WHITE: Is he hurt? (SAMPSON *bows*) Badly?

SAMPSON: Very badly. (*Turns away*)

MRS. WHITE (*with a cry*): John—! (*She instinctively moves toward* WHITE.)

MRS. WHITE: Is he in pain?

SAMPSON: He is not in pain.

MRS. WHITE: Oh, thank God! Thank God for that! Thank—(*She looks in a startled fashion at* MR. WHITE—*realizes what* SAMPSON *means, catches his arm and tries to turn him toward her*) Do you mean—? (SAMPSON *avoids her look; she gropes for her husband: he takes her two hands in his, and gently lets her sink into the armchair above the fireplace, then he stands on her right,*

336

between her and SAMPSON.)

MR. WHITE (*hoarsely*): Go on, sir.

SAMPSON: He was telling his mates a story. Something that had happened here last night. He was laughing, and wasn't noticing and—and—(*hushed*) the machinery caught him—

(*A little cry from* MRS. WHITE, *her face shows her horror and agony.*)

MR. WHITE (*vague, holding* MRS. WHITE'S *hand*): The machinery caught him—yes—and him the only child—it's hard, sir—very hard—

SAMPSON (*subdued*): The Company wished me to convey their sincere sympathy with you in your great loss—

MR. WHITE (*staring blankly*): Our—great—loss—!

SAMPSON: I was to say further—(*as if apologizing*) I am only their servant—I am only obeying orders—

MR. WHITE: Our—great—loss—

SAMPSON (*laying an envelope on the table and edging toward the door*): I was to say, the Company disclaim all responsibility, but, in consideration of your son's services, they wish to present you with a certain sum as compensation. (*Gets to the door*)

MR. WHITE: Our—great—loss—(*Suddenly, with horror*) How—how much?

SAMPSON (*in the doorway*): Two hundred pounds. (*Exit*)

(MRS. WHITE *gives a cry. The old man takes no heed of her, smiles faintly, puts out his hands like a sightless man, and drops, a senseless heap, to the floor.* MRS. WHITE *stares at him blankly and her hands go out helplessly toward him.*)

TABLEAU CURTAIN

SCENE THREE

Night. On the table a candle is flickering at its last gasp. The room looks neglected. MR. WHITE *is dozing fitfully in the armchair.* MRS. WHITE *is in the window peering through the blind.* MR. WHITE *starts, wakes, looks around him.*

MR. WHITE (*fretfully*):   Jenny—Jenny.

MRS. WHITE (*in the window*):   Yes.

MR. WHITE: Where are you?

MRS. WHITE: At the window.

MR. WHITE: What are you doing?

MRS. WHITE: Looking up the road.

MR. WHITE (*falling back*):   What's the use, Jenny? What's the use?

MRS. WHITE: That's where the cemetery is; that's where we've laid him.

MR. WHITE: Ay—ay—a week today— what o'clock is it?

MRS. WHITE: I don't know.

MR. WHITE: We don't take much account of time now, Jenny, do we?

MRS. WHITE: Why should we? He don't come home. He'll never come home again. There's nothing to think about—

MR. WHITE: Or to talk about. (*Pause*) Come away from the window; you'll get cold.

MRS. WHITE: It's colder where *he* is.

MR. WHITE: Ay—gone for ever—

MRS. WHITE: And taken all our hopes with him—

MR. WHITE: And all our *wishes*—

MRS. WHITE: Ay, and all our— (*With a sudden cry*) John! (*She comes quickly to him; he rises.*)

MR. WHITE: Jenny! What's the matter?

MRS. WHITE (*with dreadful eagerness*):   The paw! The monkey's paw!

MR. WHITE (*bewildered*):   Where? Where is it? What's wrong with it?

MRS. WHITE: I want it! You haven't done away with it?

MR. WHITE: I haven't seen it—since— why?

MRS. WHITE: I want it! Find it! Find it!

MR. WHITE (*groping on the mantelpiece*): Here! Here it is! What do you want of it? (*He leaves it there.*)

MRS. WHITE: Why didn't I think of it? Why didn't you think of it?

MR. WHITE: Think of what?

MRS. WHITE: The *other two* wishes!

MR. WHITE (*with horror*):   What?

MRS. WHITE: We've only had one.

MR. WHITE (*tragically*):   Wasn't that enough?

MRS. WHITE: No! We'll have one more. (WHITE *crosses.* MRS. WHITE *takes the paw and follows him*) Take it. Take it quickly. And wish—

MR. WHITE (*avoiding the paw*):   Wish what?

MRS. WHITE: Oh, John! John! Wish our boy alive again!

MR. WHITE: Are you mad?

MRS. WHITE: Take it. Take it and wish. (*With a paroxysm° of grief*) Oh, my boy! My boy!

MR. WHITE: Get to bed. Get to sleep. You don't know what you're saying.

MRS. WHITE: We had the first wish granted—why not the second?

MR. WHITE (*hushed*):   He's been dead ten days, and—Jenny! Jenny! I only knew him by his clothing—if you wasn't allowed to see him then—how could you bear to see him *now*?

MRS. WHITE: I don't care. Bring him back.

MR. WHITE (*shrinking from the paw*):   I daren't touch it!

MRS. WHITE (*thrusting it in his hand*): Here! Here! Wish!

MR. WHITE (*trembling*):   Jenny!

337

MRS. WHITE (*fiercely*): Wish. (*She goes on frantically whispering "Wish."*)

MR. WHITE (*shuddering, but overcome by her insistence*): I—I— wish—my— son—alive again. (*He drops it with a cry. The candle goes out. Utter darkness. He sinks into a chair.* MRS. WHITE *hurries to the window and draws the blind back. She stands in the moonlight. Pause*)

MRS. WHITE (*drearily*): Nothing.

MR. WHITE: Thank God! Thank God!

MRS. WHITE: Nothing at all. Along the whole length of the road not a living thing. (*Closes blind*) And nothing, nothing, nothing left in our lives, John.

MR. WHITE: Except each other, Jenny— and memories.

MRS. WHITE (*coming back slowly to the fireplace*): We're too old. We were only alive in him. We can't begin again. We can't feel anything now, John, but emptiness and darkness. (*She sinks into armchair.*)

MR. WHITE: 'Tisn't for long, Jenny. There's that to look forward to.

MRS. WHITE: Every minute's long, now.

MR. WHITE (*rising*): I can't bear the darkness!

MRS. WHITE: It's dreary—dreary.

MR. WHITE (*goes to dresser*): Where's the candle? (*Finds it and brings it to table*) And the matches? Where are the matches? We mustn't sit in the dark. 'Tisn't wholesome. (*Lights match; the other candlestick is close to him*) There. (*Turning with the lighted match toward* MRS. WHITE, *who is rocking and moaning*) Don't take on so, Mother.

MRS. WHITE: I'm a mother no longer.

MR. WHITE (*lights candle*): There now; there now. Go on up to bed. Go on, now—I'm a-coming.

MRS. WHITE: Whether I'm here or in bed, or wherever I am, I'm with my boy, I'm with—

(*A low single knock at the street door.*)

MRS. WHITE (*starting*): What's that!

MR. WHITE (*mastering his horror*): A rat. The house is full of 'em. (*A louder single knock; she starts up. He catches her by the arm*) Stop! What are you going to do?

MRS. WHITE (*wildly*): It's my boy! It's Herbert! I forgot it was a mile away! What are you holding me for? I must open the door!

(*The knocking continues in single knocks at irregular intervals, constantly growing louder and more insistent.*)

MR. WHITE (*still holding her*): For God's sake!

MRS. WHITE (*struggling*): Let me go!

MR. WHITE: Don't open the door! (*He drags her away.*)

MRS. WHITE: Let me go!

MR. WHITE: Think what you might see!

MRS. WHITE (*struggling fiercely*): Do you think I fear the child I bore! Let me go! (*She wrenches herself loose and rushes to the door which she tears open*) I'm coming, Herbert! I'm coming!

MR. WHITE (*cowering in the extreme corner, left front*): Don't 'ee do it! Don't 'ee do it!

(MRS. WHITE *is at work on the outer door, where the knocking still continues. She slips the chain, slips the lower bolt, unlocks the door.*)

MR. WHITE (*suddenly*): The paw! Where's the monkey's paw? (*He gets on his knees and feels along the floor for it.*)

MRS. WHITE (*tugging at the top bolt*): John! The top bolt's stuck. I can't move it. Come and help. Quick!

338

MR. WHITE (*wildly groping*): The paw! There's a wish left.

(*The knocking is now loud, and in groups of increasing length between the speeches.*)

MRS. WHITE: D'ye hear him? John! Your child's knocking!

MR. WHITE: Where is it? Where did it fall?

MRS. WHITE (*tugging desperately at the bolt*): Help! Help! Will you keep your child from his home?

MR. WHITE: Where did it fall? I can't find it—I can't find—

(*The knocking is now tempestuous, and there are blows upon the door as of a body beating against it.*)

MRS. WHITE: Herbert! Herbert! My boy! Wait! Your mother's opening to you! Ah! It's moving! It's moving!

MR. WHITE: God forbid! (*Finds the paw*) Ah!

MRS. WHITE (*slipping the bolt*): Herbert!

MR. WHITE (*has raised himself to his knees; he holds the paw high*): I wish him dead. (*The knocking stops abruptly.*) I wish him dead and at peace!

MRS. WHITE (*flinging the door open simultaneously*): Herb— (*A flood of moonlight. Emptiness. The old man sways in prayer on his knees. The old woman lies half swooning, wailing against the doorpost.*)

CURTAIN

Copies of this play, in individual paper covered acting editions, are available from Samuel French, (Canada) Ltd., 80 Richmond St., Toronto M5C 1P1, Canada.

follow-up

Discussing "The Monkey's Paw"

1. According to the sergeant, three wishes will be granted, but they will all be regretted. How does Mr. White's third wish fit this pattern?
2. When the sergeant tells the family about the monkey's paw, Mr. and Mrs. White and Herbert have different reactions to it. What are their reactions? What do those reactions tell us about each of the characters?
3. If you were offered three wishes and a warning like the one in "The Monkey's Paw," what would you do?

Premises and Possibilities

At one time or another almost every person has probably thought: "If only I could have three wishes, I could be sure of happiness for the rest of my life." The idea is appealing, perhaps because most of us have to work so hard for so many things. If we could have just three wishes—just three small gifts from the sky—just three things we could be sure of—then our problems would be over. Or would they? The writer of "The Monkey's Paw" must have felt that way himself, and he must have asked himself this question. *"Assuming that I could have three wishes, would the result be happiness? Or would it be another set of problems to deal with?"*

The idea for "The Monkey's Paw" might have grown from questions like those. The writer might well have decided to base his play on the idea that fate could and would grant a person three wishes. That's the *premise* on which the play was written. That's the premise that readers must agree to accept when they read the play or see it performed. Now, there are probably few people today who believe that a monkey's paw—or anything else, for that matter—could carry with it the power to grant wishes or to cause the problems that came with those wishes. But if you are to enjoy the play, you must agree to accept that premise—at least temporarily. You must agree to pretend that three wishes could be granted so that you can enjoy watching the story unfold.

That, of course, is exactly what you do whenever you read fiction—especially science fiction—or watch TV plays. For the moment you accept the imaginary characters in the story as real people. You accept the events acted out on the TV screen as real events. A *realistic* play, of course, requires little effort on your part to pretend that the characters and events are real. You may even be unaware that what you see did *not* actually happen. You may not stop to think that the character shot and killed in the final scene actually got up and went home to dinner with his/her family when the filming was completed. But when you read a play like "The Monkey's Paw," you are aware that you are accepting something impossible.

In the wildest, most far-fetched science fiction, however, there must be something that *is* realistic. Some aspect of the story must strike you as possible, even probable, or you'll find little satisfaction in reading it. Think back over "The Monkey's Paw." What aspect of the play seems to you to be realistic?

Almost everyone enjoys speculating about what might happen IF.... "If I had a sports car I could...." "If I had a billion dollars I would...." "If I could see into the future, I would...." Some of the best stories have been written in just that way. The writer establishes a premise—the idea around which the whole play revolves—and then explores its possibilities.

Here's a chance for you to create a short play of your own. Maybe you're a budding playwright.

Practice 1. Writing

Write a short play or dramatic scene. As you develop your play, consider your audience and your actors. Remember that your story must be presented clearly and believably through the dialogue of your characters. Remember, too, that the actors will need some direction in the script to indicate their actions and,

Depending on class arrangements and procedures, you might write your play by yourself, or you may wish to collaborate with four or five classmates.

Here are several hints to consider as you plan your drama:

1. *Characters.* Create only a few, well-defined characters for your play. Their dialogue should seem natural, reflecting their different personalities.
2. *Setting.* Your play should occur in a definite place at a specific time. Let your audience know the setting, either in what the characters say, in an opening description (as in "The Monkey's Paw"), or in the words of a narrator. Any change of setting must be made clear to the audience/reader.
3. *Conflict.* Almost all good plays and stories contain conflict. Conflict creates interest. An audience gets involved with the problems brought about by conflict. They want to know how it will turn out. Use conflict to create suspense, and then resolve the conflict at the end of your play, satisfying your audience's curiosity. The conflict may be simply two or more characters trying to reach the same goal, as in a contest. Or it may involve the struggle within a character who must make an important decision or choice.
4. *Theme.* The theme of your play may be stated by one of the characters, or it may be hinted at by what happens in the play. Theme is usually the "message" you wish to get across with your drama. For example, your play could illustrate the

idea that honesty pays or that society often is cruel to those who seem different. (In "The Monkey's Paw," the theme is this: Being granted three wishes won't guarantee happiness.)

5. *Tone*. Decide on the tone you want to use in your play. Will it be humorous or serious? Are you sympathetic or critical toward your characters?

To get you started, here are several premises on which you might base your play:

A

1. You discover the technique for travelling through time.
2. You find the secret of eternal youth.
3. You develop the ability to read others' thoughts.
4. You find suddenly that everybody else can read your mind.

But if none of those premises appeal to you, here are some other possibilities for creating a short drama:

B

From a story that you have especially liked, dramatize a scene that you think would make an effective play. Keep in mind, of course, that the action must take place in front of an audience. Thus, you may need to adapt the characters, action, and setting of the story to fit your dramatic purposes. Stage, movie, and television scripts are often successfully adapted from short stories and novels. Although you may have to change details, try to keep the flavor, tone, and theme of the original selection.

C

Write a play script by beginning with character and setting. Let the conflict grow out of the interaction of characters in a specific place and time. Follow these steps:

1. Choose two or three characters from the following list (or you may invent your own). Give them names and write a brief description of each character, including: age, physical appearance, several personality traits, interests, values, and speech habits.
2. Choose a setting from the following list (or invent your own setting). Write down more specific details about your setting, such as time, place, and description.

Characters	*Settings*
aging sports hero	restaurant
escaped convict	life boat
amnesia victim	space ship
famous actor/actress	hospital waiting room
handicapped person	busy street corner
undercover agent	courtroom
eccentric artist	crowded bench
rock star	stalled elevator
child	sports event
circus performer	funeral

3. After you have your characters and a setting, develop a conflict by imagining the problems that might emerge as a result of the interaction of the characters in that specific setting.

D

Write a play script by beginning with a conflict involving right vs. wrong. Below are some sample questions that suggest a conflict between values. Choose one of them—or invent your own—to serve as the basis for your drama. Then create characters, a setting, and details to flesh out your play. Of course, you will want eventually to resolve the conflict.

1. Should a person lie to protect a friend? (Conflicting values: honesty vs. friendship)
2. Should a person risk his/her life for a large amount of money? (Conflicting values: personal danger *vs.* financial gain)
3. In order to keep his/her friends, should a person go along with them in doing something he/she knows to be wrong? (Conflicting values: friendship *vs.* conscience)
4. Should a person steal to provide medicine for a family member? (Conflicting values: crime *vs.* love of family)
5. Should a police officer arrest a relative who has committed a crime? (Conflicting values: duty *vs.* family loyalty)

When you've finished your play, why not cast it and rehearse it? Then why not present it before a live audience—other English classes, as well as your own?

Bookshelf

Curses, Hexes, & Spells, by Daniel Cohen. Lippincott, 1974. This
collection of stories about curses spans several centuries.

The Probability of the Impossible: Scientific Discoveries and Explorations in the Psychic World, by Thelma Moss. J. P. Tarcher,
1974. Moss reports on several scientific efforts to examine
such phenomena as extrasensory perception and mental
telepathy.

Rolling Thunder, by Doug Boyd. Random House, 1974. The
writer, who learns many of the secrets of the medicine men
like Rolling Thunder, shows that they are successful.

Witchcraft and Magic: The Supernatural World of Primitive Man, by
Arthur S. Gregor. Scribner, 1972. Gregor studies the
beliefs of primitive cultures in witchcraft and magic. He
shows that some of those beliefs persist today.

23

The Immortals

forestudy

A Slice of the Action

Suppose that these two sentences appear in the first draft of a student's composition:

> The airliner approached the airport. The plane's lights blinked sleepily in the dark.

The second sentence describes something that is happening at exactly the same time as the action in the first sentence. The lights blinked *while* the airplane was approaching, not afterward. In revising the two sentences to emphasize that the two actions occurred at the same time, you could combine them in this way:

> The airliner approached the airport, *the plane's lights blinking sleepily in the dark.*

Notice that when the second sentence is changed, the verb *blinked* becomes *blinking,* which, of course, is its present participle. (For a discussion of participles, see page 280.) The subject *lights* remains the same. But *lights blinking sleepily in the dark* is obviously not a sentence. Instead, it is an ABSOLUTE. That is, it consists of a noun and a participle that add information about the thought expressed in the independent clause. The ABSOLUTE resembles the subject-verb structure of an independent clause, but it is *not quite* an independent clause.

In using an ABSOLUTE, the writer is, in effect, choosing one particular detail to give added impact to the action described in the independent clause. *Lights* singles out a specific part of the airliner; *lights blinking* adds dramatic effect to the action identified in the words "The airliner approached...." In a sense, then, an ABSOLUTE is a "slice of the entire action."

Practice 1. Discussion

1. Examine items A and B:
    A. He sat on the edge of the seat, one hand resting on the door handle.
    B. He sat on the edge of the seat. One hand rested on the door handle.
2. What is the chief difference you see between A and B?
3. Which item—A or B—has an absolute? What words make up the absolute?
4. In item B, what action—or what actions—receive emphasis? In item A, on what action does the emphasis lie?
5. In what way is the absolute a "slice of the action" described in the independent clause? If the absolute represents a slice of the action, is the action it describes more important than, just as important as, or less important than the action in the independent clause? Why?

Practice 2. Writing

Combine the pairs of sentences on page 347 into single sentences. First add a comma after the base statement, and then change the second sentence into an absolute.

> *Example*
> *Two Sentences*
>   He slumped onto the bench. His head was bowed in defeat.
> *Combined*
>   He slumped onto the bench, his head bowed in defeat.
>   (Notice that *was* is dropped, and that *head bowed* remains the same. In some sentences, however, you won't need to drop anything. But you will need to change the form of the verb to *-ing*.)

1. She turned toward me. Her face was beaming with pride. (*Hint:* Drop a word.)
2. She gasped as she looked down from the cliff. Her heart pounded with excitement. (*Hint:* An *-ing* verb form is needed.)
3. Shan got a loan from the bank. The president trusted him to repay on schedule.
4. She accepted the sweater. Admiration was reflected in her smile.
5. She said flatly that she was tired of the sweater. No smile crossed her pretty lips.

347

Be prepared to read at least one of your sentences aloud. Does everyone agree that you have used an absolute? that it is a slice of the action described in the independent clause?

Practice 3. Writing

Copy each general base statement; then add a comma and a descriptive detail in your own words. Your added detail should be an absolute, containing a noun and a verb form. If you wish, begin your addition with the italicized word(s) supplied after the *Hint.*

1. The fire finally died down. (*Hint:* What did *its embers* look like?)
2. The old man sat in his rocking chair. (*Hint:* Was *his head* bowed, or moving in any particular way?)
3. The patrolman started after the speeding sedan. (*Hint:* Would you expect action from *his siren?*)
4. The boy and girl entered the classroom together. (*Hint:* What was *each* doing while they entered?)

Be prepared to read at least one of your sentences aloud. Does your sentence contain an absolute? Have you used it effectively?

"He had been up-ended, not by a Kelvin tackle, but by a pair of snapped suspenders."

The Immortals°

Ed Kleiman

For days in the fall of forty-nine, St. John's High had buzzed with rumors about whether or not Torchy Brownstone would be allowed to play in the football game on Friday. Torchy was our first-string quarterback, a two-year veteran with the school, and if we were to have any chance of beating Kelvin—our arch-rivals from River Heights—then the team could not afford to see him sidelined with a knee injury. The injury had been sustained in a practice session last week when a second-string linebacker had gotten carried away with enthusiasm and tackled Torchy just as he was coming around the end on a double reverse. So one of our own players had done what the rest of the league would have been trying to do all through the fall.

What hurt most was that Torchy should

From a short story collection published by NeWest Publishers (Edmonton); originally appeared in *Journal of Canadian Fiction*, December, 1976. Reprinted by permission of NeWest Press.

be sidelined when we were playing Kelvin. The game itself didn't count for anything. It was an exhibition game, a warm-up before the regular season began. But what did count was that this was a contest between the North and South Ends of the city. And that was no small matter.

The North End consisted mainly of immigrants from Eastern Europe, laboring classes, small foreign-language newspapers, watch-repair shops, a Jewish theatrical company, a Ukrainian dance troupe, small choirs, tap-dancing schools, orchestral groups, chess clubs and more radical political thinkers per square block than Soviet Russia had known before the Revolution. The South End—or River Heights, as it is more fashionably called—was basically what that revolution had been against. The mayor, most of the aldermen, the chairman of the school board, and many of the civic employees—not the street sweepers, of course—lived in River Heights.

Actually, when you think about it, they had chosen a curious name for their end of town. If you've ever passed through Winnipeg, you'll realize that it rests on one of the flattest stretches of land in the world. In fact, I read in the school library once that the land falls at the rate of no more than 0.4 m/km as it extends northward towards Lake Winnipeg. So the Heights, you see, can't amount to much more than 2 m or 3 m, at the most. But people there like to think of themselves as living on a plateau overlooking the rest of the city, as in a sense they do. For the heights they've attained are built on political and economic foundations that give them a vantage point of more in the order of 200 m or 300 m.

Another way of distinguishing between the two parts of the city is by looking at the street names. In the North End, you'll find such names as Selkirk Avenue, Euclid Street, Aberdeen, Dufferin — names steeped in history, names which suggest the realm of human endeavor, anguish, accomplishment. But if you look at the street names in River Heights, what you'll find, with few exceptions, are such names as Ash Street, Elm, Oak, Willow. Vast expanses of velvet lawns, well-treed boulevards—the area looks like a garden, a retreat from the toil and anguish everywhere visible in the North End. The two cultures meet downtown, where the South End gentry immediately head for the managerial offices, and the North End rabble file past the company clocks with their time cards. After work countless numbers of expensive cars sweep grandly across the Maryland Bridge back into Eden,[1] while street cars and buses pass northward beneath the CPR subway into a grim bleak underworld of steel fences, concrete walls, locked doors, and savage dogs that seem capable of looking in three directions at once.

But at the Osborne Stadium in the fall, the traditional roles can be reversed for an evening. There, on Friday nights, the North End may once more experience the heady hours of triumph it knew during the 1919 Strike, when it seemed the World Revolution might begin right here in Winnipeg. So, you see, the fact that Torchy Brownstone had injured his knee in football practice was of major concern to us all.

And then to add insult to injury, the English teacher Mr. Rockwood caught our star tackles, Norm Mittlehaus and Sam Margolis, in Room 41 the day before the game and tried to have them disqualified

---

1. *Eden:* in the Bible, the paradise where human beings originally lived. This is an ironic description of the South End

from playing on Friday. Room 41 is Goldman's Drug Store—just across the street from the high school—and kids are always sneaking across during the day to have a soda, read a magazine, or have a smoke. And Rockwood is always catching them. Rockwood is about 158 cm and weighs about 82 kg, so he's a fairly stocky little guy with huge shoulders and a neck like a bull dog. Needless to say, Rockwood lives in River Heights, and he would have still been teaching at Kelvin if he hadn't swatted one of his pupils one day—the son of a school trustee, as it turned out—and since then he's been our affliction. He often tries to have kids expelled, banned from writing exams, or disqualified from playing football—which drives the football coach, Mr. Powalski, wild. It had always seemed to us that Mr. Rockwood would have been much happier, would have felt more free to express himself, and would have achieved a greater degree of fulfillment if he'd been a guard at Auschwitz.[2]

Anyway, as soon as Mr. Powalski learned that Rockwood had disqualified our star tackles Mittlehaus and Margolis from playing the next night, he rushed up to the principal's office and threatened to resign—again, for what must have been the tenth time that year—if they weren't reinstated.

On the Friday night of the game, the stands were packed. Would Torchy play? And what about Mittlehaus and Margolis? Even I came to the game that night, and I rarely go to football games—or any kind of sports event for that matter. As usual, I was intensely preoccupied with the finer things in life, with art and poetry, and all my evenings then were taken up by an epic poem in hexameters I was working on. But the whole school was caught up in the game that night, and Nate Samuelson, my bench partner in physics lab who had just been elected student president, finally persuaded me that I couldn't stay behind.

So there we all were, glaring across the field at the River Heights stands, where, sitting shamelessly among the staunch supporters of the opposing team, we could make out Rockwood; Peg-Leg Dobson—our physics teacher; Mr. Atkinson—our chemistry teacher; and Mr. Clearwater—the principal. Still, Kleinberg, Schultz, Rasmussen, and Pollick—all loyal North Enders—had stationed themselves prominently in our end of the stadium.

Rumors abounded. Kelvin was supposed to have all-new football equipment donated by the president of a huge department store. Their new sweaters, it was claimed, were no longer the school colors, cherry and grey, but a regal purple and gold. It was also whispered that the team had been practising secret plays to be unveiled that night. They had a new fullback —a huge two hundred pounder,[3] who would make mincemeat of our line. And, most ominous of all, there was talk that the chief referee had bet five dollars on the River Heights team.

But each new rumor of impending doom simply sent our spirits soaring higher. We shouted taunts across the field, unveiled posters that displayed a hammer and sickle, beneath which were the words, "Workers, Arise!", bombarded the officials with over-ripe tomatoes and rotten eggs which we'd saved especially for the occasion, and flung rolls of toilet paper into the playing area. Until an exasperated voice in an Oxford accent that had obviously just been acquired that summer asked us all to

2. *Auschwitz:* a Nazi concentration camp   3. *two hundred pounder:* 90.8 kg; 1 pound = 0.454 kg

stand for the National Anthem.

Then the whistle blew, and we kicked off to Kelvin and, to our horror, that two hundred pound fullback really did exist because he caught the ball and ran over three of our tacklers for a touchdown. Less than sixty seconds after the game had started, they had a converted touchdown—worth six points then—and we had three injuries. Suddenly our players in their ripped sweaters and torn pads looked like a pretty shabby lot compared to that Kelvin team, which moved with such military precision in their new uniforms and shiny helmets.

On the next kick-off, our star runner, Cramer, caught the football, and was promptly tackled by their two hundred pound fullback, whose name, we learned, was Bruno Hogg. When Cramer finally managed to get up, he was limping. A mighty groan escaped from the North End stands. Jerusalem had just been taken and we were all being marched off to captivity in Babylon. We could see Torchy, down on the sidelines, pleading with the coach to let him in—knee injury and all—but Powalski sent in Marty Klein instead.

When they first caught sight of Marty, the military discipline of the Kelvin team threatened to disintegrate. Marty's all of 158 cm and can't weigh much more than 57 kg, so his appearance caused first titters, then guffaws. Of course they didn't realize that Marty uses his size to advantage. He's the sneakiest player you'll ever see.

Right away, Marty calls a plunge by the fullback. But when they peel the players off our boy, he doesn't have the ball. Then the Kelvin line pounces on the two halfbacks, but they don't have the ball either—and so they throw them away and begin looking around with murder in their eyes for the tailback. By the time they start looking around for Marty, it's too late. He's waving to them with one hand, the ball in

the other, from behind their own goal line. Marty had jumped right out of harm's way once the ball had been snapped, and then he strolled off down the sidelines while the Kelvin team pounced upon one player after another in their frantic search for the missing football. Somehow we managed to finish the quarter with a six-all tie.

But in the second quarter, disaster struck. We'd managed to hold Kelvin in their own end of the field until they had to kick on third down. Out of their huddle they marched in that military precision of theirs, and we knew right away something tricky was up. Three of their backfielders pranced out to one side behind the kicker, who booted the ball no more than fifteen yards,[4] and those three ballet stars danced away with the ball while we were left looking like jerks, with our coach hastily thumbing through his handbook to see what it was all about. When Kelvin tried the same stunt a few plays later, all three of their ballerinas were immediately flattened. But that was strictly *verboten,* according to the officials, and we were penalized fifteen yards. Then that two hundred pound fullback of theirs got the ball again, and we were behind another six points. But at last Powalski found the section in the rule book dealing with on-side kicks and brought an end to that particular gimmick.

When we finally got the ball again, Marty Klein called another plunge by the fullback, but now the whole line piled on top of poor Marty, and so the fullback—who did have the ball this time—had already bulldozed his way more than half the length of the field when his bootlace came undone, and he tripped over the loose end. Of course Kelvin recovered the fumbled ball, and we were lucky to finish the half

only six points down.

During the intermission, more rumors swept through the stands. A doctor had been seen racing down to the stadium from the North End with a special drug and a set of splints that would enable Torchy to play in the second half. This was immediately contradicted by another rumor: the same doctor had warned that Torchy would limp for the rest of his life if he played that night.

Someone else hinted that there was a special reason for those Kelvin players moving about with such stiff, jerky motions and spastic gestures. All that talk about military precision and strict training was a bunch of nonsense. Nate Samuelson had sneaked into the Kelvin dressing room before the game and sprinkled red pepper into every one of their jock straps. A little later somebody spotted Nate sitting beside me, and soon a couple of dozen people were cheering their new student president. None of us suspected then that twenty years later, long after he had become a doctor, gotten married and had two children, he would take an overdose of drugs and walk off the MacIntyre Building smack on top of the early morning traffic jam. Nate stood up in the stands that evening, smiled in that sly way of his, and waved his hand to the cheering crowd.

Then the players came back on the field, and that two hundred pound fullback of theirs got the ball, and now we were behind twelve points. It was during the third quarter that they really began to grind our team into the turf. They seemed to be getting stronger by the minute, while our crew looked shabbier than ever. We couldn't understand it. It didn't make sense. Unless perhaps they'd discovered the red pepper. From the way they paraded and strutted

352 4. *fifteen yards:* 13.716 m; 1 yard = .9144 m

across the field, it was clear they'd be prepared for any contingency. We couldn't put anything past them.

When calling plays, they didn't huddle, as we did. Instead their team would line up in two rows, with their backs to us, and their quarterback would stand facing them and bark out the number of the play. They couldn't have cared less if we overheard or not, they were so confident. Then the centre would march out and crouch over the ball, while the rest of the team moved with just as much military precision to their positions. The ball would be snapped and—Quick March!—they had fifteen more yards, while, as likely as not, we had a few more lumps.

Just as we were getting used to the fact that they weren't trying anything fancy now—that this was going to be one of those bruising games where each side tries to pound the other into the earth—their two hundred pound fullback started to come round one end, then handed the ball off to the tailback, who scooted round the other end on a double reverse. And we were eighteen points behind.

The mood on our side of the stadium became grim. On the field the game was turning into a rout. Marty Klein, who was playing safety, as well as quarterback, got creamed when he intercepted a Kelvin pass on our one-yard line, and the Ambulance Corps had to carry him off the field. Down on the sidelines, Torchy Brownstone was still pleading with the coach to let him in.

I guess we should have known when Torchy appeared on the bench dressed for the game that the fates had decreed he would play that night. We knew it was crazy, but on to the field he limped with the first-string line: Norm Mittlehaus—

a savage tackle who was later to sing with the Metropolitan Opera and eventually become a cantor; Marvin Zimmerman — who'd recently met a bunch of pretty nurses at the General Hospital and was playing with the reckless abandon of someone determined to break a collarbone at least; Sammy Margolis—who never quite came up to expectations, and who, when he was sent to Los Angeles to study dentistry, married the daughter of a clothing manufacturer instead; and Sheldon Kunstler—who later moved to New York and got rich by inventing a machine that bent, folded, and stapled computer cards. Across the field they moved, as the voice on the P.A. system announced that Torchy Brownstone was playing against doctor's orders, and we all cheered mindlessly.

St. John's huddled behind their own goal line. A couple of Kelvin linemen— huge Goliaths that seemed to have just wandered in from the battle plains of Judaea—let long thin streams of spit slide from between their teeth to the grass. Their teammates looked no less contemptuous.

Then the St. John's huddle broke, and Izzy Steinberg, who'd played the Lord High Executioner in *The Mikado* the year before, marched with an exaggerated goose step to his position as centre. About him the rest of the team marched with stiff, jerky steps to their places also. Dressed in their torn sweaters and oversize pants, held up by bits of string and old suspenders, they turned smartly to salute Torchy, who promptly returned the salute, and then as one man they all whirled about to give a "Sieg Heil" to the members of the Kelvin team. As the full impact of the caricature was taken in by the spectators, laughter began to gather within the North **353**

End stands until it washed over the Kelvin fans.

The laughter and noise quietened into an expectant hush as Torchy began to call signals. Everyone in the stadium knew that Torchy had the largest sleight-of-hand repertoire of any high school quarterback in the city. Consequently, once the play began, anyone who could conceivably get his hands on the ball—backs, ends—all were immediately flattened by those Kelvin behemoths° that came roaring through our line. Which meant that nobody laid a hand on Torchy as he limped down the field, paused briefly to fish the ball out of the hole in his sweater, and then crossed over the River Heights goal line. The quarterback sneak had travelled the whole length of the field.

While the Kelvin players were still complaining to the officials, we could see Torchy calling the St. John's team into a huddle. I don't know what he said, but after the kick-off, our players charged down the field as if they'd been transformed. In the fading sunlight, their torn uniforms looked like golden armour, ablaze with precious stones; their helmets shone with emeralds and sapphires; and they moved with a grace and power that was electrifying. That two hundred pound River Heights fullback—who was playing both ways—caught the ball and was promptly hit by Sidney Cohen in the hardest flying tackle any of us had ever seen. After that tackle, Sidney, who had always impressed us as something of a Momma's Boy, was Papa's Boy forever.

The Kelvin fullback had fallen to the earth as if he were the Tower of Babel crumbling beneath the wrath of God. The ball bounced into the air, and Torchy . . . Torchy was where he always is during a

fumble. He would have scored touchdowns if he had had to go down the field on crutches. The same, I'm afraid, could not be said of the two hundred pound fullback. Bruno Hogg lay unconscious on the field, dreaming strange, alien dreams of knishes and gefilte fish[5], and blissfully unaware that, for once, he'd met his match and been vanquished utterly. Now we were only six points behind.

During the fourth quarter, the Kelvin line started tackling Torchy on every play. You'd see him out there, limping away from the action of the hand-off, holding up both arms to show everyone he didn't have the ball, and still they'd tackle him. So then Torchy started throwing passes—that way the whole stadium could see he didn't have the ball. But neither the Kelvin tackles nor the officials seemed to care. And that was when Torchy sent word to the bench that it was time for Luther Johnson to come out.

Luther was our secret weapon. Just recently, his family had moved up from a black ghetto in Chicago, where Luther had played end for the city high school champions. He was a lanky 196 cm, could lope along for kilometres faster than most people could sprint, and caught passes thrown anywhere within shouting distance.

Before vanishing in a melee of purple Kelvin sweaters, Torchy managed to get away a twenty-yard completion. On the next play, Luther caught a thirty-five yarder. Suddenly those River Heights players didn't seem to be strutting about so much. From the way they kept pointing, first to one player on our team, then to another,

5. *knishes and gefilte fish:* European dishes. Knishes are cakes filled with meat or cheese. Gefilte fish is a mixture of chopped fish

you could see that they were puzzling who to go after. Torchy might just choose to go limping across the goal line for the tying touchdown himself.

Our team wasn't sure, either, what to do next. You could hear them arguing about it in the huddle. Once Norm Mittlehaus's deep baritone voice could be heard demanding that they call a trick play and throw the ball to him for a change. Finally ... finally ... they came out of the conference, but before they could line up, one of the officials blew his whistle to signal they'd lost the down. Too much time in the huddle. So back they went to argue some more.

They were still arguing when they came out for the second down. Torchy looked pretty small out there as he limped into position behind the centre. Even without the limp, though, we would have recognized him by that hard whiplash voice of

his, the black hair constantly falling down into his eyes and the fluid way he managed to move once the ball was snapped—hurt leg and all. He was like a particularly graceful predatory bird that's injured a wing.

Again the ball was sent arcing through the air, and again Luther was running along in that lope of his—this time across the Kelvin goal line. Everyone on the Kelvin team seemed out to intercept the pass, and all the possible receivers were immediately encircled by River Heights players. The ball, which was soaring a good 60 cm above everyone's hands, kept rising still, and looked as if it would fall uncaught in the end zone.

Luther didn't need to leap or spring to reach the ball. Suddenly he was just there—his black face a good 90 cm higher than the distraught white ones looking up at him in disbelief. At that moment, with

the players all frozen together in a portrait of triumph and defeat, Luther must have looked—to the Kelvin team—like the Black Angel of Death himself. They hung there for a moment, Luther's eyes ablaze with laughter, his white teeth flashing savagely. Then they all broke apart and tumbled to the ground, and the roaring from the stands broke over them.

As both teams lined up again for the kick-off, Torchy moved toward the sidelines, his limp worse than ever. Though only five minutes remained, now that the score was tied, not a spectator there doubted for a moment that we would go on to win the game. Standing at the bench and looking at his teammates lining up, Torchy seemed a magician who had just worked a miraculous transformation. The fumbling rabble of players who had dragged out onto the field two hours before now looked like a company of young gods come to try their prowess on the fields of Olympus.[6]

But that was when the Kelvin team began their incredible march down the field. It all started after the kick-off, with the referee claiming that we had roughed the receiver. When Mittlehaus objected, he was promptly kicked out of the game for unsportsmanlike behavior, and the team given an additional penalty of another ten yards. On the next play, Kelvin's pass was incomplete, but we got called for being off-side. A few minutes later, and they kicked a single point from our thirty-yard line.

After a moment of doubt and disbelief, a few cheers broke, halting and uncertain, from the River Heights stands. Yet almost immediately a feverish silence gripped the stadium, preventing even the outraged protests of the North End supporters from gathering momentum. Furiously, the St. John's team gathered about the ball. There were only two minutes left in the game, barely enough time to set matters right. Torchy began calling signals, the players snapped into formation, the ball was hiked, and now they were all in motion. Every line in their bodies, the practised way in which they moved, spoke of an assurance and competence toward which they'd been building throughout the game. The fullback slashed into the line. Three yards, maybe four. Again the players gathered about the ball and signals were barked. Ends criss-crossed over the goal line, players blocked, changed direction, faked. And then the fullback—on a de-layed plunge—slashed into the line again. But the Kelvin players held as fast as the walls of Jericho before they finally came tumbling down. Five yards.

For the third down, Kelvin didn't even bother sending back receivers. The play began as another plunge, with the two lines clashing and then becoming still for a moment. Suddenly Torchy began fading back, arm raised to throw—as deadly as a cobra—while Luther burst into the open, shifted to his left, and raced downfield. Torchy waited till the last possible moment as the purple sweaters converged upon him; and then the ball was soaring free out of that jumble of players—as straight and true a pass as any receiver could hope for. Luther loped effortlessly toward where the ball would arc downward into his waiting hands, and we cheered with enough energy to split the stadium apart and bring the walls of that Philistine temple down upon our enemies' heads. And about us, the city shone as if made of molten glass— aflame in the radiance of the setting sun—

6. *Olympus:* in Greek mythology, the home of the gods

gates garnished with pearl and gold and all manner of precious stones.

In the dazzled eyes of the frenzied North End fans, Luther, in his dented helmet, torn sweater, and baggy pants, was already a figure of glory. But suddenly a look of alarm and disbelief crossed Luther's face as he was brought up short in his tracks, then pitched down, face forward, into the turf—his outstretched arms empty—the ball arcing downward to bounce mockingly across the Kelvin goal line, just beyond his fingertips.

His own disbelief was mirrored in the faces of the fans. He had been upended, not by a Kelvin tackle, but by a pair of snapped suspenders which had suddenly catapulted his pants violently downward so that they now hung about his ankles. As the stands erupted in catcalls, laughter, boos, and cheers, we glimpsed what looked like a white flag signalling defeat. And then the whistle blew to end the game.

It was right, I suppose, that we should have lost. Anything else would have been a lie. Afterwards, as we pushed and elbowed our way out the gates, we were only too aware of the outraged glances being directed at us by our teachers from across the field. While behind us, in a mighty crescendo of triumph, rose the voices from the River Heights stands:

Send him victorious,
Happy and glorious,
Long to reign over us,
God save the King!

Those voices followed us right out of the stadium, and once out of high school, we fled in every possible direction. Marvin Zimmerman raced back to the General Hospital and eventually married one of those pretty nurses; Sam Margolis got his father to mortgage the house and send him to college in Los Angeles; Nate Samuelson, who planned to become a famous heart surgeon, actually entered Medical School; Marty Klein became a delivery man for a local dairy; Luther Johnson got taken on by the CPR as a sleeping car attendant; and Torchy Brownstone just dropped out of sight. As for Mr. Rockwood, the short, heavy-set English teacher who was the terror of Room 41, he was at last allowed to return to Kelvin—after his years of penance in the North End—but almost immediately he was forced into early retirement when he swatted a grade ten student he caught sneaking out to the drugstore on Academy Road. Most of the others — players, teachers, friends — I'm afraid I've lost sight of over the years. But often, when I'm least expecting it, a familiar face that really hasn't changed all that much will stare out at me from the eleven o'clock TV news, or from the society pages of the *Free Press,* or, even occasionally now as the years pass, from the obituary columns. When that happens, I fill in a little write-up of my own beneath a photograph I keep filed away in my memory.

But not only have familiar faces disappeared, familiar landmarks have vanished also, and during the last twenty-five years it has become more and more difficult to keep track of the city I once knew. The Royal Alexandra Hotel, where we held our graduation dance, is gone. Child's Restaurant at Portage and Main, where we'd all meet after a play or movie—no more. Even Osborne Stadium, where we played our football games, has vanished, replaced by a huge, expensive insurance company. Do the shouts of former high school battles ever echo within those heavy stone walls, I wonder, or have they been filed away, along with such names as Norm Mittle- **357** haus, Nate Samuelson, Marvin Zimmerman, and the rest, as insurance statistics in grey steel filing cabinets?

With the passage of time, the North End, too, has changed. So final has its defeat become that it has even had thrust upon it a suburb with such street names as Bluebell, Marigold, Primrose, and Cherryhill. Over the years, that two hundred pound fullback has managed to race clear across the city to score a touchdown right here in our home territory. Now we also have our false Eden.

In an attempt to exact some small measure of revenge, I bought a house in River Heights a few years ago and let the lawn go to seed, allowed the back gate to fall off the hinges, let the torn screens on the veranda go unrepaired, and filled the garage and backyard with old furniture and junk from my grandmother's house. But even I know that this attempt to plant a bit of the North End in the heart of River Heights doesn't begin to restore the balance.

The only time we ever came close to holding our own—and, better still, maybe even winning—was that night years before when a lone figure with a hard whiplash voice and black hair falling into his eyes came limping onto the field for part of a football game. He was one of those figures who, at the time, are filed away in a special place in your memory and are then, unaccountably, forgotten—unless, awakened by some chance occurrence, they spring to life again.

It was just a few days ago, as I was passing a downtown parking lot early in the evening, that I heard a familiar voice barking out directions to some motorists who'd managed to snarl up traffic and block both exits at once. The dark figure of the uniformed attendant moved with a fluid grace that I was sure I had seen somewhere before. There was something familiar about that limp and the way he jerked his head to glance over the lot—like an athlete assessing a new and difficult situation. Back and forth he darted among the honking cars as he signalled some forward, others backward. Until, with a flair that—under the circumstances—was really quite surprising, he had managed to untangle them all.

In the darkness, as he started back toward the booth at the entrance to the parking lot, he seemed to merge with the figure that had limped along the sidelines of the stadium so many years ago and shouted encouragement to a grumbling rabble of players. That night, for almost thirty minutes, under the stadium lights, he had discovered to us all a grace and a strength that flashed electrically from one player to another. And then they were no longer a grumbling rabble of players. They became timeless, ancient, a group of immortals caught up in trials of strength that would never end, Greek athletes who had just come to life out of stone. That night, while we all watched in wonder, the city had flashed about us with sapphires and emeralds, jasper and amethysts. And how we had longed to believe that the city could stay like that forever.

follow-up

Discussing "The Immortals"

The story contains several glimpses of the future. Marvin Zimmerman married a nurse; Nate Samuelson became a doctor, then took his own life; Marty Klein became a delivery man for a local dairy; Luther Johnson got taken on by the CPR as a sleeping car attendant; Norm Mittlehaus became a cantor; and Sheldon Kunstler invented a machine that bent, folded and stapled computer cards. Nothing very glorious or immortal here, is there?

1. Re-read the first paragraph. Explain in your own words the irony of this opening incident. Does the opening make you want to read on?
2. Re-read the paragraph on page 351, beginning with "On the next kick-off, our star runner, Cramer, caught the football."
   a) When the writer speaks of the two teams in terms of "Jerusalem" and "Babylon," what effect does he create?
   b) Find other examples of heightened language used in the description of the game.
3. Re-read the two paragraphs on page 357 beginning "In the dazzled eyes of the frenzied North End fans…"
   The reader's sympathies are with the unlucky North End team. Still, we have to laugh at a description such as this. Why does the author use a humorous style? What other style might he have used? With what effect?

Phrase and Impression

At one point in the story, the losing team is transformed:

"In the fading sunlight, their torn uniforms *looked like golden armour, ablaze with precious stones; their helmets shone with emeralds and sapphires,* and they moved with a grace and power that was electrifying."

The uniforms are being compared (italicized above) to golden armour fit for royalty. This gives the impression of a strength that can't be overcome. This type of figurative comparison is a *simile* (see page 108). The simile serves a special purpose. It creates a vivid sensory impression and gives the phrase and the story added impact.

Later in the story when Luther managed to reach for the ball, you find this sentence:

> "*At that moment, with the players all frozen together in a portrait of triumph and defeat,* Luther must have looked—to the Kelvin team —like the Black Angel of Death himself."

Notice how the three prepositional phrases add important details that introduce the scene. The author describes the St. John's fans as they sit watching the game:

> "So there we all were, *glaring across the field at the River Heights stands,* where, *sitting shamelessly among the staunch supporters of the opposing team,* we could make out Rockwood;"

The participial phrase *glaring across the field* tells what the St. John's supporters were doing in the stands and the participial phrase *sitting shamelessly* tells how the teachers of St. John's were sitting with the opponent supporters. It gives the impression that the teachers were not supporting their own school. In the scene where Cramer was tackled by Bruno Hogg, the fullback from the Kelvin team, you no doubt noticed the following special use of a participial phrase. Notice how effectively it represents Torchy's determined character.

> "We could see Torchy, down on the sidelines, *pleading with the coach to let him in*—knee injury and all—but Powalski sent in Marty Klein instead."

In describing Luther, a writer who has less insight and imagination might write the following sentence:

> "Suddenly he was just there."

But see how sharply the impression is created as Kleiman uses the bare statement for a base and builds an image of a boy rising in power and strength above the rest of the players. The author here presents a contrast between the tall, black Luther and the other white players. You will recognize the addition of an absolute:

> "Suddenly he was just there—*his black face a good 90 cm higher than the distraught white ones looking up at him in disbelief.*"

The following sentence, also describing Luther, further emphasizes his savage determination. The addition of the two absolutes focusing on his eyes and teeth, complete the picture of his determination.

> "They hung there for a moment, *Luther's eyes ablaze with laughter, his white teeth flashing savagely.*"

In the following sentence Kleiman describes another player's strong-mindedness:

> "As both teams lined up again for the kick-off, Torchy moved toward the sidelines, *his limp worse than ever.*" (The participle *being* is understood.)

You have seen that adding a detail can create a definite impression in a sentence. The kind of detail-phrase that is added depends on the kind of information the writer wishes to add. He/she selects the kind of phrase that will fit the sentence, one that best expresses the thought or picture to be conveyed. If you know how to use these various kinds of phrases, you will be able to write and speak more expressively—much as a tennis player can improve his/her game by learning various strokes.

Practice 1. Writing

When you write narrative or description, you can add impact to what you say if you create precise, interesting impressions. You *can* create such impressions by writing cumulative sentences like those you have just examined.

Here are five sentences—base statements. Add impact to each one by adding sensory impressions expressed through one or more of the kinds of phrases we've been discussing:

1. The boy nervously shifted his weight from one foot to the other, ——.
    Hints: Why? Was he uneasy because he was the next contestant? Or: How did he appear otherwise, in face, eyes, hands, shoulders?
2. I looked straight at him for a moment, ——.
    Hints: Why did you hesitate? Were you trying to decide what to do? Or: Were you trying to think of something reassuring to say?
3. He walked out on the stage,——.
    Hints: How? like a shadow dissolved by light? like a ghost seeking new haunts? with a hurried, shuffling gait?

4. The four judges sat in the first row, _____.
   Hints: How? Were they whispering among themselves? eyeing the boy coldly? smiling expectantly?
5. The trumpet solo began, _____.
   Hints: Did the boy gain confidence? Did he flub the opening notes? Did he put heart and soul into his performance?

Be prepared to read at least one of your sentences aloud. Invite the class to say whether the phrase(s) you've added have given the entire sentence interest and impact.

Bookshelf

Lives of Girls and Women, by Alice Munro. New American Library of Canada, 1974. The story of a young girl growing up in Ontario in the 1940's. It traces the girl's transition from childhood to the fears of youth surrounded by the conservatism of a small town.

"The Fall of a City" by Alden Nowlan, in *Tigers of the Snow,* ed. by James A. MacNeil and Glen A. Sorstad. Thomas Nelson and Sons, 1972. Teddy creates a toy cardboard world of buildings and people only to have it shattered by an insensitive uncle. The story shows the destruction of childhood dreams.

The Temple on the River, by Jacques Hebert. Harvest House, 1967. The story of a young boy, the son of well-to-do parents, and his problems growing up and fighting phoniness, hypocrisy and injustice. He ends up in an institution for the mentally retarded.

interlude

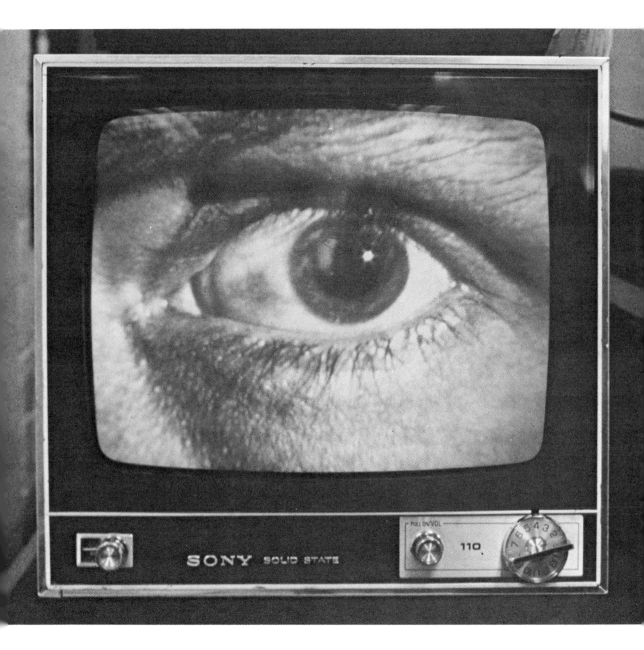

Neuteronomy

Eve Merriam

The elevator stops at every floor
and nobody opens and closes the door,
and nobody talks to his neighbor anymore
where the neuter computer goes *tick*,
where the neuter computer goes *click*.

You call the operator on the telephone
and say Help! I'm in trouble and I'm here all alone!
and all you get back is a phoney dial tone
where the neuter computer goes *clank*,
where the neuter computer goes *blank*.

There's no more teacher to be nice or mean
when you learn your lessons from a teaching machine
and plug in your prayers to the preaching machine
where the neuter computer goes *bless*,
where the neuter computer goes *yes*.

From when you are born until you are old
the facts of your life are all controlled,
put your dreams on a punch card—don't staple or fold
where the neuter computer prints *file*,
where the neuter computer prints *smile*.

There's no one to love and no one to hate,
and no more misfortune or chance or fate
in this automated obligated zero perfect state
where the neuter computer goes *think*.
where the neuter computer goes *blink*
blink think blink think blink blink blink
    blinkthink
      thinkblink
     blink
       think
        blink

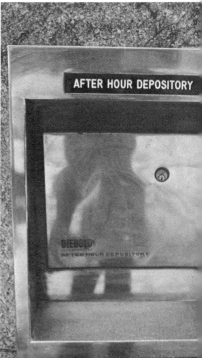

focus

Writing Business Letters

About Business Letters

Write a business letter? Who—me? You've got to be kidding. Only people who are in business—people like store managers and insurance agents and bankers—write business letters.

Does that sound like you talking? If so, you're partly right but also partly wrong. Business people do write business letters—lots of them. But they're not the only people who do. Note the following letter:

Fig. 1

```
                                        1131 North Haven Ave.
                                        Ottawa, Ontario K1P 5B5
                                        October 1, 19___

Kentucky Fried Chicken
Public Relations Department
P.O. Box 13331
Louisville, Kentucky   40213

Dear Manager:

    The members of Wig and Whiskers, the drama club
at Laurier High School, are interested in planning
money-making activities. I would appreciate your
sending me a copy of your booklet "Great Ways to
Raise Money."

    I am enclosing 25¢ to cover postage and handling.

    Thank you.

                                Yours truly,

                                Roger Herzog

                                Roger Herzog
                                Treasurer
                                Wig and Whiskers
```

Is this a business letter? Definitely, yes. Its tone is impersonal and formal. But even more important, like all business letters, it concerns a business transaction. All business letters, in fact, request or communicate information about a product or an idea or a business arrangement.

At one time or another almost all of us find it necessary to write business letters that may concern any one of a number of topics. Buying, selling, returning unsatisfactory goods, requesting information, applying for a job, explaining and describing an idea or proposal for earning one's living—all can be taken care of through business letters.

Order and Request Letters

Following are two short business letters, both addressed to the mythical Tee-Tops Company. Both are orders for merchandise.

Fig. 2

```
                                   3 Dundas Street
                                   Toronto, Ontario M5B 1C8
                                   April 20, 19___


     Tee-Tops Company
     197 Wilson Drive
     Madison, Wisconsin    53703

     Dear Sales Manager:

          Please send me the following Zodiac tee-shirt,
     which was advertised for $3.99 in the April issue of
     Today Magazine.

          One   Zodiac tee-shirt, Scorpio sign,
                medium size, blue (second
                choice, yellow)                     $3.99
                                     Postage           .85
                                     Total          $4.84

     I am enclosing a money order for $4.84.

     Thank you.

                                   Yours truly,

                                   CHRIS WASHINGTON

                                   Chris Washington
```

Fig. 3

```
                                        3 Dundas Street
                                        Toronto, Ontario M5B 1C8
                                        April 20, 19__


     Tee-Tops Company
     197 Wilson Drive
     Madison, Wisconsin    53703

     Dear Company:

         How about sending me one of your Zodiac tee-
     shirts that I saw in Today Magazine?  Make it a blue
     one printed with the sign for November.  Thanks.

                               CHRIS W.

                               Chris W.

     P.S.  Here's 4 bucks for the shirt.
```

Practice 1. Discussion

If you were an official at the Tee-Tops Company, which letter—Figure 2 or Figure 3—would you act on without delay? Why?

Millions of people shop by long distance—that is, by mail. Your letter ordering any kind of merchandise should be simple, exact, and complete. It should contain all of the information necessary to identify the item requested: the exact name of the item, the stock or catalogue number, the quantities, and (if applicable) the size, color, and style. Your order letter should also indicate the price of each item and the total cost of the order. Include sales tax and shipping and handling costs if appropriate. If you send payment with your letter, state the amount you are enclosing and the form in which you are sending it (money order, cheque, currency).

Practice 2. Writing

Write the first draft of a letter ordering or requesting items from a catalogue advertisement, or from one of the sources below. Choose merchandise that you would actually like to receive. For examples of a satisfactory letter, see Figure 2 (page 366).

Sources for Free and Inexpensive Materials

Many corporations and institutions provide free and inexpensive materials that you can obtain through the mail. Below are some sources that contain lists of "freebies." In most cases the items listed will cost you only the price of an envelope and a postage stamp. The sponsors of the items state that supplies may be limited, and that they will honor requests until their supply is exhausted. They may also request that you send a self-addressed, stamped envelope (SASE) or that you send a small amount to cover postage and handling. If you send an SASE, make sure it is a long, business-size envelope (#10). Be sure to use postal codes on all correspondence and to print your address clearly. Allow at least four weeks for your request to be filled.

The following items were selected from *1001 Valuable Things You Can Get Free,* by Harriet Saalheimer, 1978 (Pagurian Press Ltd., Suite 1106, 335 Bay St., Toronto):

The Wonderous World of Fashion

The mystery of fashion is as old as clothing itself. Fashion has always been and still is unpredictable.

The 64-page illustrated booklet, "What They Wore" (Elles ont porte"), depicts what women wore through the ages, from the cave woman to today's emancipated Ms.

Contact: Consumer Services Division, International Ladies' Garment Workers Union, 307-333 Chabanel Street W., Montreal, P.Q. H3N 2H2.

A Pleasant Personality Attracts People

Because the impression we make is so important, we must always try to be at our best.

The 4-page leaflet, "Personality Power," is a great help. It tells you which points to observe for a look of self-confidence, and it stresses the importance of cleanliness and grooming.

Your uniqueness should also be expressed in your clothes, voice, and manner of speech. Another plus in personality development is learning to listen and to be cheerful, to be polite, and to be reliable.

The folder is offered with the compliments of Shaw Colleges, 2436 Yonge Street, Toronto, Ontario M4P 2H4.

Citizen's Band Radio

General Radio Service (GRS), usually called "Citizen's Band," is becoming an increasingly popular means of communication. Thousands of Canadians now own GRS radios and use them regularly.

The 12-page bilingual "General Radio Service" ("Service général radio") booklet helps you get the most from your GRS, and offers other valuable information.

Because a licence is required to operate a two-way GRS radio, an application form is included in the book.

Contact: Information Service, Department of Communications, 300 Slater Street, Ottawa, Ontario K1A 0C8.

Like to go Hostelling?

Hostelling is an inexpensive way to travel around the world and is available to everybody.

The 12-page bilingual folder "Let's Go Hostelling" ("Allons dans les auberges de jeunesse") mentions that the world's first youth hostel was established at Bragg Creek, Alberta, in 1933. It also explains who is entitled to make use of hostel facilities. In most hostels age is no barrier.

Also available are several attractive posters which are suitable for notice boards or other places where they can be seen by a large number of people. If you request a poster, indicate where you intend to put it up, so that you receive a suitable one.

Contact: Canadian Hostelling Association, 333 River Road, Vanier, Ontario K1L 8B9.

Other sources for free and inexpensive materials are often featured in various current magazines, such as *Good Housekeeping, Ladies' Home Journal,* and *Changing Times.* Look for the "Things to Write for" section.

The government is a source for information on practically any subject. Check the public documents section of your public library, or write the following:

    Information and Public Relations
    Consumer and Corporate Affairs
    Place du Portage
    Hull, P.Q.
    K1A 0C9

Letters of Complaint

Coping with everyday problems often requires the writing of business letters. Here are two for you to examine.

Fig. 4

```
                                    836 View St.
                                    Victoria, B.C. V8W 1K2
                                    May 15, 19___


    Cheapo Sports, Inc.
    11500 Jasper Avenue
    Edmonton, Alberta T5K 0L2

    Dear Sales Manager:

        I recently ordered a Cheapo Deluxe tennis racquet,
    Model No. 633, for $5.95, as listed in your spring
    catalogue.

        I received the racquet by parcel post on May 10.
    It seemed to be in good condition when I removed it
    from the shipping carton.  But next day, I had just
    started to play tennis, when the head of the racquet
    snapped off on my first overhead shot.  Surely there
    must have been a flaw in the racquet.  I certainly did
    not abuse or mishandle it in any way--as you will see
    when you inspect it.

        I am returning the racquet--the two pieces--to
    you by separate mail.  I would appreciate it if you
    would send me a replacement--that is, another racquet
    of the same model.  If that is not possible, then I
    would like to have my $5.95 refunded.  I am enclosing
    a copy of the sales invoice.

        I would appreciate your prompt consideration of
    this matter.

        Thank you very much.

                                    Sincerely,

                                    Leslie Player
                                    Leslie Player
```

Fig. 5

```
                                        836 View St.
                                        Victoria, B.C. V8W 1K2
                                        May 15, 19___


        Cheapo Sports, Inc.
        11500 Jasper Avenue
        Edmonton, Alberta T5K 0L2

        Dear Sports, Inc:

            What do you guys think you're doing?

            Last month I ordered a Cheapo Deluxe tennis
        racquet from your company for $5.95.

            The racquet arrived yesterday.  When I went out
        to play tennis, I hit an overhead shot, and both the
        ball and the head of the racquet flew over the net,
        missing my friend by inches.

            The head of the racquet snapped off.  What kind
        of stuff do you send out, anyway?

            I'm returning the racquet in two pieces.  Either
        send me another racquet of the same model--one that's
        not cracked--or send back my $5.95.

                                Yours truly,

                                Leslie Player
                                Leslie Player
```

Practice 3. Discussion

1. If you were responsible for handling customer complaints at Cheapo Sports, Inc., which letter—Figure 4 or Figure 5— would you be likely to respond to promptly? Why?
2. How would you describe the tone of each of the letters?
3. What information does Figure 4 contain that is not found in Figure 5? Is that information important? Why? Why not?
4. From your examination of these two letters (Figures 4 and 5), what would you say are the most important features of an effective letter of complaint?

Occasionally goods or services that you have paid for turn out to be unsatisfactory. In such a case, you may need to write a letter of complaint, seeking replacement, repair, or a refund.

The complaint letter should follow the same principles as other business letters. It should be accurate, clear, concise, complete, and *courteous*. Even if you are justifiably angry, a polite tone in your letter will usually achieve faster and better results than will a sarcastic or abusive tone. Be reasonable and fair. Most companies are eager to please their customers and will respond promptly to remedy a just complaint.

Practice 4. Writing

Write the first draft of a letter of complaint. Imagine that you are a customer who has bought or ordered merchandise that turns out to be defective. Request that the firm repair or replace the item or give you a refund. For an example, see Figure 4 (page 370).

You may want to devise your own imaginary complaint, making up the specific details, such as the company's name and address, the defective item, its cost, and the situation involved. Make your letter realistic.

If you have difficulty in inventing the information needed, use one of the complaint situations (1–4) listed below. Then choose one of the fictitious companies listed below (A–D) as a target for your complaint letter. Feel free to add or change details to fit your particular complaint to make your letter effective.

Complaint Situation	*Companies*
1.	**A.**
You have bought a pair of sharp alligator shoes for $24.50. There is only one problem—they make a strange noise when you walk in them.	Bumdeal's Department Store 616 – 1st. W. Calgary, Alberta T2G 2M2
2.	**B.**
You have ordered a wrist watch (invent a brand name) for $59.00. It's a beautiful time piece, but the hands turn backwards—counter-clockwise.	Aardvark Distributors 5D Highfield St. Moncton, N.B. E1C 5N2

3.

When you get your new $30.00 hair dryer home and unpack it from its carton, you find that it does not blow hot air. To the contrary, it *draws* air like a vacuum cleaner.

C.

Finicky Enterprises
170 S. 6th Ave.
Vancouver, B.C. V5Y 1K5

4.

You have spent $23.00 for a transistor radio so that you can hear your favorite music stations. However, your radio will receive only police calls.

D.

Humdinger Industries
Box 91
Halifax, Nova Scotia
B3J 2V9

Letters of Application

Of all the business letters you may write in your lifetime, the most important could be the letter of application. Often, when applying for employment, the job-seeker's first contact with the employer is through an application letter—a special kind of business letter. In a way, the letter of application is a sales letter. The writer, in effect, is selling his/her services to a prospective employer.

Following is a list of what a typical letter of application should include:

1. A sentence or two explaining the position that you are applying for and how you learned of the job opening.
2. One or more paragraphs describing your age, qualifications, education, experience, and abilities that pertain to the work.
3. One or more paragraphs telling of your special interests and goals, if appropriate, to give the reader a glimpse of your personality and character.
4. The names, positions, addresses, and telephone numbers of two or three people (usually not related to you) to be used as references. Be sure to get their permission before listing their names.
5. A request for an interview, including information about how you may be reached.

Examine the two letters that follow:

Fig. 6

366 Park Street
Waterloo, Ontario
N2L 3G1
April 16, 19___

Mr. Frank Scott
Frank's Pharmacy
210 Main Street
Waterloo, Ontario N2L 3C5

Dear Mr. Scott:

According to Mrs. Grace Johnson, Career Counselor at Parkside High School, you are looking for a reliable student to work after school and on Saturdays, helping with deliveries and doing odd jobs at your store. I believe that I am qualified for such a job, and I would like to apply for it.

I am sixteen years old and am a junior at Parkside High School. So far I have a B average. My health is very good.

I have a driver's license, and I am a good, safe driver with an excellent record.

For the past three years I have had a newspaper route for the Waterloo Chronicle. Also last summer I helped unload produce at Farmer's Market near my neighborhood.

I was born in Waterloo and have lived here all my life, so I know the city very well.

I have permission from the following persons to refer you to them for information about my character and ability.

Mrs. Grace Johnson
Career Counselor, Parkside High School
Waterloo, Ontario N2L 3B2
Telephone: 555-2761

Mr. Anthony Martin
Distribution Director, Waterloo Chronicle
918 Front Street
Waterloo, Ontario N2L 3S2
Telephone: 555-4000

Mr. Lee Jackson
Manager, Farmer's Market
2000 Dundas Avenue
Waterloo, Ontario N2L 2C1
Telephone: 555-8559

I would be happy to come to your store for a personal interview on any weekday after 3:00 P.M., or at any time on Saturday at your convenience. My telephone number is 294-7733.

Sincerely yours,

Charles Hart

Charles Hart

Fig.7

```
                              366 Park Street
                              Waterloo, Ontario N2L 3G1
                              April 16, 19__


Mr. Frank Scott
Frank's Pharmacy
210 Main Street
Waterloo, Ontario N2L 3C5

Dear Mr. Scott:

    I heard that you are looking for a part-worker
at your store. I could use a job, so I thought I
would apply for it.

    I am going to school at Parkside High, and I am a
pretty good student. Just ask any of my teachers.

    I am also a good worker. I have had jobs at the
Chronicle and Farmer's Market. You could ask them what a
good worker I am. I also helped my uncle on his farm
one time.

    Please let me know soon about the job. I think
it would be fun to work at a drugstore. Be seeing you.

                         Sincerely yours,

                         Charles Hart

                         Charles Hart
```

Practice 5. Discussion

1. Which letter—Figure 6 or Figure 7—do you think will receive the more favorable results? Why?
2. What information does the Figure 6 letter contain that is not found in the Figure 7 letter? Is that information important? Why?
3. How would you describe the writer of each of the letters?

375

As stated earlier, a letter of application may well be the most important business letter you write in your lifetime. An effective letter of application is neat, clear, complete, courteous, and sincere. It should make a favorable impression on a prospective employer.

When there are many applicants for a job, the person who writes an effective letter will have a definite advantage. If your letter can convince the employer that you are dependable, qualified, and eager to be of service, you have a good chance of landing that job.

Practice 6. Writing

Write the first draft of a letter of application—a letter that you would actually like to send—for a part time or a summer job. Examine the Help-Wanted ads in your local newspaper for likely prospects. Or you might write to an employer in your area who traditionally hires young people. If your school has a career centre, vocational counselor, or a work experience program, check the current job listings.

If you are already employed, write your letter applying for a position—real or imaginary—that you would like to have after you complete your schooling.

Use the Figure 6 letter (p. 374) as a model for your letter—with appropriate changes to fit your purpose. In addition, you'll want to review the guidelines on page 373.

Guidelines for Business Letters

So far you have read seven different business letters, both good and bad examples. You have also written first drafts of three different types of business letters. Chances are that you now have in mind some general ideas about how to write effective business letters of all types.

Practice 7. Writing and Discussion

Using what you have learned so far in this lesson, make a list of guidelines for writing effective business letters.

Head your paper as follows: GUIDELINES FOR WRITING BUSINESS LETTERS. Two such guidelines appear on page 377. List them on your paper, using your own words. After considering them, supply at least three more of your own.

Guidelines for Writing Business Letters

1. Make your letter accurate—in both form and content. (The purpose of any business letter is to convey information. Inaccurate or incorrect information can be costly— both to the sender and the receiver of the letter.)
2. Give complete information to conduct your business. (Put yourself in the place of the intended receiver of the letter. Is there sufficient information to complete the transaction?)
3.
4.   (For you to supply.)
5.
6. ?
7. ?

Be prepared to share your guidelines with others in the class. Perhaps you'll want to develop a class set of guidelines for writing business letters.

Final Preparations

The last step in the process of writing a business letter involves revising the letter, proofreading it, and putting it in final form.

Practice 8. Writing

Choose one or more of your letters, as your teacher directs, to revise and rewrite in preparation for mailing. Proofread carefully for spelling, punctuation, sentence sense, and accuracy.

Whether you write your letter by hand or typewrite it, make it neat and legible. Allow sufficient margins to "frame" your message as if it were a picture being centred on the page. Use short, distinct paragraphs, making your letter easy to read, thus creating a favorable impression.

To illustrate the standard business letter form, an example is reproduced below, with various parts labelled. In addition, important marks of punctuation have been circled.   **377**

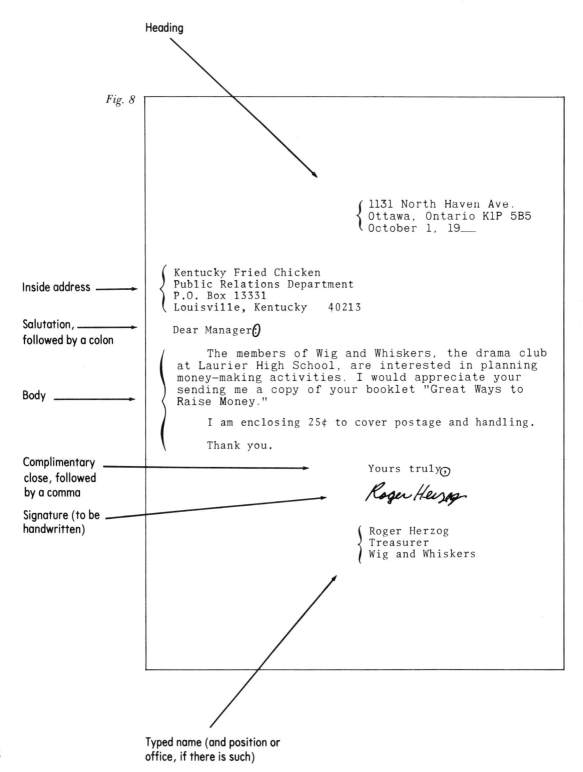

Heading

Fig. 8

1131 North Haven Ave.
Ottawa, Ontario K1P 5B5
October 1, 19___

Inside address ———→

Kentucky Fried Chicken
Public Relations Department
P.O. Box 13331
Louisville, Kentucky   40213

Salutation, ———→
followed by a colon

Dear Manager(:)

Body ———→

     The members of Wig and Whiskers, the drama club
at Laurier High School, are interested in planning
money-making activities. I would appreciate your
sending me a copy of your booklet "Great Ways to
Raise Money."

     I am enclosing 25¢ to cover postage and handling.

     Thank you.

Complimentary
close, followed
by a comma

Yours truly(,)

Roger Herzog

Signature (to be
handwritten)

Roger Herzog
Treasurer
Wig and Whiskers

Typed name (and position or
office, if there is such)

Today, more and more business letters appear in block style, set "flush left":

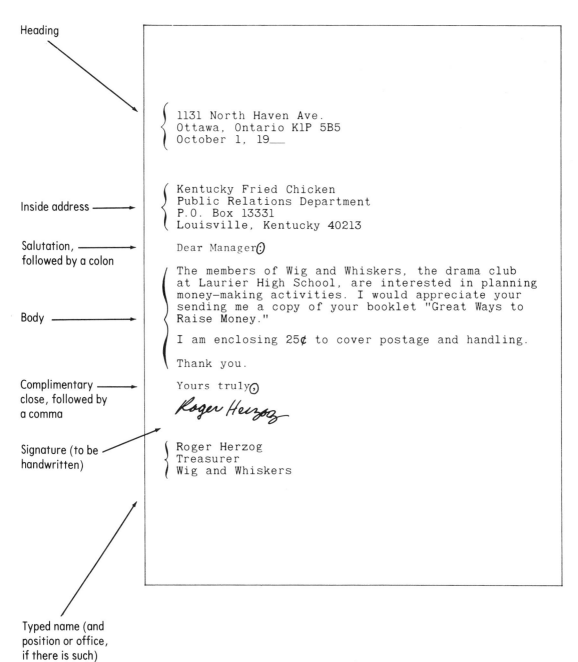

Heading

1131 North Haven Ave.
Ottawa, Ontario K1P 5B5
October 1, 19___

Inside address

Kentucky Fried Chicken
Public Relations Department
P.O. Box 13331
Louisville, Kentucky 40213

Salutation, followed by a colon

Dear Manager:

Body

The members of Wig and Whiskers, the drama club
at Laurier High School, are interested in planning
money-making activities. I would appreciate your
sending me a copy of your booklet "Great Ways to
Raise Money."

I am enclosing 25¢ to cover postage and handling.

Thank you.

Complimentary close, followed by a comma

Yours truly,

Roger Herzog

Signature (to be handwritten)

Roger Herzog
Treasurer
Wig and Whiskers

Typed name (and position or office, if there is such)

To summarize business letter form:

1. The *heading* contains:
    a. sender's address
    b. sender's city, province, and postal code
    c. date of letter.
2. The *inside address* contains:
    a. name of the person written to and his/her title (if known)
    b. company name (and department if known)
    c. address
    d. city, province, and postal code
3. The *salutation* used in greeting:
    a. an individual (formal): *Dear Sir*: or *Dear Madam*:
    b. an individual (less formal): *Dear Mr. Smith: Dear Miss Jones: Dear Ms. Hill*: (marital status not known to sender)
    c. an individual (very formal): *Sir*: or *Madam*:
    d. a firm (most common): *Gentlemen*:
    (Note that the salutation is followed by a colon.)
4. The *body* contains the message the writer wants to convey.
5. The *complimentary close*:
    a. formal (most common): *Yours truly, Yours very truly, Sincerely yours, Yours sincerely*, or just *Sincerely*,
    b. very formal: *Respectfully yours*,
    (Note that only the first word of the close is capitalized and that the close is followed by a comma.)
6. The writer's *signature* is placed directly below the complimentary close. If the letter is typewritten, the writer's name is typed directly below his/her signature.

Sending Your Letter

Practice 9. Writing

Now you are ready to send your letter(s). Prepare your envelope(s) for mailing. On page 381, Figure 10 shows the sample business envelope form. The standard *long* form is recommended for business letters.

Having addressed the envelope, fold your letter to fit into it. Fold the bottom of the sheet up approximately a third; fold the top of the sheet down slightly less than a third. Enclose your letter, seal the envelope, apply the stamp, and send your business letter on its way.

Fig. 10

```
Roger Herzog
1131 N. Haven Ave.
Ottawa, Ontario K1P 5B5




                    Kentucky Fried Chicken
                    Public Relations Department
                    P.O. Box 13331
                    Louisville, KY   40213
```

24

forestudy

The Unsung Heroine

The date: July 12, 1898

The place: Dyea, a small town a few kilometres from the Chilkoot pass from Skagway, Alaska en route to the Klondike and Dawson City, Yukon Territory.

The occasion: A young, dauntless woman named Martha Louise Black, was about to attempt a difficult challenge. She was to walk the dreaded, treacherous 68 km trail over the Chilkoot Pass to Lake Bennett. This deathtrap had taken several lives. The burden of the journey was further magnified by the transportation of thousands of kilograms of luggage and supplies. The outcome: Martha Black made it! To all her contemporaries Martha Louise Black became a symbol of female independence and determination, a woman whose daring, fearless spirit will certainly be remembered along with her varied talents and enriching career.

Autobiography

Who is better qualified to tell about a happening than the person who actually experienced it? Who knows more about the Chilkoot Pass—Dawson City journey than Martha Black herself?

Martha Louise Black wrote the book *My Seventy Years* in 1935, when she was seventy. On her ninetieth birthday she planned to reissue her book under the title *My Ninety Years*. She did not manage it before her death at 91 in 1957. Responsibility for this task was undertaken by her friend Flo Whyard, a newspaper correspondent. After much research and work with the original book along with Mrs. Black's unfinished manuscripts, Flo Whyard reissued the book

under the title *My Ninety Years,* as Martha Black would have wished.
Books like Martha Black's—that is, books in which the author tells about his/her life and experiences—are autobiographies.
This selection comes from Martha Black's autobiography.

The Trail of '98

Martha Black

We left Dyea on July 12 at noon, to walk the dreaded trail of 68 km over the Chilkoot Pass to Lake Bennett, first to Sheep Camp at the foot of the Pass, then to the summit, down to Lake Lindeman, round the shores of that beautiful lake, past the rapids and finally to the little village of Bennet.

With staff in hand, at last I had taken my place in that continuous line of pushing humans and straining animals. Before me, behind me, abreast of me almost every man toted a pack of 25 kg to 35 kg, in addition to driving dogs and horses harnessed to sleighs and carts, herding pack ponies and the odd cow, while one woman drove an ox-cart.

We were lucky enough to be travelling light. We had let out a contract to a company of packers for the transportation of our clothing, bedding, and "grub," which weighed several tonnes. After much haggling we had secured a "reduced" price of $900 spot cash—this, in the words of the packers, "a damn low figger." After I got over the Pass I agreed; it was a superhuman effort to transport those thousands of kilograms up that narrow, slippery, rocky trail of the Pass, through boulder-strewn canyons, across swampy bottomlands. It meant changing every box and bundle from steamer to wagon, to horse, to man, to sled, and finally to horse, before they were landed on the shores of Lake Bennett, where we were to wait for the building of our boat, which was to take us downriver to Dawson.

A quarter of a kilometre from Dyea we crossed a toll bridge, and after the attendant had collected our toll of $1 each, he abused us because we would not buy a $5 steering paddle to use on the lakes and rivers on the other side of the Pass. Fancy paying this price for it and carrying it over the trail too!

For eight kilometres or nine kilometres we followed a good wagon road, through cool, shady woods. We forded several clear mountain streams by stepping from stone to stone, and now and then I was carried across pick-a-back. (I weighed only 48 kg those days.) The trail became rockier, and we scrambled over piles of enormous stones and boulders, through six kilometres of a valley, with hardly a tuft of vegetation. It might have been the playground of the gods, so wild it seemed! My bulky clothes made the walking hard.

From MY NINETY YEARS by Martha Louise Black. Copyright 1976, Alaska Northwest Publishing Company, Box 4-EEE, Anchorage AK 99509.

383

My pity went out to the beasts of burden carrying their heavy loads. At three o'clock we stopped a half-hour for refreshments at a wayside cabin, kept by a widow and her little son. She brewed us a cup of strong tea, and as we ate substantial ham sandwiches, told us gruelling stories of the rush of the year before.

Refreshed and undaunted we continued, soon reaching the little settlement of Canyon City. Here we struck the mountain trail which led to Sheep Camp, at the foot of the Pass, where we planned to spend the night. As we travelled we began to realize that we were indeed on a trail of heartbreaks and dead hopes. On every side were mute° evidences—scores of dead horses that had slipped and fallen down the mountainside (so few got over the Pass), and caches of miners' outfits. We looked into a deserted shanty, where lay a mildewed ruined outfit. "Home of two brothers who died from exposure last winter," they told us.

And was I glad to call it a day when we arrived at Sheep Camp, the small shack and tent village of one street huddled between precipitous mountains. There seemed nothing permanent about it save the isolated glacier that glittered and sparkled in the sun above our heads. Before us was a huge pile of snow, ice, and rocks, the debris of the snowslide which had happened at Easter, and had crushed to death 30 such adventurers as we. We were greeted with the news that several more bodies had been discovered that day. They were buried under a large cairn of stones which was pointed out to every newcomer. As I looked at it I could not help but feel that such a sudden end—to be snuffed out without a chance to make one's peace with one's Maker, and in a mad search for

gold—was surely an ignominious death.

I looked up the Pass. I can see it yet—that upward trail, outlined on an almost perpendicular wall of ice-covered rock, alive with clinging human beings and animals, slowly mounting, single file, to the summit.

We stopped at the Grand Pacific Hotel. In writing home a description of this to Father and Mother, I said, "Look at your woodshed. Fit it up with 'standees' and you have the Grand Pacific." But I had no such uppish attitude when, weary and footsore, I staggered in, and when I left, my heart was warm with gratitude to the elderly couple who kept it. In addition to the regular supper bill of fare I had half a canned peach. I was given the only "private room" in the house—a cubicle partitioned off by a wooden wall, two-thirds the height of the room, with a built-in bunk filled with hay and covered with two pairs of grey army blankets—and comfort of comforts!—a real feather pillow!

After a wonderful night's sleep, a hearty breakfast of corn meal mush, bacon and cold-storage eggs, condensed milk, prunes, and a whole orange—the last in the camp—and settling our hotel bill (meals and bunk $1 apiece), with high hearts that glorious July morning we started to climb that 900 m of steep, narrow, icy mountain trail. The Indians said there was a curse on all who attempted it in summer, as the hot sun melted the winter snow, and it came crashing down—crushing everything before it. These avalanches had already taken toll of nearly 100 lives.

For the first hour we walked over the trail of the recent slide. In the melting snow I saw a bit of blue ribbon. Bending down, I tugged at it and pulled out a baby's bootee. Did it belong to some venturesome soul who had come to seek a fortune for wife and baby? Would those who were waiting for him wait in vain? Was this one of the hundreds of tragedies of this mad stampede?

I did not dare look around at the magnificent mountain scenery nor drink in the beauty of the tumbling torrents, for every minute the melting snow was making it more slippery under foot. The greatest of care was needed in crossing the dangerously thin ice that was often the only bridge over a mountain stream, which had paused a few moments on a narrow ledge, to drop over a precipice, hundreds of metres below.

As the day advanced the trail became steeper, the air warmer, and footholds without support impossible. I shed my sealskin jacket. I cursed my hot, high, buckram collar, my tight heavily boned corsets, my long corduroy skirt, my full bloomers which I had to hitch up with every step. We clung to stunted pines, spruce roots, jutting rocks. In some places the path was so narrow that, to move at all, we had to use our feet tandem fashion[1]. Above, only the granite walls. Below, death leering at us.

But soon, too soon, I was straining every nerve, every gram of physical endurance in that ever upward climb. There were moments when, with sweating forehead, pounding heart, and panting breath, I felt I could go no farther. At such times we dropped out of line and rested in the little snow dug-outs along the way. But such a few moments of rest! Then on with that cursing procession of men and dogs and horses, pulling sleds or toting packs.

Mush on[2]... Mush on... It beat into my brain... Cracking of whips... Wild screams of too heavily loaded pack horses which lost their footing and were dashed to the rocks below... stumbling... staggering... crawling... God pity me!

Mush on... Mush on... Another breath! Another step ... God give me strength. How far away that summit! Can I ever make it?

Mush on... Mush on... or die!

"Cheer up, cheer up, Polly!" I hear George[3] break the long silence. "Only thirty metres to go now." Thirty metres! That sheer wall of rock! Can I make it? In some inexplicable way the men of our party get round me. They push and pull me. They turn and twist me, until my very joints creak with the pain of it. "Don't look down," they warn. I have no strength to turn my head, to speak. Only three metres more! Oh, God, what a relief!

Then my foot slips! I lose my balance. I fall only a metre into a crevice in the rocks. The sharp edge of one cuts through my boot and I feel the flesh of my leg throbbing with pain. I can bear it no longer, and I sit down and do what every woman does in time of stress. I weep. "Can I help you?" "Can I help you?" asks every man who passes me. George tries to comfort me but in vain. He becomes impatient. "For God's sake, Polly, buck up and be a man! Have some style and move on!"

Was I mad? Not even allowed the comfort of tears! I bucked up all right and walked triumphantly into that broker's tent—an ancient canvas structure on the summit. I had made the top of the world, but "the wind that blew between the spheres" cut me like a knife. I was tired, faint, hungry, cold. I asked for a fire, and was answered, "Madame, wood is two bits a

---

1. *tandem fashion:* one directly behind the other

2. *Mush on:* a corruption of the French word *marchons*

3. *George:* Martha's brother, George Munzer

385

pound[4] up here." George, who was really concerned about me, spoke up: "All right. All right. I'll be a sport. Give her a $5 fire." One heavenly hour of rest. I took off my boots, washed my wounded skin and poured iodine on it. I dried my wet stockings, had a cup of tea, and got thoroughly warm.

We then went through customs, as we had now entered Canada. Around us, shivering in the cold wind, were many waiting people, their outfits partially unpacked and scattered about them in the deep snow. It was here that I met for the first time members of the North West Mounted Police, and I thought that finer, sturdier, more intelligent-looking men would be hard to find.

Then the descent! Down, ever downward. Weight of body on shaky legs, weight growing heavier, and legs shakier. Sharp rocks to scratch our clutching hands. Snake-like roots to trip our stumbling feet.

We stopped at the half-way cabin for a $2 supper of bean soup, ham and eggs (of uncertain age), prunes, bread, and butter—the bread served with the apology of the proprietor, "The middle of it ain't done, but you don't have to eat it. I hurried too much."

I had felt that I could make no greater

4. *a pound:* 0.454 kg

effort in my life than the last part of the upward climb, but the last three kilometres into Lindeman was the most excruciating° struggle of the whole trip. In my memory it will remain a hideous nightmare. The trail led through a scrub pine forest where we tripped over bare roots of trees that curled over and around rocks and boulders like great devilfishes. Rocks! Rocks! Rocks! Tearing boots to pieces. Hands bleeding with scratches. I can bear it no longer. In my agony I beg the men to leave me—to let me lie in my tracks, and stay for the night.

My brother put his arm around me and carried me most of the last kilometre. Captain Spencer hurried into the village, to the Tacoma Hotel, to get a bed for me. It wasn't much of a bed either—a canvas stretched on four logs, with a straw shakedown, yet the downiest couch in the world or the softest bed in a king's palace could not have made a better resting-place for me.

As my senses slipped away into the unconsciousness of that deep sleep of exhaustion, there surged through me a thrill of satisfaction. I had actually walked over the Chilkoot Pass!...I would never do it again, knowing now what it meant...Not for all the gold in the Klondike...And yet, knowing now what it meant, would I miss it?... No, never!...Not even for all the gold in the world!

follow-up

Discussing "The Trail of '98"

1. Martha Black discusses several difficulties she encountered on the journey. Discuss these difficulties and some of her ways of coping.
2. Martha Black seems to possess a personality of contrasts made evident by some of her actions and statements. Discuss these two contrasting sides of her personality by giving examples from the story.
3. Not only was Martha Black an adventurer, but she was also a good writer. Her writing style captures the feeling of the drama she was experiencing. By giving examples discuss the effect on the reader.
4. Re-read the last sentence of the selection. It was unusual for a woman in 1898 to leave all the comforts of a prosperous life, for one of dangerous adventure in a barren, cold land. After reading the selection, what do *you* feel motivated this woman to attempt the journey?

Kinds of Literature

FICTION/NONFICTION

Narratives about imaginary characters and events are called *fiction.* In this book, "Night Drive" and "Raymond's Run" are good examples of fiction.

"The Trail of '98" on the other hand, concerns real people and events. It is an example of *nonfiction.*

BIOGRAPHY/AUTOBIOGRAPHY

It's easy to understand the meaning of *biography,* a special kind of nonfiction, if you know what the three parts of the word mean:

bio-	means "life"
-graph	means "write"
-y	is a suffix that makes a word a noun

A biography, then, is a writing about life—specifically about a person's life. Biographies have been written about many famous persons—John A. Macdonald, William Lyon Mackenzie King, Emily Carr, Laura Secord, Albert Einstein, Louis Riel, for instance—by authors who knew them or who knew a great deal about them.

As was pointed out on page 382, "The Trail of '98" is an *autobiography*. If you know that *auto-* means "self," what does *autobiography* mean?

Practice 1. Discussion
1. How does an autobiography differ from a biography?
2. What other words do you know that have *bio-* as one of the parts? that have *-graph* as one of the parts? that have *auto-* as one of the parts? For each of those word parts, name at least three words in which it appears.

Style

From class talk about question 3 under "Discussing The Trail of '98" (page 387), you mentioned several ways in which the writer brings out the drama of the incident. In other sections of the chapter, Black uses simple, narrative style to tell what happened. For example, in describing the journey itself, she wrote merely:

> "At three o'clock we stopped a half-hour for refreshments at a wayside cabin, kept by a widow and her little son. She brewed us a cup of strong tea and as we ate substantial ham sandwiches, told us gruelling stories of the rush of the year before."

Here, Black's style—that is, her manner of writing—is concise and matter-of-fact.

In the preceding part of her adventure, Black shares the tense drama with us:

1. She describes her difficulties and pain.
2. She makes us aware of sounds and sights around her.
3. She makes us aware of what she was thinking and feeling at various points in the journey.
4. She uses short, quick, exclamatory staccato phrases that make us feel the same emotions as she felt.

Here, Black's *style* can be said to be colorful and vivid.

Practice 2. Writing

When the fire alarm went off, everyone in the theatre got up and went out into the rain.

Here is a sentence written in a concise, matter-of-fact style. Read the sentence again. Picture the event in your mind. *Exactly* what happened: *How* did the theatre-goers go out into the rain? *How* did they feel? Rewrite that sentence—you may, in fact, want to write more than one—and describe the event as vividly as you can. Give details that will help your reader (or listener) see what you see in your imagination. Try to make your reader (or listener) feel as you would feel. Be prepared to read your sentence(s) aloud; invite your listeners to comment on the vividness of your description.

Practice 3. Writing

One advantage in writing autobiography is that the author can tell exactly what it felt like to live through an experience.

Has anything ever happened to you that made you terribly angry? or sad? or jump up and down for joy? Has anything ever made you laugh so hard your sides ached?

Write a short paragraph—or two—describing your experience. Try to make your reader or listener feel exactly as you did.

Be prepared to read your paragraph(s) aloud.

Bookshelf

Angel of Hudson Bay: The True Story of Maud Watt, by William Ashley Anderson. Clarke Irwin, 1961. The biography of a Hudson Bay Company factor's wife, who devoted much of her life to the welfare of Native people on Hudson's Bay.

Joanne, by Marian Engel. Paperjacks, 1975. The story, told in diary form, is about a woman who, after eighteen years, decides to leave her husband and two children. She joins the working world and quickly adjusts to her new single life.

Klondike Kate: The Life and Legend of Kitty Rockwell, the Queen of the Yukon, by Ellis Lucia. Hastings House, 1962.

Wilderness Women, by James Polk. Canadian Portraits, 1972. Stories of women in Canada's history.

Top. Fish on the flakes, Norman Cove, Newfoundland.

Bottom. Verdisris Coulee, Alberta.

Opposite, top. Algonquin Provincial Park, Ontario.

Opposite, bottom left. Terra Nova National Park, Newfoundland.

Opposite, bottom right. Milbert's Tortoise Shell butterfly.

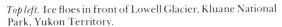

Top left. Ice floes in front of Lowell Glacier, Kluane National Park, Yukon Territory.

Bottom left. Signal Hill and the entrance to St. John's harbor, Newfoundland.

Bottom right. Moraine Lake, Banff National Park, Alberta.

Opposite, top left. Lake Baskatong, Québec.

Opposite, top right. The Badlands, Drumheller, Alberta.

Opposite, bottom left. Coon Lake, in the Kawartha Lakes area of Ontario.

Opposite, bottom right. Looking north from Okanagan Beach, British Columbia.

25

forestudy

Eyewitness Reporting

The POINT OF VIEW a writer takes depends partly on his/her purpose. The writer can assume a God-like position and tell a story from the *omniscient* point of view. (See page 212) Or the writer can assume that he/she is one of the characters and so tell the story from a first-person *participant* point of view.

But there's also a third point of view that a writer—or any narrator, for that matter—can take. You yourself have no doubt taken this point of view many times. It's the point of view of a person who is on the scene, relating what he/she experiences but not participating directly in the action. The reporter uses the first person (*I, me*), but he/she only stands on the sidelines and relates what he/she sees going on.

Practice 1. Discussion
Which of the following persons would probably relate a story from the bystander's/reporter's point of view? Why?

1. A person watching firefighters battling a blaze.
2. The fire chief, who is directing the operation.
3. A TV newscaster at a sports event.
4. A pedestrian who witnessed an automobile accident.
5. The author of "Night Drive," "The Collecting Team," "All the Years of Her Life," or "The Immortals."
6. You, who are talking with your guidance counselor or the principal of your school.
7. You, as you tell about the funny thing that happened to two classmates in the chemistry lab.

Telling about something a bystander/reporter experiences is one thing. But commenting about it—that is, saying whether the experience was good or bad or telling others what it means—is quite another. The bystander/reporter no longer is strictly a reporter. Instead, he/she becomes a commentator.

The following report by Warren Gerard and commentary by June Callwood appeared in *Maclean's,* September 15, 1980. Terry Fox, who had lost a leg to cancer, had decided early in 1980 to run across Canada in aid of the Canadian Cancer Society. In the first week of September, he was forced to stop running.

In what way does June Callwood's commentary differ from Warren Gerard's report?

The Agony and The Ecstasy of Terry Fox

Warren Gerard

He wasn't suddenly smitten, but early last week Terry Fox knew something was terribly wrong. The hopping, running 22-year-old amputee was well over the halfway mark in his coast-to-coast odyssey to show Canada he could *do* it—and to raise funds for cancer research. From April 12, when he dipped his artificial limb into the Atlantic Ocean at St. John's and began his run, until last week and 5 342 km later, Terry Fox had become a national symbol of courage, and some close to him said even stubbornness. But it wasn't to end as Terry Fox thought, and as every Canadian hoped, reminded daily as they were by the catchy jingle on radio and television, *Run Terry, Run.* Rather, it ended on the Thunder Bay bypass headed for the

Red River Road in Northern Ontario. For two days, maybe three, he hadn't felt right—but he wasn't about to quit. Then, at the 29 km point on Tuesday's run, he recalled, "There was hardness of breath. I was coughing, I started to choke. I didn't know what was going on." In severe pain, he still wouldn't quit. People were lining the road ahead and he wanted to run out of people before he quit. "There was no way I was going to stop running, not with all those people there." So he ran another kilometre and then there were no more people. And for Terry, no more road.

He was taken to Port Arthur General Hospital. Canadian Cancer Society officials had been talking about a sore ankle and then about taking x-rays of his lungs. The first set showed that his left lung had partly collapsed. "They said it could have been caused by an infection, but I could tell right away. I asked them if it could be cancer—these guys have seen this before—and they said it could be a tumor."

His parents, Rolly and Betty Fox, flew from their home in Port Coquitlam, B.C., to be with Terry. The cancer that had caused him to have his leg amputated had returned, this time to his lungs. That afternoon, his silent father on one side of a stretcher bed, his mother, unable to hold back the emotion, on the other, Terry held a press conference: "Do you want to ask questions or should I just say what I want?" He went ahead. "I didn't think this would happen, it was an unbelievable shock. I mean, I've been doing great, doing those 26 miles[1] every day, up those hills, I had less than 2,000 to go. I thought I was lucky as I could get. Well, you know I had primary cancer in my knee 3½ years ago, and now the cancer is in my lungs, and I really have to go home and have some more x-rays, and maybe an operation that will involve opening up my chest, or more drugs. I'll do everything I can. I'm gonna do my very best, I'll fight, I promise I won't give up."

Later, Rolly Fox was heard to say: "I think it's unfair. Very unfair." He said it for the nation. In homes, offices and factories, in the newspapers, on radio and television, there was an outpouring of emotion across the country: it just wasn't fair. "I don't feel that this is unfair," Terry said. "That's the thing about cancer. I'm not the only one, it happens all the time, to other people. I'm not special. This just intensifies what I did, it gives it more meaning, it'll inspire more people."

Terry and his parents flew to Vancouver on a small chartered jet. It landed and taxied to an isolated terminal where a stretcher and an ambulance were waiting. He had ordered a change in the arrival location to avoid reporters and Cancer Society officials. Later he relented and, at a press conference at the Royal Columbian Hospital in New Westminster, he spoke once more, fighting a persistent and obviously painful cough. Wearing his MARATHON OF HOPE T-shirt, he said: "I did my very best." And in his determined way he said he wanted to return to complete his journey.

During the run, Cancer Society officials found out just how stubborn and determined Terry was. Even though they made repeated requests that he have regular medical checkups, he refused: "There's no doctor in the world who has had an amputee who's doing anything on an artificial leg like I am. If I went to see a doctor, he'd have a pessimistic approach to me."

It was as if he were inspired, and nothing, no one, would change his heart. When he first thought of the idea three years ago even his mother, Betty, despite knowing intimately her son's stubborn gutsiness, told him he was "crazy." He went to see Blair MacKenzie, executive-director of the B. C. and Yukon division of the Cancer Society, who said that when he first saw the young, curly-headed youth limp into his office on a metal-and-plastic leg he was skeptical. "We get a lot of requests that are a little off-centre, so I said, fine, organize it yourself, and he did. I was really taken with him."

Terry organized a dance and approached Vancouver businessmen for support. "I'm not a dreamer," he said in his appeals for aid, "and I'm not saying that this will initiate any kind of definitive answer or cure to cancer, but I believe in

396 1. *26 miles:* 42 km; 1 mile = 1.609 km

miracles. I have to." At the same time, Terry, a B-average student at Simon Fraser University, had been training. At first he hobbled through the streets of Port Coquitlam, for almost a kilometre, then he increased the distance by the same amount each week—up to 42 km a day. He won over some skeptics, but the group that saw him off to St. John's last April was small —his family, an airline representative, Blair MacKenzie and his two children, and two other Cancer Society officials. "No one could possibly have seen the magnitude of this," MacKenzie says now. "This is the most significant thing in the 42-year history of the Cancer Society."

As Terry, in his odd hop-and-run style, moved westward, the country became more aware of what he was doing. On May 18, he was in Sherbrooke, N.S., saying the trip so far was a "piece of cake." On June 4, he was in Fredericton, N.B., losing weight and having problems with his artificial leg. But now the money was coming in—$100,000 and the $1-million mark looked good. On June 21 he was in Quebec: "At a press conference nobody knew what we were talking about."

On a couple of occasions he was nearly run off the road by transport trucks, and police barred him from the Trans-Canada Highway as a traffic hazard. He was pelted by hail-stones as big as golfballs and the leg continued to fall off, and to hurt. On his way he met Governor-General Ed Schreyer and Prime Minister Pierre Trudeau, who said he didn't have time to run with Terry. He met his hockey heroes, Darryl Sittler and Bobby Orr. Sittler later said he would carry on the run if that's what Terry wanted. In Toronto, the crowds were overwhelming—10 000 at city hall—and cops were seen to cry.

There were reports of his bad temper along the route, that he felt exploited by the Cancer Society—and others who wanted to make a buck for Terry and themselves—but he refused for himself, and he defended the Cancer Society. At the point where he stopped in Northern Ontario, out of sight of the crowds, proud, still determined, Terry Fox had done something that no individual had ever done before—he had raised almost

$2 million for cancer research.

At week's end he was still in hospital, in good spirits. Meanwhile, the country is in a flurry of fund-raising for cancer research. Contributions are coming from everywhere. Governments, cities, small communities are making pledges. The CTV network said it would open up four hours of prime-time Sunday-night television for a tribute to Terry Fox. Pledges will be taken. One radio station, CKFM, in Toronto has raised more than $236,000. The country is in a frenzy of giving—not so much, perhaps, for cancer research, but for Terry Fox.

Meanwhile, he is undergoing chemotherapy. The prognosis varies. Dr. Raymond Bush, director of the Ontario Cancer Foundation, says that during the last few years the success rate for treatment of Terry's type of cancer has improved from 20 per cent to anywhere between 60 and 70 per cent. Yet other medical experts from Vancouver say that Terry's cancer is one of the most dangerous, spreading frequently to other parts of the body, especially the lungs. One cancer expert said bone cancer hits young people between ages 10 and 30 especially hard, and that there is only a 10-per-cent survival rate over a five-year period.

Terry bravely promises to return, to finish the run he started, next year, the year after—maybe. But he accomplished what he set out to do. It was summed up by Sheila Fox (no kin to Terry) of Kitchener, Ont., a Cancer Society representative, who said: "You know, they say the United States is built on a history of heroes while Canada has none to look up to. But when I looked down the street today and saw Terry, I said, 'There's a hero.'"

"He is More Than You Can See"

June Callwood

Terry Fox is home in British Columbia now to face an uncertain future, leaving the rest of us to face our uncertain selves.

The mystery of why Terry Fox put himself into the vault of so much pain is unknowable. Terry Fox, a teen-ager endowed with fond parents, superb reflexes, handsomeness, newly crowned as his high school's athlete of the year, has a sore leg one day and three days later is mutilated, his leg cut off just above the knee. His high hopes for what Terry Fox was, a marvellous athlete, and what Terry Fox would become, something associated with sports, stopped cold. The Terry Fox he was played basketball from a wheelchair; the Terry Fox he would become wasn't clear.

How does one handle such a savage blow to self-image? One way is to deny that anything has changed. One leg is not less than two; it is more. He'll prove it. He'll run across the country in jogging shorts flaunting that declaration. He will persevere in being Terry Fox, an undiminished, unquenchable Terry Fox.

The other aspects of what was called the Marathon of Hope are real. The goal of raising money for cancer research already has realized more donations than any single effort in the Canadian Cancer Society's history. Also, Terry Fox achieved massive attitudinal change toward amputation. Also, he showed that cancer, however brutally it treats the cringing flesh, can't defeat the spirit.

The central truth, however, is that a youth wanted back the cards he had been dealing with in the beginning—all those winning cards. He wanted to feel two-legged again, an obsession that took him 5 000 km and then beyond the edge of endurance.

Fixed in our memory in this uneasy summer has been the sight of the one-legged youth, his face drained, hopping kilometre after kilometre on that punishing pavement. His quest grips us, his search for wholeness is a spiritual longing deep in us all. He asserts that he is unique. He has wonders locked within. He is more than you can see. He is not a wounded boy on an overcrowded planet. He *matters*.

People wept to see him run. They wept for his pain; they wept for his foolish pride. They wept with pity. And they wept most of all for envy to be like Terry Fox, whole-hearted and unashamed. They longed to care that much, about anything. And to go for it. All out.

---

follow-up

Discussing "The Agony and the Ecstasy of Terry Fox"

1. It takes a highly motivated individual to attempt the feat Terry Fox set out to do. He reached this decision totally on his own. What, then, do you feel motivated the 22-year-old university student?
2. Terry was successful not only in collecting money for the Cancer Research fund, but also for other reasons. Where else does Terry's success lie?
3. After reading the commentary, describe what you feel is the writer's attitude towards Terry Fox. Discuss by citing examples from the selection.
4. "But when I looked down the street today and saw Terry, I said, 'There's a hero.'"
   What characteristics do you feel a hero should possess?
   Do you agree with the above statement in relation to Terry Fox? Explain why or why not.

The Art of Writing Feature Articles

The feature article is a type of composition in which the human side of news or events is presented. The writer, by being creative and colorful, entertains and conjures up emotion in the reader.

The style is similar to the composition (p. 234) with the topic sentence (lead), body (containing several paragraphs) and conclusion.

Discuss the importance of an eye-catching title and particularly the appropriateness of the title "The Agony and the Ecstasy of Terry Fox."

Practice 1.

How does the opening sentence arouse your interest and acquaint you with the article? What effect does the lead have on you?

After reading the feature article, write your own opening sentence keeping in mind that it must make the reader *want* to read on.

Practice 2.

The body of the feature article should develop the topic sentence by adding information to the main idea. What do you feel the main idea is?

Examine the five paragraphs following the opening paragraph. Write one summary sentence for each of these paragraphs to show how each one relates to the topic of the opening sentence—Terry's dilemma.

Practice 3.

The conclusion ties up loose ends and reflects back to the opening sentence.

Examine the last paragraph. Do you feel it summarizes the essence of the article? Explain.

Practice 4. Writing the Human Interest Story

The human interest story appeals to the reader by presenting the successes or predicaments of an individual.

Think about someone who interests you. It could be someone in sports, politics, literature, or everyday life. Following the outline for feature writing, develop this into an article suitable for a magazine or newspaper feature section.

Remember to establish the mood in the opening sentence, to keep the body focused on an aspect of the person and to consider emotional appeal. You can vary your style by using questions, exclamations, and dialogue. Keep your conclusion brief, but summarize the main idea of your story.

Bookshelf

Bethune by Roderick Stewart. Paperjacks, 1973. A most intriguing biography of a colorful Canadian, Norman Bethune.

Canada's Sporting Heroes, by S. F. Wise and Douglas Fisher. General Publishing, 1974. The history of sports in Canada and the stories of Canada's sport heroes.

Nails, by R. Lance Hill. Totem Books, 1974. A thriller full of action and suspense. Joe Black's goal is total freedom, and his pursuit of it takes him into the Vancouver underworld.

Turn Him Loose by Cliff Faulknor. Western Producer Prairie Books, 1977. *The* Canadian rodeo biography of Herman Linder.

26

Virtuoso

forestudy

Trade Jargon

"Run at 30 m until 1350. Then come back to periscope depth."

"Aye, aye, sir."

"Skipper, screws bearing 0–3–9 and closing."

"OK, sonar . . . All hands: Rig for silent running. Course—right 15 degrees rudder. Shift bow and stern planes to hand power."

Maybe you're not too sure of what all that dialogue means. But if you were a submariner in the navy, you'd understand every term clearly. Expressions like "periscope depth," "aye, aye, sir," and "screws bearing 0–3–9 and closing" are peculiar to the work done by submariners. Such expressions are good examples of TRADE JARGON.

TRADE JARGON consists of language—words and expressions—developed by the people within an occupational group to describe objects and situations common primarily to them. Doctors, lawyers, musicians, teachers, carpenters, plumbers—even circus clowns—develop and use expressions that every person in the same trade or profession uses and understands.

Practice 1. Discussion

C. W. McCall's song *Convoy* has launched a sudden interest in citizen's band radios. The special terms used by C.B.'ers constitute a good example of trade jargon. How many of the following C.B. jargon terms can you explain?

1. side door
2. modulate
3. rocking chair
4. back door
5. blinkin' winkin'
6. bouncing cardboard
7. put the hammer down
8. home 20
9. 10–20
10. 50-dollar lane
11. skating rink
12. thermos bottle

Practice 2. Writing

Select a profession or trade group that interests you. List at least ten words and expressions that are part of the trade jargon of that occupational group. Then briefly explain what each expression means—so that persons outside the group can understand, too.

Be prepared to share your trade jargon terms and their explanations with your classmates.

"Virtuoso," the story that begins below, contains a good deal of trade jargon—trade jargon that musicians use. In fact, the title itself is an example!

Virtuoso

Herbert Goldstone

"Sir?"

The Maestro[1] continued to play, not looking up from the keys.

"Sir, I was wondering if you would explain this apparatus to me."

The Maestro stopped playing, his thin body stiffly relaxed on the bench. His long supple° fingers floated off the keyboard.

1. *Maestro* (mīs′ trō): 1. a musical composer, teacher, or conductor. 2. a master of any art

© 1953 by Mercury Press, Inc. Reprinted from THE MAGAZINE OF FANTASY AND SCIENCE FICTION by permission of the author.

"Apparatus?" He turned and smiled at the robot. "Do you mean the piano, Rollo?"

"This machine that produces varying sounds. I would like some information about it, its operation and purpose. It is not included in my reference data."

The Maestro lit a cigarette. He preferred to do it himself. One of his first orders to Rollo when the robot was delivered two days before had been to disregard his built-in instructions on the subject.

403

"I'd hardly call a piano a machine, Rollo," he smiled, "although technically you are correct. It is actually, I suppose, a machine designed to produce sounds of graduated pitch and tone, singly or in groups."

"I assimilated that much by observation," Rollo replied in a brassy baritone which no longer sent tiny tremors up the Maestro's spine. "Wires of different thickness and tautness struck by felt-covered hammers activated by manually operated levers arranged in a horizontal panel."

"A very cold-blooded description of one of man's nobler works," the Maestro remarked dryly. "You make Mozart and Chopin[2] mere laboratory technicians."

"Mozart? Chopin?" The duralloy sphere that was Rollo's head shone stark and featureless, its immediate surface unbroken but for twin vision lenses. "The terms are not included in my memory banks."

"No, not yours, Rollo," the Maestro said softly. "Mozart and Chopin are not for vacuum tubes and fuses and copper wire. They are for flesh and blood and human tears."

"I do not understand," Rollo droned.

"Well," the Maestro said, smoke curling lazily from his nostrils, "they are two of the humans who compose, or design successions of notes—varying sounds, that is, produced by the piano or by other instruments, machines that produce other types of sounds of fixed pitch and tone.

"Sometimes these instruments, as we call them, are played, or operated, indi-vidually; sometimes in groups—orchestras, as we refer to them—and the sounds blend together, they harmonize. That is, they have an orderly, mathematical relationship to each other which results in . . . "

The Maestro threw up his hands.

"I never imagined," he chuckled, "that I would some day struggle so mightily, and so futilely,° to explain music to a robot!"

"Music?"

"Yes, Rollo. The sounds produced by this machine and others of the same category are called music."

"What is the purpose of music, sir?"

"Purpose?"

The Maestro crushed the cigarette in an ash tray. He turned to the keyboard of the concert grand and flexed his fingers briefly.

"Listen, Rollo."

The wraithlike° fingers glided and wove the opening bars of "Clair de Lune,"[3] slender and delicate as spider silk. Rollo stood rigid, the fluorescent light over the music rack casting a bluish jewelled sheen over his towering bulk, shimmering in the amber vision lenses.

The Maestro drew his hands back from the keys and the subtle thread of melody melted reluctantly into silence.

"Claude Debussy," the Maestro said. "One of our mechanics of an era long past. He designed that succession of tones many years ago. What do you think of it?"

Rollo did not answer at once.

"The sounds were well formed," he replied finally. "They did not jar my

2. *Chopin* (shō′ păn): Frédéric. Polish-French pianist and composer (1810–1849)

3. *"Clair de Lune"* (klär′ də lōōn′) (moonlight): a piano composition by Claude Debussy

auditory senses[4] as some do." The Maestro laughed. "Rollo, you may not realize it, but you're a wonderful critic."

"This music then," Rollo droned. "Its purpose is to give pleasure to humans?"

"Exactly," the Maestro said. "Sounds well formed, that do not jar the auditory senses as some do. Marvellous! It should be carved in marble over the entrance of New Carnegie Hall."[5]

"I do not understand. Why should my definition—?"

The Maestro waved a hand. "No matter, Rollo. No matter."

"Sir?"

"Yes, Rollo?"

"Those sheets of paper you sometimes place before you on the piano. They are the plans of the composer indicating which sounds are to be produced by the piano and in what order?"

"Just so. We call each sound a note; combinations of notes we call chords."

"Each dot, then, indicates a sound to be made?"

"Perfectly correct, my man of metal."

Rollo stared straight ahead. The Maestro felt a peculiar sense of wheels turning within that impregnable° sphere.

"Sir, I have scanned my memory banks and find no specific or implied instructions against it. I should like to be taught how to produce these notes on the piano. I request that you feed the correlation between those dots and the levers of the panel into my memory banks."

The Maestro peered at him, amazed. A slow grin travelled across his face.

"Done!" he exclaimed. "It's been many years since pupils helped gray these ancient locks, but I have the feeling that you, Rollo, will prove a most fascinating student. To instill the Muse into metal and machinery . . . I accept the challenge gladly!"

He rose, touched the cool latent power of Rollo's arm.

"Sit down here, my Rolleindex Personal Robot, Model M-E. We shall start Beethoven[6] spinning in his grave—or make musical history."

More than an hour later the Maestro yawned and looked at his watch.

"It's late," he spoke into the end of the yawn. "These old eyes are not tireless like yours, my friend." He touched Rollo's shoulder. "You have the complete fundamentals of musical notation in your memory banks, Rollo. That's a good night's lesson, particularly when I recall how long it took me to acquire the same amount of information. Tomorrow we'll attempt to put those awesome fingers of yours to work."

He stretched. "I'm going to bed," he said. "Will you lock up and put out the lights?"

Rollo rose from the bench. "Yes, sir," he droned. "I have a request."

"What can I do for my star pupil?"

"May I attempt to create some sounds with the keyboard tonight? I will do so very softly so as not to disturb you."

"Tonight? Aren't you—?" Then the Maestro smiled. "You must pardon me, Rollo. It's still a bit difficult for me to realize that sleep has no meaning for you."

He hesitated, rubbing his chin. "Well, I

4. *did not jar my auditory senses:* didn't hurt my ears

5. *Carnegie Hall:* a famous concert hall in New York City

6. *Beethoven* (bā′ tō vən): Ludwig van. German composer (1770–1827)

405

suppose a good teacher should not discourage impatience to learn. All right, Rollo, but please be careful." He patted the polished mahogany. "This piano and I have been together for many years. I'd hate to see its teeth knocked out by those sledge-hammer digits of yours. Lightly, my friend, very lightly."

"Yes, sir."

The Maestro fell asleep with a faint smile on his lips, dimly aware of the shy, tentative notes that Rollo was coaxing forth.

Then gray fog closed in and he was in that half-world where reality is dreamlike and dreams are real. It was soft and feathery and lavender clouds and sounds were rolling and washing across his mind in flowing waves.

Where? The mist drew back a bit and he was in red velvet and deep and the music swelled and broke over him.

He smiled.

My recording. Thank you, thank you, thank—

The Maestro snapped erect, threw the covers aside.

He sat on the edge of the bed, listening.

He groped for his robe in the darkness, shoved bony feet into his slippers.

He crept, trembling uncontrollably, to the door of his studio and stood there, thin and brittle in the robe.

The light over the music rack was an eerie island in the brown shadows of the studio. Rollo sat at the keyboard, prim, inhuman, rigid, twin lenses focused somewhere off into the shadows.

The massive feet working the pedals, arms and hands flashing and glinting—they were living entities, separate, somehow, from the machined perfection of his body.

The music rack was empty.

A copy of Beethoven's "Appassionata" lay closed on the bench. It had been, the Maestro remembered, in a pile of sheet music on the piano.

Rollo was playing it.

He was creating it, breathing it, drawing it through silver flame.

Time became meaningless, suspended in midair.

The Maestro didn't realize he was weeping until Rollo finished the sonata.

The robot turned to look at the Maestro. "The sounds," he droned. "They pleased you?"

The Maestro's lips quivered. "Yes, Rollo," he replied at last. "They pleased me." He fought the lump in his throat.

He picked up the music in fingers that shook.

"This," he murmured. "Already?"

"It has been added to my store of data," Rollo replied. "I applied the principles you explained to me to these plans. It was not very difficult."

The Maestro swallowed as he tried to speak. "It was not very difficult . . . " he repeated softly.

The old man sank down slowly onto the bench next to Rollo, stared silently at the robot as though seeing him for the first time.

Rollo got to his feet.

The Maestro let his fingers rest on the keys, strangely foreign now.

"Music!" he breathed. "I may have heard it that way in my soul. I know Beethoven did!"

He looked up at the robot, a growing excitement in his face.

"Rollo," he said, his voice straining to remain calm. "You and I have some work to do tomorrow on your memory banks."

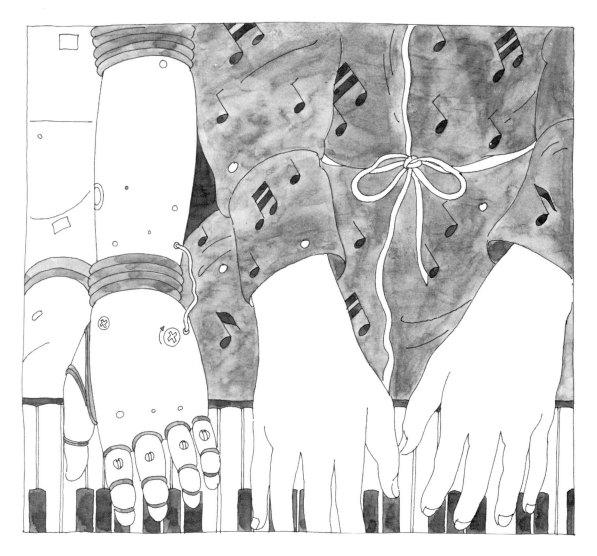

Sleep did not come again that night.

He strode briskly into the studio the next morning. Rollo was vacuuming the carpet. The Maestro preferred carpets to the new dust-free plastics, which felt somehow profane° to his feet.

The Maestro's house was, in fact, an oasis of anachronisms in a desert of contemporary antiseptic efficiency.[7]

"Well, are you ready for work, Rollo?" he asked. "We have a lot to do, you and I. I have such plans for you, Rollo—great plans!"

Rollo, for once, did not reply.

"I have asked them all to come here this afternoon," the Maestro went on. "Conductors, concert pianists, composers, my manager. All the giants of music, Rollo. Wait until they hear you play."

Rollo switched off the vacuum and stood quietly.

7. *an oasis . . . efficiency:* a nice but old-fashioned spot out of place in today's world

407

"You'll play for them right here this afternoon." The Maestro's voice was high-pitched, breathless. "The 'Appassionata' again, I think. Yes, that's it. I must see their faces!

"Then we'll arrange a recital to introduce you to the public and the critics and then a major concerto[8] with one of the big orchestras. We'll have it telecast around the world, Rollo. It can be arranged.

"Think of it, Rollo, just think of it! The greatest piano virtuoso of all time . . . a robot! It's completely fantastic and completely wonderful. I feel like an explorer at the edge of a new world."

He walked feverishly back and forth.

"Then recordings, of course. My entire repertoire,° Rollo, and more. So much more!"

"Sir?"

The Maestro's face shone as he looked up at him. "Yes, Rollo?"

"In my built-in instructions, I have the option of rejecting any action which I consider harmful to my owner," the

8. *concerto* (kən chĕr′ tō): a composition for a solo instrument and a full orchestra

robot's words were precise, carefully selected. "Last night you wept. That is one of the indications I am instructed to consider in making my decisions."

The Maestro gripped Rollo's thick, superbly molded arm.

"Rollo, you don't understand. That was for the moment. It was petty° of me, childish!"

"I beg your pardon, sir, but I must refuse to approach the piano again."

The Maestro stared at him, unbelieving, pleading.

"Rollo, you can't! The world must hear you!"

"No, sir." The amber lenses almost seemed to soften.

"The piano is not a machine," that powerful inhuman voice droned. "To me, yes. I can translate the notes into sounds at a glance. From only a few I am able to grasp at once the composer's conception. It is easy for me."

Rollo towered magnificently over the Maestro's bent form.

"I can also grasp," the brassy monotone rolled through the studio, "that this . . . music is not for robots. It is for man. To me it is easy, yes. . . . It was not meant to be easy."

follow-up

Discussing "Virtuoso"

1. Why, do you think, might Rollo's playing the piano be dangerous to the Maestro?
2. What does Rollo mean when he says that music "was not meant to be easy"?
3. Why, do you suppose, did the author choose to give his robot a name, but referred to the human being not by name, but as "The Maestro?"
4. What examples of music trade jargon did you note? Can you explain what each term means?

Reading Character

Wouldn't it be convenient if people came with full sets of descriptions? "Jones is an engineer, married with three children, lives in Calgary. He is a Protestant, a member of the Chamber of Commerce, and votes Progressive Conservative. He likes baseball and hockey but dislikes football. He has a good sense of humor, but he doesn't like jokes about engineers. Jones always rises at 6:30 and thinks anyone who sleeps beyond 7:15 has wasted the day. He believes this, feels that, thinks so-and-so, likes such-and-such. . . . " And so on. A good, thorough, detailed description would give us confidence that we understood people, wouldn't you agree? Then we wouldn't have to guess how they might respond in a certain situation. We wouldn't have to wonder what their actions meant or speculate about how to interpret their comments. All we'd need to do is consult the description. And at once we'd have the explanation we sought.

Unfortunately, most people don't come to us fully explained. If we want to understand them, we must watch them, listen to them, and try to find patterns in their behavior that reveal their motives, fears, and hopes.

It is much the same with the characters we meet in literature. Most writers do not want to present their characters to us fully explained. Instead, they want us to meet their characters as we would meet people in real life. They want us to see those characters in action and listen to them talk. And then, from the small details we observe, writers know that we'll come to our own conclusions about the characters.

Perhaps that is what Rollo did with the Maestro. Rollo concluded that if he continued to play the piano, the Maestro would be harmed. But the Maestro himself did not recognize the danger. If Rollo was correct, he noticed something that the Maestro was unaware of.

Practice 1. Discussion

What was it that Rollo noticed about the Maestro? Look back over the story to see whether you can find the details that Rollo's internal computer must have recorded and analysed. If you wish, you might try to answer the following questions, as an aid in discovering those details:

1. How did the Maestro feel about calling the piano a "machine?"
2. What did the Maestro say about Chopin and Mozart?
3. How did the Maestro react when he found out how much Rollo had learned during the night?
4. What did the Maestro's house tell you about him?
5. What did the nickname, "Maestro," tell you about the man himself?
6. Why, then, did Rollo conclude, from these observations, that his playing the piano would harm the Maestro?

Character and Theme

The Maestro was a man who loved music and worked very hard to become "the master." Then he found that his robot could learn, in one night's time, everything that it had taken him a lifetime to learn. Because the Maestro loved music, he wanted the robot to learn and to perform. But Rollo refused because he saw that becoming an accomplished musician was not meant to be easy, that *his* easy success would drain all significance from the Maestro's lifetime of work.

But what does all that mean? What general idea about life is the author expressing?

Practice 2. Discussion

Before you try to state the theme—the general meaning—of the story, consider these statements. With which do you think the writer would agree? Why?

1. "It matters not how you played the game—only whether you won or lost."
2. "The goal of life is comfort and ease."
3. "The journey is more important than the destination."
4. "An accomplishment should be judged, in part, by the effort it required."

Practice 3. Writing

Now, in one sentence, state the meaning of the story. You might do that by completing this statement: "In Virtuoso: Goldstone is saying that _____."

Be prepared to share your statement of the theme with your classmates. Do they agree with you? If not, what do they suggest? Do you agree with them?

Bookshelf

Computer Coach, by Stephen R. Lewinstein. Westminster, 1971. A computer expert takes a job as baseball coach, counting on his unusual brain to transform a losing team into a winner.

The Joy of Music, by Leonard Bernstein. New American Library, 1967 (originally, 1959). Bernstein writes entertainingly about music. He explains the art of conducting and discusses various kinds of music.

The Thinking Computer: Mind Inside Matter, by Bertram Raphael. W. H. Freeman, 1976. Raphael explains how computers work and how they are used. He also has a section on robots.

Turn It Up: (I Can't Hear the Words), by Bob Sarlin. Simon & Shuster, 1974. A discussion of modern rock and roll performers.

27

Meihem in ce Klasrum

forestudy

The Trouble with Spelling

If you find the title "Meihem in ce Klasrum" hard to read, don't panic. It is! That's because you're not familiar with the spelling system used. Dolton Edwards, the author, is simply trying to show you how "easy" reading would become if all words were spelled exactly the way they sound.

Practice 1. Discussion
See what you can do about reading these sentences from "Meihem in ce Klasrum" aloud.

1. For, as is wel known, the horible mes of "e's" apearing in our writen languag is kaused prinsipaly bai the present nesisity of indikeiting whether a vowel is long or short.
2. Kontinuing cis proses, year after year, we would eventuali hav a reali sensibl writen languag.

Reading phonetically—that is, sound by sound, is not as easy as some people might think. Although English-speaking people have no major problems learning their language—just as the French have no major problems reading French, or Russians reading Russian, or Israeli people reading Hebrew, or Chinese people deciphering Chinese characters—language experts claim that English is one of the most difficult languages for a non-native speaker to learn. Irregularity in spelling is one reason.

English is essentially a Germanic language. Many of our English words have kept their German spelling, without their German pronunciation: *knight, night, delicatessen*. Other words have come into English from French, maintaining French

412

spelling: *buffet, bouquet, chandelier, marquis, cliché.* In America, the Westward Movement introduced Native North American words into the language: *tobacco, hammock, skunk, raccoon, toboggan.* From the Spanish colonization of Florida and the Southwest have come Spanish terms and Spanish spellings: *rodeo, corral, tamale, coyote.*

Words used in science and medicine have come from Latin: *genes, vacuum, data, bacteria.* Even today, space age technology is adding new words to the language: *interballistic, intergalactic, transistor.*

Is there any wonder then, that spelling in English is often difficult?

Practice 2. Discussion/Writing

Try to pronounce the following words aloud. Next, check your pronunciation in the dictionary by copying the pronunciation information on a sheet of paper. Also, if your dictionary has this information, see what languages these words come from. Then write down the meaning of each.

1. debris
2. yacht
3. paroxysm
4. poltergeist
5. croissant

Be prepared to discuss your findings with the class.

In "Meihem in ce Klasrum" Dolton Edwards claims to have found a solution to *all* of your spelling problems. Has he?

Meihem in
ce Klasrum

Dolton Edwards

He: I M A B.
She: U R!
He: S, R U A B 2?
She: O S, I M A B 2. R U N TV?
He: S, I M A TV B.
She: G!
—Children's Primer
New Style

Because we are still bearing some of the scars of our brief skirmish with 11-B English, it is natural that we should be enchanted by Mr. George Bernard Shaw's[1] proposal for a simplified alphabet.

Obviously, as Mr. Shaw points out, English spelling is in much need of a general overhauling and streamlining. However, our own resistance to any changes requiring a large expenditure of mental effort in the near future would cause us to view with some apprehension the possibility of some day receiving a morning paper printed in—to us—Greek.

Our own plan would achieve the same end as the legislation proposed by Mr. Shaw, but in a less shocking manner, as it consists merely of an acceleration of the normal processes by which the language is continually modernized.

As a catalytic agent,[2] we would suggest that a "National Easy Language Week" be proclaimed, which the President would inaugurate, outlining some short-cut to concentrate on during the week, and to be adopted during the ensuing year. All school children would be given a holiday, the lost time being the equivalent of that gained by the spelling shortcut.

In 1972, for example, we would urge the elimination of the soft "c," for which we would substitute "s". Sertainly, such an improvement would be selebrated in all sivic-minded sircles as being suffisiently worth the trouble, and students in all sities in the land would be reseptive toward any change eliminating the nesessity of learning the differense between the two letters.

In 1973, sinse only the hard "c" would be left, it would be possible to substitute "k" for it, both letters being pronounsed identikally. Imagine how greatly only two years of this prosess would klarify the konfusion in the minds of students. Already we would have eliminated an entire letter from the alphabet. Typewriters and linotypes kould all be built with one less letter, and all the manpower and materials previously devoted to making "c's" kould be turned toward raising the national standard of living.

In the fase of so many notable improvements, it is easy to forsee that by 1974 "National Easy Language Week" would be a pronounsed sukses. All skhool tshildren would be looking forward with konsiderable exsitement to the holiday, and in a blaze of national publisity it would be announsed that the double konsonant "ph" no longer existed, and that the sound would henseforth be written "f" in all words. This would make sutsh words as "fonograf" twenty persent shorter in print.

By 1975, publik interest in a fonetik alfabet kan be expekted to have inkreased to the point where a more radikal step forward kan be taken without fear of undue kritisism. We would therefore urge the elimination at that time of al unesesary double leters, whitsh, although quite harmles, have always ben a nuisanse in the language and a desided deterent to akurate speling. Try it yourself in the next leter you write, and se if both writing and reading are not fasilitated.

With so mutsh progres already made, it might be posible in 1976 to delve further into the posibilities of fonetik speling.

After due konsideration of the reseption aforded the previous steps, it should be expedient by this time to spel al difthongs[3] fonetikaly. Most students do not realize that the long "i" and "y," as in "time" and "by," are aktualy the difthong "ai," as it is writen in "aisle," and that the long "a" in "fate," is in reality the difthong "ei" as in "rein." Although perhaps not imediately aparent, the saving in taime and efort will be tremendous when we leiter elimineite the sailent "e," as meide posible bai this last tsheinge.

For, as is wel known, the horible mes of "e's" apearing in our writen language is kaused prinsipaly bai the present nesesity of indikeiting whether a vowel is long or short. Therefore, in 1977 we kould simply elimineit al sailent "e's," and kontinu to read and wrait merily along as though we wer in an atomik ag of edukation.

In 1978 we would urg a greit step forward. Sins bai this taim it would have ben four years sins anywun had used the leter "c," we would sugest that the "National Easy Languag Wek" for 1978 be devoted to substitution of "c" for "th." To be sur it would be some taim befor peopl would bekom akustomd to reading ceir newspapers and buks wic sutsh sentenses in cem as "Ceodor caught he had cre cousand cistls crust crough ce cik of his cumb."

In ce seim maner, bai meiking eatsh leter hav its own sound and cat sound only, we kould shorten ce languag stil mor. In 1979 we would elimineit ce "y"; cen in 1980 we kould us ce leter to indikeit ce "sh" sound, cerbai klarifaiing words laik yugar and yur, as wel as redusing bai wun mor leter al words laik "yut,"

3. *difthongs—diphthongs* (dĭf′ thôngz): a speech sound beginning with one vowel sound and moving to another vowel sound within the same syllable, as *ei* in *vein*

415

"yore," and so forc. Cink, cen, of al ce benefits to be geind bai ce distinktion whitsh wil cen be maid between words laik:

ocean	now written oyean
machine	now written mayin
racial	now written reiyial

Al sutsh divers weis of wraiting wun sound would no longer exist, and whenever wun kaim akros a "y" sound he would know exaktli what to wrait.

Kontinuing cis proses, year after year, we would eventuali hav a reali sensibl writen languag. By 1995, wi ventyur tu sei, cer wud bi no mor uv ces teribli trublsum difikultis, wic no tu leters usd to indikeit ce seim nois, and laikwais no tu noises riten wic ce seim leter. Even Mr. Yaw wi beliv, wud be hapi in ce noleg cat his drims fainali keim tru.

follow-up

Discussing "Meihem in ce Klasrum"

1. Did u have eni trubl reding ce words speld az cis aucor rekomendz? Whai?
2. Du u cink cat cis nu fonetic alfabet wil werk satisfactorili for everibodi? Whai? Whai not?
3. What speling problem or problemz—if eni—du u cink ce aucor mei hav overlooked?
4. What is "meihem" (mayhem)? Why "meihem" in the classroom? What do you suppose Mr. Edwards had in mind in giving his article this title?
5. Do you think Mr. Edwards is serious in his proposal? Or he is simply pulling your leg? Why?

In a Comical Tone

Tone, as you know, refers to the writer's attitude toward the subject and the audience as reflected in the language used. The writer's attitude is revealed through the details he/she chooses and through whatever receives emphasis.

The writer's tone can be serious—as in "Especially Worthy" (page 181)), and "Cranes Fly South" (page 316). Or it can be wistful as in "When I Was One-and-Twenty" (page 44), and "It's Raining in Love (page 272). Or it can be exuberant as in "The Song My Paddle Sings" (page 175). It can be personal and sentimental—as in "Scent of Apples" (page 97). It can be mysterious and foreboding—as in "The Monkey's Paw" (page 325). Or it can be comical—as in "An Ounce of Cure" (page 53).

Practice 1. Discussion

What word do you think best describes the tone of "Meihem in ce Klasrum"? Why? What passages in the article support your point of view?

Bookshelf

Body Language, by Julius Fast. Pocket Books, 1971. About non-verbal communication—the way we reveal ourselves in our movements, our postures, and our facial expressions.

Danger—Men Talking! by Stuart Chase. Parents, 1969. Chase discusses the way people use language to communicate—and to avoid communicating.

Queries & Theories: Game of Science & Language, by Layman E. Allen, Peter Kugel, and Joan Ross. Wff 'n Proof, 1970. Not a book, but a game, based on the principles of linguistics. It is, in fact, many games, from very simple to very difficult.

Stuff, Etc., by John Gordon. Lippincott, 1970. Gordon discusses the corruption of language that has been brought about largely by advertising.

Handbook

Contents

Introduction

This *Handbook* offers you help with your language. It does so with the understanding that many language rules can only approximate the rules which the majority of North Americans seem to be observing in their speech and writing at the present time.

Spoken language and written language differ in many ways. Most speech—at least everyday conversation—is informal. The speaker changes pitch, pace, quality, and loudness of his/her voice, and he/she often depends on gestures and facial expressions to communicate his/her meaning. The writer usually writes down what he/she has to express; then he/she rereads, corrects, and polishes what has been written. The writer pays attention to conventions such as spelling, punctuation, careful sentence structure, and well-organized paragraphs. Speech tends to be spontaneous; writing is carefully planned and revised. Both the speaker and the writer, however, have the same goal: to be understood.

English "rules," if they are to be really useful, must allow for the variations of informal and formal usage in writing, as well as in speech. The appropriateness of one usage over another, like one mode of dress over another, depends on the occasion. In this *Handbook*, you will find examples of standard informal and formal expressions considered suitable for various occasions. Nonstandard usages are also included so that you can avoid using them.

Our language is used in many different ways, but none of these ways is always right or wrong, or even necessarily good or bad. The similarities in the ways that English-speaking people use their language are far greater than the differences. In fact, for practical purposes you need to concentrate on only relatively few problems which result from these differences. These problem areas are explained and illustrated in this *Handbook*.

Carefulness

You can prevent many faults in your speech and writing if you are careful. The General Guide Questions listed in the box below are like self-checks. Referring to them frequently will help you say what you mean and mean what you say.

After the General Guide Questions you will find a convenient treatment of the specific problems, alphabetically arranged, that most often trouble students; refer to any of those items whenever you need to or when your teacher directs you to.

> ## General Guide Questions
>
> 1. Do I make a habit of listening to my own speech to detect nonstandard expressions?
> 2. Have I checked with a dictionary every doubtful spelling of a word?
> 3. Have I carefully reexamined every separate sentence I have written?
> 4. Have I used the right words and the right punctuation to make my meaning clear?
> 5. Have I clearly and directly followed through with my thought from sentence to sentence and from paragraph to paragraph, "thinking ahead" for a rhythmic flow of words?
> 6. Have I read my writing aloud, making corrections, to insure saying interestingly and precisely what I intended to say?

1. Agreement: pronoun-antecedent.

Use that pronoun which agrees in number with the word it refers to (its antecedent).

    a. If the antecedent is singular, use a singular pronoun to refer to it.

    George can succeed in mathematics if *he* tries.

    Mary forgot *her* student pass, so *she* had to pay at the gate.

      (1) Use a singular pronoun to refer to these singular antecedents: *any, anybody, anyone, each, either, everybody, everyone, everything, neither, no one, nobody, somebody, someone.* See 2a (1).

      Each of the boys will bring *his* own canteen.

      Neither of the cats moved *its* ears.

      Everybody should bring *his/her* own materials to class.

      Everyone in the girls' gym class did *her* stunt.

      But: Everyone is going to the game, and *they* will have to buy *their* tickets in advance. (*Everyone* and *everybody* are sometimes used in the plural sense.)

      (2) Use a singular pronoun to refer to singular antecedents which are formed like plurals: *corps, mathematics, measles, mumps, news.*

      He flunked *mathematics* because *it* was too hard for him.

      Measles caused her permanent injury because *it* wasn't detected soon enough.

    b. If the antecedent is plural, use a plural pronoun to refer to it.

    The *kids* worked harder on the prom than *they* ever had before.

420

c. If the antecedent is a word that can be used as either singular or plural, use a singular or plural pronoun, depending on the sense.

Singular Sense	*Plural Sense*
The *group* planned *its* annual picnic. (The group acted together as a unit.)	The *group* couldn't agree on *their* plans. (The group members acted individually.)
The *jury* gave *its* verdict. (The jury acted as a unit.)	The *jury* took *their* seats. (The jury members acted individually.)

2. Agreement: subject-verb.

Use that verb which agrees in number with its subject.

a. If the subject is singular, use a singular verb.

Nonstandard	*Standard*
S V	S V
He don't understand the map.	*He doesn't understand* the map.
S V	S V
He run on the track every day.	*He runs* on the track every day.

(1) Use a singular verb to agree with these singular words: *any, anybody, anyone, each, either, everybody, everyone, everything, neither, no one, one, somebody, someone.* (See also Section 1a (1).)

    S   V
Everyone was invited to the sports assembly.

    S   V
One of my favorite subjects *is* English.

    S   V
Each of my friends *enjoys* the movies.

(2) Use a singular verb to agree with singular words which are formed like plurals: *corps, mathematics, measles, mumps, news.*

    S   V
Mathematics is a fascinating subject for people who have logical minds.

   S   V
Mumps is a painful disease.

b. If the subject is plural, use a plural verb.

Nonstandard	*Standard*
S V	S V
We was about to give you up for lost.	*We were* about to give you up for lost.
S V	S V
They wasn't supposed to be here.	*They weren't supposed* to be here.

421

(1) If two or more subjects are joined by *and*, use a plural verb when the combined subjects give a plural sense.

S   S   V

Sue and *Jackie are* on the volleyball team.

S   V

But: Macaroni and cheese is my favorite dish. (In combination, *macaroni and cheese* is considered a single food.)

  c. Some words can be used in either the singular or plural sense. Use either the singular or plural verb to agree with such words, depending on the sense. Examples of these words are *all, any, most, none, some.*

Singular Sense	Plural Sense
S V	S V
None of the ice cream *was eaten*.	*None* of the players *were injured*.
S LV	S LV
All is not lost.	*All are* young adults.

  d. In phrasing questions, use that verb which agrees with the subject, even though part of the verb comes first.

Nonstandard	Standard
V S S V	V S S V
Was Sally <u>and</u> *her sister permitted* to skate?	*Were Sally* <u>and</u> *her sister per-* mitted to skate?
V S V	V S V
Wasn't we taught that lesson last year?	*Weren't we taught* that lesson last year?

  e. In verb-subject (V–S) sentences introduced by *there* and *here*, use that verb which agrees with the subject.

V   S

There *are* four *things* you have to know for the test.

V   S

Here *is* the *list* of items you asked for.

  f. Be sure to make the verb agree with the actual subject, not with a noun that comes between the subject and verb.

S   V

A *group* of determined, happy soldiers *is marching* up the avenue. (*Group* is the subject, not *soldiers*. *Soldiers* is the object of the preposition *of*.)

S   V

The old *man*, not the two young boys, *is* prepared to work all day. (The verb agrees with the subject *man*, not with *boys*.)

g. In the S-LV-SC (noun) sentence pattern, make the LV agree with the subject, not with the noun or nouns following the LV.

      S   LV

The *problem was* the rioters who were throwing bottles and rocks. (The linking verb *was* agrees with the singular subject *problem*, not with the subject complement *spectators*.)

3. Apostrophe.

Use either the apostrophe (') or the apostrophe and *s* ('s) according to the following rules:

a. Use the apostrophe alone—

   (1) in contractions at the exact place where you have left letters out, including *o'clock* (of the clock).

      I've (I have)   I'm (I am)   you're (you are)
      they're (they are) we'll (we will) it's (it is)

   (2) to show the possessive form of all singular and plural nouns ending in *s*.

      babies' shoes   Charles' report

b. Use the apostrophe and *s* ('s)—

   (1) to show the possessive form of all singular nouns and those plural nouns not ending in *s*.

      the boy's hat   women's liberation
      Alaska's climate   children's toys

   (2) to show the possessive form of these pronouns: *anybody, anyone, else, everybody, everyone, nobody, no one, one, somebody, someone.*

      It was someone else's fault.
      It was no one's business.
      Someone's purse was lying on the sidewalk.

c. Do *not* use the apostrophe in verbs or in forming plural nouns.

     He *comes* and he *goes*. (verbs)
     Four *cars* were parked outside. (plural noun)
     Jerry has four *brothers* and *sisters*. (plural nouns)

4. Capital letters.

Use capital letters—

a. to begin the first word of a sentence.

     Were you planning to discuss the matter?

b. to begin a quoted sentence used with an explainer.

     She said, "The information you requested is in the enclosed envelope."

c. in letter writing to begin the first and last words in a salutation and the first word of a complimentary close.

Dear Sir: Sincerely yours,

d. in titles:

Title	Example
works of literature	"Another Solution" (short story) *Adventures of Huckleberry Finn* (novel)
publications	*Edmonton Journal* *Miss Chatelaine*
musical compositions	"Rhapsody in Blue"
works of art	the *Mona Lisa*
titles of persons, when used before the name, but not otherwise	Premier Peter Lougheed *But*: Peter Lougheed, premier of Alberta
offices of high distinction	the Secretary-General the Prime Minister of Canada

Note: Do not capitalize articles (*a, an, the*), coordinating words (*and, but, for, nor, or, yet*), or prepositions of fewer than five letters unless they appear at the beginning or at the end of the title.

e. in proper names:

Name	Example
persons	George Brown, Mr. Eric Blohm, Ms. Effie Trask Ms. Eva Retamos
family names when not used with possessives	Aunt Mary. *But*: my aunt Mary Father. *But:* my father
nationalities, races, and languages	Hindu, German, Negro, Indian, English, American, French, Caucasian
days of the week	Sunday, Friday
months of the year	May, October. *But* not the seasons: spring, summer, autumn, winter.
holidays	Christmas, Remembrance Day Easter, New Year's Day

5. Clearness.

Write clearly so that your reader can understand exactly what you mean.

Unclear	*Clear*
She was hit in the game by a pitched ball.	In the game she was hit by a pitched ball.
George saw a red barn strolling down the road.	Strolling down the road, George saw a red barn.
Beating the dust away, the rug became cleaner and brighter.	The rug became cleaner and brighter as my brother beat the dust from it.
Gnawing on a bone, Iola found the lost pup.	Iola found the lost pup gnawing on a bone.
Our desire for the truth has impelled us to search for it. This has made us better than the lower animals.	Our urge and ability to search for the truth distinguishes us from the lower animals.

6. Colon.

Use the colon (:)—

    a. after the salutation of a business letter or any formal letter.

        Dear Manager: To whom it may concern:

    b. to introduce a list after such expressions as *the following, as follows.*

        Please come prepared with the following items: pen, paper, eraser, and pencil.

    c. to introduce an explanation or a result.

        The speaker expressed his opinion in three words: "It is deplorable."

        Note: Many writers do not begin an independent explanatory clause with a capital unless the clause has independent meaning, as in the preceding example.

        We now have one goal: We must complete the decorations by four o'clock.

7. Comma.

Use a comma (,)—

    a. to separate—

        (1) parts of addresses (except the postal code) and dates.
            Waterloo, Ontario N2L 3G1   July 1, 1867

        (2) salutations in friendly social letters; the complimentary close in all letters.
            Dear Suzie,   Love,   Sincerely yours,

(3) equal items in a series.

Dad brought bread, milk, and ice cream home from the store.
The children got up early, sneaked downstairs, and went out
into the yard.

(4) two or more adjectives when *and* could be substituted for the
comma.

It was a huge, rambling house. (It was a huge *and* rambling
house.)
Mr. Jones is a little old man. (No comma; "a little and old man"
does not sound natural.)

(5) two or more simple sentences joined by *and, but, for, nor, or, yet.*

George wanted to spend his summer earnings on a car, but he
found he needed the money for college.

(6) the explainer *he said* or *she said* (or its equivalent) from the directly quoted sentence (unless a question mark or an exclamation point is used).

He said, "I won't be forced into such a deal."
"I won't," he said, "be forced into such a deal."
"I won't be forced into such a deal," he said.
But: "Is that you?" she asked.
     "That's nonsense!" she shouted.

(7) an interrogative phrase that changes a statement into a
question.

The Yankees are going to win, *aren't they?*
You saw the tall ships, *didn't you?*

b. to set off certain words and groups of words which introduce or
interrupt the sentence—

(1) introductory phrases.

Standing in line, I looked around and saw an old friend.
After he had paid the bill, he left.
On the contrary, not all mushrooms are poisonous.

(2) introductory words such as *yes, no, well, oh*.

Yes, I'll be there.   *No,* she can't come.
Well, wait here.   *Oh,* I didn't know.

(3) interrupting words.

Mary, *my sister,* is an electrician.
Aspirin, *which is a simple compound,* is good for headaches.
We can't, *however,* be sure.

(4) direct address.

Lloyd, where have you been?
Jump, *Ken,* before the boat sinks!
Are you going to the game, *Betty?*

c. to make your writing clear, to prevent misleading or confusing your reader.

Misleading	*Clear*
After eating Grandfather sat in his rocking chair and read the newspaper.	After eating, Grandfather sat in his rocking chair and read the newspaper.
As he tripped the dish fell out of his hands. (Did he trip the dish?)	As he tripped, the dish fell out of his hands.

8. Conciseness.

a. Get to the point directly, using the fewest words necessary.

Wordy	*Concise*
Of all of the problems that I have in writing, my biggest problem is spelling. (15 words)	My biggest writing problem is spelling. (6 words)
We followed the path to *the place where* the world's tallest tree *is located.* (14 words)	We followed the path to the world's tallest tree.(9 words)

b. Avoid needless repetition of words or thought.

Repetitive	*Concise*
The water looked sanitary but when I tasted it, *it tasted* as if it were not *sanitary.* (repeated words)	The water looked sanitary but tasted bad.
Modern students *of today* have greater respect for *true* facts. (repeated thought)	Modern students have greater respect for facts.

9. Consistency.

Maintain one approach.

a. Do not shift needlessly from one tense to another.

Inconsistent	*Consistent*
He *goes* to the garage and *came* back with a new fan belt.	He *went* to the garage and *came* back with a new fan belt.
I *asked* her to join us, but she *says* she was too busy.	I *asked* her to join us, but she *said* she was too busy.

(1) In narrative writing, ordinarily use the past tense.

   She *glanced* at the ebony clock and *saw* that it was time to leave.

(2) When you are writing about literature, use the present tense to describe what the author does, regardless of when he lived.

   Shakespeare *creates* characters that live.
   John Steinbeck *uses* symbolism.
   The Iliad, an epic poem, *tells* about the fall of Troy.

427

(3) When expressing an idea that is true for all time, use the present tense even if you have been using another tense.

Columbus proved that the world *is* round.
There *are* 24 hours in a day.

b. Keep to the same point of view.

Inconsistent	*Consistent*
I climbed to the top of the mountain, and *you* could see everything.	*I* climbed to the top of the mountain, and *I* could see everything.
A person should do what *they* think is right.	*A person* should do what *he* or *she* thinks is right.

10. Dash.

Use the dash—

a. to set off a group of words containing commas.

All our equipment—rods, reels, bait—was lost when the boat tipped over. (The dashes are like very strong commas.)

b. to show an afterthought, as in a sudden twist in meaning.

They are mountain climbers—within reason, of course.

c. to show an abrupt break in thought, as when writing dialogue.

"But you—you are the one that—"

d. to emphasize a sentence interrupter.

Mr. Phelps—he's the one I told you about—asked me for a book.

11. Demonstratives

Demonstratives are words that point out: *this, that, these,* and *those.*

a. When used as adjectives, *this, these, that,* and *those* should agree with the words they modify.

This type of story is my favorite.
These types of stories are my favorites.
That kind of music makes me want to dance.
Those kinds of records are hard to find.

Caution: Avoid such expressions as *those kind of peaches.* The demonstrative modifies the singular noun *kind,* not the object of the preposition (*peaches*). The demonstrative must be singular: *that kind* of peaches.

Nonstandard	*Standard*
I don't like *those* kind of movies.	I don't like *that* kind of movies.
Those kind of people make me happy.	*That* kind of people makes me happy.
	Those kinds of people make me happy.

b. Avoid using *them* as a demonstrative. Use *those*.

Nonstandard	*Standard*
Them days are gone forever.	*Those* days are gone forever.
Where did you get all *them* apples?	Where did you get all *those* apples?

c. Avoid using words *here* or *there* with demonstratives. Such words are unnecessary. They waste your time, as well as the time of your listener or reader.

Nonstandard	*Standard*
This here rake is broken	*This* rake is broken.
That there temperature chart is wrong.	*That* temperature chart is wrong.
These here are my best shoes.	*These* are my best shoes.
I think skis like *those there* are best.	I think skis like *those* are best.

12. End Punctuation.

Use end punctuation (. ? !) according to the following rules:

a. Use a period (.) after—

    (1) a statement.

        She is a pretty girl.

    (2) an indirect question.

        I asked Carl whether he could go.

    (3) a command or direction.

        Leave the room, please.

b. Use a question mark (?) after—

    (1) a direct question.

        Who is she?

    (2) a direct question following a statement.

        He likes fish, doesn't he?

c. Use an exclamation point (!) after—

    (1) a statement showing strong feeling.

        Help!

    (2) a statement showing great surprise.

        It was you all the time!

    (3) a strongly worded opinion.

        What a horrible time we had!

Caution: Do not overuse the exclamation point, and never use more than one at the end of an expression.

13. Fragments.

Make sure that every sentence you write is grammatically complete.

    a. Correct a fragment by supplying the missing subject or verb or both.

Fragment	*Complete*
	S
Went to a ball game.	*Amy* went to the ball game.
The girl in the blue suit.	The girl in the pink dress
	V
	answered the door.

    b. Correct a fragment by joining it to the sentence of which it should be a part.

Fragment	*Complete*
Last year we had to get by with few luxuries. *Because we lived too far from civilization*	Last year we had to get by with few luxuries, *because we lived too far from civilization.*

Note: Occasionally an experienced writer may introduce a sentence fragment in order to create a particular effect. However, it is better for the inexperienced writer to avoid using a fragment.

14. Hyphen.

Use a hyphen (-)—

    a. at the end of a line to divide a word between its syllables, as with—

        (1) a prefix or suffix and a root word.

            pre-fer, social-ism

        (2) parts of a compound word.

            master-mind

        (3) double letters.

            inflam-mable

        (4) two consonants between vowels.

            chief-tain, foun-dation

    b. with prefixes *all-*, *ex-* (former), *self-*; with any prefix before a prop-er name; and with the suffix *-elect*.

        all-purpose, ex-member, self-pity, anti-Communist, mid-June, mayor-elect

    c. to avoid confusion between words of similar spelling.

        re-cover (to cover again)   re-lay (re-lay the tile)
        But: recover (to regain)   *But*: relay (a relay race)

    d. to avoid an awkward joining of letters.

        semi-invalid (*not* semiinvalid)   co-owner (*not* coowner)

e. to join compound numbers from twenty-one to ninety-nine, and written fractions when used as modifiers.

thirty-five   two-thirds majority

f. to join words which form a single unit: a *major-league* team.

Caution: Never divide—

(1) a one-syllable word.

help, name, their, your

(2) a proper name.

Jones, Washington

(3) a single-letter syllable.

about (*not* a-bout), heavy (*not* heav-y)

Note: Use a dictionary when in doubt as to syllable division.

15. Modifiers

a. Use adjectives to modify nouns and pronouns; use adverbs to modify verbs, adjectives, and other adverbs.

Nonstandard	*Standard*
He does *good* in sports.	He does *well* in sports.
Helen felt *badly* about the game. (This use means that something was wrong with her sense of touch.)	Helen felt *bad* about the game. (She was a bad-feeling person.)
I feel *some* better today.	I feel *somewhat* better today.

b. Use the appropriate forms of adjectives and adverbs.

(1) When you compare two things—

(a) add *-er* to modifiers of one syllable.

great—great*er*   small—small*er*

(b) put *more* or *less* before modifiers of three or more syllables.

beautiful—*more* beautiful   agreeable—*less* agreeable

(c) treat a two-syllable modifier either way.

often—oft*ener*   or   *more* often

(2) When you compare three or more things—

(a) add *-est* to modifiers of one syllable

great—great*est*   small—small*est*

(b) put *most* or *least* before modifiers of three or more syllables.

beautiful—*most* beautiful   agreeable—*least* agreeable

(c) usually, treat a two-syllable modifier either way.

quiet—quiet*est*   or   *most* quiet

431

16. Numbers, symbols, and abbreviations.

Use words, numerals, symbols, and abbreviations as follows:

a. Write out those numbers and symbols that can be expressed in one or two words. This rule applies to most writing in which numbers and symbols occur only occasionally.

There are *twenty-eight* students present.

The teachers said that *seventy plus* was a passing grade.

b. Use numerals and symbols instead of spelling them out whenever your writing includes them frequently, as in statistical reports.

Judge Springer stated that in San Francisco 50 marriages out of 100 end in divorce. This is a 50% divorce rate.

c. Use only commonly accepted abbreviations.

USA and USSR; A.M. and P.M.; Mr., Mrs., Ms.; Dr.; St. (Saint); Jr. and Sr. *as part of a person's name;* UN, UNICEF, *well-known organizations*

d. Note these variations in the previous rules:

(1) Write out any number, no matter how large, if it occurs first in the sentence.

One hundred and twenty-five people failed to vote.

(2) Spell out amounts of money only when you can do so in *one or two words*.

three dollars. *But:* $3.40; $2.50

(3) Use numerals for dates unless the month follows the day.

June 15, 1960; June 15 (not 15th) of that year.

But: the fifteenth of the month

(4) Use numerals for the complete decade designations.

in the 1960s. *But:* in the sixties

(5) Write out the numbers of centuries.

the nineteenth century

(6) Write out time when giving the hour or using "o'clock."

Be here at four o'clock. We leave at five. The show is over at half-past nine.

But: Use numerals when using A.M. and P.M.

at 8:15 A.M.; at 3 P.M.

(7) Use numerals when listing pages and parts of a book.

Chapter 12, page 178, column 2, line 17

(8) Use numerals when giving street, room, highway, and track numbers.

15 Thirty-sixth Street (*Thirty-sixth* is written out to separate it from *15*); room 15; Highway 99; Track 14

(9) Use numerals when giving percentages.

over 10 percent

(10) Use numerals when giving decimals.

exactly 3.58 inches

(11) Use numerals when giving scores.

Our team won, 14–12.

17. Parentheses.

Use parentheses to set off incidental or less important material.

We drove all the way from Halifax (where we were born and raised) to Vancouver.

Note: Parentheses play down an item; dashes emphasize it.

18. Parts of speech

Words are classified according to the jobs they do in sentences:

a. Words that name—persons, places, animals, things, ideas—are *nouns.*

George sits here; *Mattie* sits over there.
We live in *Canada.*
Honesty is the best *policy.*
Cats meow.
Sticks and *stones* were scattered over the *yard.*

b. Words that substitute for nouns are *pronouons.*

I am your friend.
She called *him.*
Nobody knows the combination.
Who can answer the question?
Everyone sang.

c. Words that show action or the condition of something are *verbs.*

The ball *sailed* over the fence.
Our team *scored* two goals.
Bob *is* Joan's cousin.
I *could have broken* my neck!
That *seems* obvious.

d. *Modifiers* change the meaning of other words. There are two kinds.

(1) Words that tell <u>what kind</u> or <u>which one</u> or <u>how many</u> modify nouns and are called *adjectives.*

Man, what a *smooth* talker he is! (what kind)
That book is mine. (which one)
There are *twenty* kids in our class. (how many)

433

(2) Words that tell <u>how</u>, <u>when</u>, <u>where</u>, <u>why</u>, and <u>how much</u> are called *adverbs*. They can modify verbs or adjectives or other adverbs.

I'm going *out*! (*Out* tells where I'm going.)

You're driving *too fast*. (*Fast* tells how you are driving. *Too* tells how fast.)

Mrs. Burns is *very* young. (*Very* tells how young.)

I've heard that song *before*. (*Before* tells when.)

e. Words that show relationships between other words are *prepositions*.

Gramps' feet were *on* the table. (*On* shows the relationship between *feet* and *table*.)

We'll eat *after* the game. (*After* shows the relationship between our eating and the game.)

f. Words that join words and ideas are *conjunctions*.

Angie *and* Moe will be here soon.

I like chocolate, *but* it doesn't like me.

Neither fire *nor* flood could keep us away.

We don't like cabbage *or* turnips.

Don't sing *until* the moon comes up.

When the bells rings, open the oven door *and* take the pie out.

g. Words that show strong emotion are *interjections*.

Man! What a day!

Ouch! Why don't you step on your own feet!

What! The guy's crazy!

19. Pronoun usage.

Use the form of a pronoun required by its function in the sentence.

a. Use *I, we, he, she, they, who* (the nominative case) when the pronoun is used—

(1) as the subject of a verb.

Nonstandard—Faulty	Standard
Her, him, and *me* are on the committee.	*She, he,* and *I* are on the committee. (subjects of verb *are*)
Mary and *me* were late to class.	Mary and *I* were late to class. (subjects of verb *were*)
Us boys will help.	*We* boys will help. (subject of verb *will help*)
She is older than *him*.	She is older than *he (is)*. (subject of "understood" verb *is*)
My son is as tall as *me*.	My son is as tall as *I (am)*. (subject of "understood" verb *am*)

434

(2) after the linking verbs *is, am, are, was, were, be, being, been.*

Nonstandard—Faulty	*Standard*
It *was him* who brought the surfboard.	It *was he* who brought the surfboard.
It *is him (her, them).*	*It is he (she, they).*

Note: It's me, an apparent exception to this rule, is now considered acceptable informal English.

b. Use *her, hers, his, its, mine, my, mine, our, ours, your, yours, their, theirs, whose* (the possessive case) to show ownership. Do *not* use an apostrophe with those words.

Whose pen is that?   That book is *hers*, not *yours*.

c. Use *her, him, me, them, us, whom* (the objective case)—

(1) after verbs of action.

Nonstandard	*Standard*
The usher seated *she* and *I* in the back.	The usher seated *her* and *me* in the back.

Nonstandard	*Standard*
The principal asked *we* girls to move to the balcony.	The principal asked *us* girls to move to the balcony.
Let George and *I* sit there.	Let George and *me* sit there.

(2) after prepositions.

Nonstandard	*Standard*
The tickets were handed to Charles and *I*.	The tickets were handed to Charles and *me*.
Save the money for *we* girls.	Save the money for *us* girls.
This will be a secret between you and *I*.	This will be a secret between you and *me*.

20. Punctuation in sequence.

Use punctuation marks together according to the following rules:

a. Place period (.) or comma (,)—

(1) before the closing quotation marks.

He said, "I'm leaving."
"I'm leaving," he said.

(2) after parentheses.

He wrote, "I'm going to leave on Saturday (at least, I hope to)."
But: Place a period inside parentheses if the words within the parentheses are not joined to the preceding sentence.
I am leaving on Saturday. (At least, I hope to leave then.)   **435**

b. Place question mark (?), exclamation point (!), or dash (—)—

    (1) inside the closing quotation marks or parentheses if it applies to the quotation or to the item within the parentheses.

        She asked, "Are you leaving?"
        He screamed, "Help!"
        "I'm leaving—" he began.
        The two-year-old boy (or was he three?) created a disturbance.

    (2) outside quotation marks or parentheses if it refers to the whole sentence.

        Did he say, "I'm leaving"? (The entire sentence is a question.)
        What a time to say, "I'm leaving"! (The entire sentence is an exclamation.)
        He said, "I'm leaving"—and he left. (The dash applies to the entire sentence, not to the quotation.)

c. Place colon (:) or semicolon (;) outside quotation marks.

    Frost makes this statement in his poem "Fire and Ice": "I think I know enough of hate. . . . "
    He said, "I am here"; then he left the room.

21. Quotation marks.

Use quotation marks (" ") to—

    a. quote directly what someone has said.

        Larry said, "I'm not coming home for dinner."

Note: Do not use quotation marks for an indirect quotation.

    Larry said that he wasn't coming home for dinner.

    b. enclose titles of selections less than book length (short stories, poems, articles, essays, editorials, chapters of books), titles of one-act plays, and of songs. (See Section 30a for book titles.)

    "Flight" is a powerful short story by John Steinbeck.
    I have read "Mending Wall," a poem by Robert Frost.
    "Humiliating the Matterhorn" is a chapter in Richard Halliburton's book.

22. Reference of pronouns

    a. Make sure that the antecedent of every pronoun is clear and unmistakable.

Confusing	*Clear*
If you put the candy bar into your purse, *it* is probably messy by now. (What is messy, the purse or the candy bar?)	If you put the candy bar into your purse, you probably have a messy purse by now.
	or
	The candy bar you put in your purse is probably messy by now.

	Driving away, Marge waved to her aunt.
Marge waved to her aunt as *she* drove away. (Who drove away, Marge or her aunt?)	*or*
	As her aunt drove away, Marge waved.

b. Be sure to supply an antecedent for each pronoun. If there is no antecedent, use an appropriate noun instead of the pronoun.

Antecedent lacking	*Noun substituted*
In looking at the new models, a person can see that *they* have improved refrigerator designs. (Who are *they*?)	In looking at the new models, a person can see that *manufacturers* have improved refrigerator designs.

c. Avoid using pronouns that aren't needed for clear reference.

Nonstandard—Faulty	*Standard*
That woman *she* bought five turkeys.	That woman bought five turkeys.
In the paper, *it* said that rain is expected tonight.	The paper said that rain is expected tonight.

23. Run-on sentences.

Do not run together two separate sentences without punctuation. Do not run together two separate sentences with only a comma between them.

Not: We went to the beach we saw a whale. (*no punctuation*)
Not: We went to the beach, we saw a whale. (*comma-splice*)

a. To correct run-on sentences—

(1) separate the sentences with end punctuation.
We went to the beach. We saw a whale.

(2) join closely related sentences with a semicolon.
We went to the beach; we saw a whale.

(3) join closely related sentences with a comma *plus* a coordinating conjunction (*and, but, for, nor, or, yet*).
We went to the beach, and we saw a whale.

(4) subordinate one idea.
When we went to the beach, we saw a whale.

b. Use a semicolon (or a period followed by a capital letter) to separate two sentences joined by such words as *consequently, however, moreover, nevertheless, so, then, therefore, thus*.

Comma-splice	*Corrected*
She says she is fourteen years old, however, she looks much older.	She says she is fourteen years old; however, she looks much older.

437

24. Semicolon
Use the semicolon to join sentences closely related in thought—
  a. when no connecting word is used.

    The days are hot; the nights are cold. (contrasting ideas)

  b. when the sentences are connected by such words as *consequently, however, nevertheless, so, then, therefore.* (See also Section 25b.)

    It was snowing; therefore, we drove carefully.

  c. when the sentences connected by *and, but, for, nor, or, yet* are long and contain commas.

    Jerry Phelps, the captain of the hockey team, awaited the big game of the season; but since his wrist was swollen, he was not sure he could play.

  d. when needed to separate groups of words which themselves contain commas.

    Newly elected officers include Marcia Jones, president; Skip Miller, secretary; and James Pettit, treasurer.

25. Sentence patterns
In the English language there are seven basic sentence patterns. Every sentence—written or spoken—is constructed according to one of those patterns.
  a. S-V: SUBJECT-VERB

        S   V
    Monkeys chatter.

        S   V
    Everyone in the class laughed.

  b. S-V-DO: SUBJECT-VERB-DIRECT OBJECT

      S   V   DO
    Boy meets girl.

      S   V   DO
    We saw them at the game.

                S   V   DO
    The glee club sang three songs.

  c. S-LV-SC (noun): SUBJECT-LINKING VERB-SUBJECT COMPLEMENT (noun)

      S   LV   SC(noun)
    Mike is my brother.

      S   LV   SC (noun)
    Peg was the captain of the team.

          S LV   SC (noun)
    And that's a tummy!

            S   LV   SC (noun)
    Hafton High has been our rival for many years.

d. S-LV-SC(adjective): SUBJECT-LINKING VERB-SUBJECT COMPLEMENT (adjective)

         S   LV   SC (adj.)

The water seems warm.

      S   LV   SC (adj.)

They are all crazy.

      S   LV   SC (adj.)

You can be sure with mistletoe.

         S   LV SC (adj.)

The cake tastes salty.

e. S-V-IO-DO: SUBJECT-VERB-INDIRECT OBJECT-DIRECT OBJECT

      S   V   IO   DO

Sara told the children a story.

      S   V   IO   DO

We did them a favor.

      S   V   IO   DO

Dad baked Mom a cake for her birthday.

f. S-V-DO-OC (noun): SUBJECT-VERB-DIRECT OBJECT-OBJECT COMPLEMENT (noun)

        S   V   DO   OC (noun)

The Nelsons named their daughter Trixie.

        S   V   DO OC (noun)

The class elected Tina president.

        S   V   DO OC (noun)

The coach made Bob captain of the hockey team.

g. S-V-DO-OC (adj.): SUBJECT-VERB-DIRECT OBJECT-OBJECT COMPLEMENT (adjective)

      S   V   DO OC (adj.)

That just makes me mad.

     S   V   DO OC (adj.)

We found him reliable.

      S   V   DO OC (adj.)

They painted the town red.

      S   V   DO   OC (adj.)

The referee kept the crowd waiting for ten minutes.

26. Spelling.

Spell all words correctly. If you are in doubt about the spelling of a word, look it up in a dictionary. In your notebook, keep a list of the words you have misspelled. Write these words correctly several times to get the "feel" of them. The following hints may help you become a better speller. **439**

a. Spell a word syllable by syllable.

   (1) Pronounce a troublesome word slowly, one syllable at a time.

man-u-al	sub-mar-ine
plan-ta-tion	ri-dic-u-lous
rec-og-nize	li-brar-y

   (2) Know prefixes and suffixes. Do not drop or add letters when combining prefixes and suffixes with the root words.

Prefix		Root		Result
dis	+	approve	=	disapprove
dis	+	service	=	disservice
mis	+	fortune	=	misfortune
mis	+	spell	=	misspell
un	+	natural	=	unnatural

Root		Suffix		Result
eager	+	ness	=	eagerness
sudden	+	ness	=	suddenness
sure	+	ly	=	surely
final	+	ly	=	finally

b. Spell by rule, if a rule applies.

   (1) The following rules apply to the final-letter problems.

     (a) With words ending in silent *e*, drop the *e* when adding a suffix beginning with a vowel.

Root		Suffix		Result
advise	+	ing	=	advising
fame	+	ous	=	famous
desire	+	able	=	desirable

Exceptions: dyeing, canoeing, hoeing, singeing.

     (b) With words ending in silent *e*, keep the *e* when adding a suffix beginning with a consonant.

Root		Suffix		Result
arrange	+	ment	=	arrangement
care	+	ful	=	careful
strange	+	ness	=	strangeness
complete	+	ly	=	completely

Exceptions: duly, judgment, truly.

     (c) With words ending in *ce* and *ge*, keep the *e* when adding a suffix beginning with *a* or *o*.

Root		Suffix		Result
change	+	able	=	changeable
peace	+	able	=	peaceable
courage	+	ous	=	courageous

(d) With words ending in *y* preceded by a consonant, change the *y* to *i* when adding any suffix except one beginning with *i*.

Root		*Suffix*		*Result*
try	+	ed	=	tried
worry	+	ed	=	worried
busy	+	ly	=	busily
mercy	+	ful	=	merciful

But:

worry	+	ing	=	worrying
study	+	ing	=	studying

(e) Double the final consonant before adding a suffix that begins with a vowel if both of the following conditions exist:
1. The word has only one syllable or is accented on the last syllable.
2. The word ends in a single consonant preceded by a single vowel.

Double Consonant

run	+ ing	= running
stop	+ ed	= stopped
swim	+ er	= swimmer
refer	+ ed	= referred
omit	+ ed	= omitted

(2) The following rules apply to the *ei* and *ie* problems.

(a) Use *ie* when the sound is *ee* as in *see*.
believe, chief, field, grief, yield.
Exceptions: either, leisure, neither, seize, weird.

(b) Use *ei* when the *ee* sound comes after *c*.
ceiling, conceit, deceive, receipt, receive.
Exceptions: financier, species.

(c) In certain words use *ei* when the sound is not *ee*.
eight, foreign, freight, height, their, heir, neighbor, vein, weigh.
Exceptions: fiery, friend, handkerchief, mischief, sieve. view.

(3) The following rules apply to the spelling of plural nouns:

(a) Add *s* to most singular nouns to make them plural.

Singular	*Plural*
pencil	pencils
paper	papers
sister-in-law	sisters-in-law

(b) Add *es* if the plural form adds a syllable to the singular form. This occurs with nouns ending in *s, sh, ch, x*.

glass	glass*es*
flash	flash*es*
tax	tax*es*

(c) Add *es* if the singular ends in *o* preceded by a consonant.

| hero | hero*es* |
| potato | potato*es* |

Exception: Add *s* to music words ending in *o*.

| piano | piano*s* |
| soprano | soprano*s* |

(d) Add *es* if the singular ends in *y* preceded by a consonant (but first change the *y* to *i*).

| fly | fli*es* |
| lady | ladi*es* |

Note: For words ending in *ay, ey,* or *oy*, merely add *s* for the plural.

tray	tray*s*
monkey	monkey*s*
boy	boy*s*

(e) Form the plural of singular nouns that end in *f* in two ways:

When the plural form is pronounced *fs*, merely add *s*.

chief	chief*s*
gulf	gulf*s*
reef	reef*s*

When the plural form is pronounced *vz*, drop the *f* plus any letters following it and add *ves*.

leaf	lea*ves*
life	li*ves*
wife	wi*ves*
loaf	loa*ves*

(f) Note that some nouns have special ways of forming plurals.

deer	deer
foot	feet
goose	geese
child	children
mouse	mice
woman	women

27. Transformations

Section 25—"Sentence Patterns" (page 438)—uses short simple sentences to illustrate basic sentence structure. Luckily basic sentence patterns can be combined and manipulated in lots of ways. Such combining and manipulation makes it possible to produce millions of sentences, no two of which need be exactly alike.

When we combine and manipulate basic sentence patterns, we are *transforming*—changing—those patterns. We call those changes *transformations*.

a. Negative transformations

Torbey did *not* go to the game.
I *never* said that.
If you ask me *no* questions, I'll tell you *no* lies.

b. Request/Command transformations

Please close the window. (The subject *you* is understood.)
Get out of here! (*You*, the subject, is understood.)

c. Question transformations

(1) Questions to which the answer is yes or no.
Did you see the Dan Abbott TV show last night?
Is the narrator of that story crazy?
Will Harold Trueheart rescue Patience Golightly in time?

(2) Questions that seek information.
What time is it?
What did you tell Amy about me?
When will they return?
How do you feel today?
Why doesn't that bus come?

d. Expletive (*there*) transformations

     LV   S
There are seven holes in your head.

     LV   S
There was a lot of school spirit last year.

e. Inverted order transformations.

     V   S
Pop goes the weasel.

              V   S
Round and round went the top.

          DO S V IO
One perfect rose he gave her.

f. Passive transformations

          S   V

The new road was paved yesterday. (The subject is the receiver of the action.)

            S   V

Three wishes were made by the old woman. (The subject is the receiver of the action. The doer—or agent—is the object of the preposition *by*.)

           S   V

Three sails have been sighted off the starboard bow. (The subject is the receiver of the action.)

       S   V   DO

Aretha was given a vote of thanks. (The subject is the receiver of the direct—or retained—object.)

g. Progressive transformations

The students *have been writing* for two hours.
Tabor *is skating* now.
I *am going* to the school play.
Nothing *is being done* about the fire hazard. (A passive transformation, as well as a progressive transformation.)

h. Emphatic transformations

Yes, I *do see* the need for immediate action.
He *doesn't understand* the problem. (A negative transformation, as well as an emphatic transformation.)
Maria *did play* the harp at yesterday's assembly.

28. Underlining.

Use underlining according to the following rules. (Underlining in handwriting or typing corresponds to *italics* in printing.)

a. Underline titles of books, newspapers, magazines, and full-length musical works, plays, films, and radio or television series. (See Section 23 for titles of selections of less than book length.)

I went to the library and checked out copies of <u>Life</u> and <u>Macbeth</u>.

The Carol Burnett Show is my favorite TV program.

Exception: Sacred books are not underlined, nor are portions of them underlined.
the Bible, the Koran, Genesis.

b. Underline words, letters, numbers, and symbols referred to as such.

<u>If</u>, <u>and</u>, and <u>but</u> are small but important words.
The <u>e</u> is silent in <u>bone</u>.
His <u>7</u>s looked like <u>9</u>s.

c. Underline words and phrases for special emphasis only where needed to add meaning.

He told me that it was <u>his</u> book, not yours.

But not: It was such a <u>pretty</u> sight. (The word *pretty* does not need emphasis for further meaning.)

29. Variety in sentence length and structure.

Vary sentence patterns instead of repeating them.

    a. Vary the length of your sentences to prevent monotony.

The story which the little boy made up did not fool his mother. She knew the truth. (A short sentence follows a long one, for contrast.)

Mae learned fast. After two months of apprenticeship, she was able to step into her brother's position. (A long sentence follows a short sentence.)

Phil's sister was a singer. His brother was a pianist. Phil was a cartoonist. In fact there wasn't one member of the Feldson family that wasn't talented in one way or another. (One long sentence follows a series of short sentences.)

In examining the character of his older brother Morris, John found that there was very little to admire. Morris cheated. He lied. He was lazy. (Short sentences follow one long sentence.)

    b. Vary the structure of your sentences by using—

    (1) simple sentences with or without modifiers.

Stop!
We walked in the redwood forest.
At about sundown we saw two spoonbills flying over the tops of the trees.

    (2) compound sentences.

We arrived at the park at sundown, and we camped under the giant redwoods.
Ozzie may be late, but he will get here sometime.
You'll have to dive into that 60 cm tank, or we'll cancel your contract.

    (3) sentences with subordinate clauses (complex sentences).

While I was eating breakfast, the doorbell rang.
Joel can't go to the game because he's sick.
Annie said that she'd like to see you.
After Uncle John had slammed the door, he stepped on a banana peel which someone had unthinkingly thrown on the path. (There are two subordinate clauses in this sentence.)

445

c. Invert the word order of some of your sentences.

S-V order	*V-S (inverted) order*
S V	V
A silver plane streaked across the sky.	Across the sky streaked a S silver plane.

30. Verb forms.

Use the appropriate verb form.

Use the correct tense, or time. Verbs have three principal parts or forms that show time: the present form, the past form, and the past participle.

    a. Most verbs regularly form the past and third form (the past participle) simply by adding *d* or *ed* to the present form. These are called regular verbs.

Present	*Past*	*Past Participle*
		(Used with a helping form of *have* or *be*.)
ask	asked	asked
drown	drowned	drowned
live	lived	lived
talk	talked	talked
use	used	used

Some verbs form the past and third form in special ways. Following is a reference list of irregular verbs. Consult a dictionary for tense forms of any other verbs.

Present	*Past*	*Past Participle*
		(Used with a helping form of *have* or *be*.)
beat	beat	beaten
become	became	become
begin	began	begun
bite	bit	bitten, bit
blow	blew	blown
break	broke	broken
bring	brought	brought
buy	bought	bought
choose	chose	chosen
come	came	come
cut	cut	cut
do	did	done
draw	drew	drawn
drink	drank	drunk
drive	drove	driven
eat	ate	eaten
fall	fell	fallen
fly	flew	flown

446

Present	Past	Past Participle
		(Used with a helping form of *have* or *be*.)
freeze	froze	frozen
get	got	got, gotten
give	gave	given
go	went	gone
grow	grew	grown
know	knew	known
lay (to place)	laid	laid
lie (to rest)	lay	lain
ride	rode	ridden
ring	rang	rung
rise	rose	risen
run	ran	run
see	saw	seen
shake	shook	shaken
show	showed	shown, showed
shrink	shrank	shrunk
sing	sang	sung
speak	spoke	spoken
steal	stole	stolen
stick	stuck	stuck
swim	swam	swum
take	took	taken
tear	tore	torn
throw	threw	thrown
wear	wore	worn
write	wrote	written

c. Use the past tense to show that an action occurred at some time in the past. Do not confuse the past tense with the third form (past participle).

Nonstandard—Faulty	Standard
Joe actually *done* his work	Joe actually *did* his work.
I *seen* your brother.	I *saw* your brother.
Who *drunk* my lemonade?	Who *drank* my lemonade?
It *begun* to rain.	It *began* to rain.

d. Use the third form—the past participle—with a form of *have* or *be*—

(1) when an action began in the past and is still going on.

Nonstandard—Faulty	Standard
Uncle Max *has drove* a taxi for eighteen years.	Uncle Max *has driven* a taxi for eighteen years.
The phone *has rang* six times in the past hour, and now it is ringing again.	The phone *has rung* six times in the past hour, and now it is ringing again.

447

(2) when a recently completed action has a direct influence on the present.

Nonstandard—Faulty	Standard
I *have did* the dishes, so now we can go.	I *have done* the dishes, so now we can go.
Jerry can't come with us, because he *has went* to a friend's house.	Jerry can't come with us, because he *has gone* to a friend's house.
We *ain't saw* you for years!	We *haven't seen* you for years!

e. Use the past participle (with *had*) to show an action started (and sometimes completed) before another action in the past.

When I first met Aunt Tillie, she *had been* in a wheel chair for four years.
By the time Anne arrived at the picnic, we *had eaten* all of the food.

Nonstandard—Faulty	Standard
If he *would have come* to class on time, he would not have missed the assignment.	If he *had come* to class on time, he would not have missed the assignment.

31. Words: Confused/misused.

Be sure the word you use is the appropriate one.

a. Use *a* before a word beginning with a consonant sound; use *an* before a word beginning with a vowel sound.

Give me *a* minute to explain. (*a* before the consonant sound *m*)
She bought *an* apple. (*an* before the vowel sound *a*)
It took her *an* hour to get ready. (The *h* in *hour* is a silent consonant; *hour* begins with a vowel sound.)
There was *a* hum in the engine. (The *h* in *hum* is pronounced.)
Dad bought *an* umbrella. (*Umbrella* begins with a vowel sound.)
Anna is *a* university student. (*University* begins with the consonant *y* sound.)

b. Be careful not to confuse two or more words because they are similar in sound or spelling, or because they are so frequently misused that they may "sound right." Following is a list of words commonly confused, with their meanings and examples given.

(1) accept (to take or receive)	Will you *accept* a cheque?
except (but, not)	Everybody went *except* Sue.
except (to leave out)	We *excepted* him from the list.
(2) advice (counsel, words of wisdom)	Please help me; I need *advice*.
advise (to give advice)	I will *advise* you.

(3) affect (to influence something)	The rain will *affect* the crops.
effect (a result)	The bad weather had a gloomy *effect* on her mood.
effect (to bring about)	Can the doctor *effect* a cure?
(4) all ready (all prepared)	They were *all ready* to begin writing.
already (referring to time; when)	Have you *already* eaten?
(5) brake (device to stop a machine)	When she jammed on the *brake*, the car slid.
break (to fracture or shatter)	Do not *break* any dishes.
(6) breath (air inhaled and exhaled)	He held his *breath* for two minutes.
breathe (to draw air in and let it out)	It is difficult to *breathe* at high altitudes.
(7) buy (to purchase)	Did she *buy* that shirt?
by (a preposition)	He drove *by* her house.
	By that time things had changed.
(8) cite (to refer to)	I wish to *cite* an example from today's paper.
sight (a view)	The mountains are a beautiful *sight*.
site (a piece of land)	Mr. Johnson bought the *site* near the reservoir.
(9) choose (to make a selection)	What kind of book will you *choose*?
chose (past tense of *choose*)	Last week I *chose* three new records.
(10) coarse (rough; crude)	The material was so *coarse* it irritated the baby's skin.
course (path of action)	What *course* should be taken in the face of these difficulties?
(11) desert (dez′ərt) (an expanse of arid land)	The Sahara is a vast *desert*.
desert (di zėrt′) (to abandon)	Above all, don't *desert* your post.
dessert (last course of a meal)	We had ice cream for *dessert*.
(12) hear (to listen)	Can you *hear* that noise?
here (telling where)	I am going to stay *here* until she comes.

(13) in (inside)
into (from outside to inside)

The dog was *in* the house.
The dog walked *into* the house.

(14) its (possessive)
it's (contraction of *it is*)

Give the cat *its* milk.
Do you think *it's* going to rain?

(15) later (comparative of adjective *late*)
latter (the second of two)

She arrived *later* than he did.
Of the two stories, the *latter* is the more powerful.

(16) lay, laid, laid (to place)

She *laid* your book on the table. (*Laid* takes an object.)

lie, lay, lain (to rest)

If I could just *lie* down for a moment, I'm sure I would feel better. (*Lie* does not take an object.)

(17) lead (lēd) (to guide)
lead (led) (name of mineral)
led (past tense of *lead*, to guide)

I will go where you *lead* me.
Lead is a heavy metal.

The captain *led* the way.

(18) lose (to fail to keep, or to fail to win)
loose (opposite of secure or tight)

Did Jim *lose* his money?

The boxer has a *loose* tooth because he didn't wear his mouthpiece.

(19) past (referring to time; beyond)

During the *past* week she has used his car.
He drove *past* her house.

passed (past tense of pass)

She *passed* the test.

(20) peace (absence of trouble)

People should be able to live in *peace*.

picce (a part of something)

I will take a small *piece* of pie.

(21) plain (not fancy; flat area of land; clear)

I want to get a *plain* suit.
The buffalo galloped across the *plain*.
Difficult information can be made *plain*.

plane (a flat surface; tool; airplane)

Plane geometry deals with two-dimensional figures.
A *plane* is used to smooth the surface of wood.
The Chicago *plane* landed.

450

(22) principal (main or most important; the head of a school)

The *principal* food is rice.
The school *principal* talked to the students.

principle (a theory or basic idea)

It was against her *principles* to lie.

(23) quiet (absence of noise)

The teacher asked the students to be *quiet*.

quite (to a great extent, really, completely)

It was *quite* noisy in the classroom.

quit (to stop; to resign)

The worker *quit* because of poor pay.

(24) right (correct; opposite of left)

You are *right*. He is *right*-handed.

write (to form letters)

Will you *write* out your answers, please?

rite (a custom)

They had a strange burial *rite*.

(25) set (to put, to place)

Please *set* the box on the floor. (*Set* takes an object unless it means "to become firm," as "Her hair was *set*," or refers to heavenly bodies, as "The sun *set*.")

sit (to get into a sitting position)

Sit over here by me. (*Sit* does not take an object unless it means "to put something in a sitting position," as "*Sit* the baby on the bed.")

(26) stair (a flight of steps)

The *stairs* were poorly lighted.

stare (to look at intently)

Do not *stare* at strangers.

(27) teach (to instruct)

Let the older students *teach* the younger ones.

learn (to gain knowledge)

People *learn* from experience.

(28) than (used in comparison)

I like the seashore better *than* the desert.

then (later, afterwards, subsequently)

He swung; *then* he ran.

(29) their (possessive)
there (telling where; a fill-in word)

Their shoes were wet.
If you go *there*, take plenty of food.
There is a meeting today.

they're (contraction of *they are*)

They're likely to ask you to stay with them.

451

(30) thorough (complete, carefully done)	She did a *thorough* job of washing the car.
through (a preposition; finished)	She jumped *through* the window.
	Are you *through* with it?
threw (past tense of *throw*)	She *threw* her shoes into the closet.
(31) to (a preposition; used with a verb)	Are you going *to* the carnival?
	I would like *to* go.
too (also; more than enough)	Can you go *too*?
	It isn't *too* far.
two (number)	It will cost only *two* dollars.
(32) waist (middle of a person,	Bend from the *waist*, please.
waste (unused or unusable material; to squander)	The liquid *waste* was thrown into the sink.
	He tends to *waste* his money on trifles.
(33) which (refers only to things)	The car *which* I saw was red.
who (refers only to people)	The man *who* was driving is wanted by the police.
(34) who's (a contraction of *who is* or *who has*)	*Who's* running for president of the club?
whose (possessive of *who*)	This is the girl *whose* dog is lost.
(35) your (possessive)	When did you lose *your* book?
you're (contraction of *you are*)	*You're* the first student with the correct answer.

c. Use the appropriate word for its function in your sentence.

    (1) Be sure that the word you choose really means what you intend it to. When in doubt, consult a dictionary.

Inappropriate	*Appropriate*
The story *relates* the author's personality.	The story *reveals* the author's personality.
The old man was a *sadist*: he always felt sorry for himself.	The old man was a *sadist*: he enjoyed hurting others.

    (2) Use *have*, not *of*, with verbs such as *could, would, may, might,* and *must.* The contraction *could've*, for example, sounds like "could of."

Nonstandard—Faulty	*Standard*
I could *of* gone.	I could *have* gone.

452

d. To express a negative meaning, use only one negative word.

Nonstandard—Faulty	*Standard*
I *haven't* got *no* pencil.	I have *no* pencil. *Or*: I *don't* have a pencil.
He *can't* seem to do *nothing* right.	He *can't* seem to do anything right.
She *didn't* do *nothing*.	She *didn't* do anything. *Or*: He did *nothing*.
It *doesn't hardly* matter.	It *hardly* matters. *Or*: It *doesn't* matter.

e. Avoid needless repetitive expressions. (See also Section 9b)

Nonstandard—Faulty	*Standard*
Where is it *at*?	Where is it?
In this book *it* traces the history of the Apache *Indians*.	This book traces the history of the Apaches.
The workers *they* are on strike.	The workers are on strike.
This man *he* became successful *as* as doctor.	This man became a successful doctor.

f. Avoid using *ain't*. Words like *isn't, aren't, haven't, hasn't,* express the intended meaning much better.

Nonstandard—Faulty	*Standard*
I *ain't* going.	I'm *not* going.
She *ain't* been here for several days.	She *hasn't been* here for several days.
We *ain't* the ones who broke the window.	We *aren't* (we're not) the ones who broke the window.

Correction Follow-Up

After your paper has been corrected and returned, you may find certain comments on it, including helpful suggestions and perhaps praise for how well you have met the assignment. In addition, your attention may be directed to errors you overlooked, marked in either of two ways:

Correction method 1. The correction is supplied, along with the problem number.

She laid awake, thinking of the comeing day.
32   28   453

Correction method 2. The *Handbook* section number is supplied, but the correction is left for you to look up after you have found the appropriate rule. (See Contents to the *Handbook*.)

She laid awake, thinking of the comeing day.
32b,d   28b

To help you profit from the corrections, a convenient plan follows.

Method of Correction Follow-Up

Whichever way your teacher indicates your problems, you will want to follow them up so that they are less likely to occur in your future writing. One effective method is this:

First: In a spelling section of your notebook, list the correct spelling of each misspelled word. Keep this list up to date and review it often.

Second: Use the *Handbook* to review each error noted on your paper. Locate the rule which best applies to your error. In either your own words or in the words of the book, write the rule and illustrate it with the correction of your error, underlining the correction. Save your lists for review.

32b,d. Laid means "having put"; the past tense of lie, "to rest," is lay: She lay awake.

28b(1)(a). Drop the final silent e before adding a suffix beginning with a vowel: coming.

Third: After your teacher has examined and returned your corrected paper, keep it to use as a reference when you write your next paper.

dictionary

This dictionary is provided as a convenient means for looking up unfamiliar words in this book. These words are indicated in the selection by superior marks (°). In most cases words that are footnoted in the text are not included here. The order and kinds of information to be found in an entry are given below:

1. Syllable division. Divided into syllables. *Example*: **des•ig•nate**.
2. Pronunciation. In standard dictionaries you may find several pronunciations of a word. We have used only one pronunciation. *Example*: **hu•mil•i•ty** (hū mil′ ə tē).
3. The part of speech and, when required, a listing of different tense forms. *Example*: **break**...*v.* **broke**, **broken**.
4. Definition. The word is always defined according to its use in the book. Other commonly used meanings may also be given.
5. Alternate spellings. *Example*: **bos'n** (Also **bo•sun**, **bo′•sun**).

In using this dictionary and doing the dictionary lessons, you will need to know the following abbreviations:

adj.	adjective	n.	noun
adv.	adverb	prep.	preposition
conj.	conjunction	v.	verb

Pronunciation Key*

a, act; ā, able; ã, air; ä, art; b, back; ch, chief; d, do; e, ebb; ėr, earth; ē, equal; f, fit; g, give; h, hit; i, if; ī, ice; j, just; k, kept; l, low; m, my; n, now; ng, sing; o, box; ō, over; oi, oil; ü, ooze; ou, out; p, page; r, read; s, see; sh, shoe; t, ten; th, thin, that; u, up; ū, use; v, voice; w, west; y, yes; z, zeal; zh, vision; ə = *a* in *alone*, e in *system*, i in *easily,* o in *gallop*, u in *circus*.

The pronunciation system in this book is that of The Gage Canadian Dictionary, Copyright© Gage Publishing Limited, 1979, 1973, 1967.

A

af•flic•tion (ə flik′ shən), *n*. a state of pain or distress.

am•a•to•ry (am′ ə to rē), *adj*. of love, causing love.

an•gu•lar (ang′ gyə lər), *adj*. bony; gaunt.

an•ni•hi•la•tion (ə ni ə lā′ shən), *n*. complete destruction.

an•ti•cli•max (an′ ti klī′ maks), *n*. a sudden descent from the significant to the inconsequential; a flop.

a•pol•o•get•i•cal•ly (ə pol′ ə jet′ ik lē), *adv*. in the manner of offering excuses.

ar•o•mat•ic (ar′ ə mat′ ik), *adj*. fragrant; sweet-smelling; spicy.

ar•ro•gant•ly (ar′ ə gənt lē), *adv*. haughtily; proudly.

ar•se•nal (är′ sə nəl), *n*. a building for storing or manufacturing weapons.

as•sur•ance (ə sh r′ əns), *n*. confidence; freedom from doubt.

a•wry (ərī′), *adv. adj*. with a twist or turn.

B

be•he•moths (bi hē′ moths), *n.pl*. in the Bible, huge and powerful animals.

bi•zarre (bi zär′), *adj*. strikingly unusual or odd in appearance, especially in fashion, design, or color.

C

cas•ti•gate (kas′ tə gāt′), *v*. criticize severely.

cen•te•nar•i•an (sen′ tə när′ ē ən), *adj*. 100-year-old person.

cir•cum•stan•tial (sur′ kəm stan′ shəl), *adj*. pertaining to the conditions of time and place; dependent on circumstances.

com•pla•cent (kəm plā′ sənt), *adj*. pleased with oneself.

con•strict•ed (kən strik′ tid), *v., adj.—v*. grew tightened. *—adj*. made narrow or small by being squeezed together.

con•tempt (kən tempt′), *n*. disgust; scorn.

con•tin•gen•cy (kən tin′ jən sē), *n*. chance happening.

con•vul•sive (kən vul′ siv), *adj*. spastic, violently disturbing.

cre•ma•tion (krē mā′ shən), *n*. burning a dead body to ashes.

cryp•ti•cal•ly (krip′ tə klē), *adv*. in a hidden or secret manner; in a manner which hints at a hidden meaning.

curt (kurt), *adj*. short; rude in speech or manner.

D

de•lu•sion (di lü′ zhən), *n*. a mistaken belief or opinion; self-deception.

de•vi•ous (dē′ vē əs), *adj*. roundabout; departing from the direct path.

dis•con•so•late•ly (dis kon′ sə lit lē), *adv*. in an unhappy manner.

E

em•bod•i•ment (em bod′ ē mənt), *n*. having a body; the essential part of something.

er•rat•ic (ə rat′ ik), *adj*. uncertain, irregular.

ev•o•lu•tion•ar•y (ev′ ə lü′ shə ner′ ē), *adj*. developing or changing over a period of time.

ex•cru•ci•at•ing (eks krü′ shē āt ing), *adj*. very painful.

ex•ploit•ing (eks ploit′ ing), *v*. use selfishly for one's own ends.

ex•ult•ing (eg zul′ ting), *v*. rejoicing greatly.

F

fa•nat•i•cism (fə nat′ ə siz′ əm), *n*. an unreasonable enthusiasm.

feigned (fānd), *past participle as adjective*. false; pretended.

feral (fir′ əl), *adj*. **1**. wild, or existing in a state of nature. **2**. having gone back to the wild state after contact with civilization. **3**. of or characteristic of wild animals.

fret•ting (fret ting), *v*. eating away, wearing.

fu•tile•ly (fū′ təl lē), *adv*. in vain; uselessly.

G

gen•ial (jēn′ yəl), *adj*. cordial; kindly.

gib•ber•ing (jib′ ər ing), *v*. chattering; speaking inarticulately.

gird (gird), *v*. get ready for action.

H

hu•mil•i•ty (hū mil′ ə tē), *n*. **1**. the state or quality of being modest. **2**. freedom from pride; not conceited.

hy•poc•ri•sy (hi pok′ rə sē), *n*. pretense of virtue; false goodness.

hy•poth•e•sis (hī poth′ ə sis), *n*. something not proved but assumed true for purposes of argument, further study, or investigation.

hys·ter·i·cal·ly (his ter′ ə klē), *adv.* acting in a very emotional way; in the manner of a person who has lost his/her mind.

I

ig·no·min·i·ous (ig no min′ ē əs), *adj.* disgraceful, dishonorable.

il·lu·sive (i lü′ siv), *adj.* like a dream; imagined.

im·mor·tals (i mȯr′ təlz), *n.* beings who will live forever, gods.

im·pas·sive·ly (im pas′ iv lē), *adv.* with indifference; with no show of emotion.

im·po·si·tion (im′ pə zish′ ən), *n.* any excessive, overly burdensome requirement or demand.

im·preg·na·ble (im preg′ nə bəl), *adj.* not capable of being captured.

im·promp·tu (im promp′ tū), *adj.* without preparation, without previous study.

im·pro·vised (im′ pro vīzd), *v.* prepared on the spur of the moment.

in·ar·tic·u·late (in′ är tik′ yə lit), *adj.* not clear; not understandable.

in·cred·i·ble (in kred′ ə bəl), *adj.* unbelievable.

in·dig·na·tion (in′ dig nā′ shən), *n.* displeasure; anger aroused by something unjust.

in·fi·nite (in′ fə nit), *adj.* immeasurable; without limit.

in·fir·ma·ry (in fur′ mə rē), *n.* hospital or dispensary.

in·so·lent (in′ sə lənt), *adj.* impertinent; insulting; rude.

i·tin·er·ant (ī tin′ ər ənt), *adj.* travelling from place to place.

L

lag·gard (lag′ ərd), *n.* one who moves too slowly or falls behind.

lan·guish (lang′ guish), *v.* become weak or weary.

M

mal·let (mal′ it), *n.* a hammer having a head of wood, rubber or other fairly soft material.

mea·gre (mē′ gər), *adj.* poor, scanty.

me·lee (mel′ ā), *n.* a state of hectic confusion.

me·thod·i·cal (mə thod′ ə kəl), *adj.* systematic, orderly.

mien (mēn), *n.* bearing, as showing character

and feeling; facial expression.

mirth·less·ly (murth les lē), *adv.* without joy; gloomily.

mor·bid (mȯr′ bid), *adj.* not sound or healthy; unwholesome and gloomy.

mot·ley (mot′ lē), *adj.* of various mixed kinds or parts; *n.* an outer garment of many colors.

mute (mūt), *adj.* not making any sound.

N

neb·u·lous (neb′ yə ləs), *adj.* cloudy; hazy; vague; with unclear outlines.

non·con·form·ist (non′ kən fȯr′ mist), *n.* one who refuses to be bound by the accepted rules or beliefs of a group.

non·en·ti·ty (non en′ tə tē), *n.* a person or thing of no importance.

O

om·i·nous (om′ ə nəs), *adj.* threatening.

os·mo·sis (ŏz mō′ sis), *n.* any gradual, often unconscious, process of absorbing something.

P

pal·ing (pāl′ ing), *n.* fencing material.

pal·sied (pol′ zēd), *adj.* paralysed.

pan·to·mime (pan′ tə mīm′), *n.* a play or entertainment in which the players express themselves only in silent gestures.

pa·ral·y·sis (pə ral′ ə sis), *n.* inability to move.

par·ox·ysm (par′ ək siz′ əm), *n.* **1.** any sudden violent outburst. **2.** a severe attack of shivering and shaking.

per·cep·ti·ble (pər sep′ tə bəl), *adj.* capable of being seen or otherwise noticed.

pet·ty (pet′ ē), *adj.* small; mean.

pith·y (pith′ ē), *adj.* short but to the point.

pla·cat·ing·ly (plā′ kāt ing lē), *adv.* in a soothing manner.

plat·i·tu·di·nous (plat′ ə tū′ də nəs), *adj.* having the quality of a dull, insipid remark; corny.

plum·met (plum′ it), *v.* plunge, drop.

poign·ant·ly (poin′ ənt lē), *adv.* mentally or emotionally appealing.

pon·der·ous (pon′ dər əs), *adj.* very heavy; difficult to understand.

pre·cip·i·ta·ted (pri sip′ ə tā′ tid), *v.* fell, like rain or snow; produced; resulted in.

457

preg•nant (preg′ nənt), *adj.* filled with meaning; very significant.

pre•oc•cu•pa•tion (prē ok′ yə pā′ shən), *n.* the state of being completely engrossed in thought; absorbed.

pre•pos•ter•ous (pri pos′ tər əs), *adj.* foolish; absurd; contradicting common sense or experience.

pro•cured (prō kūrd′), *v.* gotten with care and effort.

pro•fane (prə fān′), *adj.* common; vulgar. *v.* abuse, debase.

pro•fi•cient (prə fish′ ənt), *adj.* skilled; expert.

pro•pri•e•tar•y (prə prī′ ə ter′ ē), *adj.* characterized by attitudes of an owner; focused on one's own self-interest.

Q

qui•es•cent (kwī es′ ənt), *adj.* at rest; still; motionless.

R

rad•i•cal (rad′ ə kəl), *n.* one who holds or follows extreme principles; an extremist; one who is for violent political and social revolution.

rau•cous (ro′ kəs), *adj.* harsh of voice or sound; hoarse.

re•ac•tion•ar•y (rē ak′ shə ner′ ē), *n.* one who opposes progress; one who resists all kinds of change.

re•fined (ri fīnd′), *adj.* showing good manners.

rem•i•nis•cent (rem′ ə nis′ ənt), *adj.* recalling past events.

rep•er•toire (rep′ ər twär′), *n.* a list of pieces an actor or musician can perform.

re•pres•sing (rē pres′ ing), *v.* forcing from consciousness ideas, feelings, or memories; prohibiting.

S

sab•o•taged (sab′ ə täzhd′), *adj.* destroyed by an unknown enemy; undermined by discontented workers or undercover agents.

sac•ris•ty (sak′ ris tē), *n.* a room in a church where sacred objects are stored.

sa•li•ent (sā′ lē ənt), *adj.* important.

sal•vos (sal′ vōz), *n.pl.* discharges of several guns.

scru•ti•ny (skrü′ tə nē), *n.* a close examination.

scull (skul), *n.* an oar worked with a side twist over the end of a boat.

se•pul•chral (sə pul′ krəl), *adj.* deep and gloomy; dismal.

sin•glet (sing glət), *n.* a kind of undershirt worn by men.

snuf•fled (snuf′ əld), *v.* breathed noisily through a partly clogged nose.

so•lic•it•ous•ness (sə lis′ ə təs nəs), *n.* the quality of being concerned or anxious about something; anxious desire or care.

sov•er•eign•ty (sov′ rən tē), *n.* supreme power or authority.

spews (spūz), *v.* pours forth; gushes.

strewn (strün), *v.* covered with something scattered or sprinkled.

sub•ter•fuge (sub′ tər fūj), *n.* a trick or excuse used to escape something unpleasant.

sup•ple (sup′ əl), *adj.* limber; flexible.

sur•rep•ti•tious•ly (sər′ əp tish′ əs lē), *adv.* stealthily; secretly.

syn•thet•ics (sin thet′ iks), *n.* artificial ingredients or products.

T

taint•ed (tānt′id), *adj.* discredited, corrupted.

tan•gent (tan′ jənt), *n.* a sudden change of thought or course.

throt•tled (throt′ əld), *v.* checked or stopped the flow of.

tol•er•ance (tol′ ər əns), *n.* the capacity to be patient and fair toward those with differing opinions; freedom from bigotry.

tot•ter•ing (tot′ ər ing), *adj.* shaking.

U

un•in•flec•ted (un′ in flek′ tid), *adj.* not changing in pitch or loudness.

un•in•hib•it•ed (un′ in hib′ ə tid), *adj.* not held back; unrestrained; open.

V

val•e•dic•tion (val′ ə dik′ shən), *n.* bidding farewell.

W

whee•dling (wē′ dling), *adj.* persuasive.

wraith•like (rāth′ līk′), *adj.* lifelike.

index

For additional information about language conventions, refer to the Contents for the *Handbook,* page 418.

459

credits

Cover Design

Gregory Fossella Associates

Production

James Rigney, Inc.

Illustration

Patrick Blackwell, 170, 275, 407
Penny Carter, 29, 33, 35
Brenda Clarke, 48, 53, 57, 61
Navah Haber-Schaim, 413
Dorothy Kegel, 70, 247
Judith Dufour Love, 261, 264
Theresa Manchester, 351, 355
Marilyn Mets, 111, 183, 186, 204,
    207, 211
Les Morrill, 214, 217
Mary Ellen Podgorsky, 122
Deborah Taylor, 143
George Ulrich, 79, 85
Candy Walters, 248
John Whalley, 119, 121, 329, 334,
    336, 339

Photography

The photographs were obtained
    through the courtesy of the
    following sources:
Alberta Provincial Parks, 390(b)
Brian K. Allen, 21
Christopher Barnes, 162, 163
Jon Chase, 42
de Lange, FPG, 129(tr)
Dobo, Stock, Boston, 103(b)
Peter H. Dreyer, 13, 94(l, r), 101,
    151
Sherry Fendell, 126(t)
Robert Forget, 270, 287, 290
Foster, FPG, 309(t)
Kevin Galvin, 98, 310(tl)
Bohdan Hrynewych, 12, 16, 134,
    139, 156
Morris Huberland, 128(bl)

Image Bank/John de Visser, 73
Bernard F. Jackson, 390(t)
Johnson, Stock, Boston, 363
Lanks, FPG, 103(t)
Mark Lipman, 273
Stephen G. Maka, 126(l)
Mazzaschi, Stock, Boston, 127(l),
    169
Terry McKoy, 305, 310(tr), 311(br)
Miller Services/Hans L. Blohm,
    393(tl)
Miller Services/Camerique, 392(br)
Miller Services/Tom Hall, 393(br)
Miller Services/Richard
    Harrington, 392(tl)
Miller Services/Brian D. Minielly,
    392(bl)
Miller Services/Nicholas Morant,
    393(tr)
Miller Services/Neil Newton,
    393(bl)
Miller Services/Eberhard E. Otto,
    391(bl)
Morocco Flowers Photography
    1977, 286, 364(b)
Parks & Recreation, Queen's Park,
    391(t)
The Picture Cube, 259
Rebbot, Stock, Boston, 126(br)
A. Glen Ryan, 391(br)
Schuyler, Stock, Boston, 20
Mark Sexton, 127(t,r)
Sage Sohier, 277
Tinker, FPG, 102
U.P.I., 308(br), 309(m)
Vandermark, Stock, Boston, 308(tr)
Wide World Photos, Inc., 271,
    308(l)
Wing, Stock, Boston, 311(tr)
Wolinsky, Stock, Boston, 309(b)
Zimmerman, A.P.A., 311(l)

ABCDEF 0854321
Printed in Canada